also by america's test kitchen

The New Essentials Cookbook

Cook's Illustrated Revolutionary Recipes

Dinner Illustrated

Tasting Italy: A Culinary Journey

The Complete Diabetes Cookbook

The Complete Slow Cooker

The Complete Make-Ahead Cookbook

The Complete Mediterranean Cookbook

The Complete Vegetarian Cookbook

The Complete Cooking for Two Cookbook

Cooking at Home with Bridget and Julia

Just Add Sauce

How to Roast Everything

Nutritious Delicious

What Good Cooks Know

Cook's Science

The Science of Good Cooking

The Perfect Cake

The Perfect Cookie

Bread Illustrated

Master of the Grill

Kitchen Smarts

Kitchen Hacks

100 Recipes: The Absolute Best Ways to Make the True Essentials

The New Family Cookbook

The America's Test Kitchen Cooking School Cookbook

The Cook's Illustrated Meat Book

The Cook's Illustrated Baking Book

The Cook's Illustrated Cookbook

The America's Test Kitchen Family Baking Book

The Best of America's Test Kitchen (2007–2019 Editions)

The Complete America's Test Kitchen TV Show Cookbook 2001–2019

Air Fryer Perfection

Cook It in Your Dutch Oven

Sous Vide for Everybody

Multicooker Perfection

Food Processor Perfection

Pressure Cooker Perfection

Vegan for Everybody

Naturally Sweet

Foolproof Preserving

Paleo Perfected

The How Can It Be Gluten-Free Cookbook: Volume 2

The How Can It Be Gluten-Free Cookbook

The Best Mexican Recipes

Slow Cooker Revolution Volume 2: The Easy-Prep Edition

Slow Cooker Revolution

The Six-Ingredient Solution

The America's Test Kitchen D.I.Y. Cookbook

THE COOK'S ILLUSTRATED ALL-TIME BEST SERIES

All-Time Best Brunch

All-Time Best Dinners for Two

All-Time Best Sunday Suppers

All-Time Best Holiday Entertaining

All-Time Best Appetizers

All-Time Best Soups

COOK'S COUNTRY TITLES

One-Pan Wonders

Cook It in Cast Iron

Cook's Country Eats Local

The Complete Cook's Country TV Show Cookbook

FOR A FULL LISTING OF ALL OUR BOOKS

CooksIllustrated.com

AmericasTestKitchen.com

praise for america's test kitchen titles

"It's all about technique and timing, and the ATK crew delivers their usual clear instructions to ensure success. . . . The thoughtful balance of practicality and imagination will inspire readers of all tastes and skill levels."
PUBLISHERS WEEKLY (STARRED REVIEW) ON HOW TO ROAST EVERYTHING

"This encyclopedia of meat cookery would feel completely overwhelming if it weren't so meticulously organized and artfully designed. This is Cook's Illustrated at its finest."
THE KITCHN ON THE COOK'S ILLUSTRATED MEAT BOOK

"*The Perfect Cookie* . . . is, in a word, perfect. This is an important and substantial cookbook. . . . If you love cookies, but have been a tad shy to bake on your own, all your fears will be dissipated. This is one book you can use for years with magnificently happy results."
THE HUFFINGTON POST ON THE PERFECT COOKIE

Selected as one of the 10 Best New Cookbooks of 2017
THE LA TIMES ON THE PERFECT COOKIE

Selected as the Cookbook Award Winner of 2017 in the Baking category
INTERNATIONAL ASSOCIATION OF CULINARY PROFESSIONALS (IACP) ON BREAD ILLUSTRATED

Selected as one of Amazon's Best Books of 2015 in the Cookbooks and Food Writing category
AMAZON ON THE COMPLETE VEGETARIAN COOKBOOK

"This book upgrades slow cooking for discriminating, 21st-century palates—that is indeed revolutionary."
THE DALLAS MORNING NEWS ON SLOW COOKER REVOLUTION

"A beautifully illustrated, 318-page culinary compendium showcasing an impressive variety and diversity of authentic Mexican cuisine."
MIDWEST BOOK REVIEW ON THE BEST MEXICAN RECIPES

"Some 2,500 photos walk readers through 600 painstakingly tested recipes, leaving little room for error."
ASSOCIATED PRESS ON THE AMERICA'S TEST KITCHEN COOKING SCHOOL COOKBOOK

"This book is a comprehensive, no-nonsense guide . . . a well-thought-out, clearly explained primer for every aspect of home baking."
THE WALL STREET JOURNAL ON THE COOK'S ILLUSTRATED BAKING BOOK

"If there's room in the budget for one multicooker/Instant Pot cookbook, make it this one."
BOOKLIST ON MULTICOOKER PERFECTION

"The book offers an impressive education for curious cake makers, new and experienced alike. A summation of 25 years of cake making at ATK, there are cakes for every taste."
THE WALL STREET JOURNAL ON THE PERFECT CAKE

"Some books impress by the sheer audacity of their ambition. Backed up by the magazine's famed mission to test every recipe relentlessly until it is the best it can be, this nearly 900-page volume lands with an authoritative wallop."
CHICAGO TRIBUNE ON THE COOK'S ILLUSTRATED COOKBOOK

"The 21st-century *Fannie Farmer Cookbook* or *The Joy of Cooking*. If you had to have one cookbook and that's all you could have, this one would do it."
CBS SAN FRANCISCO ON THE NEW FAMILY COOKBOOK

"The go-to gift book for newlyweds, small families, or empty nesters."
ORLANDO SENTINEL ON THE COMPLETE COOKING FOR TWO COOKBOOK

"The sum total of exhaustive experimentation . . . anyone interested in gluten-free cookery simply shouldn't be without it."
NIGELLA LAWSON ON THE HOW CAN IT BE GLUTEN-FREE COOKBOOK

"A one-volume kitchen seminar, addressing in one smart chapter after another the sometimes surprising whys behind a cook's best practices. . . . You get the myth, the theory, the science, and the proof, all rigorously interrogated as only America's Test Kitchen can do."
NPR ON THE SCIENCE OF GOOD COOKING

"This impressive installment from America's Test Kitchen equips readers with dozens of repertoire-worthy recipes. . . . This is a must-have for beginner cooks and more experienced ones who wish to sharpen their skills."
PUBLISHERS WEEKLY (STARRED REVIEW) ON THE NEW ESSENTIALS COOKBOOK

HOW TO BRAISE EVERYTHING

EVERYTHING

Classic, Modern, and Global Dishes
USING A TIME-HONORED TECHNIQUE

America's Test Kitchen

Library of Congress Cataloging-in-Publication Data

Names: America's Test Kitchen (Firm), author.
Title: How to braise everything : classic, modern, and global dishes using a time-honored technique / America's Test Kitchen.
Description: Boston, MA : America's Test Kitchen, [2019] | Includes index.
Identifiers: LCCN 2018033789 | ISBN 9781945256714 (hardcover)
Subjects: LCSH: Braising (Cooking) | LCGFT: Cookbooks.
Classification: LCC TX686 .H69 2019 | DDC 641.7/3--dc23
LC record available at https://lccn.loc.gov/2018033789

AMERICA'S TEST KITCHEN
21 Drydock Avenue, Boston, MA 02210
Manufactured in the United States of America

10 9 8 7 6 5 4 3 2 1

Distributed by Penguin Random House
Publisher Services
Tel: 800.733.3000

Pictured on front cover: French-Style Pot-Roasted Pork Loin (page 142)

Pictured on back cover: Braised Brisket with Pomegranate, Cumin, and Cilantro (page 48), Sicilian White Beans and Escarole (page 306), Chicken Scarpariello (page 195), and Braised Red Potatoes with Lemon and Chives (page 373)

Editorial Director, Books ELIZABETH CARDUFF
Senior Editor SACHA MADADIAN
Editorial Assistants KELLY GAUTHIER AND ALYSSA LANGER
Art Director, Books LINDSEY CHANDLER
Deputy Art Director ALLISON BOALES
Associate Art Director KATIE BARRANGER
Graphic Designer SARAH HORWITCH DAILEY
Production Designer REINALDO CRUZ
Photography Director JULIE BOZZO COTE
Photography Producer MEREDITH MULCAHY
Senior Staff Photographer DANIEL J. VAN ACKERE
Staff Photographers STEVE KLISE AND KEVIN WHITE
Additional Photography KELLER + KELLER AND CARL TREMBLAY
Food Styling CATRINE KELTY, CHANTAL LAMBETH, KENDRA MCKNIGHT, MARIE PIRAINO, ELLE SIMONE SCOTT, AND SALLY STAUB
Photoshoot Kitchen Team
     Photo Team and Special Events Manager TIMOTHY MCQUINN
     Lead Test Cook DANIEL CELLUCCI
     Test Cook JESSICA RUDOLPH
     Assistant Test Cooks SARAH EWALD, ERIC HAESSLER, AND DEVON SHATKIN
Production Manager CHRISTINE SPANGER
Imaging Manager LAUREN ROBBINS
Production and Imaging Specialists DENNIS NOBLE AND JESSICA VOAS
Copy Editor CHERYL REDMOND
Proofreader ANN-MARIE IMBORNONI
Indexer ELIZABETH PARSON

Chief Creative Officer JACK BISHOP
Executive Editorial Directors JULIA COLLIN DAVISON AND BRIDGET LANCASTER

CONTENTS

ix Welcome to America's Test Kitchen

x What Is Braising?

34 **Beef**

106 **Lamb and Veal**

130 **Pork**

176 **Poultry**

234 **Seafood**

266 **Vegetarian Mains**

294 **Beans**

332 **Vegetable Sides**

374 Nutritional Information for Our Recipes

380 Conversions and Equivalents

382 Index

Welcome to America's Test Kitchen

This book has been tested, written, and edited by the folks at America's Test Kitchen. Located in Boston's Seaport District in the historic Innovation and Design Building, it features 15,000 square feet of kitchen space, including multiple photography and video studios. It is the home of *Cook's Illustrated* magazine and *Cook's Country* magazine and is the workday destination for more than 60 test cooks, editors, and cookware specialists. Our mission is to test recipes over and over again until we understand how and why they work and until we arrive at the best version.

We start the process of testing a recipe with a complete lack of preconceptions, which means that we accept no claim, no technique, and no recipe at face value. We simply assemble as many variations as possible, test a half-dozen of the most promising, and taste the results blind. We then construct our own recipe and continue to test it, varying ingredients, techniques, and cooking times until we reach a consensus. As we like to say in the test kitchen, "We make the mistakes so you don't have to." The result, we hope, is the best version of a particular recipe, but we realize that only you can be the final judge of our success (or failure). We use the same rigorous approach when we test equipment and taste ingredients.

All of this would not be possible without a belief that good cooking, much like good music, is based on a foundation of objective technique. Some people like spicy foods and others don't, but there is a right way to sauté, there is a best way to cook a pot roast, and there are measurable scientific principles involved in producing perfectly beaten, stable egg whites. Our ultimate goal is to investigate the fundamental principles of cooking to give you the techniques, tools, and ingredients you need to become a better cook. It is as simple as that.

To see what goes on behind the scenes at America's Test Kitchen, check out our social media channels for kitchen snapshots, exclusive content, video tips, and much more. You can watch us work (in our actual test kitchen) by tuning in to *America's Test Kitchen* or *Cook's Country* on public television or on our websites. Listen in to test kitchen experts on public radio (SplendidTable.org) to hear insights that illuminate the truth about real home cooking. Want to hone your cooking skills or finally learn how to bake—with an America's Test Kitchen test cook? Enroll in one of our online cooking classes. However you choose to visit us, we welcome you into our kitchen, where you can stand by our side as we test our way to the best recipes in America.

facebook.com/AmericasTestKitchen

twitter.com/TestKitchen

youtube.com/AmericasTestKitchen

instagram.com/TestKitchen

pinterest.com/TestKitchen

google.com/+AmericasTestKitchen

AmericasTestKitchen.com
CooksIllustrated.com
CooksCountry.com
OnlineCookingSchool.com

WHAT IS BRAISING?

2 **Introduction**

3 **Braising Defined**

4 **A Look in the Braising Pot**

6 **Braising How-Tos**

8 **Braising Time: How Long Is Long Enough?**

9 **Make It Ahead**

10 **All About Beef**

14 **All About Lamb**

16 **All About Pork**

19 **All About Veal**

20 **All About Fish and Shellfish**

24 **Braising Beans and Vegetables**

27 **Soak It Up**

30 **Equipment**

Introduction

Braised foods bring people to the table. The most comforting dishes in your repertoire—think beefy pot roasts, shredded pork for tacos, sauce-coated chicken parts, aromatic vegetable stews—are braised. They're family favorites like onion-smothered Brisket Carbonnade, bistro classics like elegant Coq au Vin, and spiced global dishes like Lamb Vindaloo. Braising is elemental and universal. Every culture braises much in the same way, with differences lying mainly in the flavor profiles. And the technique's ease makes it seem like magic: Raw, tough ingredients go into a pan with liquid; they're cooked, often low, slow, and (happily) unattended; and they emerge something else entirely—tender and deeply flavorful, with a glossy sauce.

But as we know in the test kitchen, cooking isn't magic; it's an art and a science. And just because braising is simple, convenient, and time-honored doesn't mean there isn't a right way to do it. So we've aggregated all we've learned about the technique over the years in one volume. And that means a lot of recipes. These aren't just stews and roasts, and the flavors are interesting and lively. In addition to our Simple Pot Roast, which we make better than the rest, there are vegetable braises that keep their fresh green color, like our light, crisp, and buttery Braised Spring Vegetables with Tarragon. Monkfish Tagine is sweet and sour (and simple) in a Dutch oven; Lemon-Braised Chicken Thighs with Chickpeas and Fennel is a fresh one-skillet dinner that boasts crisp chicken skin. While we include classic red wine–braised short ribs, we also make pomegranate-braised ribs with prunes pureed into the sauce for earthy sweetness.

We'll walk you through the common traditional method for achieving these results—sear protein, sauté aromatics, add liquid, cover, cook—but also share tips and tricks for optimizing this routine or streamlining it by browning meat while you braise rather than in advance (keep the lid off and let the oven's heat brown exposed pieces), brining beans before cooking them (the saltwater soak results in tender skins and creamy interiors), and using the *en cocotte* method, which braises food in a covered pot without added liquid—just the ultraconcentrated liquid created by the food's exuded juices. You'll learn when it's best to braise in the oven and when to simmer on the stove, which cuts of meat and seafood take best to braising, and what to look for in a Dutch oven. All of this education means you'll serve up soul-satisfying dishes for everything from beans to veal every time you braise.

Braising Defined

To braise is to cook a main ingredient—meat, vegetable, legume—in a closed environment to break down its proteins or fibers and achieve ultratender results.

Other common cooking techniques like roasting, sautéing, and frying all use high heat to create flavor through changes to foods' proteins and sugars—in effect, they add to food to make it taste good. But braising unlocks the delicious flavor already inherent in the food you're cooking: The tough collagen of marbled pork butt roast in Cider-Braised Pork Roast (page 137) breaks down so its tender meat tastes deeply rich and faintly sweet, enhanced by a sauce whose flavor comes from cooking with the meat itself. Chicken in a Pot with Red Potatoes, Carrots, and Shallots (page 202) is a whole bird that cooks in a closed pot so it braises in its own juices—all the flavor stays inside. Beets with Lemon and Almonds (page 338) taste more like beets—earthy and sweet—when cooked in a small amount of water in a sauté pan than when boiled (which washes out flavor). But what does this mean practically? Why do you want to take the time to braise?

BRAISING BENEFITS

steady, even cooking

Cooking in liquid maintains a temperature in the cooking vessel that can't possibly reach higher than 212 degrees, the boiling point of water. This allows and coaxes collagen—the main protein that makes up the chewy connective tissue that surrounds meat's muscle fibers—to melt into gelatin without the worry of one part of the meat cooking too fast or too slow on its path to ultimate tenderness. The gelatin lubricates the muscle fibers rather than hold them together (as collagen does), giving the protein a soft, tender texture. The conversion of collagen to gelatin is both temperature- and time-dependent; the longer the food is held in the ideal temperature range the more collagen will break down.

a lustrous sauce

That gelatin doesn't benefit just the texture of the meat; it also lends body to the braising liquid, which thickens to a lovely lacquering sauce: The wine in Red Wine–Braised Short Ribs with Bacon, Parsnips, and Pearl Onions (page 60) becomes beefy-tasting and glossy from the gelatin-rich meat and bones and beautifully coats the tender ribs; Smothered Pork Chops (page 152) taste deeply porky in a thick but not cloying sauce.

cooking without hands

The simplicity of braising is its most immediate draw. Without the flipping required of searing, the frequent temperature checks of roasting, or the mess of frying, it's nearly hands-off, save for a bit of prep. Whether it's the long, low cooking of bubbling meat dishes or the faster finish of seafood dinners or vegetable sides, a braised dish is left alone for its self-improvement. There's little possibility for user error; just let the moderate oven or stovetop simmer do the work of coaxing out food's flavor.

COOKING *EN COCOTTE*

When we talk about braising, we're usually talking about cooking in liquid—whether it be the large amount for a stew, the moderate amount for a roast, or the shallow pool for Brussels sprouts. The liquid turns to steam that helps cook the food from all sides. But there doesn't need to be liquid in a pot to gently heat food. Braising in a pot without liquid is called *en cocotte*, French for covered cooking "in a casserole." Here, the liquid released from the food itself creates a moist environment, in effect braising the item in its own juices. The muscle fibers break down and a shallow sauce forms, ultraconcentrated in savory flavor. There's less of a buffer for overcooking, but it's a great method when we want foods to maintain their structural integrity but still be ultratender. Beef en Cocotte with Caramelized Onions (page 56), for example, emerges a juicy, rosy-red medium-rare; instead of pull-apart meat, we get beautiful slices of satisfying roast beef with deep savor.

A Look in the Braising Pot

Just put meat and water in a pot and cook it low and slow until the meat reaches the proper internal temperature, and you have a braise—a pretty bland one. Most successful braises—whether the highly spiced tagines of North Africa or the whole roasts of Italy—include the same components. They're added in a predictable sequence and build on one another to create a dish with remarkable flavor. Look inside this Dutch oven, and you'll see the steps to building flavorful Braised Lamb Shanks with Lemon and Mint (page 111); below, learn how these steps correspond to nearly every braise.

1 AROMATICS

Braises benefit from a base of aromatic flavor. It can be simple: Sautéeing onion alone can add sweetness and complexity to a dish. These ingredients will cook with the dish the whole time, perfuming it with flavor. A common trinity of vegetables in many cuisines—carrot, celery, and onion—provide a balance of sweet and vegetal. Sometimes we chop the vegetables; here, we keep them chunkier because they become part of the plated meal. The judicious amount of garlic in this recipe sweetens and grows in complexity through cooking.

Common examples Onion, carrot, celery, bell pepper, garlic, shallot, ginger, chiles, hardy herbs

2 BEEFY BOOSTERS

Braising unlocks the flavor inherent in a main ingredient, but sometimes after long cooking this ingredient needs even more enhancement. That's when we turn to umami-boosting ingredients that increase the perception of meatiness; a small amount makes savory items taste even more like themselves. We typically incorporate these earlier in the process to bloom or brown them before we add liquid. Here, we sauté glutamate-packed tomato paste with the aromatics, and it adds meaty depth, sweetness, and richness.

Common examples Tomato paste, anchovies, soy sauce, mushrooms, Parmesan cheese rind

3 LIQUID

The braising liquid coaxes out and transfers flavors; its reduction forms the sauce. It's important stuff! We rarely use just water (unless in combination with fruity canned tomatoes)—why not get the most flavor? We like to use chicken, beef, or vegetable stock. Store-bought works just fine. (Our favorites are Swanson Chicken Stock, Better Than Bouillon Roasted Beef Base, and Orrington Farms Vegan Chicken Flavored Broth Base & Seasoning, respectively.) Even for red meats, we often use chicken broth or a combination of beef and chicken broth for rounder, fuller meaty flavor; store-bought beef broth alone can be, oddly enough, not as beefy. For these lamb shanks, we use a combination of wine and chicken broth—the red meatiness coming from the deeply-flavored, collagen-rich shanks themselves. We never make seafood stock; some broth or water bolstered by bottled clam juice and the flavor of the seafood at hand does the job much more easily.

Common examples Chicken broth, beef broth, vegetable broth, wine, canned tomatoes, bottled clam juice

4 MAIN EVENT

All of these ingredients come together to braise something. In this recipe we're talking about protein, the lamb shanks. (Learn more about other items we braise in pages 10–25.) As you'll learn, we often braise tough, fattier cuts with more connective tissue. We brown these lamb shanks in the pot before the ingredients are added.

Common examples Beef, pork, and lamb roasts; short ribs; lamb and pork chops; sausages; whole chicken; chicken parts; turkey breast; fish and shellfish; beans; legumes; vegetables

5 FINISHING TOUCHES

Braised food gets cooked through fully until tender, often for hours. It can use a bright flavor touch at the end or something to provide a textural contrast to the fall-apart tender meat. This usually involves whisking together a quick, flavorful sauce; sprinkling on some fresh herbs; or passing lemon wedges at the table. These small touches work wonders for both the flavor and the visual appeal of our meals. For our lamb shanks, some lemon zest and mint freshen up the supersavory braise.

Common examples A smattering of fresh herbs, a squeeze of lemon juice, a pour of vinegar, a sprinkle of nuts, a stir-in of gremolata, a dollop of a rouille or chutney

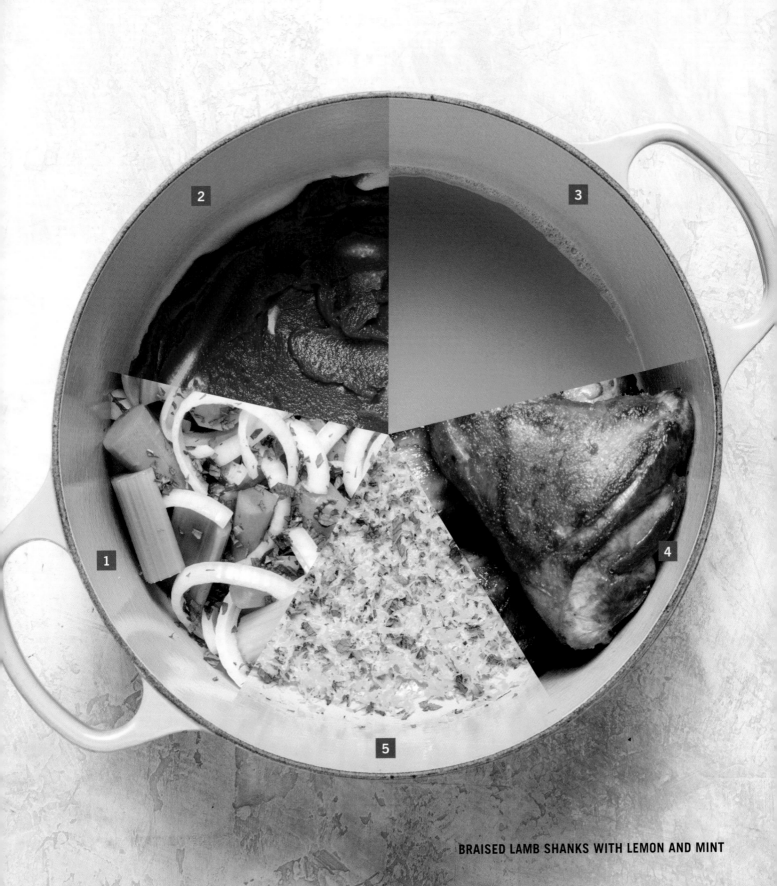

BRAISED LAMB SHANKS WITH LEMON AND MINT

Braising How-Tos

While braised dishes mostly follow a universal model, there are still techniques to learn that differ from braise to braise.

WHERE TO BRAISE: OVEN VERSUS STOVETOP

It's possible to braise in a covered pot on the stove, but we find that the direct heat of the burner is intense, specific, and often too efficient. It can cook the meat quickly and unevenly as well as affect the consistency of the braising liquid, breaking down added starch (like flour) on the bottom of the pan, creating a too-thin sauce. The oven, however, uses indirect and less efficient heat. This translates to gentle, even cooking in the closed environment of a covered pot and allows for a silky and luxurious sauce. The sweet spot is usually around 300 degrees, depending on the recipe, and always between 225 and 350. Low and slow, as they say.

While they are few in number, there are notable exceptions to our own oven-braise rule. We use the stove for thin, quick-cooking, or lean cuts, or seafood of any kind; these don't get any extra benefit from the more gentle environment of a slow oven braise. These are dishes like Steak Tips with Mushroom-Onion Gravy (page 71), with its small pieces of moderately lean, beefy sirloin steak, or the boneless, skinless chicken breasts in Chicken with Pumpkin Seed Sauce (page 200). Recipes that require frequent stirring, like Sweet-and-Sour Pork Ribs (page 147), or multiple staggered additions, like Lamb Curry with Whole Spices (page 121), make oven cooking cumbersome. Many vegetables, like the delicate green asparagus and peas in our Braised Spring Vegetables with Tarragon (page 334), would turn gray or mushy covered in the oven.

TO BROWN OR NOT TO BROWN

The claim that searing meat or fish "seals in juices" simply isn't true. It does develop browning and flavor through the Maillard reaction and creates fond in the pan that gives braising liquid depth, but it has nothing to do with juiciness. (In fact, the perception of juiciness is almost entirely determined by two factors: the fat content and the internal temperature of the food.) So you could skip this step and get a braise with meltingly tender meat. And we do on occasion: In the French veal stew Blanquette de Veau (page 128), the goal is a dish without browning and a remarkably clean flavor. Seafood is meant to be delicate and evenly cooked from top to bottom. Sometimes for ease in already-robust dishes like Guinness Beef Stew (page 84), we get a beefy boost simply by deeply browning the vegetables and adding a glutamate-rich ingredient like tomato paste.

But usually, browning the meat is one of the first steps in our braises, as the process forms thousands of new flavor compounds that we build on when developing the dish. We think it's so important that in many of our chicken dishes, where soft skin would be undesirable in the finished dish, we brown the chicken to get browned bits on the bottom of our pan and then discard the skin once it has served this foundational flavor-boosting purpose.

Some recipes are so packed with bold spices or aromatics that traditional browning—heating oil and sautéing pieces of meat in it—just isn't necessary for flavor, like our Catalan-Style Beef Stew with Mushrooms (page 92). Here, we brown while we braise. How? Over time, if a pot is left uncovered in the oven, the dry top layer of meat reaches 300 degrees—the temperature at which meat begins to brown. Only the top of the meat will brown. Sometimes that's enough and sometimes we'll stir during cooking to expose new meat to browning.

For fattier (and more unwieldy) cuts, or large-yield recipes, we'll achieve browning through another cooking technique: roasting. By precooking short ribs or oxtails in a hot oven we achieve browning, and we render a lot more fat at the start rather than in the braise.

SAUCE TALK

In a traditional meat braise, much of the silky body achieved in the sauce comes from the gelatin in the meat's bones, which transfers to the sauce. So if a cut of meat exists on the bone, you'll usually want to use the bone-in cut for our recipe.

Sometimes bone-in cuts will take too long for a weeknight and you want a boneless version, like Braised Boneless Beef Short Ribs (page 58); sometimes the ones called for in traditional versions of a recipe—like the pig trotters in French-Style Pot-Roasted Pork Loin (page 142)—aren't readily available or are hard to cook; sometimes the bones that are in the recipe aren't very rich in gelatin, like those in Pork Chops with Vinegar Peppers (page 155). Here are our methods for thickening stews or adding body to sauces when bones aren't enough.

powdered gelatin

Powdered gelatin is an easy way to create the exact same body you'd get from bones. Just hydrate and melt the gel into your liquid like the real thing. French-Style Pot Roast (page 40) usually calls for adding extraneous veal and pork parts to the pot for body; some powdered gelatin is our modern solution.

starches

Starches like flour or cornstarch, whisked with some liquid to form a slurry before entering the pot, thicken liquids with ease. Stirring flour into our Chicken Bouillabaisse (page 204) thickens the liquid but allows it to remain brothy, as is appropriate for the dish.

reduction

Reduction is a technique you'll commonly see in our braising recipes. Once the main ingredients are cooked we often simmer the sauce rapidly to concentrate its flavors and thicken it. We remove the chops from our Braised Lamb Shoulder Chops with Tomatoes and Red Wine (page 108) when they're done cooking and simmer the wine- and tomato-based braising liquid for a few minutes until perfectly pourable.

pureeing

Pureeing the softened aromatic vegetables with a little of the braising liquid before serving creates a hearty sauce. Our Simple Pot Roast (page 36) gets a sauce with gravy consistency from blended vegetables; as a bonus they release their earthiness and sweetness.

SKIM THE FAT

Collagen-rich braising cuts are often on the fattier side. Fat means flavor, but we don't want a greasy braise. Trimming all the fat before cooking would result in dry meat, so we often need to do so after cooking is done. There are three ways to do this.

spoon it

If you let the braise sit for a few minutes after cooking, some of the grease molecules will come out of emulsion and rise to the top of the pot. A large, wide spoon is best for skimming over the surface to remove the grease before reducing the liquid or serving the dish.

chill out

Many braises taste great the next day, but in addition to convenience, a bonus of making a braise in advance is that, with time, even more grease rises and the fat hardens in the fridge, making it simple to take off.

separate it

An immediate and thorough solution is to use a fat separator (see our favorite on page 32); you pour stock or sauce into the separator through a built-in strainer at the top and wait a few minutes for the fat to rise to the top of the liquid. Then you pour off liquid until only the fat remains in the separator.

Braising Time: How Long Is Long Enough?

When you're braising a chuck roast or meaty chicken thighs, you're essentially doing something you've been taught is bad: overcooking. In many cases, overcooking, however, is what makes braised food taste so good. Because when you're braising, at least as it pertains to more marbled or fattier cuts of meat and chicken, collagen doesn't even start to break down until meat reaches 140 degrees. As meat heats, protein molecules bond together tighter, pushing out moisture; as the temperature creeps up, the meat is drier and seems tougher. But "overcook" a collagen-rich cut even more, past this point, and the collagen melts into gooey gelatin, which lubricates the fibers, making the meat tender—even more tender than before the moisture was pushed out. And in the gentle environment of the no-higher-than-212-degree liquid (water's boiling point), the meat doesn't dry out as its temperature climbs—it normally tops out at an ideal 180 to 195 degrees, the temperature of simmering liquid. Sure, your braised blade steak won't be rosy-pink inside, but it will break into buttery slices under your knife.

This principle makes the method very forgiving, but you can't ignore the pot completely. There's a point at which you can go too far, when, often in the case of red meat, all the moisture is cooked out, or, as in the case of chicken, the meat completely falls off the bone and loses all flavor to the surrounding liquid. And forget slicing; an overcooked braised roast can only be shredded. Delicate white fish can overcook and become dry; vegetables can become mush.

175 degrees
Meat is fully cooked but clings to the bone.

Below see chicken thighs braised to three temperatures. At 175 degrees—the conventional recommended doneness temperature for safely consuming dark meat chicken—the chicken is just fine. It's tender but doesn't have the succulence of meat we associate with liquid-braised dishes; it clings to the bone when you try to pull it. The thigh cooked to 195 degrees— a full 20 degrees higher—is something else: meltingly tender, yielding and pullable, and succulent, with rich poultry flavor. Take the thighs too far, to 210, and they slump off the bone, can look gray, and taste bland; they've been sapped of savor.

195 degrees
Meat is meltingly tender.

210 degrees
Meat is bland, stringy, and falls off the bone.

Make It Ahead

Braises are nearly impossible to overcook (for more information on this, see page 6), and they often taste better the next day, when the flavors have mingled even longer. Plus, braising liquid and sauces are easier to defat after chilling. These factors make braised dishes perfect for entertaining guests or simply for meal planning during busy weeks. As a general rule meat, poultry, and bean braises can be stored in the refrigerator for three days and certain dishes can be frozen. Braised fish and delicate vegetable sides can be reheated at your discretion, but we don't consider them great options for make-ahead cooking. Here are our tips for storing and reheating braises.

keep it together

When you're storing a braised dish with distinguishable major components—protein and sauce—there's no need to separate them. First, this makes it simple to reheat without mess. Second, flavor transfer will continue to take place—at a much-decelerated rate—in the cold refrigerator. And the meat will stay moist within the liquid. Scrape off the fat that's risen to the top after refrigerating before reheating the dish.

reheating meat

Braises take well to reheating, but all require that you take a gentle approach so that the meat comes up to temperature slowly and evenly. And don't heat the food until scorching hot; this will raise the doneness temperature, squeezing out more moisture so the made-ahead dish is drier than the original. Large roasts (think: pot roast) do well in a 325-degree oven for 30 to 45 minutes, depending on the roast's size. Pieces of meat, often with a bone (think: oxtails, short ribs, or chicken parts), are easier to monitor and rearrange on the stove. Heat them covered in their liquid at a gentle simmer until heated through, 1 to 1½ hours, redistributing occasionally.

A large, flat brisket can soak up a lot of goodness if sliced before reheating; then you can serve it right in the luxurious sauce. After storing, remove the brisket from the sauce and scrape the fat from the surface of the sauce. Slice the brisket into ¼-inch-thick slices and return to the baking dish with the sauce. Cover the baking dish with aluminum foil and reheat in a 350-degree oven until heated through, 1 to 1½ hours.

freezer friend: stews and chilis

Stews and chilis, with their small cuts of meat, are perfect for the refrigerator or the freezer. If you're freezing the stew, divide it among individual airtight containers, freeze for up to a month, and let thaw in the refrigerator before simmering it over low heat, stirring occasionally.

brighten up the flavor

We often add acid to a braised recipe in the form of lemon juice or vinegar. But storing can dull its flavor. If a braised recipe calls for stirring in an acidic ingredient at the end, leave it out before storing and stir it in when reheating the sauce. Similarly, sometimes peas or another green vegetable or herbs finish a braised dish with freshness. If braising ahead, leave these out and heat them for the required time (or stir them in at the end) when reheating the dish.

All About Beef

Many parts of the cow contain lots of connective tissue, making them just right for braising. Braised beef dishes come in many forms: a pot roast that cuts into buttery pieces, wide slices of juicy brisket, cubes of tender meat in a stew, individual servings of short ribs (on or off the bone), and if we're cooking *en cocotte*, even rosy-red medium-rare roast beef. Many of these cuts, because of all that intramuscular fat and tissue, are the most inexpensive options at the butcher shop. Here are the techniques and shopping tips to get you braising with beef.

PRIMAL CUTS

Before choosing a cut of beef for braising, it helps to understand the anatomy of a cow. Eight different cuts of beef are sold at the wholesale level. From this first series of cuts, known in the trade as primal cuts, butchers make the retail cuts that you find at the market.

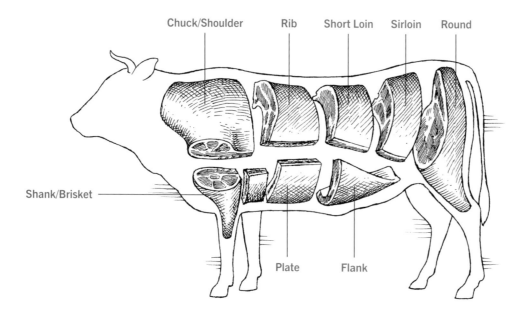

Chuck/Shoulder The chuck (also called the shoulder) runs from the neck down to the fifth rib. There are four major muscles in this region. Meat from here tends to be flavorful and fairly fatty, and contains a good amount of connective tissue.

Rib The rib section extends along the back of the animal from the sixth to the 12th rib. The prime rib comes from this area, as do rib-eye steaks. Rib cuts have beefy flavor and are quite tender, making them the best for roasting or searing.

Short Loin The short loin (also called the loin) extends from the last rib back through the midsection of the animal to the hip area. It contains two major muscles—the tenderloin and the shell. The tenderloin is mild and extremely tender. The shell is much larger and has a more robust flavor as well as more fat.

Sirloin The sirloin contains relatively inexpensive cuts that are sold as both steaks and roasts. Sirloin cuts are fairly lean and tough. They're good cut into pieces for quick braises, or cooked en cocotte until medium-rare.

Round Roasts and steaks cut from the round are usually sold boneless. They are quite lean and can be tough.

Shank/Brisket, Plate, and Flank Moderately thick boneless cuts are removed from the three primal cuts that run along the underside of the animal. The brisket (also called shank) is rather tough and contains a lot of connective tissue, which usually requires a long braise to become tender. The plate is rarely sold at the retail level (it is used to make pastrami). The flank is a leaner cut that tastes great as a steak.

BEEF CUTS FOR BRAISING

Here are the test kitchen's top picks for beef braises. We've also listed the primal cut from which the roast is cut when it's not obvious.

**CHUCK-EYE ROAST
(Chuck/Shoulder)**

This tender, juicy boneless roast is cut from the center of the first five ribs and it contains an abundant amount of fat. It's also called boneless chuck roll and boneless chuck fillet. We like the chuck-eye roast for its compact, uniform shape, deep flavor, and tenderness in braised applications. This roast is often tied (see page 13 for tying instructions) when braised whole, or cut into cubes for stews and chilis.

**BLADE STEAK
(Chuck/Shoulder)**

Top blade (or simply blade) steak is a small shoulder cut. While we don't braise steak often—most steaks are best seared—blade steaks take well to the technique as they're well-marbled and taste best and are most juicy when cooked well-done. Blade steak can also be cut into cubes for stew meat; be sure to remove the line of gristle before doing so.

TOP SIRLOIN ROAST

Other parts of the sirloin are lean and tough, but top sirloin roast is a great inexpensive cut. This cut from the hip area tastes incredibly meaty and has plenty of marbling, which makes for a succulent braise. Aside from an unpleasant vein of gristle that runs through it, this roast is tender and juicy with big, beefy flavor.

BEEF SHANK

Shank (also called shin), a cut from the upper portion of a steer's legs, is incredibly beefy-tasting but also quite lean, so the cooking liquid requires little, if any, skimming. It's loaded with collagen, giving the meat and the cooking liquid a silky richness. It's a bargain cut, cheaper than both chuck and short ribs. Shank is typically sold in two forms: boneless long-cut and crosscut, which can be sold with or without the bone. We prefer long-cut because it contains more collagen.

BRISKET

This large, rectangular cut is often divided into two subcuts, the flat cut and the point cut, the knobby point cut overlapping the rectangular flat cut. Because the flat cut is easy to find, cheap, and fairly uniform in shape, it's the cut we generally prefer. Make sure to trim the fat cap according to the instructions in whatever recipe you are using for the best flavor and texture.

FLANK STEAK (Flank)

Flank steak is intensely flavorful, so it stands up to a long cooking time. It's on the leaner side so shouldn't be overcooked.

SHORT RIBS

These meaty ribs can be cut from various locations on the cow, although they commonly come from the underside of the animal. English-style short ribs are 2- to 4-inch lengths of bone with a wide piece of fatty meat attached. They are easy to find at the supermarket and usually cheaper than flanken, so we prefer them in the test kitchen. Flanken-style short ribs are about ¾ inch thick, cut across the ribs and grain, and they include two or three segments of rib bone. We find them harder to eat than English-style short ribs; thus, we don't recommend them.

OXTAILS

Inexpensive oxtails are a very gelatin-rich cut of meat that makes up the actual tail area of a steer raised for meat (as tails of oxen are no longer available). All of that gelatin makes them perfect for low, slow cooking, and oxtail braises have luxurious body. Depending on which part of the tail they come from, oxtail pieces can vary in diameter from ¾ inch to 4 inches. (Thicker pieces are cut close to the body; thinner pieces come from the end of the tail.) Try to buy oxtail packages with pieces approximately 2 inches thick and between 2 and 4 inches in diameter; they will yield more meat and lend more flavor to the broth. Oxtails are often found in the freezer section of the grocery store; if using frozen oxtails, be sure to thaw them completely before using.

BUYING BEEF

There are not only a large number of beef cuts to choose from, but there are a variety of other factors (and price tags) to consider when picking one out at the butcher's counter. Here's what is helpful to know when buying beef.

buy choice or prime

The U.S. Department of Agriculture (USDA) assigns different quality grades to beef, and beef that is graded should bear a USDA grade stamp, though it may not be visible to the consumer. Most meat available to consumers is confined to the top three grades: prime, choice, and select. Prime is the highest grade and the meat is heavily marbled with intramuscular fat, which makes for a tender, flavorful steak. Choice is the second-highest grade and it's generally moderately marbled with intramuscular fat; the majority of graded beef is choice. Select is the third-highest grade and it has little marbling. In a blind tasting of all three grades (using rib steaks), we found that prime ranked first for its tender, buttery texture and rich beefy flavor, followed by choice with good meaty flavor and a little more chew. The select beef was ranked last, with a tough stringy texture and barely acceptable flavor. If you can find and afford prime quality beef, go for it, but choice quality is a fine option.

buy organic

The government regulates the use of the term "organic" on beef labels, but producers set their own guidelines when it comes to the term "natural." If you want to ensure that you're buying meat raised without antibiotics or hormones and fed an organic diet (and no mammalian or aviary products), then look for the USDA's organic seal.

grain-fed versus grass-fed beef

Most U.S. beef is raised on grain but grass-fed beef is becoming an increasingly popular option. Grain-fed beef is generally considered to be richer and fattier, while grass-fed beef is leaner, chewier, and more gamy—or at least that's the conventional wisdom. In our taste tests, we pitted grain-fed and grass-fed rib-eye steaks and strip steaks against each other. We found differences among the various strip steaks to be quite small. The grain-fed rib eyes had a milder flavor compared with the nutty, complex flavor of the grass-fed beef, but our tasters' preferences were evenly split. The texture of all samples was similar, but we did find that the grass-fed beef cooked slightly faster than grain-fed beef, so be sure to check the meat for doneness at the beginning of a recommended time range.

WHAT'S WAGYU?

What do the terms "Kobe beef," "Wagyu beef," and "American Wagyu" mean exactly? Wagyu is a breed of cattle raised in Kobe, the capital city of Japan's Hyogo prefecture. Wagyu have been bred for centuries for their rich intramuscular fat, the source of the buttery-tasting, supremely tender meat. Wagyu cattle boast extra fat since they spend an average of one year longer in the feedlot than regular cattle, and end up weighing between 200 and 400 pounds more at slaughter. What's more, the fat in Wagyu beef is genetically predisposed to be about 70 percent desirable unsaturated fat and about 30 percent saturated fat, while the reverse is true for conventional American cattle.

In order to earn the designation "Kobe beef," the Wagyu must come from Kobe and meet strict production standards that govern that appellation. Despite what you may see on a menu, however, Wagyu consumed stateside is nearly always domestically raised—so it can't possibly be Kobe beef. The "American Wagyu" or "American-Style Kobe Beef" is usually a cross between Wagyu and Angus, but the U.S. Department of Agriculture requires that the animal be at least 50 percent Wagyu and remain in the feedlot for at least 350 days to receive these designations.

Snake River Farms, located in Idaho, has one of the largest herds of American Wagyu. When we tasted its beef ($18 to $50 per pound, depending on the cut) against regular prime beef ($13 to $30 per pound), the Wagyu proved itself a delicacy worthy of an occasional splurge: It was strikingly rich, juicy, and tender. The prime beef was also very good, but its texture and taste weren't quite as luxuriant. That said, braising does the job of making almost any meat luxuriant, so this is a splurge we'd likely leave for searing or roasting.

two ways to tie a roast

Most roasts are unevenly shaped, which leads to uneven cooking. For long, more cylindrical cuts, such as beef sirloin roast or pork loin, we even out thickness with a series of ties down the length. For squat roasts such as the chuck-eye roast, we wrap longer pieces of kitchen twine around the perimeter to cinch in the sides and give the roast a neater shape.

For Long Roasts

Wrap piece of kitchen twine around roast and fasten with double knot, repeating along length of roast, spacing ties about 1½ inches apart.

For Squat Roasts

Wrap piece of kitchen twine around roast about 1 inch from bottom and tie with double knot. Repeat with second piece of twine, wrapping it about 1 inch from top.

trimming beef

Even though fat gives beef flavor, sometimes we like to trim some of the exterior fat on beef cuts; if you cut the fat before cooking, the grease won't end up in the braise.

cutting stew meat

Stay away from precut cubes of "stewing" meat in the supermarket; you don't know exactly what cut you're getting—and you could end up with dry stew. We prefer to purchase a whole cut of meat—most often marbled chuck-eye roast—and cut it into stew meat ourselves. This also ensures even-size pieces (and therefore even cooking) and allows us to cut away any gristle or unnecessary extra fat.

1 Pull apart roast at major seams (delineated by lines of fat and silverskin). Use knife as necessary.

2 Trim excess fat and silverskin.

3 Cut meat in cubes or pieces as directed in specific recipes.

salting meat

Salting meat and letting it sit in advance of cooking is a technique we sometimes use to help meat retain its moisture (and season it deeply). The salt draws moisture to the meat's surface. The moisture dissolves the salt, and then the meat reabsorbs it; the salt changes the protein structure so that the meat better holds on to this moisture. One cut we like to salt in particular is brisket; the muscle fibers on a flat-cut brisket are very tight. Because it's particularly dense, we like to poke the brisket with holes using a fork or skewer, so the salt better penetrates. And then we let the salt do its thing for at least 6 hours before cooking. Other cuts, like pieces of flap meat for sirloin steak tips, require just a toss with salt and a brief sit.

All About Lamb

Lamb is undergoing a renaissance of late and is no longer relegated to the Easter table. And for good reason. Many cuts are perfect for braising, and its rich flavor can't be beat.

PRIMAL CUTS

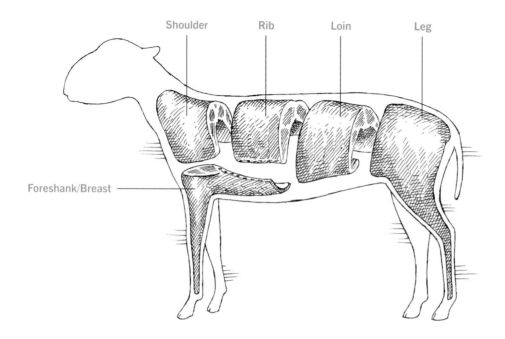

Shoulder   Rib   Loin   Leg

Foreshank/Breast

Shoulder This area extends from the neck through the fourth rib. Meat from this area is flavorful and contains a fair amount of connective tissue. Chops, roasts, and boneless stew meat all come from the shoulder.

Rib The rib area is directly behind the shoulder and extends from the fourth to the 12th rib. The rack (all eight ribs from this section) is cut from the rib. When cut into individual chops, the meat is called rib chops. Meat from this area has a fine, tender grain and a mild flavor.

Loin The loin extends from the last rib down to the hip area. The loin chop is the most familiar cut from this part of the lamb. Like the rib chop, it is tender and has a mild, sweet flavor.

Leg The leg area runs from the hip down to the hoof. It may be sold whole or broken into smaller roasts and shanks (one comes from each hind leg). These roasts may be sold with the bones in, or they may be butterflied and sold boneless.

Foreshank/Breast The foreshank and breast is cut from the underside of the animal. This area includes the two front legs (each yields a shank) as well as the breast, which is rarely sold in supermarkets.

LAMB CUTS FOR BRAISING

These are the test kitchen's favorite lamb cuts for braising.

BLADE CHOPS
(Shoulder)

There are two kinds of shoulder chop. The blade chop is roughly rectangular in shape and contains a piece of the chine bone (the backbone) and a thin piece of the blade bone (the shoulder blade). They are rich in fat, and their bold, gutsy flavor stands up to all the liquid in a braise.

ROUND CHOPS
(Shoulder)

The round-bone, or arm, chop is oval in shape. Round-bone chops contain less fat and fewer muscles than blade chops, making them easier to cut into pieces for stews.

LAMB SHANK

Don't let the odd shape of a shank intimidate you; they are incredibly flavorful and inexpensive to boot. Logically enough, shanks can come from either the front legs (fore shanks) or back legs (hind shanks) of the lamb. The two shanks are basically interchangeable as far as cooking technique is concerned.

LEG OF LAMB

Up near the hip is the butt end of the leg (which includes the sirloin, or hip meat); below that is the shank end, with the shank (or ankle) at the very bottom. We prefer the shank end, which is easier to work with and yields more meat. For an impressive roast, we like to braise boneless leg of lamb. There are two methods butchers use to remove the bone, referred to as corkscrewed and butterflied; we find the corkscrewed type much easier to work with, but a butterflied leg of lamb will also work. We also cut it into pieces for stews and curries.

BUYING LAMB

Lamb is becoming more popular. It can be relatively inexpensive and is easy to turn into something special with the right recipes. Note that most markets contain just a few of our favorite cuts, so you may need to special-order lamb.

buy young lamb

Most lamb sold in the supermarket has been slaughtered when 6 to 12 months old. When the animal is slaughtered past the first year, the meat must be labeled mutton. Generally, younger lamb has a milder flavor that most people prefer. The only indication of slaughter age at the supermarket is size. A whole leg of lamb weighing 9 pounds is likely to have come from an older animal than a whole leg weighing just 6 pounds.

domestic versus imported lamb

While almost all the beef and pork sold in American markets is raised domestically, you can purchase imported as well as domestic lamb. Domestic lamb is distinguished by its larger size and milder flavor, while lamb imported from Australia or New Zealand has a stronger, gamier taste. The reason for this difference in taste boils down to diet and the chemistry of lamb fat. Imported lamb is pasture-fed on mixed grasses, while lamb raised in the United States begins on a diet of grass but finishes with grain.

KEY PREP TIPS

trimming boneless leg of lamb

Trimming the lamb of excess fat and silverskin will give it a cleaner flavor, as lamb's gaminess largely comes from its fat, and the meat will be less chewy.

Place lamb on cutting board with fat cap facing down. Using sharp knife, trim any pockets of fat and connective tissue from underside of lamb.

trimming lamb shanks

Lamb shanks can be quite fatty and it's important to trim them before braising so the dish doesn't become too greasy.

Using boning knife, remove excess fat from exterior of shanks.

All About Pork

We love the meaty, almost sweet flavor of pork in all of its forms, from large shoulder roasts to weeknight-friendly pork chops. With the exception of the loin (and we cover the best way to braise that, too), much of the pig contains the intramuscular fat and connective tissue that we like for braising cuts and which result in ultratender braised dishes with rich flavor.

PRIMAL CUTS

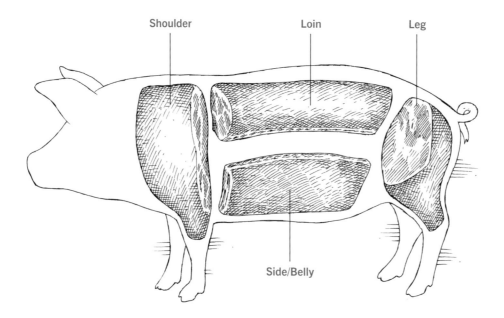

Shoulder Cuts from the upper portion of the shoulder (called the blade shoulder) are well marbled with fat and contain a lot of connective tissue, making them ideal candidates for braising or barbecuing. Cuts from the arm, or picnic shoulder, are a bit more economical than those from the blade area but are otherwise quite similar.

Loin The area between the shoulder and back legs is the leanest, most tender part of the animal. Rib and loin chops are cut from this area, as are pork loin roasts and tenderloin roasts.

Leg The rear legs are often referred to as "ham." This primal cut is sold as large roasts and is available fresh or cured.

Side/Belly The underside is the fattiest part of the animal and is the source of bacon and spareribs.

PORK CUTS FOR BRAISING

These are the cuts of pork we braise most often in the test kitchen. This chart helps you understand their differences so you can shop with confidence.

PORK BUTT (Blade Shoulder)

This large, flavorful cut (often labeled Boston butt or pork shoulder) can weigh as much as 8 pounds when sold with the bone in. Many markets take out the bone and sell this cut in smaller chunks. This cut is ideal for slow-roasted shredded pork dishes.

BLADE CHOP (Loin)

All chops are cut from the loin, so it's important to be specific. Cut near the fatty shoulder end, this chop's high proportion of marbled dark meat and connective tissue makes it ideal for braising. Because of these qualities, we braise blade chops longer than we do rib chops.

RIB CHOP (Loin)

Cut from the rib section of the loin, these chops have a large eye of loin muscle but enough fat to stay succulent. They're easily identified by the bone that runs along one side and the one large eye of loin muscle. They need less cooking time than blade chops.

BONELESS BLADE-END LOIN ROAST

This boneless roast is cut from the shoulder end of the loin and has plenty of fat and flavor. Unfortunately, this cut can be hard to find, but the more readily available boneless center-cut loin roast serves as a strong stand-in.

BONELESS CENTER-CUT LOIN ROAST

This boneless roast is widely available but less fatty and flavorful than the blade-end roast; make sure to buy a center-cut roast with a decent fat cap on top. The two can usually be used interchangeably.

COUNTRY-STYLE PORK RIBS

Country-style ribs aren't ribs at all: They come from the region where the loin meets up with the blade, or shoulder, of the animal. Therefore, they contain a mix of lean light meat from the loin, rich dark meat from the shoulder, and, if bone-in, part of the shoulder blade or rib bone. They're meaty and boast rich pork flavor.

HAM HOCKS

Ham hocks give porky (and sometimes smoky) flavor to soups, stews, and pots of long-simmered greens. Cut from the lower portion of the pig's hind leg, the hock has lots of fat, bone, and connective tissue, plus a little meat, so it requires long cooking to release flavor and tenderize. Ham hocks are usually sold smoked or cured, although fresh ones are available, too.

BUYING PORK

The majority of pork sold in today's supermarkets bears little resemblance to the pork our grandparents consumed. New breeding techniques and feeding systems have slimmed down the modern pig, which contains a third less fat than it did 30 years ago. As you might imagine, leaner pork is not as flavorful and is prone to drying out as it cooks. Here's what you need to know when buying pork.

buy pink pork

Raw pork can range in color from a pasty white to a deep pink, and color is an indication of quality. The color of pork reflects the meat's pH, and even small differences in pH can have a significant impact on flavor and texture. In fact, a high pH can be even more important than fat in determining flavor. Compared to rosy-pink high-pH pork, pork with low pH is paler, softer, and relatively bland. So don't be fooled into thinking that pork is "the other white meat," but rather pick out the pinkest pork you can find at the market.

buy unenhanced or natural pork

Because modern supermarket pork is so lean and prone to dryness, many producers now inject their fresh pork products with a sodium solution. So-called enhanced pork is now the only option at many supermarkets, especially for lean cuts like the tenderloin. To be sure, read the label; if the pork has been enhanced it will have an ingredient list.

berkshire pork

Chefs and consumers pay top dollar for specialty heritage pork breeds, such as Berkshire (known as Kurobuta in Japan) and Duroc. They are touted as being fattier, juicier, and much more flavorful. Putting this claim to the test, we tasted both Berkshire and Duroc pork in a side-by-side test against regular supermarket pork. The Berkshire pork consistently came out on top for being the juiciest and most intensely flavored. Some stores carry Berkshire pork and you can order it online, but it does costs much more than supermarket pork.

KEY PREP TIPS

---

preventing curled pork chops

Pork chops come covered in a thin layer of fat and connective tissue (or silverskin). This layer contracts faster than the rest of the meat, causing buckling and leading to unevenly cooked chops. Cutting slits in this layer solves the problem.

For each chop, cut 2 slits about 2 inches apart through fat and connective tissue.

---

tying a pork loin

Tying a pork loin helps maintain its shape during cooking so that it cooks evenly.

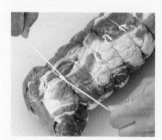

Wrap piece of kitchen twine around roast and fasten with double knot, repeating along length of roast, spacing ties about 1½ inches apart.

---

cutting a crosshatch into a beef or pork roast

To help the meat absorb a salt rub and help the fat render during cooking, we score a crosshatch pattern into the fat cap of the roast.

Using sharp knife, cut evenly spaced slits in crosshatch pattern in fat cap, being careful not to cut into meat.

All About Veal

We don't cook veal often but when we do, it's a treat. We braise flavorful shanks (osso buco) and use shoulder for stew. But veal can be controversial. "Natural" is the term used to inform the consumer that the calves move freely, without the confines of stalls as with milk-fed veal. Natural veal is generally raised on grass (the calves can forage) and without hormones or antibiotics. Natural veal is darker, meatier, and more like beef. Milk-fed veal is milder, paler in color, and more tender. Each has its supporters.

PRIMAL CUTS OF VEAL

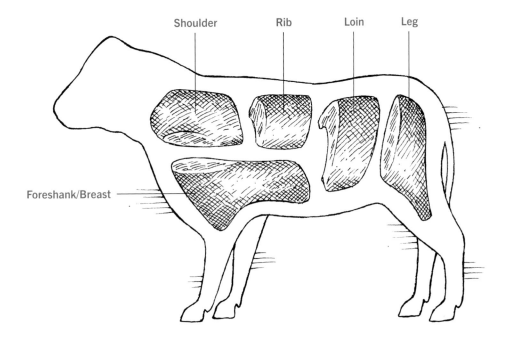

Shoulder   Rib   Loin   Leg

Foreshank/Breast

Shoulder This area includes the front of the animal and runs from the neck through the fifth rib. Boneless shoulder roast is our favorite for stews since the roast is meaty and doesn't contain too much gristle or fat.

Rib This prime area of the calf includes ribs 6 through 12 along the top half of the animal. Expensive rib chops are ideal candidates for grilling.

Loin Farther back from the rib, the loin section runs along the top half of the animal and extends from the 13th rib back to the hip bone. Meat from this area is tender and lean. It is also very expensive and best suited to grilling.

Leg The section includes both the sirloin (the hip) and the actual leg. Cuts from this section often contain multiple muscles and connective tissue. Veal cutlets, known as scaloppini, come from this portion of the animal.

Foreshank/Breast The underside of the animal yields various cuts, most of which require prolonged cooking to make tender. Veal shanks, also known as osso buco, come from this area, which is also home to the breast roast. Make sure not to buy veal shanks boneless; we love how the marrow-packed bone adds flavor and body to the braising medium.

All About Fish and Shellfish

Braising might not be the first cooking technique that comes to mind for delicate fish, but the ocean's the limit when it comes to braising fish and seafood. Braising simmers and steams anything from lean, meaty halibut fillets to oily fish like salmon to small pieces of shellfish until tender but still succulent. As a moist-heat cooking method, braising is gentle and thus forgiving, all but guaranteeing moist fish.

BUYING

Buying top-quality fish is just as important as utilizing the proper cooking technique. Here's what to look for either from a fishmonger or at the supermarket.

buy fresh fish

Buying fresh fish is key for good flavor and texture. Try to always buy fish from a trusted source, preferably one with a high volume to help ensure freshness. Both the store, and the fish in it, should smell like the sea (not fishy or sour), and all the fish should be on ice or properly refrigerated. Fillets and steaks should look bright, shiny, and firm, not dull or mushy. It is always better to have your fishmonger slice steaks and fillets to order rather than buying precut pieces that may have been sitting around.

keep it cold

It is important to keep your fish very cold. If you have a long ride home, ask for a plastic bag of ice that you can put under the fish. Because fish is so perishable, it's best to buy it the day it will be cooked. If that's not possible, unwrap the fish, pat it dry, put it in a zipper-lock bag, press out the air, and seal the bag. Set the fish on a bed of ice in a bowl or container (to hold the water once the ice melts), and place it in the back of the fridge, where it is coldest. If the ice melts before you use the fish, replenish it. The fish should keep for one day.

buy mussels and oysters with closed shells

The key to buying bivalves is freshness. They should smell clean and the shells should look moist. Look for tightly closed shells and avoid any that are broken or sitting in a puddle of water. Some clam and mussel shells may gape slightly, but they should close when they are tapped. Discard any that won't close; they may be dead and should not be eaten. Every bag of mussels and clams that is harvested commercially must be tagged by the grower. And the retailer is required to keep the tag attached to the original container until that container is empty. Any legitimate seller will show you the tag upon request, and if the date is within a couple of days of your purchase, you know you have a fresh product.

store bivalves properly

Storing mussels and clams properly will ensure that they stay fresh before serving. They need to be kept moist and cold and have access to oxygen. Do not place them inside a sealed plastic bag or submerge them in water or they'll die. Store mussels and clams in a colander of ice set over a bowl with a damp towel draped over the top. Stored properly, they should keep for up to three days.

buy frozen shrimp

Virtually all shrimp sold in supermarkets today were frozen at some point. Because it's hard to know how long "fresh" (defrosted) shrimp have been sitting at the fish counter, we recommend buying bags of still-frozen shrimp and defrosting them at home. Shell-on shrimp tend to be sweeter. Make sure your shrimp are preservative-free (shrimp should be the only thing on the ingredient list). Shrimp are sorted and sold by size; see below for more information.

SORTING OUT SHRIMP SIZES

Shrimp are sold both by size (small, medium, etc.) and by the number needed to make 1 pound, usually given in a range. Choosing shrimp by the numerical rating is more accurate, because the size labels vary from store to store. Here's how the two sizing systems generally compare:

Small	51 to 60 per pound
Medium	41 to 50 per pound
Medium-Large	31 to 40 per pound
Large	26 to 30 per pound
Extra-Large	21 to 25 per pound
Jumbo	16 to 20 per pound

FISH AND SHELLFISH FOR BRAISING

Here we list all the fish and shellfish that are best suited for braising and that have recipes in the book. We explain what they are and show what you can expect to see at the supermarket.

COD

Cod is a white fish with a medium-firm, meaty texture and a clean, mild flavor. We like braising skinless cod fillets.

BASS

Sea bass is a sweet, mild white fish with a medium-firm texture, also good in many dishes that call for firm white fish.

HALIBUT

Sold as whole steaks, belly steaks, and fillets, this firm, lean white fish is mild but rich, ideal for robust flavor pairings, and it holds up well and provides contrast in seafood soups and stews. We braise fillets with vegetables and cook whole steaks *en cocotte*.

HADDOCK

Usually sold as skin-on fillets, haddock is a very mild white fish with a medium-firm texture. It's a good substitute for cod.

HAKE

We use hake fillets for braising. They're meaty with a clean, mild flavor, and also a good substitute for cod.

SALMON

We cook salmon fillets en cocotte for evenly cooked, moist salmon every time. We like the mild flavor and silky texture of marbled farm-raised salmon more often than leaner wild salmon. When filleted, salmon is most often sold deboned, but it's prudent to check for pin bones (see page 22).

SWORDFISH

Swordfish is incredibly meaty, and steaks of it indeed cook up like steak when braised using an *en cocotte* method. Swordfish steaks can stand up to robust flavors.

MONKFISH

Monkfish is nice for braising because it's quite firm, almost impervious to breaking apart in the braising liquid. It's purchased as skinless, boneless loin-shaped pieces cut from the tail. It has a hearty, rich, slightly musky flavor.

CLAMS

There are many varieties of clams available throughout the United States, but they generally fall into two categories: hard-shelled and soft-shelled. Hard-shell clams have thick, hard shells; the two most common varieties are littleneck clams and cherrystone clams. Soft-shell clams have thin, brittle shells and common varieties include steamers and razor clams. Make sure that shells are tightly closed and avoid any that are open or gaping; they may be dying or dead. Clams must be scrubbed to remove sand and grit before cooking (see page 22).

MUSSELS

The two main varieties you will see at the store are the Atlantic blue mussel and the Pacific green-lipped (also called New Zealand) mussel. These mussels are interchangeable when it comes to cooking, although some think the green-lipped mussels are slightly chewier. Most mussels sold today are farmed or rope-cultured, which is good because they are less gritty. Make sure that shells are tightly closed and avoid any that are open or gaping; they may be dying or dead.

SCALLOPS

We use larger sea scallops (not seasonal tiny bay scallops) in braises since they can withstand the cooking time. And they're in markets year-round. They're shucked at sea, so before cooking, simply remove the crescent-shaped muscle that attaches the scallop to the shell. Avoid "wet" scallops (ask at the store), which are treated with a solution of water and sodium tripolyphosphate to preserve them. But if wet is all you can find, soak them in 1 quart of cold water, ¼ cup of lemon juice, and 2 tablespoons of salt for 30 minutes to mask any chemical flavors.

SHRIMP

Sweet shrimp are great in seafood stews. Shrimp are sold by size as well as by the number needed to make 1 pound, usually given in a range. Choosing shrimp by the numerical rating is more accurate, because the size label can vary from store to store.

SQUID

Squid is perfect for braising because its naturally chewy texture becomes more tender and its mild flavor is the perfect vehicle for a host of bold flavors as in tomato-based stews. We typically separate the body from the tentacles before cutting the body into rings.

OCTOPUS

Octopus is great for braising as it's tough and collagen-rich. An octopus has a large sac on its head, which is surrounded by eight muscular, sucker-bearing arms. There are more than 300 different species of these cephalopods. We've had the most success using frozen octopus from either Spain or Portugal. (Frozen octopus is actually preferable to fresh because the ice crystals help to break down the muscle fibers.) Frozen octopus is cleaned during processing, but it's necessary to rinse the suckers well to rid them of dirt. Octopus is made up of 50 to 80 percent salt water; the finished volume of your dish could be less than half of what you started with and very salty if you don't follow the recipe.

KEY PREP AND SERVING TIPS

Here's what you should do when getting ready to braise fish and shellfish.

removing skin from a fish fillet

Some recipes recommend removing the skin from the fish before cooking.

Using tip of boning knife or sharp chef's knife, cut skin away from fish at corner of fillet. When sufficient skin is exposed, grasp skin firmly with paper towel, hold it taut, and slice remaining skin off flesh.

removing pin bones from salmon

Pin bones can sometimes be hidden inside a piece of salmon. Always check the salmon for these bones before cooking.

1 Drape fillet over inverted bowl to help any pin bones protrude. Then, working from head end to tail end, locate pin bones by running your fingers along length of fillet (they will feel like tiny bumps).

2 Use needle-nose pliers or tweezers to grasp tip of bone. To avoid tearing flesh, pull slowly but firmly at slight angle in direction bone is naturally pointing rather than straight up. Repeat until all pin bones are removed.

cutting salmon into fillets

Buying a large piece of salmon and cutting it into fillets at home ensures that the pieces are the same thickness and will cook at the same rate.

Using sharp chef's knife, cut whole salmon fillet into even-size portions.

scrubbing mussels and clams

Bivalves often have fine bits of sand and grit stuck within the crags of their shells and need to be scrubbed before cooking.

Place mussels or clams in colander and scrub briefly with vegetable brush under cold running water. Discard any that are cracked or open.

debearding mussels

There can be a small, weedy beard protruding from the side of the mussel that needs to be removed before cooking.

Holding mussel in your hand, pull beard firmly out of shell, using your thumb and side of paring knife to grip it firmly.

peeling and deveining shrimp

It's better to buy shrimp with their shells intact and then peel and devein them yourself because the shrimp will have better flavor.

1 Break shell on underside, under swimming legs, which will come off as shell is removed. Leave tail intact, if desired, or tug tail to remove shell.

2 Use paring knife to make shallow cut along back of shrimp to expose vein.

3 Using tip of knife, lift vein out. Discard vein by wiping knife blade against paper towel.

preparing octopus

For our Red Wine–Braised Octopus (page 252) and other braised octopus dishes, we like to simmer the octopus first in water to remove some of its salty juices. A bonus: The octopus is easier to clean and cut after this step.

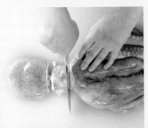

1 Using sharp knife, separate octopus mantle (large sac) and body (lower section with tentacles) from head (midsection containing eyes); discard head.

3 Using your fingers, grasp skin at base of each tentacle and pull toward tips to remove. Be careful not to remove suction cups from tentacles.

2 After simmering in water, while octopus is still warm, use paring knife to cut mantle into quarters (or halves), then trim and scrape away skin and interior fibers.

4 Cut tentacles from around core of body in 3 sections; discard core. Separate tentacles.

Braising Beans and Vegetables

Braising is easy to define and illustrate using cuts of beef; Simple Pot Roast (page 36) and Modern Beef Stew (page 78) made with chuck-eye roast—and their many variations—are probably the most commonly recognized braises. Of course, however, the concept translates to other main ingredients—lamb, veal, pork, poultry, and even delicate seafood. But braising isn't just for proteins: Beans and vegetables can be braised as well with great results. In the pages that follow, we outline the unique properties of vegetables and beans and how best to braise them.

BRAISING WITH BEANS

Some of the most appealing braises combine beans and meat, like hearty Ultimate Chili (page 102) or rich Moroccan Braised White Beans with Lamb (page 114). And classic bean braises are canvases for flavors from around the world: Hearty Tuscan White Bean Stew (page 297) features creamy cannellini beans (cooking them perfectly is a point of pride in Tuscany); the beans in Chickpeas with Spinach, Chorizo, and Smoked Paprika (page 311) are a counterpoint to bold smoke and spice; Spiced Red Lentils (*Masoor Dal*) (page 325) become creamy and comforting and redolent with the flavors of traditional Indian *masoor dal*. Rushing bean cooking causes the starches to swell unevenly and the skins to burst: That's why we braise rather than boiling, as we do with pasta. As with many of our meat braises, we often use the oven to cook bean recipes because it's easy to maintain a gentle simmer and because the heat is more evenly distributed so the beans on the bottom of the pot don't cook too quickly.

brining beans

If we're braising dried beans, we like to brine them—soak them in a saltwater solution—for at least 8 hours or up to 24 hours. The water alone does a job: It starts the hydration process so soaked beans cook faster than unsoaked (as much as 45 minutes faster), and they absorb water more evenly for a creamier end result. But this doesn't do much for the skin, which can still be a tough shield around even the most perfectly creamy beans. In addition to being tough, they're also rigid, so beans can burst since they expand as they cook. That's where the salt comes in: It causes the beans to cook up with soft skins. Why? The sodium weakens the pectin bonds that keep the bean skins intact. That's why a soak isn't enough; you want to brine your beans.

adding baking soda to beans

Even if you're brining your beans, they still take some time to cook. But there is a shortcut: adding baking soda at the start of cooking. The alkaline environment created in the pot by adding the baking soda forces the pectin strands to break down, which weakens the cell walls and allows water to be absorbed at a faster rate for a quickly cooked bean. It's important to use baking soda sparingly, however: Too much can give the beans a bitter, soapy flavor.

In addition, baking soda can be used to set the color of black beans, as in our Brazilian Black Bean and Pork Stew (page 328), preventing them from turning a grayish-purple color when cooked. The coating of black beans contains anthocyanins (colored pigments) that change color with alterations in pH: A more alkaline broth makes them darker.

cooking canned beans

We most often braise dried beans because they soak up the flavor of the broth readily in the longer cooking time. But we like the ease of canned beans, too, and while they can save time, they still should be cooked—even though they're already fully cooked. Cooking them twice allows for flavor absorption and produces beans that meld into the dish much better.

Soaked Beans
Tough skins burst
during cooking.

Brined Beans
Soft, elastic skins
remain intact.

BRAISING WITH VEGETABLES

We know vegetables can be sautéed, roasted, and steamed. So why would we want to cover the pot on vegetables and braise them? Braising vegetables causes them to cook in their own juices, turning them perfectly tender and ensuring earthy sweetness—they taste most like themselves, neither too sweet nor washed-out. The slow, gentle technique also allows heartier vegetables to break down slowly and evenly: Think about rugged kale turning silky and hard cubes of butternut squash creamy. The long cooking also mellows the flavors of more sulfurous cruciferous vegetables so they're universally enjoyable.

pectin, again

Pectin is a soluble fiber and is therefore present in high amounts in many fiber-full vegetables just as it is in beans. The pectin acts like glue that holds the cell walls together, giving raw vegetables snap, or even a hard texture. During cooking, however, the pectin breaks down, weakening the structure of the cell walls, which then collapse, creating a tender vegetable. That means many of the same pH principles apply. And for vegetables with high amounts of pectin, you can manipulate cooking with the addition of acid or baking soda, as with our Mediterranean Braised Green Beans (page 364), in which we use both.

two-part cooking

Braised vegetables don't have to have the untouched appearance of vegetables out of the steamer basket. Just like with meat, browning can make vegetables taste good because of the caramelization of their abundant sugars. When we braise vegetables in a skillet or sauté pan, we can evaporate water quickly (typically we don't want stewy vegetable side dishes), and we can turn up the heat at this point to achieve the browning of sautéed vegetables. In our Braised Red Potatoes with Lemon and Chives (page 373), for example, we cover and cook halved new potatoes in liquid with butter until tender and then crank the heat to evaporate the liquid and let the cut sides sizzle in the buttery pan until crispy and browned like roasted potatoes. As with other foods, we also brown vegetables at the beginning of the process by adding fat to the pan and sautéeing before pouring in liquid and covering, as with our Braised Cauliflower with Garlic and White Wine (page 357), which get nutty browning.

PICK YOUR POTATO

Depending on the recipe, sometimes we want our potatoes to break down to add body to the braise, as in Brunswick Stew (page 219); here we use workaday russet potatoes, the starchiest at the supermarket. Sometimes creaminess or a rustic feel is what we're after, so we use buttery-tasting medium-starch Yukon Gold potatoes, as in Modern Beef Stew (page 78) or Carne Guisada (page 89). But other times, whether braised on their own or as a secondary ingredient in a meat braise, we want the potatoes to completely hold their shape; that's when we choose waxy red potatoes. Red potatoes not only maintain their shape when cooked for long periods of time; they cook up incredibly creamy and smooth.

In Braised Red Potatoes with Lemon and Chives (page 373), we cook halved red potatoes for as long as 35 minutes—by which point we'd expect them to be overcooked. Instead they were creamy throughout—a trait we don't always associate with low-starch red potatoes. And when we tried to cook russets this way, they broke down and turned crumbly and mushy. Why?

A little-known but key difference between waxy potatoes (red or new potatoes) and starchy potatoes (russets) is that they contain different ratios of two different starches: amylopectin and amylose. Waxy potatoes contain very little amylose; as they cook, the starch granules in waxy potatoes burst, releasing very sticky amylopectin, which in essence glues the potato structure together, giving the impression of creaminess. In a russet or other starchy potato, there is a higher ratio of the second starch—amylose—which is made up of smaller molecules that are less sticky. Despite the fact that, overall, russets contain more starch than do waxy potatoes (hence they are often described as being "high starch"), russets simply fall apart once overcooked since most of the starch is the less sticky amylose.

Crumbly
"Overcooked" starchy russets break apart.

Creamy
"Overcooked" waxy new potatoes hold together.

Soak It Up

One of the beauties of braised dishes like Brisket Carbonnade (page 45) or Red Wine–Braised Pork Chops (page 150) is that they create a rich, velvety sauce, perfect for pouring over fluffy mashed potatoes, creamy polenta, or buttery noodles. Here are our favorite starchy sides for soaking up flavorful sauces.

CLASSIC MASHED POTATOES

serves 4 to 6

Russet potatoes make fluffier mashed potatoes, but Yukon Golds have an appealing buttery flavor and can be used. Mashed potatoes are a good match for just about any braise.

2 pounds russet potatoes, unpeeled

8 tablespoons unsalted butter, melted

1 cup half-and-half, warmed

Salt and pepper

1 Place potatoes in large saucepan and cover with cold water by 1 inch. Bring to boil over high heat, reduce heat to simmer, and cook until potatoes are just tender (paring knife can be slipped in and out of potatoes with little resistance), 30 to 45 minutes. Drain.

2 Using potholder or folded dish towel to hold potatoes, peel skins from potatoes with paring knife. For slightly chunky texture, return peeled potatoes to now-empty pot and mash smooth using potato masher. For creamy texture, set ricer or food mill over now-empty pot; cut peeled potatoes into large chunks and press or mill into saucepan in batches. Stir in melted butter until incorporated. Gently whisk in half-and-half and season with salt and pepper to taste. Serve.

Mashed Potatoes with Scallions and Horseradish

Stir ¼ cup prepared horseradish and 3 minced scallions, green parts only, into warm half-and-half before adding to mashed potatoes.

Garlic Mashed Potatoes

Toasting the garlic is essential for mellowing it. Avoid using unusually large garlic cloves, as they will not soften.

Toast 20 unpeeled garlic cloves in covered 8-inch skillet over lowest heat possible until spotty dark brown and slightly softened, about 22 minutes. Off heat, let sit, covered, until fully softened, 15 to 20 minutes. Peel and mince garlic, then stir into mashed potatoes with half-and-half. (If using ricer or food mill, softened garlic cloves can be processed along with potatoes.)

BOILED RED POTATOES WITH BUTTER AND HERBS

serves 4 to 6

We prefer to use small red potatoes measuring 1 to 2 inches in diameter. If using larger potatoes, halve or quarter the potatoes and adjust the cooking time as needed. Boiled potatoes work just as well with dishes that make small amounts of sauce as with those with abundant liquid.

2 pounds small red potatoes, unpeeled

2 tablespoons unsalted butter

Salt and pepper

1 tablespoon minced fresh chives, tarragon, or parsley

Place potatoes in large pot and cover with cold water by 1 inch. Bring to boil over high heat. Reduce heat to simmer and cook until potatoes are tender, 20 to 25 minutes. Drain potatoes well, then toss gently with butter in large bowl until butter melts. Season with salt and pepper to taste, sprinkle with chives, and serve.

MASHED POTATOES AND ROOT VEGETABLES

serves 4 to 6

Russet potatoes will yield a slightly fluffier, less creamy mash, but they can be used in place of the Yukon Gold potatoes. It is important to cut the potatoes and root vegetables into evenly sized pieces so they cook at the same rate. The sweetness of the roots are a nice foil to savory beef or rich pork.

1½ pounds Yukon Gold potatoes, peeled, quartered lengthwise, and cut crosswise into ¼-inch-thick slices

4 tablespoons unsalted butter

8 ounces carrots, parsnips, turnips, and/or celery root, peeled (carrots and parsnips cut into ¼-inch-thick half-moons, turnips and celery root cut into ½-inch dice)

⅓ cup vegetable broth

Salt and pepper

¾ cup half-and-half, warmed

3 tablespoons minced fresh chives

1 Rinse potatoes using 3 or 4 changes of cold water, then drain well. Melt butter in large saucepan over medium heat. Add root vegetables and cook, stirring occasionally, until butter is browned and vegetables are dark brown and caramelized, 10 to 12 minutes. (If after 4 minutes vegetables have not started to brown, increase heat to medium-high.)

2 Stir in potatoes, broth, and ¾ teaspoon salt, cover, and reduce heat to low. Simmer gently, stirring occasionally and adjusting heat as needed, until potatoes fall apart easily when poked with fork and all liquid has been absorbed, 25 to 30 minutes. Remove pan from heat, remove lid, and allow steam to escape for 2 minutes.

3 Gently mash potatoes and root vegetables in saucepan with potato masher (do not mash vigorously). Gently fold in warm half-and-half and chives. Season with salt and pepper to taste, and serve.

SIMPLE WHITE RICE

serves 4 to 6

A nonstick saucepan works best here, although a traditional saucepan will also work. This is a good all-purpose white rice recipe.

1 tablespoon unsalted butter or vegetable oil

2 cups long-grain white rice, rinsed

3 cups water

Salt and pepper

1 Melt butter in large saucepan over medium heat. Add rice and cook, stirring constantly, until grains become chalky and opaque, 1 to 3 minutes. Add water and 1 teaspoon salt, increase heat to high, and bring to boil, swirling pot to blend ingredients. Reduce heat to low, cover, and simmer until all liquid is absorbed, 18 to 20 minutes.

2 Remove pot from heat and lay clean folded dish towel underneath lid. Let sit for 10 minutes. Fluff rice with fork, season with salt and pepper to taste, and serve.

BASMATI RICE PILAF

serves 4 to 6

Long-grain white, jasmine, or Texmati rice can be substituted for the basmati. A nonstick saucepan works best here, although a traditional saucepan will also work. Aromatic basmati rice is nice with Indian and Middle Eastern dishes.

1 tablespoon extra-virgin olive oil

1 small onion, chopped fine

Salt and pepper

1½ cups basmati rice, rinsed

2¼ cups water

1 Heat oil in large saucepan over medium heat until shimmering. Add onion and ¼ teaspoon salt and cook until onion is softened, about 5 minutes. Stir in rice and cook, stirring often, until grain edges begin to turn translucent, about 3 minutes. Stir in water and bring to simmer. Reduce heat to low, cover, and continue to simmer until rice is tender and water is absorbed, 16 to 18 minutes.

2 Remove pot from heat and lay clean folded dish towel underneath lid. Let sit for 10 minutes. Fluff rice with fork, season with salt and pepper to taste, and serve.

CLASSIC COUSCOUS

serves 4 to 6

Do not substitute large-grain couscous (also known as Israeli couscous) here; it requires a much different cooking method. To make this dish vegetarian, substitute vegetable broth for the chicken broth. Couscous is a classic pairing for Moroccan tagines but goes nicely with other North African and Middle Eastern dishes.

2 tablespoons unsalted butter

2 cups couscous

1 cup water

1 cup chicken broth

Salt and pepper

Melt butter in medium saucepan over medium-high heat. Add couscous and cook, stirring frequently, until grains are just beginning to brown, about 5 minutes. Add water, broth, and ½ teaspoon salt and stir briefly to combine. Cover, remove pan from heat, and let stand until grains are tender, about 7 minutes. Uncover, fluff grains with fork, and season with salt and pepper to taste. Serve.

Couscous with Garlic, Lemon, and Herbs

Stir 2 minced garlic cloves and 1 teaspoon grated lemon zest into toasted couscous and cook until fragrant, about 15 seconds, before adding liquids and salt. Gently fold 2 tablespoons minced fresh parsley (or tarragon, chives, or cilantro) and 1 tablespoon lemon juice into couscous before serving.

CREAMY PARMESAN POLENTA

serves 4 to 6

Coarse-ground degerminated cornmeal such as yellow grits (with grains the size of couscous) works best in this recipe. Avoid instant and quick-cooking products, as well as whole-grain, stone-ground, and regular cornmeal. Do not omit the baking soda—it reduces the cooking time and makes for a creamier polenta. If the polenta bubbles or sputters even slightly after the first 10 minutes, the heat is too high and you may need a flame tamer. A flame tamer keeps polenta and sauces from simmering too briskly. You can buy one or easily make one. Shape a sheet of heavy-duty foil into a 1-inch-thick ring that fits on your burner, making sure the ring is of even thickness. Polenta is a nice alternative to mashed potatoes with most dishes, especially French- or Italian-style ones.

7½ cups water

Salt and pepper

Pinch baking soda

1½ cups coarse-ground cornmeal

4 ounces Parmesan cheese, grated (2 cups), plus extra for serving

2 tablespoons unsalted butter

1 Bring water to boil in large, heavy-bottomed saucepan over medium-high heat. Stir in 1½ teaspoons salt and baking soda. Slowly pour cornmeal into water in steady stream while stirring back and forth with wooden spoon. Bring mixture to boil, stirring constantly, about 1 minute. Reduce heat to lowest setting and cover.

2 After 5 minutes, whisk polenta to smooth out any lumps that may have formed, about 15 seconds. (Make sure to scrape down sides and bottom of pan.) Cover and continue to cook, without stirring, until grains of polenta are tender but slightly al dente, about 25 minutes longer. (Polenta should be loose and should barely hold its shape but will continue to thicken as it cools.)

3 Off heat, stir in Parmesan and butter and season with salt and pepper to taste. Let stand, covered, for 5 minutes. Serve with extra Parmesan.

CARAWAY AND BUTTERED EGG NOODLES

serves 4 to 6

Gently chopping the caraway seeds brings out their flavor. Egg noodles are commonly served with French, German, or other Central European dishes. The caraway flavor goes particularly well with pork.

12 ounces (7¾ cups) egg noodles

Salt

4 tablespoons unsalted butter, cut into 4 pieces

1 teaspoon caraway seeds, chopped

2 tablespoons finely chopped fresh dill or chives

1 Bring 4 quarts water to boil in large pot. Add noodles and 1 tablespoon salt and cook until al dente. Drain noodles and return to pot.

2 Meanwhile, melt 3 tablespoons butter in small saucepan over medium-low heat. Add caraway seeds and cook, swirling pan occasionally, until butter is nutty brown and fragrant, about 5 minutes. Add browned butter mixture, dill, and remaining 1 tablespoon butter to pot with noodles and toss to combine. Season with salt to taste, and serve.

Equipment

Dutch Oven

A Dutch oven just might be the most important—and versatile—cooking vessel you can own. Dutch ovens can go on the stove and in the oven, making them ideal for braising meat. These kitchen workhorses make cooking in one pan a breeze, as you can sear, sauté, and simmer away in these heavy-duty pots. They're made from a range of materials but you want cast iron, which retains heat well, and enameled, which makes the pot easy to clean.

OUR FAVORITES Le Creuset 7¼ Quart Round Dutch Oven ($368) and Cuisinart 7 Qt. Round Covered Casserole ($71) (Best Buy)

Roasting Pan

It might have the word "roasting" in the name, but the roasting pan serves a variety of uses in braising: Render the fat from short ribs or oxtails before braising, brown and braise a large batch of beef stew, or slow-cook a brisket.

OUR FAVORITE Calphalon Contemporary Stainless Roasting Pan with Rack ($99.99)

Traditional Skillet

Skillet-braising in a stainless-steel skillet results in the formation of flavorful fond in the bottom of the pan. Buy a good traditional skillet and you will have it for a lifetime of cooking. Look for an ovensafe model with balanced weight, sturdy construction, and flared sides for good evaporation. It's also good to have a tight-fitting lid.

OUR FAVORITE All-Clad 12-Inch Stainless Steel Fry Pan with Lid ($120)

Nonstick Skillet

Look for an ovensafe model with a broad cooking area, a dark finish, and a grippy, stay-cool handle. It's also good to have a tight-fitting lid to keep the steam in the braise. A nonstick skillet is good for ensuring that delicate braised vegetables won't stick to the bottom of the pan.

OUR FAVORITE OXO Good Grips Non-Stick 12-inch Open Frypan ($40)

Baking Dish

We often cover brisket with sauce and braise it in a shape-flattering 13- by 9-inch baking dish. We don't broil after braising, but a broiler-safe dish is also a good investment for other cooking.

OUR FAVORITES Pyrex Easy Grab 3-Quart Oblong Baking Dish ($7.29), HIC Porcelain Lasagna Baking Dish ($56) (Broiler-Safe)

Oven Thermometer

For reliable, consistent results when braising, an accurate oven thermometer is critical to ensure your oven is calibrated perfectly.

OUR FAVORITE CDN Pro Accurate Oven Thermometer ($6)

Digital Instant-Read Thermometer

There is nothing worse than braising a great cut of meat for an extended amount of time and then worrying about over- or undercooking it. This problem is easily solved by buying a good instant-read thermometer—an absolute essential in our opinion and an indispensable tool in your braising arsenal.

OUR FAVORITES ThermoWorks Thermapen Mk4 ($99) and ThermoWorks ThermoPop ($29) (Best Buy)

KNIVES AND OTHER TOOLS

Chef's Knife

A sturdy, sharp 8-inch blade and a comfortable grip make this knife useful for everything from mincing herbs and chopping aromatics to butchering chicken to carving a finished roast.

OUR FAVORITE Victorinox Swiss Army 8-inch Fibrox Pro Chef's Knife ($41)

Boning Knife

When it comes to the intricate work of skinning fish fillets or removing the breast from a whole chicken, a boning knife is best. A good boning knife will be at least 6 inches long, very sharp, and agile, letting you maneuver nimbly around joints and bones.

OUR FAVORITE Victorinox Swiss Army 6-inch Fibrox Pro Flexible Boning Knife ($22)

DO YOU NEED A TAGINE?

We have four Moroccan-style tagines in this book; we love their aromatic, richly spiced, and sweet and savory character. The vessel they're traditionally cooked in goes by the same name. The tagine has a distinctive conical lid; as steam rises during cooking, it condenses in the tip of the relatively cool lid (it's farther from the heat source than most lids) and drips back into the stew, conserving water in the process. Less steam loss means you can start off with less liquid and therefore end up with more concentrated flavors. When we tested our Chicken Tagine with Olives and Lemon (page 212) in both tagines and Dutch ovens, however, we found that while the amount of liquid left behind in the stews varied, that variance translated to little flavor difference. If you're a stickler for tradition, choose a tagine with a heavy, tight-fitting lid. But a Dutch oven will do the job just as well.

Slicing/Carving Knife

The long, thin blade of this knife makes slicing a large roast or turkey breast safe and easy.

OUR FAVORITE Victorinox Swiss Army 12-inch Fibrox Pro Granton Edge Slicing/Carving Knife ($58)

Carving Fork

This tool holds pieces of meat in place while carving and makes for neater serving.

OUR FAVORITE Mercer Culinary Genesis 6-inch High-Carbon Carving Fork ($26)

Twine

Essential for tying roasts into shape and birds' legs together, this strong, no-fray cotton twine stays in place without splitting during braising.

OUR FAVORITE Librett Cotton Butcher's Twine ($8)

Tongs

A good pair of tongs is essential for grabbing and turning all kinds of food on the stovetop or in the oven.

OUR FAVORITE OXO Good Grips 12-Inch Locking Tongs ($12.09)

Fat Separator

A fat separator defats braising liquids almost immediately for grease-free sauces.

OUR FAVORITE Cuisipro Fat Separator ($22)

Fine-Mesh Strainer

A stable and durable—and comfortable to hold— fine-mesh strainer is great for straining braising liquids and sauces so they're silky-smooth.

OUR FAVORITE Rösle Fine Mesh Strainer, Round Handle, 7.9 inches, 20 cm ($39)

Cutting Board

The right durable cutting board ensures safe slicing and dicing.

OUR FAVORITES Proteak Edge Grain Teak Cutting Board ($105) and OXO Good Grips Carving & Cutting Board ($25)

Carving Board

Designed with trenches to contain braising juices and a well to hold a roast in place, this board is essential for slicing a wide variety of meats.

OUR FAVORITE J.K. Adams Maple Reversible Carving Board ($69.95)

Ladle

Serving a stew or chili may seem straightforward—until you try to do it with a poorly designed ladle. A ladle with a pouring rim, a hook for resting on the Dutch oven, and an offset handle ensure mess-free serving.

OUR FAVORITE Rösle Hook Ladle with Pouring Rim ($29)

Blender

Sometimes we blend the braising liquid at the end of cooking to combine the flavors and use the ingredients in the braise—softened vegetables—to thicken and add body to the sauce. There is quite a range of blenders on the market so you'll want to choose based on how many other kitchen tasks you turn to your blender for. (Nut butter or hummus enthusiasts, pureed soup makers, and smoothie drinkers will want a higher-end blender and will love the luxury of a Vitamix, while those using a blender mainly for drinks, soups, and braise sauces can purchase an inexpensive blender).

OUR FAVORITE Vitamix 5200 ($442) (High-End) and Black + Decker Performance FusionBlade Blender ($151) (Inexpensive)

Food Processor

A food processor with a good motor and sharp blade that doesn't leak will make quick work of preparing large amounts of vegetables for braises, pureeing onions or chiles for the base of stews or chilis, creating fillings for stuffed meats or vegetables, or making toppings to finish a braise.

OUR FAVORITE Cuisinart Custom 14-Cup Food Processor ($159)

BEEF

Italian Pot Roast

36 **Simple Pot Roast**
with Root Vegetables

39 **Italian Pot Roast**

40 **French-Style Pot Roast**

42 **Beef in Barolo**

45 **Brisket Carbonnade**

46 **Atlanta Brisket**

48 **Braised Brisket with Pomegranate, Cumin, and Cilantro**
Beer-Braised Brisket with Prunes and Ginger
Red Wine—Braised Brisket with Thyme

51 **Oaxacan-Style Beef Brisket**

52 **Home-Corned Beef and Cabbage**

55 **Braised Beef with Red Wine and Cherries**

56 **Beef en Cocotte with Caramelized Onions**

58 **Braised Boneless Beef Short Ribs**
with Guinness and Prunes

60 **Red Wine—Braised Short Ribs with Bacon, Parsnips, and Pearl Onions**
Porter-Braised Short Ribs with Prunes and Brandy

62 **Pomegranate-Braised Short Ribs with Prunes and Sesame**

64 **Chinese-Style Braised Short Ribs**

66 **Shredded Beef Tacos (Carne Deshebrada)**

68 **Braised Oxtails with White Beans, Tomatoes, and Aleppo Pepper**
Roman Braised Oxtails

71 **Steak Tips with Mushroom-Onion Gravy**

72 **Braised Steaks with Root Vegetables**
Braised Steaks with Mushrooms and Tomatoes

74 **Braciole**

77 **Cuban Braised Shredded Beef (Ropa Vieja)**

78 **Modern Beef Stew**

80 **Beef Stew with Parsnips, Kale, and Mushrooms**

83 **Big Batch Beef Stew**

84 **Guinness Beef Stew**

86 **Modern Beef Burgundy**

89 **Carne Guisada**

90 **Daube Provençal**

92 **Catalan-Style Beef Stew with Mushrooms**

95 **Chinese-Style Red-Cooked Beef**

97 **Portuguese-Style Beef Stew (Alcatra)**

98 **Sichuan Braised Tofu with Beef (Mapo Tofu)**

100 **Flank Steak in Adobo**

102 **Ultimate Chili**

105 **Beef Short Rib Ragu**

SIMPLE POT ROAST

serves 6 to 8

1 (3½- to 4-pound) boneless beef chuck-eye roast, trimmed and tied at 1-inch intervals

Salt and pepper

2 tablespoons vegetable oil

1 onion, chopped fine

1 small carrot, peeled and chopped

1 small celery rib, chopped

2 garlic cloves, minced

2 teaspoons sugar

1 cup chicken broth

1 cup beef broth

1 sprig fresh thyme

¼ cup dry red wine

Why This Recipe Works Pot roast is one of the most fundamental examples of a hearty, comforting braise: Slow-cooking an economical roast in liquid with vegetables and aromatics until it's succulent is an accessible technique, and some version of this is seen in most every culture. We wanted to achieve a supremely tender roast along with a deliciously savory sauce to spoon over mashed potatoes or egg noodles. After testing various cuts of meat, we determined that chuck-eye roast is the best choice for pot roast; its fat and connective tissue break down and keep the meat moist during the long braise. (For more information on chuck roast, see page 11.) For the braising liquid, equal amounts of beef and chicken broth tasted best, and we added just enough water for the liquid to come about halfway up the sides of the roast and prevent it from drying out. When it comes to cooking a pot roast, there are two typical approaches: Cook it on the stove or in the oven. After a few rounds of stovetop cooking, we felt that it was too difficult to maintain a steady, low temperature with the flame from below. We transferred the Dutch oven, covered with foil under the lid for a tight seal, to a 300-degree oven where the roast could cook more evenly. When we tested the roast with a fork and it met no resistance, we were rewarded with moist, flavorful meat. Use a good-quality, medium-bodied wine, such as a Côtes du Rhône or a Pinot Noir, for this dish.

1 Adjust oven rack to middle position and heat oven to 300 degrees. Pat roast dry with paper towels and season with salt and pepper.

2 Heat oil in Dutch oven over medium-high heat until shimmering. Brown roast on all sides, 8 to 10 minutes, reducing heat if fat begins to smoke. Transfer roast to large plate.

3 Reduce heat to medium; add onion, carrot, and celery to pot and cook, stirring occasionally, until beginning to brown, 6 to 8 minutes. Add garlic and sugar; cook until fragrant, about 30 seconds. Add chicken broth, beef broth, and thyme sprig, scraping up any browned bits.

4 Return roast and any accumulated juices to pot; add enough water to come halfway up sides of roast. Bring liquid to simmer over medium heat. Place large piece of aluminum foil over pot and cover tightly with lid; transfer pot to oven. Cook, turning roast every 30 minutes, until fully tender and fork slips easily in and out of meat, 3½ to 4 hours.

5 Transfer roast to carving board and tent with foil. Let liquid in pot to settle for about 5 minutes, then use wide spoon to skim fat from surface; discard thyme sprig. Bring liquid to boil over high heat and cook until reduced to about 1½ cups, about 8 minutes. Add wine to pot and cook until reduced to 1½ cups, about 2 minutes. Season with salt and pepper to taste.

6 Remove twine from roast. Slice meat against grain into ½-inch-thick slices or pull apart into large pieces. Transfer meat to serving platter and pour about ½ cup sauce over meat. Serve, passing remaining sauce separately.

Simple Pot Roast with Root Vegetables

Add 1½ pounds carrots, sliced ½ inch thick; 1½ pounds small red potatoes, halved if larger than 1½ inches in diameter; and 1 pound parsnips, sliced ½ inch thick, to Dutch oven after cooking beef for about 3 hours, submerging them in liquid. Continue to cook until vegetables are almost tender, 30 minutes to 1 hour longer. Transfer roast to carving board and tent with aluminum foil. Let liquid in pot to settle for about 5 minutes, then use wide spoon to skim fat from surface; remove thyme sprig. Add wine and salt and pepper to taste; boil over high heat until vegetables are tender, 5 to 10 minutes. Using slotted spoon, transfer vegetables to warmed serving platter. Slice meat against grain into ½-inch-thick slices or pull apart into large pieces; transfer meat to bowl or platter with vegetables and pour about ½ cup sauce over meat and vegetables. Serve, passing remaining sauce separately.

ITALIAN POT ROAST

serves 4 to 6

1 (3½- to 4-pound) boneless beef chuck-eye roast, trimmed and tied at 1-inch intervals

Salt and pepper

2 tablespoons vegetable oil

1 onion, chopped

1 celery rib, minced

1 pound cremini or white mushrooms, trimmed and quartered

2 tablespoons tomato paste

1 (14.5-ounce) can diced tomatoes

1 cup red wine

½ cup canned tomato sauce

½ cup water

1 large garlic head, outer papery skins removed, halved

2 teaspoons sugar

1 sprig fresh thyme

1 sprig fresh rosemary

Why This Recipe Works The bolder Italian American cousin of classic pot roast, Italian pot roast trades the potatoes, carrots, and gravy for mushrooms, onion, and a thick sauce made from tomatoes, red wine, garlic, and herbs. As with our Simple Pot Roast (page 36), we went with chuck-eye roast for the cut of meat since the method and end goal aren't all that different. Since Italian pot roast is all about its sauce, we wanted to make sure it was big in flavor but also balanced: The acidic tomatoes and red wine and the potent garlic should complement one another and not overpower the beefy taste of the roast. We found we needed to employ tomatoes in three forms—diced, sauce, and paste—for the thick, rich sauce we were looking for; a double dose of red wine added depth and brightness. Simmering a whole head of garlic with our roast ensured that the meat and sauce were infused with a mellow (not overwhelming) garlic flavor. Start checking the roast for doneness after 2 hours; if there is a little resistance when prodded with a fork, it's done. Use a light, sweeter wine, such as a Merlot or Beaujolais, for this dish.

1 Adjust oven rack to middle position and heat oven to 300 degrees. Pat roast dry with paper towels and season with salt and pepper.

2 Heat oil in Dutch oven over medium-high heat until just smoking. Brown roast on all sides, 8 to 10 minutes. Transfer roast to large plate. Reduce heat to medium; add onion, celery, mushrooms, and tomato paste; and cook until vegetables begin to soften, about 8 minutes. Add diced tomatoes and their juices, ½ cup wine, tomato sauce, water, garlic, sugar, and thyme sprig. Return roast and any accumulated juices to pot. Bring liquid to simmer over medium-high heat. Place large piece of aluminum foil over pot and cover tightly with lid; transfer pot to oven.

3 Cook until roast is just fork-tender, 2½ to 3½ hours, turning roast after 1 hour. Remove lid and foil and let roast rest for 30 minutes, skimming fat from surface of liquid after 20 minutes. Transfer roast to carving board and tent with foil.

4 Remove and reserve garlic head and skim remaining fat. Add remaining ½ cup wine to pot, bring to boil over medium-high heat, and cook until sauce begins to thicken, about 12 minutes. Meanwhile, carefully squeeze garlic cloves from their skins and mash into paste. Add rosemary to pot and simmer until fragrant, about 2 minutes. Remove rosemary and thyme sprigs, stir in mashed garlic, and season with salt and pepper to taste.

5 Remove twine from roast. Slice meat against grain into ½-inch-thick slices or pull apart into large pieces. Transfer meat to serving platter and pour ¾ cup sauce over meat. Serve, passing remaining sauce separately.

FRENCH-STYLE POT ROAST

serves 6 to 8

1 (4- to 5-pound) boneless beef chuck-eye roast, pulled apart at seams and trimmed

Kosher salt and pepper

1 (750-ml) bottle red wine

10 sprigs fresh parsley, plus 2 tablespoons minced

2 sprigs fresh thyme

2 bay leaves

3 slices thick-cut bacon, cut into ¼-inch pieces

1 onion, chopped fine

3 garlic cloves, minced

1 tablespoon all-purpose flour

2 cups beef broth

4 carrots, peeled and cut on bias into 1½-inch pieces

3 tablespoons unsalted butter

2 cups frozen pearl onions, thawed

2 teaspoons sugar

10 ounces white mushrooms, trimmed and halved if small or quartered if large

1 tablespoon unflavored gelatin

Why This Recipe Works French-style pot roast (*boeuf à la mode*) is richer and deeper in flavor than its American cousin and dates back to a time when a multiday recipe was the rule rather than the exception. The elegant dish calls for a full bottle of wine for flavor, adds collagen-rich veal and pork parts for body, and has a separately prepared mushroom-onion garnish. To skip the time-consuming accessories, we started with our well-marbled pot roast choice, chuck; split it in half to expose more surface area; and salted the meat for an hour to ramp up the meaty flavor by drawing moisture out of the meat and forming a shallow brine that was then reabsorbed. This resulted in particularly luxurious meat. Traditionally the beef is marinated in the wine before cooking, but we found the step unnecessary; the roast tasted fruity and rich just from braising in the wine. Reducing the wine rather than simply pouring in the bottle gave it extra complexity. The gelatin from the additional bones gives French pot roast a rich, saucy braising liquid rather than a brothy one. To keep the ingredient list as streamlined as possible, we went straight to the source: powdered gelatin. The sauce reduced to a rich and velvety consistency. Use a medium-bodied, fruity red wine, such as a Côtes du Rhône or Pinot Noir, for this recipe.

1 Season beef with 2 teaspoons salt, place on wire rack set in rimmed baking sheet, and let stand at room temperature for 1 hour.

2 Meanwhile, bring wine to simmer in large saucepan over medium-high heat. Cook until reduced to 2 cups, about 15 minutes. Using kitchen twine, tie parsley sprigs, thyme sprigs, and bay leaves into bundle.

3 Pat beef dry with paper towels and season generously with pepper. Using 3 pieces of kitchen twine for each piece of beef, tie crosswise to form even roasts.

4 Adjust oven rack to lower-middle position and heat oven to 300 degrees. Cook bacon in Dutch oven over medium-high heat, stirring occasionally, until crispy, 6 to 8 minutes. Using slotted spoon, transfer bacon to paper towel–lined plate and reserve. Pour off all but 2 tablespoons fat from pot; heat fat over medium-high heat until beginning to smoke. Brown roasts on all sides, 8 to 10 minutes. Transfer roasts to large plate.

5 Reduce heat to medium; add onion and cook, stirring occasionally, until beginning to soften, 2 to 4 minutes. Add garlic, flour, and reserved bacon; cook, stirring constantly, until fragrant, about 30 seconds. Add broth, reduced wine, and herb bundle, scraping up any browned bits. Return beef and any accumulated juices to pot; increase heat to high and bring to simmer. Place large sheet of aluminum foil over pot and cover tightly with lid; transfer pot to oven. Cook, turning beef every hour, until fork slips easily in and out of meat, 2½ to 3 hours, adding carrots to pot after 2 hours.

6 While beef cooks, bring butter, pearl onions, ½ cup water, and sugar to boil in 12-inch skillet over medium-high heat. Reduce heat to medium, cover, and cook until onions are tender, 5 to 8 minutes. Uncover, increase heat to medium-high, and cook until all liquid evaporates, 3 to 4 minutes. Add mushrooms and ¼ teaspoon salt; cook, stirring occasionally, until vegetables are browned and glazed, 8 to 12 minutes. Remove from heat and set aside. Sprinkle gelatin over ¼ cup water in bowl and let sit until gelatin softens, about 5 minutes.

7 Transfer beef to carving board and tent with foil. Let liquid in pot settle for about 5 minutes, then use wide spoon to skim fat from surface. Discard herb bundle and stir in onion-mushroom mixture. Bring liquid to simmer over medium-high heat and cook until mixture is slightly thickened and reduced to 3¼ cups, 20 to 30 minutes. Season sauce with salt and pepper to taste. Add softened gelatin and stir until completely dissolved.

8 Remove twine from roasts. Slice meat against grain into ½-inch-thick slices. Divide meat among warmed bowls or transfer to platter; arrange vegetables around meat, pour sauce over top, and sprinkle with minced parsley. Serve.

BEEF IN BAROLO

serves 6

1 (3½- to 4-pound) boneless beef chuck-eye roast, pulled apart at seams and trimmed

Salt and pepper

2 (¼-inch-thick) slices pancetta (4 ounces), cut into ¼-inch pieces

2 onions, chopped

2 carrots, peeled and chopped

2 celery ribs, chopped

3 garlic cloves, minced

1 tablespoon tomato paste

1 tablespoon all-purpose flour

½ teaspoon sugar

1 (750-ml) bottle Barolo wine

1 (14.5-ounce) can diced tomatoes, drained

10 sprigs fresh parsley

1 sprig fresh rosemary

1 sprig fresh thyme, plus 1 teaspoon minced

Why This Recipe Works Beef in Barolo is a hearty yet elegant braise enjoyed in households across the Piedmont region of Italy for special occasions. This pot roast is supreme because it's cooked in a full bottle of Barolo, often called the king of wines. Rich, full-bodied, and velvety, the wine reduces to an ultraluxurious and complex-tasting sauce that can't be achieved with a lighter-bodied wine. *Bresato al Barolo*'s purpose is to highlight this ingredient, so we sought to do justice to this regal wine. We started with our favorite cut for braises, chuck-eye roast, but it has a line of fat in the middle that doesn't easily break down. Separating the meat at the seam enabled us to discard excess fat before braising and create two roasts, which cooked quicker than one large roast. We kept the aromatics simple, and to temper the Barolo's bold flavor, we also added a can of diced tomatoes, plus just ½ teaspoon of sugar balanced the wine's acidity. After 3 hours of braising in a low oven (which provided even, consistent heat), a dark, full-flavored, and lustrous sauce bestowed nobility on our humble cut of meat.

1 Adjust oven rack to middle position and heat oven to 300 degrees. Pat beef dry with paper towels and season generously with pepper. Using 3 pieces of kitchen twine for each piece of beef, tie crosswise to form even roasts.

2 Cook pancetta in Dutch oven over medium-low heat until browned and fat is rendered, about 8 minutes. Using slotted spoon, transfer pancetta to bowl. Pour off all but 2 tablespoons fat from pot. Heat fat left in pot over medium-high heat until just smoking. Brown roasts on all sides, 8 to 10 minutes. Transfer roasts to large plate.

3 Add onions, carrots, and celery to fat left in pot and cook over medium heat until softened and lightly browned, 6 to 8 minutes. Stir in garlic, tomato paste, flour, sugar, and pancetta and cook until fragrant, about 1 minute. Slowly whisk in wine, scraping up any browned bits and smoothing out any lumps. Stir in tomatoes, parsley sprigs, rosemary sprig, and thyme sprig. Nestle roasts into pot along with any accumulated juices and bring to boil. Place large sheet of aluminum

foil over pot and cover tightly with lid; transfer pot to oven. Cook, turning roasts every 45 minutes, until beef is tender and fork slips easily in and out of meat, about 3 hours.

4 Transfer roasts to carving board and tent with foil. Let liquid in pot settle for 5 minutes, then use wide spoon to skim fat from surface. Stir in minced thyme. Bring liquid to boil and cook, whisking vigorously to help vegetables break down, until thickened and reduced to about 3½ cups, about 18 minutes. Strain sauce through fine-mesh strainer into bowl, pressing on solids to extract as much liquid as possible; you should have about 1½ cups strained sauce (if necessary, return strained sauce to pot and continue to boil until sauce reduces to 1½ cups). Discard solids. Season sauce with salt and pepper to taste.

5 Remove twine from roasts. Slice meat against grain into ½-inch-thick slices. Transfer meat to serving dish. Spoon half of sauce over meat and serve, passing remaining sauce separately.

BRISKET CARBONNADE

serves 6

4 large onions

1 (3½-pound) beef brisket, flat cut,
fat trimmed to ¼ inch

Salt and pepper

2 tablespoons vegetable oil

1 tablespoon tomato paste

2 garlic cloves, minced

1 tablespoon all-purpose flour

1½ cups beer

1 tablespoon packed brown sugar

1 tablespoon cider vinegar

4 sprigs fresh thyme

2 bay leaves

1 teaspoon Dijon mustard

Why This Recipe Works Brisket with onions is generally a simple dish, but we thought a bit outside the box to elevate it. To that end, we turned to *carbonnade à la flamande*, a Flemish dish in which beef and browned onions are braised in Belgian beer to a deep, dark, malty finish. To translate its flavors into a fine sauce for sliced brisket, we started by browning a flat-cut beef brisket. (For more information on brisket, see page 11.) Weighing the meat down with a Dutch oven ensured an evenly browned crust and created plenty of flavorful fond in the skillet. Brisket is different than stew meat in that it has a more assertive, mineral-y taste, so this would need to be more strongly flavored than the traditional carbonnade sauce. Skipping broth and upping the beer created a sauce with extra maltiness that complemented the brisket nicely. As for the onions, we increased their amount and sliced them extra-thick to ensure they wouldn't disappear in the sauce. Pureeing an onion thickened and further flavored the sauce; cider vinegar, mustard, and a little brown sugar rounded it out. Letting the brisket rest in the juices for an hour ensured that it was moist and tender. Use a wheat beer, lager, or pilsner for this recipe.

1 Adjust oven rack to lower-middle position and heat oven to 325 degrees. Halve and slice 3 onions ½ inch thick. Puree remaining onion in food processor, about 10 seconds. Pat brisket dry with paper towels and season liberally with salt and pepper. Heat 1 tablespoon oil in 12-inch skillet over medium-high heat until just smoking. Place brisket in skillet; weigh down with Dutch oven or cast-iron skillet and cook until well browned, about 4 minutes per side. Transfer brisket to 13 by 9-inch baking dish.

2 Heat remaining 1 tablespoon oil in now-empty skillet over medium heat until shimmering. Add sliced onions and ½ teaspoon salt and cook, stirring occasionally, until soft and golden brown, about 15 minutes. Stir in tomato paste and garlic and cook until fragrant, about 30 seconds. Stir in flour until onions are evenly coated and flour is lightly browned, about 2 minutes. Stir in pureed onion and cook until mixture has thickened, about 2 minutes. Stir in beer, sugar, vinegar, thyme sprigs, and bay leaves, scraping up any browned bits. Increase heat to medium-high and bring to boil.

3 Pour onion mixture over brisket and cover dish tightly with aluminum foil. Bake until brisket is tender and fork easily slips in and out of meat, about 3 hours. Let brisket rest in liquid, uncovered, for 1 hour.

4 Transfer brisket to carving board. Using wide spoon, skim fat from surface of sauce and discard thyme sprigs and bay leaves. Whisk mustard into sauce and season with salt and pepper to taste. Slice brisket against grain into ¼-inch-thick slices and return to dish with sauce. Serve.

getting a great sear

To prevent flat brisket from curling up during searing, weigh it down with a heavy Dutch oven to ensure an even, thorough sear.

ATLANTA BRISKET

serves 6

1 (3½-pound) beef brisket, flat cut, fat trimmed to ¼ inch thick

Salt and pepper

4 teaspoons vegetable oil

1 pound onions, halved and sliced ½ inch thick

2 cups cola

1½ cups ketchup

4 teaspoons onion powder

2 teaspoons packed dark brown sugar

1 teaspoon garlic powder

1 teaspoon dried thyme

Why This Recipe Works Coca-Cola was once just a local Atlanta specialty. Today, Southerners don't just drink more soda than people in other parts of the country (so says the U.S. Department of Agriculture)—they cook with it, too. Atlanta brisket is a Southern braise featuring onion soup mix, ketchup, and Atlanta's own Coca-Cola. We wanted to keep the regional charm but update the flavor derived from mostly convenience products. Marinating the brisket in the sweet, acidic cola didn't tenderize the brisket as many recipes claim; instead it made it spongy and dry. Piercing it with a fork, salting it, and letting it sit overnight was much more effective. Finally, for a braising liquid characteristic of the original, we mixed cola and ketchup and replaced the artificial-tasting soup mix with our own blend of sautéed onions, onion and garlic powders, brown sugar, and dried thyme. The mixture both flavored the meat and became a sweet, tangy sauce for serving. Parchment paper provides a nonreactive barrier between the cola-based braising liquid and the aluminum foil. This recipe requires refrigerating the salted meat for at least 6 hours before cooking.

1 Using metal skewer or paring knife, poke holes all over brisket. Rub entire surface of brisket with 1 tablespoon salt. Wrap brisket in plastic wrap and refrigerate for at least 6 hours or up to 24 hours.

2 Adjust oven rack to lower-middle position and heat oven to 325 degrees. Pat brisket dry with paper towels and season with pepper. Heat 2 teaspoons oil in 12-inch nonstick skillet over medium-high heat until just smoking. Place brisket in skillet; weigh down brisket with Dutch oven or cast-iron skillet and cook until well browned, about 4 minutes per side. Transfer brisket to large plate.

3 Heat remaining 2 teaspoons oil in now-empty skillet over medium heat until shimmering. Add onions and cook, stirring occasionally, until soft and golden brown, 10 to 12 minutes. Transfer onions to 13 by 9-inch baking dish and spread in even layer.

4 Combine cola, ketchup, onion powder, sugar, garlic powder, thyme, 1 teaspoon salt, and 1 teaspoon pepper in bowl. Place brisket fat side up on top of onions and pour cola mixture over brisket. Place parchment paper over brisket and cover dish tightly with aluminum foil. Bake until tender and fork slips easily in and out of meat, 3½ to 4 hours. Let brisket rest in liquid, uncovered, for 30 minutes.

5 Transfer brisket to carving board. Using wide spoon, skim fat from surface of sauce. Slice brisket against grain into ¼-inch-thick slices and return to baking dish. Serve with sauce.

BRAISED BRISKET WITH POMEGRANATE, CUMIN, AND CILANTRO

serves 6 to 8

1 (4- to 5-pound) beef brisket, flat cut, fat trimmed to ¼ inch

Kosher salt and pepper

2 tablespoons vegetable oil

2 large onions, chopped

¼ teaspoon baking soda

6 garlic cloves, minced

4 anchovy fillets, rinsed, patted dry, and minced to paste

1 tablespoon tomato paste

1 tablespoon ground cumin

1½ teaspoons ground cardamom

⅛ teaspoon cayenne pepper

¼ cup all-purpose flour

2 cups pomegranate juice

1½ cups chicken broth

3 bay leaves

2 tablespoons unflavored gelatin

1 cup pomegranate seeds

3 tablespoons chopped fresh cilantro

Why This Recipe Works We know well that braising brisket breaks down what can be a tough cut into something satisfyingly tender. For a foolproof modern take on a timeless cooking method, we wanted to spare no detail for the ultimate brisket dish—one that stood apart from the rest for the holidays or an elegant dinner party. For braised brisket that would be both tender and moist, we started by salting the meat (halved lengthwise for quicker cooking and easier slicing and poked all over to allow the salt to penetrate) and letting it sit for at least 16 hours, which helped it retain moisture as it cooked; the salt also seasoned it. From there, we brought the meat to 180 degrees—the sweet spot for the collagen breakdown that is necessary for the meat to turn tender— relatively quickly in a 325-degree oven and then lowered the oven temperature to 250 degrees so that the brisket finished cooking gently and retained as much moisture as possible. We reduced the braising liquid (chicken broth, pomegranate juice, lots of onions and garlic, anchovies, tomato paste, herbs, and spices) in the pan to achieve rich flavor. Reducing the sauce also built body, which we enhanced with flour and gelatin for a velvety consistency. This recipe requires salting the brisket for at least 16 hours; if you have time, you can salt it for up to 48 hours. If you have a probe thermometer, we recommend using it to monitor the temperature of the brisket as it cooks.

1 Place brisket, fat side down, on cutting board and cut in half lengthwise with grain. Using metal skewer or paring knife, poke each roast 20 times, pushing all the way through roast. Flip roasts and repeat on second side.

2 Sprinkle each roast evenly on all sides with 2½ teaspoons salt (5 teaspoons salt total). Wrap each roast in plastic wrap and refrigerate for at least 16 hours or up to 48 hours.

3 Adjust oven rack to middle position and heat oven to 325 degrees. Heat oil in large roasting pan over medium heat until shimmering. Add onions and baking soda and cook, stirring frequently, until onions have started to soften and break down, 4 to 5 minutes. Add garlic and cook until fragrant, about 30 seconds. Stir in anchovies, tomato paste, cumin, cardamom, cayenne, and ½ teaspoon pepper. Add flour and cook, stirring constantly, until onions are evenly coated and flour begins to stick to pan, about 2 minutes.

Stir in pomegranate juice, broth, and bay leaves, scraping up any browned bits. Stir in gelatin. Increase heat to medium-high and bring to boil.

4 Unwrap roasts and place in pan. Cover pan tightly with aluminum foil, transfer to oven, and cook until meat registers 180 to 185 degrees at center, about 1½ hours. Reduce oven temperature to 250 degrees and continue to cook until fork slips easily in and out of meat, 2 to 2½ hours longer. Transfer roasts to baking sheet and wrap sheet tightly in foil.

5 Strain braising liquid through fine-mesh strainer set over large bowl, pressing on solids to extract as much liquid as possible; discard solids. Let liquid settle for 10 minutes, then use wide spoon to skim fat from surface. Wipe roasting pan clean with paper towels and return defatted liquid to pan.

6 Increase oven temperature to 400 degrees. Return pan to oven and cook, stirring occasionally, until liquid is reduced by about one-third, 30 to 40 minutes. Remove pan from oven and use wooden spoon to draw liquid up sides of pan and scrape browned bits around edges of pan into liquid.

7 Transfer roasts to carving board. Slice brisket against grain into ¼-inch-thick slices and transfer to wide serving platter. Season sauce with salt and pepper to taste and pour over brisket. Tent platter with foil and let stand for 5 to 10 minutes to warm brisket through. Sprinkle with pomegranate seeds and cilantro and serve.

Beer-Braised Brisket with Prunes and Ginger

Omit ground cumin and ground cardamom. Stir in 1 teaspoon five-spice powder with anchovies in step 3. Substitute 1½ cups beer for pomegranate juice and increase chicken broth to 2 cups. Stir in 2 tablespoons Dijon mustard and 1 (3-inch) piece ginger, peeled and sliced thin, with chicken broth in step 3. Stir 1½ cups pitted prunes into braising liquid before returning roasting pan to oven in step 6. Omit pomegranate seeds and substitute parsley for cilantro.

Red Wine–Braised Brisket with Thyme

Omit ground cumin and ground cardamom. Substitute 1 cup red wine for pomegranate juice and increase chicken broth to 2 cups. Add 6 thyme sprigs with bay leaves in step 3. Omit pomegranate seeds and cilantro.

the slice is right

The thinner blade of a carving knife (also called a slicing knife) cuts the brisket more gently than a thicker chef's knife would.

preparing the brisket

Place brisket, fat side down, on cutting board and cut in half lengthwise with grain. Using paring knife or metal skewer, poke each roast 20 times, pushing all the way through roast. Flip roasts and repeat on second side.

OAXACAN-STYLE BEEF BRISKET

1 (3½-pound) beef brisket, flat cut, fat trimmed to ¼ inch

Salt and pepper

4 pasilla chiles, stemmed, seeded, and torn into ½-inch pieces (1 cup)

1 tablespoon vegetable oil

2 onions, chopped

8 garlic cloves, peeled and smashed

1 tablespoon dried oregano

2 teaspoons ground cumin

2 teaspoons dried thyme

1 teaspoon ground coriander

¼ teaspoon ground cloves

1 cup chicken broth

1 (28-ounce) can diced tomatoes

Why This Recipe Works Looking to add some international interest to our brisket repertoire, we decided to make a tender, juicy beef brisket with bold Mexican flavor—the flavor of the southern region of Oaxaca, to be specific. To ensure that our brisket turned out tender, we cooked it fat side up so it would self-baste as it cooked, and we covered it with foil to hold in moisture. We infused our aromatic cooking liquid with toasted mild but deep-flavored and multidimensional pasilla chiles—the prime chile of Oaxaca—and lots of Mexican herbs and spices: dried oregano, ground cumin, dried thyme, ground coriander, and ground cloves. Blending the cooking liquid to a smooth consistency made an ample quantity of rich sauce to spoon over the meat. You will need 18-inch-wide heavy-duty aluminum foil for this recipe. This recipe requires refrigerating the salted meat for at least 6 hours before cooking.

1 Using metal skewer or paring knife, poke holes all over brisket. Rub entire surface of brisket with 1 tablespoon salt. Wrap brisket in plastic wrap and refrigerate for at least 6 hours or up to 24 hours.

2 Adjust oven rack to lower-middle position and heat oven to 325 degrees. Pat brisket dry with paper towels and season with pepper. Toast pasilla chiles in 12-inch skillet over medium heat, stirring frequently, until fragrant, 2 to 6 minutes; transfer to bowl.

3 Heat oil in now-empty skillet over medium-high heat until just smoking. Place brisket fat in skillet; weigh down brisket with Dutch oven or cast-iron skillet and cook until well browned, about 4 minutes per side. Transfer brisket to large plate.

4 Pour off all but 1 tablespoon fat from skillet. Add onions and cook over medium heat until softened, 8 to 10 minutes. Stir in garlic, oregano, cumin, thyme, coriander, cloves, and 1 teaspoon pepper and cook until fragrant, about 1 minute. Stir in broth, tomatoes and their juice, and toasted chiles, scraping up any browned bits, and bring to simmer. Transfer to 13 by 9-inch baking dish.

5 Nestle browned brisket fat side up into dish and spoon some sauce over top. Cover dish tightly with aluminum foil and bake until tender and fork easily slips in and out of meat, 3½ to 4 hours. Remove dish from oven and let brisket rest, covered, for 1 hour.

6 Transfer brisket to carving board and tent with foil. Strain cooking liquid through fine-mesh strainer into bowl; transfer solids to blender. Let liquid settle for 5 minutes, then skim fat from surface. Add defatted liquid to blender and puree until smooth, about 2 minutes. Season sauce with salt and pepper to taste.

7 Slice brisket against grain into ¼-inch-thick slices and return to dish. Pour sauce over top and serve.

HOME-CORNED BEEF AND CABBAGE

serves 8 to 10

Corned Beef

¾ cup salt

½ cup packed brown sugar

2 teaspoons pink curing kosher salt #1

1 (4½- to 5-pound) beef brisket, flat cut, fat trimmed to ⅛ inch

6 garlic cloves, peeled

6 bay leaves

5 allspice berries

2 tablespoons black peppercorns

1 tablespoon coriander seeds

Vegetables

6 carrots, peeled, halved crosswise, thick ends halved lengthwise

1½ pounds small red potatoes, unpeeled

1 head green cabbage (2 pounds), uncored, cut into 8 wedges

Why This Recipe Works You can make a decent corned beef dinner by buying a corned beef brisket, simmering it in a pot of water for a few hours, and adding vegetables at the end of cooking. But you can make superb New England–style corned beef if you skip the commercially made stuff and "corn" the meat yourself. When this curing process is done properly, the meat isn't just generically salty; it's seasoned but balanced, with complex flavor thanks to the presence of aromatics and spices. Although the process takes several days, we found that it's almost entirely hands-off: After a six-day soak in a brine made with both table and pink curing salt, and flavored with sugar, whole spices, and garlic, the seasonings had penetrated to the core of the meat. To break down the brisket's collagen, we gently simmered the meat in a low oven, adding carrots, potatoes, and cabbage to the pot while the meat rested so that they simmered briefly in the seasoned cooking liquid. Pink curing salt #1, which can be purchased online or in stores specializing in meat curing, is a mixture of table salt and nitrites; it is also called Prague Powder #1, Insta Cure #1, or DQ Curing Salt #1. In addition to the pink salt, we use table salt here. If using Diamond Crystal kosher salt, increase the salt to 1½ cups; if using Morton kosher salt, increase to 1⅛ cups. Choose a uniformly thick brisket. The brisket will look gray after curing but will turn pink once cooked. This recipe requires refrigerating the brined brisket for six days.

1 For the corned beef Dissolve salt, sugar, and curing salt in 4 quarts water in large container. Add brisket, 3 garlic cloves, 4 bay leaves, allspice berries, 1 tablespoon peppercorns, and coriander seeds to brine. Weigh brisket down with plate, cover, and refrigerate for 6 days.

2 Adjust oven rack to middle position and heat oven to 275 degrees. Remove brisket from brine, rinse, and pat dry with paper towels. Cut 8-inch square triple thickness of cheesecloth. Place remaining 3 garlic cloves, remaining 2 bay leaves, and remaining 1 tablespoon peppercorns in center of cheesecloth and tie into bundle with kitchen twine. Place brisket, spice bundle, and 2 quarts water in Dutch oven. (Brisket may not lie flat but will shrink slightly as it cooks.) Bring to simmer over high heat, cover, and transfer to oven. Cook until fork inserted into thickest part of brisket slides in and out with ease, 2½ to 3 hours.

3 Remove pot from oven and turn off oven. Transfer brisket to large ovensafe platter, ladle 1 cup of cooking liquid over meat, cover, and return to oven to keep warm.

4 For the vegetables Add carrots and potatoes to pot and bring to simmer over high heat. Reduce heat to medium-low, cover, and simmer until vegetables begin to soften, 7 to 10 minutes.

5 Add cabbage to pot, increase heat to high, and return to simmer. Reduce heat to low, cover, and simmer until all vegetables are tender, 12 to 15 minutes.

6 While vegetables cook, transfer brisket to cutting board. Slice brisket against the grain into ¼-inch-thick slices. Return brisket to platter. Using slotted spoon, transfer vegetables to platter with beef. Moisten with additional broth and serve.

BRAISED BEEF WITH RED WINE AND CHERRIES

6 slices bacon, finely chopped

1 (3½- to 4-pound) boneless beef chuck roast, pulled apart at seams, trimmed, and cut into 2-inch pieces

Salt and pepper

3 onions, halved and sliced

2 cups red wine

1½ cups (6 ounces) dried cherries

2 tablespoons minced fresh parsley

Why This Recipe Works Braised dishes don't have to involve a slew of ingredients; much of the flavor of braised beef is coaxed from the meat itself during a long, low cooking process. This recipe is a perfect example: We made a superstreamlined sweet-and-savory braise with chuck-eye roast—and you'd never know it's only six ingredients long. Smoky bacon laid down a base of flavor and provided ample fat for sautéing thinly sliced onions. Braising our beef chunks in red wine in a low oven worked to infuse them with intense flavor and allowed them to cook through gently. Uncovering the pot halfway through the cooking time enabled the exposed beef to brown, thereby eliminating the time-consuming step of searing it beforehand. Dried cherries, stirred in toward the end of cooking, infused the sauce with their sweet, tart flavor. To finish our dish and brighten the flavor of the sauce, we added more red wine; minced parsley provided freshness and contrasting color.

1 Adjust oven rack to middle position and heat oven to 300 degrees. Cook bacon in Dutch oven over medium heat until crisp, 5 to 7 minutes. Using slotted spoon, transfer bacon to paper towel–lined plate. Season beef with 1 teaspoon salt and ½ teaspoon pepper.

2 Add onions to fat left in pot. Add ¼ teaspoon salt and cook over medium heat until onions are softened, 5 to 7 minutes. Slowly whisk in 1¾ cups wine, scraping up any browned bits. Stir in beef and half of bacon. Cover and bring to simmer; transfer pot to oven. Cook for 1 hour.

3 Stir in cherries and continue to cook stew in oven, uncovered, until meat is tender, 1½ to 2 hours longer. Stir in remaining ¼ cup wine and season with salt and pepper to taste. Sprinkle parsley and remaining bacon over stew and serve.

BEEF EN COCOTTE WITH CARAMELIZED ONIONS

serves 6 to 8

1 (3- to 4-pound) top sirloin beef roast, trimmed and tied once around middle

Salt and pepper

3 tablespoons vegetable oil

3 onions, halved, and sliced thin

3 garlic cloves, peeled and crushed

¼ cup dry sherry

2 cups chicken broth

1 tablespoon unsalted butter

Why This Recipe Works Cooking *en cocotte* (cooking in a casserole) is a French technique that's a variation on braising: It uses a covered pot, a low oven temperature, and an extended cooking time to yield tender, flavorful meat or poultry. Where it differs? No liquid is added to the pan. Instead, the meat cooks in its own juices. The great thing about beef en cocotte is it gives you the best of braising and roasting—the low, slow cooking encourages muscle fibers to break down so the meat is ultra-tender, but, as with roasting, you can cook it to your desired doneness (for us, medium-rare). Without all the liquid, cooking en cocotte does the job quicker than traditional braising; this wasn't enough time for more-marbled chuck roast or eye round to become tender, so we chose top sirloin, which has concentrated, beefy flavor. We balanced the flavors with the sweetness of caramelized onions, cooking the onions after we seared the beef. To boost their flavor, we added some garlic and then deglazed the pot with sherry, scraping up the fond as the liquid reduced. We cooked the steaks on top of the onions; when they were done we added chicken broth to the onions and reduced the mixture to a flavorful sauce. Trim the beef well so the sauce isn't greasy.

1 Adjust oven rack to lowest position and heat oven to 250 degrees. Pat roast dry with paper towels and season with salt and pepper.

2 Heat 2 tablespoons oil in Dutch oven over medium-high heat until just smoking. Brown roast on all sides, 7 to 10 minutes, reducing heat if pot begins to scorch. Transfer beef to large plate.

3 Add remaining 1 tablespoon oil to pot and heat over medium heat until shimmering. Add onions and garlic, cover, and cook until softened and wet, about 5 minutes. Remove lid and continue to cook onions, stirring often, until dry and well browned, 10 to 12 minutes. Stir in sherry, scraping up any browned bits, and cook until almost all of liquid has evaporated, about 1 minute.

4 Off heat, nestle beef into pot and add any accumulated juices. Place large sheet of aluminum foil over pot and cover tightly with lid; transfer pot to oven. Cook until very center of the roast registers 120 to 125 degrees for medium-rare, 20 to 30 minutes.

5 Transfer roast to carving board, tent with foil, and let rest for 20 minutes. Stir broth into onions and simmer over medium-high heat until slightly thickened, about 2 minutes. Off heat, whisk in butter, season with salt and pepper to taste, and cover to keep warm.

6 Remove twine from roast, slice meat against grain into ¼-inch-thick slices, and transfer to serving platter. Spoon sauce over meat and serve.

BRAISED BONELESS BEEF SHORT RIBS

serves 6

3½ pounds boneless beef short ribs, trimmed

Kosher salt and pepper

2 tablespoons vegetable oil

2 large onions, sliced thin

1 tablespoon tomato paste

6 garlic cloves, peeled

2 cups red wine

1 cup beef broth

4 large carrots, peeled and cut into 2-inch pieces

4 sprigs fresh thyme

1 bay leaf

½ teaspoon unflavored gelatin

Why This Recipe Works Braised short ribs are a warm, hearty dinner on a cold day—but they often take a fair amount of that day to execute. We wanted to cut the usual long cooking time so that short ribs, with a silky, grease-free sauce, could make more frequent appearances at our dinner table. The first, easiest step to eliminating hours of cooking was starting with boneless short ribs. The only problem with omitting bones is that our braising liquid lacked the viscosity usually provided by the bones, so we added powdered gelatin ourselves to get a silky sauce that nicely napped the ribs. Wine, once reduced, added depth and intensity to the braise, and to supplement it, we chose beef broth to balance the wine. Make sure that the ribs are at least 4 inches long and 1 inch thick. We recommend a bold red wine such as a Cabernet Sauvignon.

1 Adjust oven rack to lower-middle position and heat oven to 300 degrees. Pat short ribs dry with paper towels and sprinkle with 2 teaspoons salt and 1 teaspoon pepper. Heat 1 tablespoon oil in Dutch oven over medium-high heat until smoking. Add half of short ribs and cook, without moving them, until well browned, 4 to 6 minutes. Turn short ribs and continue to cook on second side until well browned, 4 to 6 minutes longer, reducing heat if fat begins to smoke. Transfer short ribs to bowl. Repeat with remaining 1 tablespoon oil and remaining short ribs.

2 Reduce heat to medium, add onions, and cook, stirring occasionally, until softened and beginning to brown, 12 to 15 minutes. (If onions begin to darken too quickly, add 1 to 2 tablespoons water to pot.) Add tomato paste and cook, stirring constantly, until it browns on sides and bottom of pot, about 2 minutes. Add garlic and cook until fragrant, about 30 seconds. Increase heat to medium-high, add wine, and simmer, scraping up any browned bits, until reduced by half, 8 to 10 minutes. Add broth, carrots, thyme sprigs, and bay leaf. Add short ribs and any accumulated juices to pot, cover, and bring to simmer; transfer pot to oven. Cook, turning short ribs twice during cooking, until fork slips easily in and out of meat, 2 to 2½ hours.

3 Sprinkle gelatin over ¼ cup water in bowl and let sit until gelatin softens, about 5 minutes. Using tongs, transfer short ribs and carrots to serving platter and tent with aluminum foil. Strain cooking liquid through fine-mesh strainer into fat separator or bowl, pressing on solids to extract as much liquid as possible; discard solids. Let liquid settle for 5 minutes, then skim fat from surface. Return cooking liquid to pot and cook over medium heat until reduced to 1 cup, 5 to 10 minutes. Remove from heat and stir in gelatin mixture; season with salt and pepper to taste. Pour sauce over short ribs and serve.

Braised Boneless Beef Short Ribs with Guinness and Prunes
Substitute 1 cup full-flavored porter or stout for wine and omit wine reduction time in step 2. Add ⅓ cup pitted prunes to pot along with broth.

RED WINE–BRAISED SHORT RIBS WITH BACON, PARSNIPS, AND PEARL ONIONS

serves 6

Short Ribs

6 pounds bone-in English-style short ribs, trimmed

Salt and pepper

3 cups dry red wine

3 large onions, chopped

2 carrots, peeled and chopped

1 large celery rib, chopped

9 garlic cloves, chopped

¼ cup all-purpose flour

4 cups chicken broth

1 (14.5-ounce) can diced tomatoes, drained

1½ tablespoons minced fresh rosemary

1 tablespoon minced fresh thyme

3 bay leaves

1 teaspoon tomato paste

Bacon, Parsnips, and Pearl Onions

6 slices bacon, cut into ¼-inch pieces

10 ounces parsnips, peeled and cut on bias into ¾-inch pieces

8 ounces frozen pearl onions

¼ teaspoon sugar

¼ teaspoon salt

6 tablespoons chopped fresh parsley

Why This Recipe Works Our flavorful Braised Boneless Beef Short Ribs (page 58) save some time and fuss, but traditional bone-in braised short ribs are a luxurious and elegant treat. Short ribs are a terrific option when cooking for company because you can make them ahead—in fact, it's actually best to rest them overnight before serving. Most recipes call for a cumbersome stovetop browning strategy, but we wanted a simpler option. We opted to brown the short ribs all at once in the oven, which allowed the ribs to spend more time in the heat, maximizing the amount of fat rendered (and therefore minimizing the greasiness of our final sauce). To supplement the flavor, we made sure to add a lot of savory ingredients to the mix—a hefty amount of garlic, red wine, rosemary, thyme, and tomato paste made the cut. Although we had rendered a fair amount of fat in the oven, plenty still came out in the braise, so we let the ribs rest to allow the fat to separate out and solidify. Once solidified, the fat was easy to scoop off the top before we re-employed the braising liquid to finish cooking the vegetables and rewarm the ribs. Crisped bacon and sautéed pearl onions and parsnips added crunch and sweetness to our tender, succulent short ribs.

1 For the short ribs Adjust oven rack to lower-middle position and heat oven to 450 degrees. Arrange short ribs bone side down in single layer in large roasting pan; season with salt and pepper. Roast until meat begins to brown, about 45 minutes; drain off all liquid and fat. Return short ribs to oven and continue to roast until meat is well browned, 15 to 20 minutes longer. Transfer short ribs to large plate. Pour rendered fat into small bowl.

2 Reduce oven temperature to 300 degrees. Place now-empty pan over 2 burners set at medium heat; add wine and bring to simmer, scraping up any browned bits. Set aside.

3 Heat 2 tablespoons reserved fat in Dutch oven over medium-high heat; add onions, carrots, and celery and cook, stirring occasionally, until vegetables soften, about 12 minutes. Add garlic and cook until fragrant, about 30 seconds. Stir in flour until combined, about 45 seconds. Stir in broth, tomatoes, rosemary, thyme, bay leaves, tomato paste, and reserved wine. Season with salt and pepper to taste. Bring to boil and add short ribs, completely submerging meat in liquid. Return to boil and cover; transfer pot to oven. Cook until short ribs are tender, 2 to 2½ hours. Transfer pot to wire rack and let cool, partially covered, until warm, about 2 hours.

4 Transfer short ribs to serving platter, removing any vegetables that cling to meat; discard loose bones that have fallen away from meat. Strain braising liquid through fine-mesh strainer set over bowl, pressing on solids to extract all liquid; discard solids. Refrigerate short ribs and liquid separately, covered with plastic wrap, for at least 8 hours or up to 3 days.

5 For the bacon, parsnips, and pearl onions Cook bacon over medium heat in Dutch oven until just crispy, 8 to 10 minutes; using slotted spoon, transfer bacon to paper towel–lined plate. Add parsnips, onions, sugar, and salt to pot; increase heat to high and cook, stirring occasionally, until browned, about 5 minutes.

6 Spoon off and discard solidified fat from reserved braising liquid. Add defatted liquid to pot and bring to simmer, stirring occasionally; season with salt and pepper to taste. Submerge short ribs in liquid and return to simmer. Reduce heat to medium and cook, partially covered, until short ribs are heated through and vegetables are tender, about 5 minutes; gently stir in bacon. Divide short ribs and sauce among serving bowls, sprinkle each bowl with 1 table-spoon parsley, and serve.

Porter-Braised Short Ribs with Prunes and Brandy

Substitute 3 cups porter for red wine, omit rosemary, and substitute 2 tablespoons Dijon mustard and 2 teaspoons Worcestershire sauce for tomato paste. Continue with recipe through step 3. For garnish, bring ½ cup brandy to boil in small saucepan; off heat, add 8 ounces pitted prunes, halved, and let stand until plump and softened, about 15 minutes. Meanwhile, spoon off and discard fat from braising liquid. Bring liquid to boil in Dutch oven over medium-high heat, stirring occasionally. Add prunes, brandy, and 2 teaspoons packed brown sugar; season with salt and pepper to taste. Submerge ribs in liquid and return to simmer. Reduce heat to medium-low and cook until ribs are heated through, about 5 minutes longer; gently stir in 2 teaspoons grated lemon zest. Divide ribs and sauce among serving bowls, sprinkle each bowl with 1 tablespoon parsley, and serve.

POMEGRANATE-BRAISED SHORT RIBS WITH PRUNES AND SESAME

serves 4 to 6

4 pounds bone-in English-style short ribs, trimmed

Salt and pepper

4 cups unsweetened pomegranate juice

1 cup water

2 tablespoons extra-virgin olive oil

1 onion, chopped fine

1 carrot, peeled and chopped fine

2 tablespoons ras el hanout

4 garlic cloves, minced

¾ cup pitted prunes, halved

1 tablespoon red wine vinegar

2 tablespoons toasted sesame seeds

2 tablespoons chopped fresh cilantro

Why This Recipe Works This dish takes its cue from a popular combination in Moroccan tagines: meltingly tender beef and sweet, tangy prunes. We found that using pomegranate juice as the braising liquid gave our sauce the perfect touch of tartness to balance the meatiness of the beef and the sweetness of the prunes. A good dose of *ras el hanout*, a warm, complex North African spice blend, added a pleasing, piquant aroma. After defatting the cooking liquid, we blended it with the vegetables and part of the prunes to create a velvety sauce that coated the ribs nicely. We added the remaining prunes to the sauce and garnished the dish with toasted sesame seeds and fresh-tasting cilantro. The flavor and spiciness of store-bought ras el hanout can vary greatly by brand, so we recommend making your own (recipe follows).

1 Adjust oven rack to lower-middle position and heat oven to 450 degrees. Pat short ribs dry with paper towels and season with salt and pepper. Arrange ribs bone side down in single layer in large roasting pan and roast until meat begins to brown, about 45 minutes; drain off all liquid and fat. Return short ribs to oven and continue to roast until meat is well browned, 15 to 20 minutes longer. Transfer ribs to bowl and tent with aluminum foil; set aside. Stir pomegranate juice and water into pan, scraping up any browned bits; set aside.

2 Reduce oven temperature to 300 degrees. Heat oil in Dutch oven over medium heat until shimmering. Add onion, carrot, and ¼ teaspoon salt and cook until softened, about 5 minutes. Stir in ras el hanout and garlic and cook until fragrant, about 30 seconds.

3 Stir in pomegranate mixture from roasting pan and half of prunes and bring to simmer. Nestle short ribs bone side up into pot. Return to simmer and cover; transfer pot to oven and cook until ribs are tender and fork slips easily in and out of meat, about 2½ hours.

4 Transfer short ribs to bowl, discarding any loose bones that have fallen away from meat, and tent with aluminum foil. Strain braising liquid through fine-mesh strainer into fat separator; transfer solids to blender. Let braising liquid settle for 5 minutes, then pour defatted liquid into blender with solids and process until smooth, about 1 minute.

5 Transfer sauce to now-empty pot and stir in vinegar and remaining prunes. Return short ribs and any accumulated juices to pot, bring to gentle simmer over medium heat, and cook, spooning sauce over ribs occasionally, until heated through, about 5 minutes. Season with salt and pepper to taste. Transfer short ribs to serving platter, spoon 1 cup sauce over top, and sprinkle with sesame seeds and cilantro. Serve, passing remaining sauce separately.

RAS EL HANOUT
makes about ½ cup

If you can't find Aleppo pepper, you can substitute
½ teaspoon paprika and ½ teaspoon red pepper flakes.

16 cardamom pods
4 teaspoons coriander seeds
4 teaspoons cumin seeds
2 teaspoons anise seeds
½ teaspoon allspice berries
¼ teaspoon black peppercorns
4 teaspoons ground ginger
2 teaspoons ground nutmeg
2 teaspoons ground dried Aleppo pepper
2 teaspoons ground cinnamon

1 Toast cardamom, coriander, cumin, anise, allspice, and
peppercorns in small skillet over medium heat until fragrant,
shaking skillet occasionally to prevent scorching, about
2 minutes. Let cool to room temperature. Remove seeds
from cardamom pods.

2 Transfer toasted spices, cardamom seeds, ginger, nutmeg,
Aleppo, and cinnamon to spice grinder and process to fine
powder. (*Ras el hanout* can be stored in airtight container
at room temperature for up to 1 year.)

CHINESE-STYLE BRAISED SHORT RIBS

serves 6

6 tablespoons fermented black beans, rinsed

2 tablespoons soy sauce

2 tablespoons Chinese rice wine or dry sherry

4 garlic cloves, minced

6 pounds bone-in English-style short ribs, trimmed

Pepper

2 tablespoons vegetable oil

2 tablespoons cornstarch

Why This Recipe Works Short ribs and black bean sauce (made with fermented black beans) are a classic combination in Chinese cuisine, and it's no wonder—the rich short ribs perfectly pair with the musky, salty beans. Marrying the two, we found, wasn't as easy as simply tossing some of these beans into the pot. The beans are quite pungent and salty, so they need to be rinsed and soaked before cooking—and used with restraint. Because of their strong flavor, we could use water as our braising liquid. To enhance the flavor of the sauce, we added soy sauce for color and rich, meaty flavor, and rice wine for a bit of brightness, relying on cornstarch as a thickener. Fermented black beans can be found in Asian markets and some well-stocked supermarkets. Because the braising liquid doesn't cover all of the ribs in the pot, be sure to move the ribs around during the cooking to ensure they are evenly cooked and flavored. Once cooked, the ribs can sit in the finished sauce to stay warm for up to an hour before serving.

1 Adjust oven rack to lower-middle position and heat oven to 325 degrees. Soak fermented black beans in 2 cups warm tap water for 20 minutes. Drain beans; toss with soy sauce, rice wine, and garlic; and set aside.

2 Meanwhile, pat short ribs dry with paper towels and season with pepper. Heat 1 tablespoon oil in Dutch oven over medium-high heat until just smoking. Add half of ribs and brown on all sides, 7 to 10 minutes, reducing heat if pot begins to scorch. Transfer ribs to large plate and repeat with remaining 1 tablespoon oil and remaining ribs; transfer to plate.

3 Pour off fat from pot, add fermented black bean mixture to pot, and cook over medium heat until fragrant, about 1 minute. Stir in 5¾ cups water, scraping up browned bits, and bring to simmer.

4 Nestle short ribs bone side up into pot and add any accumulated juices. Return to simmer and cover; transfer pot to oven. Cook until short ribs are tender and fork slips easily in and out of meat, 2½ to 3 hours, rearranging ribs halfway through cooking so that all ribs become moistened with braising liquid.

5 Transfer short ribs to large plate, discarding any loose bones that have fallen away from the meat, and tent with foil. Strain braising liquid through fine-mesh strainer into fat separator. Let braising liquid settle for 5 minutes, then pour defatted liquid into now-empty pot and bring to simmer over medium-high heat. Whisk cornstarch with ¼ cup water to dissolve, then whisk into simmering sauce. Continue to simmer, whisking constantly, until thickened, about 4 minutes. Return ribs to sauce and simmer until ribs are rewarmed through. Serve.

SHREDDED BEEF TACOS (CARNE DESHEBRADA)

serves 6 to 8

1½ cups beer

4 dried ancho chiles, stemmed, seeded, and torn into ½-inch pieces (1 cup)

½ cup cider vinegar

2 tablespoons tomato paste

6 garlic cloves, lightly crushed and peeled

3 bay leaves

2 teaspoons ground cumin

2 teaspoons dried oregano

Salt and pepper

½ teaspoon ground cloves

½ teaspoon ground cinnamon

1 large onion, sliced into ½-inch-thick rounds

3 pounds boneless beef short ribs, trimmed and cut into 2-inch cubes

18 (6-inch) corn tortillas, warmed

1 recipe Cabbage-Carrot Slaw (recipe follows)

4 ounces queso fresco, crumbled (1 cup)

Lime wedges

Why This Recipe Works *Carne deshebrada*, literally meaning "shredded beef," is a common offering at Mexican taco stands. It's made by braising a large cut of beef until ultratender and then shredding the meat and tossing it with a flavorful *rojo* sauce made with tomatoes and/or dried chiles. Although short ribs are a bit nontraditional, their ultrabeefy flavor made them an excellent choice. To achieve flavorful browning, we raised the beef up out of the braising liquid by resting it on onion rounds; the ambient heat browned the short ribs just enough for this dish. Next, we created a braising liquid that would infuse the beef with flavor and later act as a base for our rojo sauce. Beer and cider vinegar provided depth and brightness, and tomato paste boosted savory flavor. Smoky-sweet ancho chiles gave the sauce a rounder flavor and a gentle, spicy kick. Cumin, cinnamon, cloves, oregano, and bay leaves added warmth and complexity. Once the beef had finished cooking, we pureed the braising liquid into a sauce with a smooth, luxurious consistency. A bright, tangy slaw provided a nice counterbalance to the rich meat. Use a full-bodied lager or ale such as Dos Equis or Sierra Nevada.

1 Adjust oven rack to lower-middle position and heat oven to 325 degrees. Combine beer, anchos, vinegar, tomato paste, garlic, bay leaves, cumin, oregano, 2 teaspoons salt, ½ teaspoon pepper, cloves, and cinnamon in Dutch oven. Arrange onion rounds in single layer on bottom of pot. Place beef on top of onion rounds in single layer. Cover and cook until meat is well browned and tender, 2½ to 3 hours.

2 Using slotted spoon, transfer beef to large bowl, cover loosely with aluminum foil, and set aside. Strain liquid through fine-mesh strainer into 2-cup liquid measuring cup (do not wash pot). Discard onion rounds and bay leaves. Transfer remaining solids to blender. Let strained liquid settle for 5 minutes, then skim any fat from surface. Add water as needed to equal 1 cup. Pour liquid into blender with reserved solids and blend until smooth, about 2 minutes. Transfer sauce to now-empty pot.

3 Using 2 forks, shred beef into bite-size pieces. Bring sauce to simmer over medium heat. Add beef and stir to coat. Season with salt to taste. (Beef can be refrigerated for up to 2 days; gently reheat before serving.)

4 Spoon small amount of beef into each warm tortilla and serve, passing slaw, queso fresco, and lime wedges separately.

CABBAGE-CARROT SLAW
makes about 8 cups

1 cup cider vinegar

½ cup water

1 tablespoon sugar

1½ teaspoons salt

½ head green cabbage, cored and sliced thin (6 cups)

1 onion, sliced thin

1 large carrot, peeled and shredded

1 jalapeño chile, stemmed, seeded, and minced

1 teaspoon dried oregano

1 cup chopped fresh cilantro

Whisk vinegar, water, sugar, and salt in large bowl until sugar is dissolved. Add cabbage, onion, carrot, jalapeño, and oregano and toss to combine. Cover and refrigerate for at least 1 hour or up to 24 hours. Drain slaw and stir in cilantro right before serving.

BRAISED OXTAILS WITH WHITE BEANS, TOMATOES, AND ALEPPO PEPPER

serves 6 to 8

4 pounds oxtails, trimmed

Salt and pepper

4 cups chicken broth

2 tablespoons extra-virgin olive oil

1 onion, chopped fine

1 carrot, peeled and chopped fine

6 garlic cloves, minced

2 tablespoons tomato paste

2 tablespoons ground dried
Aleppo pepper

1 tablespoon minced fresh oregano

1 (28-ounce) can whole peeled tomatoes

1 (15-ounce) can navy beans, rinsed

1 tablespoon sherry vinegar

Why This Recipe Works Oxtails are succulent, beefy, and hugely underutilized, so we gave them star status in our spin on a Turkish dish, *etli kuru fasulye,* or "white beans with meat," which is often served with rice pilaf and pickled vegetables. In our version, the white beans offer a creamy, nutty counterpoint to hearty oxtails. To be sure our braise didn't turn out greasy, we started by roasting the oxtails in the oven for an hour, rather than browning them in a Dutch oven; this way, we rendered and discarded a significant amount of fat (about a half-cup!). We then transferred the oxtails to the pot and deglazed the roasting pan with chicken broth to create a flavorful liquid for braising. To give the braising liquid its character, we added a simple yet flavorful trio of eastern Mediterranean elements: sweet whole tomatoes, warm and earthy Aleppo pepper, and pungent oregano. After braising, we were careful to remove the fat (about another half-cup) from the cooking liquid using a fat separator. We added canned navy beans, sherry vinegar, and fresh oregano to create a hearty sauce in which we reheated the oxtails. Try to buy oxtails that are approximately 2 inches thick and 2 to 4 inches in diameter. Oxtails can often be found in the freezer section of the grocery store; if using frozen oxtails, thaw them completely before using. If you can't find Aleppo pepper, you can substitute 1½ teaspoons paprika and 1½ teaspoons finely chopped red pepper flakes.

1 Adjust oven rack to lower-middle position and heat oven to 450 degrees. Pat oxtails dry with paper towels and season with salt and pepper. Arrange oxtails cut side down in single layer in large roasting pan and roast until meat begins to brown, about 45 minutes.

2 Discard any accumulated fat and juices in pan and continue to roast until meat is well browned, 15 to 20 minutes. Transfer oxtails to bowl and tent with aluminum foil; set aside. Stir chicken broth into pan, scraping up any browned bits; set aside.

3 Reduce oven temperature to 300 degrees. Heat oil in Dutch oven over medium heat until shimmering. Add onion and carrot and cook until softened, about 5 minutes. Stir in garlic, tomato paste, Aleppo pepper, and 1 teaspoon oregano and cook until fragrant, about 30 seconds.

4 Stir in broth mixture from roasting pan and tomatoes and their juice and bring to simmer. Nestle oxtails into pot and bring to simmer and cover; transfer pot to oven. Cook until oxtails are tender and fork slips easily in and out of meat, about 3 hours.

5 Transfer oxtails to bowl and tent with foil. Strain braising liquid through fine-mesh strainer into fat separator; return solids to now-empty pot. Let braising liquid settle for 5 minutes, then pour defatted liquid into pot with solids.

6 Stir in beans, vinegar, and remaining 2 teaspoons oregano. Return oxtails and any accumulated juices to pot, bring to gentle simmer over medium heat, and cook until oxtails and beans are heated through, about 5 minutes. Season with salt and pepper to taste. Transfer oxtails to serving platter and spoon 1 cup sauce over top. Serve, passing remaining sauce separately.

Roman Braised Oxtails

As with many braises, there is a very similar oxtail dish, *coda alla vaccinara*, made by Roman peasants, that can be easily replicated with a change in ingredients.

Add 2 ribs celery, cut into 1-inch lengths, to pot with onion and carrot in step 3. Reduce garlic to 3 cloves and substitute ⅛ teaspoon cloves for Aleppo pepper. Before stirring in broth in step 4, stir in ½ cup wine and cook until nearly all liquid is evaporated, about 2 minutes. Stir in 2 tablespoons chopped raisins along with broth and tomatoes. Omit beans, vinegar, and oregano. When oxtails are done, transfer to serving dish and tent loosely with aluminum foil. Spoon 1 cup of sauce over top of oxtails and sprinkle with pine nuts.

STEAK TIPS WITH MUSHROOM-ONION GRAVY

serves 4 to 6

1 tablespoon soy sauce

1 teaspoon sugar

1½ pounds sirloin steak tips, trimmed and cut into 1½-inch chunks

1¾ cups beef broth

¼ ounce dried porcini mushrooms, rinsed

Salt and pepper

2 tablespoons vegetable oil

1 pound white mushrooms, trimmed and sliced ¼ inch thick

1 large onion, halved and sliced thin

4 teaspoons all-purpose flour

1 garlic clove, minced

½ teaspoon minced fresh thyme

1 tablespoon chopped fresh parsley

Why This Recipe Works Steak tips smothered in mushroom and onion gravy is an American classic, but this dish is too often plagued by chewy beef, bland gravy, and prefab ingredients like canned cream of mushroom soup. We wanted tender, meaty steak and gravy flavored with fresh mushrooms and onions. Cutting the steak tips to just the right size—in this case, 1½-inch chunks—created enough surface area to brown without risking overcooking. To beef up the steak flavor and juiciness, we soaked the chunks in soy sauce for an hour; the salty soy sauce drew juices out of the steak, and the reverse happened as the soy sauce, along with the moisture, flowed back in, bringing their flavor with them. To achieve deep mushroom flavor in our gravy without overloading the pan, we added a few dried porcini in addition to our pound of fresh white mushrooms. The best part? We needed just one pan. In fact, it was ideal; giving the meat a sear in a skillet left a fond, which provided a meaty base for the gravy. And allowing the meat to finish cooking in the gravy blended the flavors. If you can find only cubes or strips rather than whole steak tips, reduce the cooking time slightly to avoid overcooking any smaller or thinner pieces. Cremini mushrooms can be used in place of the white mushrooms.

1 Combine soy sauce and sugar in bowl. Add beef, toss well, and marinate for at least 30 minutes or up to 1 hour, tossing once more.

2 Meanwhile, microwave ¼ cup broth and porcini mushrooms in covered bowl until steaming, about 1 minute. Let sit until softened, about 5 minutes. Drain porcini mushrooms in fine-mesh strainer lined with coffee filter, reserve liquid, and mince porcini mushrooms. Set aside porcini mushrooms and liquid.

3 Pat beef dry with paper towels and sprinkle with ½ teaspoon pepper. Heat 1 tablespoon oil in 12-inch skillet over medium-high heat until just smoking. Add beef and cook until well browned on all sides, 6 to 8 minutes. Transfer to large plate and set aside.

4 Add remaining 1 tablespoon oil to now-empty skillet and heat over medium-high heat. Add white mushrooms, minced porcini mushrooms, and ¼ teaspoon salt; cook, stirring frequently, until all liquid has evaporated and mushrooms start to brown, 7 to 9 minutes, scraping up any browned bits.

Add onion and ¼ teaspoon salt; cook, stirring frequently, until onion begins to brown and dark bits form on pan bottom, 6 to 8 minutes longer. Add flour, garlic, and thyme; cook, stirring constantly, until vegetables are coated with flour mixture, about 1 minute. Stir in porcini soaking liquid and remaining 1½ cups broth, scraping up any browned bits, and bring to boil. Nestle beef into mushroom-onion mixture and add any accumulated juices to skillet. Reduce heat to medium-low and simmer until beef registers 130 to 135 degrees (for medium), 3 to 5 minutes, turning beef several times. Season with salt and pepper to taste, sprinkle with parsley, and serve.

steak tips nomenclature

Although "tips" is plural, steak tips are not always sold this way. Flavorful sirloin steak tips, cut from the area just before the cow's hip, also known as flap meat, are sold as whole steaks, cubes, and strips. To ensure uniform pieces that cook evenly, we prefer to purchase whole steaks and cut them ourselves.

BRAISED STEAKS WITH ROOT VEGETABLES

serves 6

6 (6-ounce) top blade steaks,
¾ to 1 inch thick, trimmed

Salt and pepper

4 teaspoons vegetable oil

2 onions, halved and sliced thin

3 garlic cloves, minced

1 tablespoon minced fresh thyme
or 1 teaspoon dried thyme

1½ cups beef broth

1 cup water

½ cup dry white wine

12 ounces red potatoes, cut into
¾-inch pieces

4 carrots, peeled and sliced ½ inch thick

4 parsnips, peeled and sliced
½ inch thick

2 tablespoons minced fresh parsley

1 tablespoon fresh lemon juice

Why This Recipe Works We don't typically think of braising steaks: What could beat a thick steak with a browned crust from a hard sear? But tough blade steaks turn meltingly tender when simmered in liquid, which produces an accompanying sauce full of beefy flavor. To achieve this effect, we purposely "overcooked" the meat—a 2-hour braise allowed nearly all of the fat and connective tissue to dissolve, giving each bite a soft, silky texture. We seared the meat to get the browning we'd expect on steaks and set it aside while we built a balanced braising liquid. Then we returned the steaks to the pot and let them simmer in the oven undisturbed until the final 30 minutes of cooking when we added potatoes, carrots, and parsnips so we could easily get a full dinner out of one vessel. And at the very end we reduced the braising liquid to spoon over both the steaks and vegetables before serving. Top blade steak may sometimes be labeled as "flat iron" steak. Make sure to buy steaks that are about the same size to ensure even cooking.

1 Adjust oven rack to lower-middle position and heat oven to 325 degrees. Pat steaks dry with paper towels and season with salt and pepper.

2 Heat 2 teaspoons oil in Dutch oven over medium-high heat until smoking. Brown steaks well on all sides, 7 to 10 minutes. Transfer steaks to large plate.

3 Add remaining 2 teaspoons oil to pot and heat over medium heat until shimmering. Add onions and cook until softened, 8 to 10 minutes. Stir in garlic and thyme and cook until fragrant, about 30 seconds. Stir in broth, water, and wine, scraping up any browned bits, and bring to simmer.

4 Nestle steaks, along with any accumulated juice, into pot. Spoon sauce over steak. Return to simmer and cover; transfer pot to oven. Cook for 1½ hours.

5 Add potatoes, carrots, and parsnips to pot and continue to cook until steak and vegetables are tender, about 30 minutes. Transfer steaks and vegetables to large platter, tent with aluminum foil, and let rest while finishing sauce.

6 Simmer sauce over medium-high heat until slightly thickened, 2 to 4 minutes. Off heat, stir in parsley and lemon juice and season with salt and pepper to taste. Spoon sauce over steaks and vegetables and serve.

Braised Steaks with Mushrooms and Tomatoes

Omit carrots and parsnips. Before cooking onions in step 3, add 4 chopped portobello mushroom caps and cook, covered, until they begin to soften and release their liquid, about 5 minutes. Remove lid, add onions, and cook until onions and mushrooms are softened and browned, 10 to 12 minutes. Reduce water to ½ cup, substitute 2 teaspoons minced fresh rosemary for thyme, and add one 14.5-ounce can diced tomatoes with their juice with broth.

BRACIOLE

serves 4 to 6

1 (2-pound) flank steak, trimmed

¼ cup extra-virgin olive oil

10 garlic cloves, sliced thin

½ cup golden raisins, chopped coarse

1 ounce Parmesan cheese, grated
(½ cup), plus extra for serving

½ cup chopped fresh basil

¼ cup chopped fresh parsley

1 teaspoon dried oregano

½ teaspoon red pepper flakes

Salt and pepper

1 onion, chopped

3 tablespoons tomato paste

2 (28-ounce) cans crushed tomatoes

Why This Recipe Works Braciole is a staple for many Italian Americans (especially those whose ancestors came from southern Italy). It's thin beef that's rolled around a savory, slightly sweet filling and then browned and simmered in tomato sauce. For our take on this Sunday supper, we used flank steak, which we found had the beefiest flavor, and pounded it to an even ½-inch thickness. Many recipes call for a bread-based filling, presumably to bind it, but these were stodgy: A simple mixture of sweet raisins, fresh parsley and basil, and savory Parmesan cheese was tacky enough, and brushing the meat with oil before applying the filling helped it stay put while we rolled the steak. An easy way to add another layer of flavor was infusing the oil with the garlic from our filling; this also took away the garlic's harsh raw flavor. A quick sear gave the meat bundle nice browning, and a long braise in a quick homemade tomato sauce infused it with more flavor and kept it tender. Some supermarkets sell meat labeled specifically for braciole, but we recommend buying flank steak and trimming it yourself. Look for flank steak of even thickness, without tapered ends. Braciole is usually served with pasta; our recipe makes enough sauce for at least 1 pound of pasta.

1 Adjust oven rack to middle position and heat oven to 325 degrees. Position steak on cutting board so long edge is parallel to counter edge. Cover with plastic wrap and pound to even ½-inch thickness. Trim any ragged edges to create rough rectangle about 11 by 9 inches. Pat steak dry with paper towels.

2 Combine oil and garlic in bowl and microwave until fragrant, about 1 minute. Let cool slightly, then remove garlic from oil with fork. Separately reserve garlic and garlic oil. Combine raisins, Parmesan, ¼ cup basil, parsley, ½ teaspoon oregano, ¼ teaspoon pepper flakes, and half of garlic in bowl.

3 Brush exposed side of steak with 1 tablespoon garlic oil and season with ¾ teaspoon pepper and ½ teaspoon salt. Spread raisin mixture evenly over steak, pressing to adhere, leaving 1-inch border along top edge. Starting from bottom edge and rolling away from you, roll steak into tight log, finally resting it seam side down. Tie braciole crosswise with kitchen twine at 1-inch intervals.

4 Heat 1 tablespoon garlic oil in 12-inch nonstick skillet over medium-high heat until just smoking. Add braciole, seam side down, and cook until lightly browned all over, about 5 minutes. Transfer to 13 by 9-inch baking dish.

5 Reduce heat to medium and add onion, remaining garlic oil, remaining ½ teaspoon oregano, and remaining ¼ teaspoon pepper flakes to now-empty skillet. Cook until onion just begins to soften, about 3 minutes. Stir in tomato paste and remaining garlic and cook until fragrant and tomato paste is lightly browned, about 1 minute. Stir in tomatoes, bring to simmer, and pour sauce over braciole. Cover dish tightly with aluminum foil and bake until fork slips easily in and out of braciole, 1½ to 1¾ hours. Transfer dish to wire rack, spoon sauce over braciole, re-cover, and let rest in sauce for 30 minutes.

6 Transfer braciole to carving board, seam side down. Discard twine and slice braciole ¾ inch thick. Stir remaining ¼ cup basil into sauce and season with salt and pepper to taste. Ladle 2 cups sauce onto serving platter. Transfer braciole slices to platter. Serve, passing remaining sauce and extra Parmesan separately.

preparing braciole

1 Pound trimmed flank steak to even ½-inch thickness.

2 Brush steak with garlic oil, season with salt and pepper, and spread with filling, leaving 1-inch border at top. Roll steak away from you into tight log.

3 Place log seam side down and tie crosswise with kitchen twine at 1-inch intervals.

CUBAN BRAISED SHREDDED BEEF (ROPA VIEJA)

serves 6 to 8

1 (2-pound) beef brisket, fat trimmed to ¼ inch

Salt and pepper

5 tablespoons vegetable oil

2 onions, halved and sliced thin

2 red bell peppers, stemmed, seeded, and sliced into ¼-inch-wide strips

4 garlic cloves, minced

2 anchovy fillets, rinsed, patted dry, and minced

2 teaspoons ground cumin

1½ teaspoons dried oregano

½ cup dry white wine

2 cups chicken broth

1 (8-ounce) can tomato sauce

2 bay leaves

¾ cup pitted green olives, chopped coarse

¾ teaspoon white wine vinegar, plus extra for seasoning

Why This Recipe Works A comforting Cuban dish of braised and shredded beef, sliced peppers and onions, chopped green olives, and a brothy sauce, *ropa vieja* is as hearty as it is rustic. Traditionally, the dish requires making a beef stock and then using the meat and some of the liquid to make a separate sauté with onion, pepper, and spices. To simplify it, we combined the two cooking methods and did everything in the same Dutch oven, which also meant that all of the beef's juices ended up in the final dish. We eschewed traditional flank steak in favor of brisket, which contains the right mix of beefy flavor and collagen to guarantee tender, flavorful, juicy shreds. We cut the brisket ahead of time into 2-inch-wide strips, which sped up cooking and made shredding a breeze. To mimic the meatiness that commonly comes from an MSG-spiked seasoning blend, we chose to sear the meat before braising, and we added glutamate-rich anchovies to the mix. Slowly caramelizing the onion and pepper strips gave them deep flavor, and the final addition of briny chopped green olives and a splash of white vinegar brought all the flavors into sharp focus. Look for a brisket that is 1½ to 2½ inches thick.

1 Adjust oven rack to middle position and heat oven to 300 degrees. Cut brisket against grain into 2-inch-wide strips. Cut any strips longer than 5 inches in half crosswise. Season beef on all sides with salt and pepper.

2 Heat ¼ cup oil in Dutch oven over medium-high heat until just smoking. Brown beef on all sides, 7 to 10 minutes. Transfer brisket to large plate; set aside. Add onions and bell peppers to pot and cook over medium-high heat until softened and pan bottom develops fond, 10 to 15 minutes. Transfer vegetables to bowl; set aside.

3 Add remaining 1 tablespoon oil to now-empty pot, then add garlic, anchovies, cumin, and oregano and cook until fragrant, about 30 seconds. Stir in wine, scraping up any browned bits, and cook until mostly evaporated, about 1 minute. Stir in broth, tomato sauce, and bay leaves. Return beef and any accumulated juices to pot and bring to simmer over high heat; transfer pot to oven. Cook, covered, until beef is just tender, 2 to 2¼ hours, flipping meat halfway through cooking.

4 Transfer beef to cutting board; when cool enough to handle, shred into ¼-inch-thick pieces. Meanwhile, add olives and reserved vegetables to pot and bring to boil over medium-high heat; simmer until thickened and measures 4 cups, 5 to 7 minutes. Stir in beef. Add vinegar. Season with salt, pepper, and extra vinegar to taste; serve.

MODERN BEEF STEW

serves 6 to 8

2 garlic cloves, minced

4 anchovy fillets, rinsed and minced

1 tablespoon tomato paste

1 (4-pound) boneless beef chuck-eye roast, pulled apart at seams, trimmed, and cut into 1½-inch pieces

2 tablespoons vegetable oil

1 large onion, halved and sliced ⅛ inch thick

4 carrots, peeled and cut into 1-inch pieces

¼ cup all-purpose flour

2 cups red wine

2 cups chicken broth

4 ounces salt pork, rinsed

2 bay leaves

4 sprigs fresh thyme

1 pound Yukon Gold potatoes, cut into 1-inch pieces

1½ cups frozen pearl onions, thawed

2 teaspoons unflavored gelatin

½ cup water

1 cup frozen peas, thawed

Salt and pepper

Why This Recipe Works Every culture has its version of beef stew, but for our all-American stew, we didn't want to settle for the commonplace: We sought a superlatively rich-tasting but approachable beef stew with tender meat, flavorful vegetables, and a rich brown gravy. We planned to take a no-holds-barred attitude toward the ingredient list. To begin, we chose to break down our own chuck roast instead of using prepackaged cut-up lean stew meat, and we browned it properly, taking care not to crowd the meat in the pan. Along with traditional stew components like onion, carrots, garlic, red wine, and chicken broth, we added glutamate-rich tomato paste, anchovies, and salt pork. Glutamates are compounds that give meat its savory taste, and they contribute considerable flavor to the dish. To mimic the luxurious, mouth-coating texture of beef stews made with homemade stock (collagen in bone is transformed into gelatin when simmered and gives the liquid body), we included powdered gelatin and flour. Potatoes, pearl onions, and peas rounded out our rich-tasting yet updated beef stew. Use a good-quality, medium-bodied red wine, such as a Côtes du Rhône or Pinot Noir, for this stew. Try to find beef that is well marbled with white veins of fat; meat that is too lean will come out slightly dry. Look for salt pork that is roughly 75 percent lean.

1 Adjust oven rack to lower-middle position and heat oven to 300 degrees. Combine garlic and anchovies in small bowl; press with back of fork to form paste. Stir in tomato paste and set aside.

2 Pat beef dry with paper towels (do not season). Heat 1 tablespoon oil in Dutch oven over high heat until just smoking. Add half of beef and cook until well browned on all sides, about 8 minutes. Transfer beef to large plate. Repeat with remaining 1 tablespoon oil and remaining beef, leaving second batch of beef in pot after browning.

3 Reduce heat to medium and return first batch of beef to pot. Stir in onion and carrots and cook, scraping up any browned bits, until onion is softened, 1 to 2 minutes. Add garlic mixture and cook, stirring constantly, until fragrant, about 30 seconds. Add flour and cook, stirring constantly, until no dry flour remains, about 30 seconds.

4 Slowly add wine, scraping up any browned bits. Increase heat to high and simmer until wine is thickened and slightly reduced, about 2 minutes. Stir in broth, salt pork, bay leaves, and thyme sprigs. Bring to simmer and cover; transfer pot to oven. Cook for 1½ hours.

5 Remove pot from oven; discard salt pork, bay leaves, and thyme sprigs. Stir in potatoes, cover, return pot to oven, and continue to cook until potatoes are almost tender, about 45 minutes.

6 Using wide spoon, skim fat from surface of stew. Stir in pearl onions; cook over medium heat until potatoes and pearl onions are cooked through and fork slips easily in and out of beef (meat should not be falling apart), about 15 minutes. Meanwhile, sprinkle gelatin over water in bowl and let sit until gelatin softens, about 5 minutes.

7 Increase heat to high, stir in gelatin mixture and peas, and simmer until gelatin is fully dissolved and stew is thickened, about 3 minutes. Season with salt and pepper to taste, and serve.

BEEF STEW WITH PARSNIPS, KALE, AND MUSHROOMS

serves 4 to 6

2 pounds boneless beef chuck-eye roast, trimmed and cut into 1½-inch pieces

Salt and pepper

5 teaspoons vegetable oil

1 large portobello mushroom cap, cut into ½-inch pieces

2 onions, chopped fine

3 garlic cloves, minced

1 tablespoon minced fresh thyme or 1 teaspoon dried

3 tablespoons all-purpose flour

1 tablespoon tomato paste

1½ cups dry red wine

2 cups chicken broth

2 cups beef broth

2 bay leaves

12 ounces red potatoes, unpeeled, cut into 1-inch pieces

4 carrots, peeled, halved lengthwise, and sliced 1 inch thick

4 parsnips, peeled, halved lengthwise, and sliced 1 inch thick

1 pound kale, stemmed and sliced into ½-inch-wide strips

½ cup frozen peas

¼ cup minced fresh parsley

Why This Recipe Works Beef stew doesn't have a strict definition; beyond the beef, you can braise a host of ingredients. Peas, carrots, and pearl onions might be expected, and we elevate that classic in our ultimate stew, Modern Beef Stew (page 78). However, sometimes we want a stew where the vegetables are as hearty as the meat, so we developed this vegetable-heavy stew. Not only did the extra vegetables add nutrition, they also lent their own clean, fresh, earthy flavors to the gravy. Using two types of broth, chicken and beef, provided a meaty flavor to this vegetable-heavy stew, but the combination was neutral enough that it didn't overtake the beefiness of the chuck roast or obscure the flavor of the vegetables. Red wine added nice depth to the braise. And we still kept the peas and parsley of traditional stew for verdant freshness: Stirred in at the end, the peas didn't lose their color or texture and the generous amount of parsley brightened the whole dish with a pleasant grassiness. With so many vegetables, this plant-boosted stew was just as filling and satisfying as traditional beef stew. Use a red wine made from a blend of grapes, such as Côtes du Rhône, for this dish.

1 Adjust oven rack to lower-middle position and heat oven to 300 degrees. Pat beef dry with paper towels and season with salt and pepper. Heat 1 teaspoon oil in Dutch oven over medium-high heat until just smoking. Brown half of meat on all sides, 5 to 10 minutes; transfer to bowl. Repeat with 1 teaspoon oil and remaining beef; transfer to bowl.

2 Add mushroom pieces to fat left in pot, cover, and cook over medium heat until they've softened and released their liquid, about 5 minutes. Uncover and continue to cook until mushroom pieces are dry and browned, 5 to 10 minutes.

3 Stir in remaining 1 tablespoon oil and onions and cook until softened, 5 to 7 minutes. Stir in garlic and thyme and cook until fragrant, about 30 seconds. Stir in flour and tomato paste and cook until flour is lightly browned, about 1 minute.

4 Slowly whisk in wine, scraping up any browned bits. Slowly whisk in chicken broth and beef broth until smooth. Stir in bay leaves and browned meat and bring to simmer. Cover; transfer pot to oven. Cook for 1½ hours.

5 Stir in potatoes, carrots, and parsnips; cover; return pot to oven and continue to cook until meat and vegetables are tender, about 1 hour. Stir in kale and continue to cook in oven until tender, about 10 minutes. Remove stew from oven and remove bay leaves. Stir in peas and parsley and let stew sit for 5 to 10 minutes. Season with salt and pepper to taste. Serve.

preparing kale

1 Cut away leafy portion from either side of stalk or stem using chef's knife.

2 Slice kale into strips.

BIG BATCH BEEF STEW

serves 12 to 14

4 tablespoons unsalted butter

4 onions, chopped coarse

Salt and pepper

2 tablespoons tomato paste

5 garlic cloves, minced

1 cup all-purpose flour

1 cup red wine

4 cups chicken broth

7 pounds boneless beef chuck-eye roast, pulled apart at seams, trimmed, and cut into 1-inch chunks

2 pounds carrots, peeled and sliced 1 inch thick

3 bay leaves

1½ tablespoons minced fresh thyme or 1½ teaspoons dried

3 pounds red potatoes, unpeeled, cut into 1-inch chunks

1 cup frozen peas

½ cup minced fresh parsley

Why This Recipe Works Few things are as satisfying as a hearty bowl of old-fashioned beef stew—except perhaps being able to share it with a dozen or so of your closest friends and family. Whether you're cooking for a party or just to stock the freezer, a roasting pan makes for a super-easy way to turn out a big batch of classic beef stew with fall-apart meat and tender vegetables draped in a rich brown gravy. We bypassed the need to sear a whopping 7 pounds of meat by doing something much less messy: Browning plenty of onions on the stovetop developed fond we could scrape up to enhance the flavor of our braising liquid. Garlic and tomato paste added a considerable boost as well. We seasoned the meat with salt and pepper before placing it in the pan, along with carrots, bay leaves, and thyme, and then we covered the pan and popped it in the oven to give the meat and carrots a head start. After an hour and a half we added potatoes and roasted everything for another 2 hours, ensuring that the spuds wouldn't fall apart. With minimal fuss, we had created a simple but intensely flavored old-fashioned beef stew, with plenty to share.

1 Adjust oven rack to lower-middle position and heat oven to 325 degrees. Melt butter in 16 by 12-inch roasting pan over medium-high heat (over 2 burners, if possible). Add onions and 1½ teaspoons salt and cook until onions are softened and lightly browned, 10 to 15 minutes.

2 Stir in tomato paste and garlic and cook until fragrant, about 30 seconds. Stir in flour and cook, stirring constantly, until golden, about 1 minute. Slowly whisk in wine, scraping up any browned bits. Gradually whisk in broth, smoothing out any lumps. Season meat with salt and pepper and add to pan. Add carrots, bay leaves, and thyme.

3 Bring stew to simmer. Off heat, cover roasting pan loosely with aluminum foil; transfer pan to oven. Cook stew for 1½ hours.

4 Stir in potatoes, cover, return pan to oven, and continue to cook until meat is tender, 2 to 2½ hours.

5 Remove pan from oven. Discard bay leaves. Stir in peas and let heat through, about 5 minutes. Stir in parsley and season with salt and pepper to taste. Let cool for 15 minutes before serving.

GUINNESS BEEF STEW

serves 6 to 8

1 (4-pound) boneless beef chuck-eye roast, pulled apart at seams, trimmed, and cut into 1½-inch pieces

Salt and pepper

3 tablespoons vegetable oil

2 onions, chopped fine

1 tablespoon tomato paste

2 garlic cloves, minced

¼ cup all-purpose flour

3 cups chicken broth

1¼ cups Guinness Draught

1½ tablespoons packed dark brown sugar

1 teaspoon minced fresh thyme

1½ pounds Yukon Gold potatoes, unpeeled, cut into 1-inch pieces

1 pound carrots, peeled and cut into 1-inch pieces

2 tablespoons minced fresh parsley

Why This Recipe Works Both Guinness and beef stew have deep, roasted, delicious flavor. However, Guinness beef stew often captures only the bitterness of the dark Irish beer and none of the caramelized flavors. Cooked beer can be especially bitter; introducing some of the beer before cooking created a restrained bitter background, and adding the rest just before serving gave us a robust, complex stout flavor. We also added a little dark brown sugar, which balanced some of the bitterness with sweetness and bolstered flavor with its molasses notes. We loved the idea of just dumping the meat into the pot without searing, but the flavor was lacking. To compensate, we first browned the onions and tomato paste, and then we cooked the stew uncovered so that the meat could brown in the oven. Doing this not only bypassed the searing step but also let the sauce evaporate, concentrating its flavor. (Learn more about this technique on page 7.) Use Guinness Draught, not Guinness Extra Stout, which is too bitter.

1 Adjust oven rack to lower-middle position and heat oven to 325 degrees. Season beef with salt and pepper. Heat oil in Dutch oven over medium-high heat until shimmering. Add onions and ¼ teaspoon salt and cook, stirring occasionally, until well browned, 8 to 10 minutes.

2 Add tomato paste and garlic and cook until rust-colored and fragrant, about 2 minutes. Stir in flour and cook for 1 minute. Whisk in broth, ¾ cup Guinness, sugar, and thyme, scraping up any browned bits. Bring to simmer and cook until slightly thickened, about 3 minutes. Stir in beef and return to simmer; transfer pot to oven. Cook, uncovered, for 1½ hours, stirring halfway through cooking.

3 Stir in potatoes and carrots, cover, return pot to oven, and continue to cook until beef and vegetables are tender, about 1 hour, stirring halfway through cooking. Stir in remaining ½ cup Guinness and parsley. Season with salt and pepper to taste, and serve.

MODERN BEEF BURGUNDY

serves 6 to 8

1 (4-pound) boneless beef chuck-eye roast, pulled apart at seams, trimmed, and cut into 1½-inch pieces, scraps reserved

Salt and pepper

6 ounces salt pork, cut into ¼-inch pieces

3 tablespoons unsalted butter

1 pound cremini mushrooms, trimmed and halved if medium or quartered if large

1½ cups frozen pearl onions, thawed

1 tablespoon sugar

⅓ cup all-purpose flour

4 cups beef broth

1 (750-ml) bottle red Burgundy or Pinot Noir

5 teaspoons unflavored gelatin

1 tablespoon tomato paste

1 teaspoon anchovy paste

2 onions, chopped coarse

2 carrots, peeled and cut into 2-inch lengths

1 garlic head, cloves separated, unpeeled, and smashed

½ ounce dried porcini mushrooms, rinsed

10 sprigs fresh parsley, plus 3 tablespoons minced

6 sprigs fresh thyme

2 bay leaves

½ teaspoon black peppercorns

Why This Recipe Works Julia Child once wrote that *boeuf bourguignon* "is the best beef stew known to man." One of the most defining dishes in French cuisine, beef Burgundy is probably the ultimate example of how rich, savory, and satisfying a beef stew can be: By gently simmering large chunks of well-marbled meat in beef broth and a good amount of red wine, you end up with fork-tender beef and a braising liquid that's transformed into a silky, full-bodied sauce. We wanted all of that— without all the work that traditional recipes require: browning beef, cooking garnishes, braising, combining, cooking further. To eliminate the time-consuming step of searing the beef, we cooked the stew uncovered in a roasting pan in the oven so that the exposed meat browned as it braised. This method worked so well that we also used the oven, rather than the stovetop, to render the salt pork and to caramelize the traditional mushroom and pearl onion garnish. Salting the beef before cooking and adding some anchovy paste and porcini mushrooms enhanced the meaty savoriness of the dish without making our recipe too fussy. If the pearl onions have a papery outer coating, remove it by rinsing them in warm water and gently squeezing individual onions between your fingertips. Two minced anchovy fillets can be used in place of the anchovy paste.

1 Toss beef and 1½ teaspoons salt together in bowl; let sit at room temperature for 30 minutes.

2 Adjust oven racks to lower-middle and lowest positions and heat oven to 500 degrees. Place beef scraps, salt pork, and 2 tablespoons butter in large roasting pan. Roast on upper rack until well browned and fat has rendered, 15 to 20 minutes.

3 While beef scraps and salt pork roast, toss cremini mushrooms, pearl onions, sugar, and remaining 1 tablespoon butter on rimmed baking sheet. Roast on lower rack, stirring occasionally, until moisture released by mushrooms evaporates and vegetables are lightly glazed, 15 to 20 minutes. Transfer vegetables to large bowl, cover, and refrigerate.

4 Remove roasting pan from oven and reduce temperature to 325 degrees. Sprinkle flour over rendered fat and whisk until no dry flour remains. Whisk in broth, 2 cups wine, gelatin, tomato paste, and anchovy paste until combined. Add onions, carrots, garlic, porcini mushrooms, parsley sprigs, thyme sprigs, bay leaves, and peppercorns to pan. Arrange beef in single layer on top of vegetables. Add water as needed to come three-quarters up sides of beef pieces (beef should not be submerged). Return roasting pan to oven and cook until meat is tender, 3 to 3½ hours, stirring after 1½ hours and adding water to keep meat at least half-submerged.

5 Using slotted spoon, transfer beef to bowl with cremini mushrooms and pearl onions; cover and set aside. Strain braising liquid through fine-mesh strainer set over large bowl, pressing on solids to extract as much liquid as possible; discard solids. Stir in remaining wine. Let liquid settle for 10 minutes, then use wide spoon to skim fat from surface.

6 Transfer liquid to Dutch oven and bring mixture to boil over medium-high heat. Simmer briskly, stirring occasionally, until sauce has thickened to consistency of heavy cream, 15 to 20 minutes. Reduce heat to medium-low, stir in beef and mushroom-onion mixture, cover, and cook until just heated through, 5 to 8 minutes. Season with salt and pepper to taste. Stir in minced parsley and serve.

CARNE GUISADA

serves 8 to 10

3 pounds boneless beef chuck-eye roast, trimmed and cut into 1-inch pieces

Salt and pepper

2 tablespoons vegetable oil

2 onions, chopped

2 tablespoons tomato paste

4 garlic cloves, minced

1 tablespoon chili powder

1 tablespoon dried oregano

2 teaspoons ground coriander

1½ teaspoons ground cumin

1 tablespoon all-purpose flour

1 (14.5-ounce) can diced tomatoes, drained

1 cup chicken broth

1 pound Yukon Gold potatoes, peeled and cut into ½-inch pieces

2 green bell peppers, stemmed, seeded, and cut into ¼-inch strips

24 flour tortillas, warmed

Fresh cilantro leaves

Lime wedges

Why This Recipe Works Braised beef and potatoes is as classic as, well, meat and potatoes. *Carne Guisada* is a bold and intensely satisfying Texas stew that punches up this familiar combination with tomato, chiles, and warm spices. It's commonly served as tacos (our favorite way to eat it), or as a stew with beans, rice, or tortillas on the side. We turned to our go-to stew cut, beef chuck and kicked out hard-to-find varieties of fresh and dried chiles that we saw in some recipes in favor of the simple but delicious mix of chili powder, oregano, cumin, and coriander—no fresh chiles necessary. Choosing chicken broth for our braising liquid let the flavor of what would become meltingly tender beef shine—there were already strong flavors in this stew. We added the potatoes and bell peppers partway through cooking to guarantee the vegetables were tender but that they didn't disintegrate. Finally, cutting back on the amount of liquid and adding a tablespoon of flour gave our stew the perfect texture, making it equally delicious as a taco filling or served on a plate with beans and rice.

1 Adjust oven rack to lower-middle position and heat oven to 325 degrees. Pat beef dry with paper towels and season with salt and pepper. Heat oil in Dutch oven over medium-high heat until just smoking. Add half of beef and cook until browned on all sides, 7 to 10 minutes; transfer to plate.

2 Reduce heat to medium-low, add onions and 1 teaspoon salt to pot, and cook until softened, about 5 minutes. Stir in tomato paste, garlic, chili powder, oregano, coriander, and cumin and cook until fragrant, about 30 seconds. Stir in flour and cook for 1 minute. Stir in tomatoes and broth and bring to simmer, scraping up any browned bits. Stir in all of beef and any accumulated juices and cover; transfer pot to oven. Cook for 1½ hours.

3 Remove pot from oven and stir in potatoes and bell peppers. Cover, return pot to oven, and continue to cook until beef and potatoes are tender, about 45 minutes longer.

4 Season with salt and pepper to taste. Spoon small amount of stew into center of each tortilla, top with cilantro, and serve with lime wedges.

DAUBE PROVENÇAL

serves 4 to 6

2 cups water

¾ ounce dried porcini mushrooms, rinsed

1 (3½-pound) boneless beef chuck-eye roast, pulled apart at seams, trimmed, and cut into 2-inch pieces

1½ teaspoons salt

1 teaspoon pepper

¼ cup olive oil

2 onions, halved and cut into ⅛-inch-thick slices

4 large carrots, peeled and cut into 1-inch-thick rounds

5 ounces salt pork, rind removed

2 tablespoons tomato paste

4 garlic cloves, sliced thin

⅓ cup all-purpose flour

1 (750-ml) bottle red wine

1 cup chicken broth

1 cup pitted niçoise olives

3 anchovy fillets, minced

4 (3-inch) strips orange zest, cut into thin strips

5 sprigs thyme, tied together with kitchen twine

2 bay leaves

1 (14.5-ounce) can whole peeled tomatoes, drained and cut into ½-inch pieces

2 tablespoons minced fresh parsley

Why This Recipe Works *Daube Provençal*, also known as *daube niçoise*, has all the elements of an outstanding stew—tender beef, a luxurious sauce, and complex flavors—but is infused with the flavors of Provence: olive oil, olives, garlic, wine, herbs, oranges, tomatoes, mushrooms, and anchovies. The result is a bold, brash, and full-flavored beef stew. Our technique for stews is strong; we concentrated on selecting and managing the complex blend of ingredients that defines this dish. We chose briny niçoise olives, bright tomatoes, floral orange peel, and the regional flavors of thyme and bay leaf. In addition, a few anchovies added complexity without a fishy taste, and salt pork contributed rich body. A whole bottle of wine added bold flavor and needed just a little cooking to tame its raw bite. Finally, to keep the meat from drying out during the long braising time required to create a complex-tasting sauce, we cut it into relatively large 2-inch pieces. Use a Dutch oven that holds 7 quarts or more for this recipe. If niçoise olives are not available, kalamata olives, though not authentic, can be substituted. We like to use Cabernet Sauvignon for this dish, but Côtes du Rhône and zinfandel also work.

1 Microwave 1 cup water and mushrooms in covered bowl until steaming, about 1 minute. Let sit until softened, about 5 minutes. Drain mushrooms in fine-mesh strainer lined with coffee filter, reserve liquid, and set mushrooms and liquid aside.

2 Adjust oven rack to lower-middle position and heat oven to 325 degrees. Pat beef dry with paper towels and season with salt and pepper. Heat 2 tablespoons oil in Dutch oven over medium-high heat until shimmering. Add half of beef and cook, without moving pieces, until well browned, about 2 minutes on each side, for total of 8 to 10 minutes, reducing heat if fat begins to smoke; transfer beef to bowl. Repeat with remaining 2 tablespoons oil and remaining beef.

3 Reduce heat to medium and add onions, carrots, salt pork, tomato paste, and garlic to now-empty pot; cook, stirring occasionally, until light brown, about 2 minutes. Stir in flour and cook, stirring constantly, about 1 minute. Slowly add wine, scraping up any browned bits. Add broth, remaining 1 cup water, and beef and any accumulated juices. Increase heat to medium-high and bring to simmer. Add ½ cup olives, anchovies, orange zest, thyme sprigs, bay leaves, and mushrooms and their liquid, distributing ingredients evenly and arranging beef so that it is completely covered by liquid and partially cover pot; transfer pot to oven. Cook until fork inserted in beef meets little resistance (meat should not be falling apart), 2½ to 3 hours.

4 Discard salt pork, thyme sprigs, and bay leaves. Add tomatoes and remaining ½ cup olives; cook over medium-high heat until heated through, about 1 minute. Cover pot and let stew settle for about 5 minutes, then skim fat from surface with wise spoon. Stir in parsley and serve.

CATALAN-STYLE BEEF STEW WITH MUSHROOMS

serves 4 to 6

Stew

3 tablespoons olive oil

2 large onions, chopped fine

½ teaspoon sugar

Kosher salt and pepper

2 plum tomatoes, halved lengthwise, pulp grated on large holes of box grater, and skins discarded

1 teaspoon smoked paprika

1 bay leaf

1½ cups dry white wine

1½ cups water

1 large sprig fresh thyme

¼ teaspoon ground cinnamon

2½ pounds boneless beef short ribs, trimmed and cut into 2-inch cubes

8 ounces oyster mushrooms, trimmed

1 teaspoon sherry vinegar

Picada

¼ cup whole blanched almonds

1 tablespoon olive oil

1 slice hearty white sandwich bread, crust removed, torn into 1-inch pieces

2 garlic cloves, peeled

3 tablespoons minced fresh parsley

Why This Recipe Works Spanish cuisine is remarkably complex, with influences from ancient Greece and Rome, North Africa, and even the Americas. A multilayering of flavors and textures is particularly apparent in the meat stews from the easternmost region of Catalonia. They begin with a slow-cooked jam of onions and tomatoes known as *sofrito* and end with the stirring in of *picada*, a pesto-like paste that includes fried bread, herbs, and ground nuts and gives the stew body and even more dimension. Cinnamon and smoked paprika are also common, along with a sherry-like fortified wine known as *vi ranci*. Spanish cooks employ a variety of cuts like flank, skirt, or blade steak or short ribs in their stews, and we loved the short ribs; boneless short ribs were easy to butcher, boasted outstanding beef flavor, and became supremely tender and moist after a long, slow simmer. We deeply caramelized the onions for the sofrito, so we thought the vi ranci or sherry made the stew cloying. We preferred wine, and less-assertive white wines were best; they complemented rather than overpowered the flavor of the meat. We didn't want to overload this beef dish with vegetables, but some additional element felt appropriate. It only made sense to feature a popular Catalan ingredient: oyster mushrooms. While we developed this recipe with Albariño, a dry Spanish white wine, you can also use a Sauvignon Blanc. Remove the woody base of the oyster mushroom stems before cooking. An equal amount of quartered white mushrooms may be substituted for the oyster mushrooms.

1 For the stew Adjust oven rack to middle position and heat oven to 300 degrees. Heat 2 tablespoons oil in Dutch oven over medium-low heat until shimmering. Add onions, sugar, and ½ teaspoon salt; cook, stirring often, until onions are deeply caramelized, 30 to 40 minutes. Add tomato pulp, paprika, and bay leaf; cook, stirring often, until darkened and thick, 5 to 10 minutes.

2 Add wine, water, thyme sprig, and cinnamon to pot, scraping up any browned bits. Season short ribs with 1½ teaspoons salt and ½ teaspoon pepper and add to pot. Increase heat to high and bring to simmer; transfer pot to oven. Cook, uncovered, for 1 hour. Stir stew to redistribute meat, cover, return to oven, and continue to cook until meat is tender, 1½ to 2 hours longer.

CHINESE-STYLE RED-COOKED BEEF

serves 6

1½ tablespoons unflavored gelatin

2½ cups plus 1 tablespoon water

½ cup dry sherry

⅓ cup soy sauce

3 scallions, white and green parts separated, green parts sliced thin on bias

2 tablespoons hoisin sauce

2 tablespoons molasses

1 (2-inch) piece ginger, peeled, halved lengthwise, and crushed

4 garlic cloves, peeled and smashed

1½ teaspoons five-spice powder

1 teaspoon red pepper flakes

3 pounds boneless beef short ribs, trimmed and cut into 4-inch lengths

1 teaspoon cornstarch

Why This Recipe Works Think of red-cooked beef as the high-energy Chinese version of American beef stew: tender chunks of beef in a potent, exotically fragrant sauce, which is redolent with flavorings such as ginger, cinnamon, star anise, Sichuan peppercorns, and cardamom. Red-cooked beef doesn't actually turn out red, even though it comes from the notion that beef simmered in a lightly sweetened broth of soy sauce and spices takes on a ruddy hue. Regardless, this dish is comfort food at its best. But the comfort factor diminishes a bit if the recipe is fussy. We simplified the dish for the American kitchen. For meat that cooked up rich and tender, we used readily available boneless beef short ribs. Then we eliminated a traditional cooking step: blanching the meat, which is said to remove impurities. While this does provide clearer stock by sloughing away free proteins from the beef's surface, we were reducing our liquid to a concentrated sauce, so translucency didn't matter. Browning in the Western tradition wasn't necessary either—the dish was plenty flavorful without it. A pair of thickeners—gelatin and cornstarch—added body to the sauce and created a lacquered glaze on the meat. Five-spice powder provided characteristic flavors without the bother of whole spices, and a combination of hoisin sauce and molasses contributed the underlying sweetness that completes the dish. With its generous amount of soy sauce, this dish is meant to taste salty, which is why we pair it with Simple White Rice (page 28) or plain steamed rice.

1 Sprinkle gelatin over 2½ cups water in Dutch oven and let sit until gelatin softens, about 5 minutes. Adjust oven rack to middle position and heat oven to 300 degrees.

2 Heat softened gelatin over medium-high heat, stirring occasionally, until melted, 2 to 3 minutes. Stir in sherry, soy sauce, scallion whites, hoisin, molasses, ginger, garlic, five-spice powder, and pepper flakes. Stir in beef and bring to simmer. Remove pot from heat. Place large piece of aluminum foil over pot and cover tightly with lid; transfer pot to oven. Cook until beef is tender, 2 to 2½ hours, stirring halfway through cooking.

3 Using slotted spoon, transfer beef to cutting board. Strain sauce through fine-mesh strainer into fat separator. Wipe pot clean with paper towels. Let liquid settle for 5 minutes, then return defatted liquid to now-empty pot. Cook liquid over medium-high heat, stirring occasionally, until thickened and reduced to 1 cup, 20 to 25 minutes.

4 While sauce reduces, break beef into 1½-inch pieces with 2 forks. Whisk cornstarch and remaining 1 tablespoon water together in small bowl.

5 Reduce heat to medium-low, whisk cornstarch mixture into reduced sauce and cook until sauce is slightly thickened, about 1 minute. Return beef to sauce and stir to coat. Cover and cook, stirring occasionally, until beef is heated through, about 5 minutes. Sprinkle scallion greens over top. Serve.

PORTUGUESE-STYLE BEEF STEW (ALCATRA)

3 pounds boneless long-cut beef shanks

Salt and pepper

5 garlic cloves, peeled and smashed

5 allspice berries

4 bay leaves

1½ teaspoons peppercorns

2 large onions, halved and sliced thin

2¼ cups dry white wine

¼ teaspoon ground cinnamon

8 ounces Spanish-style chorizo sausage, cut into ¼-inch-thick rounds

Why This Recipe Works *Alcatra*, a simple and meaty Portuguese beef stew, features tender chunks of beef braised with onions, garlic, spices, and wine. Unlike beef stews that require searing the beef to build savory flavor or adding flavor boosters like tomato paste and anchovies, this recipe skips those steps and ingredients, highlighting the warm and bright flavors of the spices and wine as much as the meatiness of the beef. We used beef shank because it's lean (which meant the cooking liquid didn't need to be skimmed) and full of collagen, which broke down into gelatin and gave the sauce full body. Submerging the sliced onions completely in the liquid under the meat caused them to form a meaty-tasting compound that amped up the savory flavor of the broth. Slices of smoky-sweet Spanish chorizo sausage matched up perfectly with the other flavors in the stew. You can substitute 4 pounds of bone-in crosscut shank if that's all you can find. Remove the bones before cooking and save them for another use. Crosscut shank cooks more quickly, so check the stew for doneness in step 2 after 3 hours. A 3½- to 4-pound chuck roast, trimmed of fat and cut into 2½-inch pieces, can be substituted for the shanks.

1 Adjust oven rack to middle position and heat oven to 325 degrees. Trim away any fat or large pieces of connective tissue from exterior of shanks (silverskin can be left on meat). Cut each shank crosswise into 2½-inch pieces. Sprinkle meat with 1 teaspoon salt.

2 Cut 8-inch square of triple-thickness cheesecloth. Place garlic, allspice berries, bay leaves, and peppercorns in center of cheesecloth and tie into bundle with kitchen twine. Arrange onions and spice bundle in Dutch oven in even layer. Add wine and cinnamon. Arrange shank pieces in single layer on top of onions. Cover and cook until beef is tender, about 3½ hours.

3 Remove pot from oven and add chorizo. Using tongs, flip each piece of beef over, making sure that chorizo is submerged. Cover and let stand until chorizo is warmed through, about 20 minutes. Discard spice bundle. Season with salt and pepper to taste, and serve.

buying beef shank

Beef shank is sold both crosscut and long-cut (with and without bones). We prefer long-cut since it has more collagen.

Long-cut beef shank

Crosscut beef shank

SICHUAN BRAISED TOFU WITH BEEF (MAPO TOFU)

serves 4 to 6

1 tablespoon Sichuan peppercorns

12 scallions

28 ounces soft tofu, cut into ½-inch cubes

2 cups chicken broth

9 garlic cloves, peeled

1 (3-inch) piece ginger, peeled and cut into ¼-inch rounds

⅓ cup Asian broad bean chili paste

1 tablespoon fermented black beans

6 tablespoons vegetable oil

1 tablespoon Sichuan chili powder

8 ounces 85 percent lean ground beef

2 tablespoons hoisin sauce

2 teaspoons toasted sesame oil

2 tablespoons water

1 tablespoon cornstarch

Why This Recipe Works Think tofu is bland and boring? Surely not if you've tried this braise of custardy curds cloaked in a garlicky, spicy meat sauce—the signature dish of the Sichuan province. Our version of *mapo* tofu is bold in flavor, with a balanced spiciness. We started with cubed soft tofu, poaching it gently in chicken broth to help the cubes stay intact in the braise. For the sauce base, we used plenty of ginger and garlic along with four Sichuan pantry powerhouses: Asian broad bean chili paste, fermented black beans, Sichuan chili powder, and Sichuan peppercorns. A small amount of ground beef acted as a seasoning, not as a primary component of the dish. In place of the chili oil often called for, we used a generous amount of vegetable oil, extra Sichuan chili powder, and toasted sesame oil. We finished the dish with just the right amount of cornstarch to create a velvety thickness. Ground pork can be used in place of beef, if desired. Asian broad bean chili paste (or sauce) is also known as *doubanjiang* or *toban djan*. Our favorite, Pixian, is available online; Lee Kum Kee Chili Bean Sauce is a good supermarket option. If you can't find Sichuan chili powder, an equal amount of Korean red pepper flakes (*gochugaru*) is a good substitute. In a pinch, use 2½ teaspoons of ancho chile powder and ½ teaspoon of cayenne pepper. If you can't find fermented black beans, you can use an equal amount of fermented black bean paste or sauce or 2 additional teaspoons of Asian broad bean chili paste.

1 Place peppercorns in small bowl and microwave until fragrant, 15 to 30 seconds. Let cool completely. Once cool, grind in spice grinder or mortar and pestle (you should have 1½ teaspoons).

2 Using side of chef's knife, lightly crush white parts of scallions, then cut scallions into 1-inch pieces. Place tofu, broth, and scallions in large bowl and microwave, covered, until steaming, 5 to 7 minutes. Let stand while preparing remaining ingredients.

3 Process garlic, ginger, chili paste, and black beans in food processor until coarse paste forms, 1 to 2 minutes, scraping down sides of bowl as needed. Add ¼ cup vegetable oil, chili powder, and 1 teaspoon peppercorns and continue to process until smooth paste forms, 1 to 2 minutes longer; transfer spice paste to bowl.

4 Heat 1 tablespoon vegetable oil and beef in large saucepan over medium heat; cook, breaking up meat with wooden spoon, until meat just begins to brown, 5 to 7 minutes; transfer beef to bowl.

5 Add remaining 1 tablespoon vegetable oil and spice paste to now-empty saucepan and cook, stirring frequently, until paste darkens and oil begins to separate from paste, 2 to 3 minutes. Gently pour tofu with broth into saucepan, followed by hoisin, sesame oil, and beef. Cook, stirring gently and frequently, until dish comes to simmer, 2 to 3 minutes. Whisk water and cornstarch together in small bowl. Add cornstarch mixture to saucepan and continue to cook, stirring frequently, until thickened, 2 to 3 minutes longer. Transfer to serving dish, sprinkle with remaining peppercorns, and serve.

FLANK STEAK IN ADOBO

serves 4 to 6

Adobo

1½ ounces dried ancho chiles, stemmed and seeded

1 ounce dried pasilla chiles, stemmed and seeded

¾ cup salsa verde

¾ cup chicken broth

½ cup orange juice

⅓ cup packed brown sugar

¼ cup lime juice (2 limes)

1½ teaspoons dried oregano

1 teaspoon salt

½ teaspoon pepper

Flank Steak

2½–3 pounds flank steak, trimmed and cut into 1½-inch cubes

Salt and pepper

2 tablespoons vegetable oil

1 onion, chopped fine

8 garlic cloves, minced

1 tablespoon ground cumin

4 ounces queso fresco, crumbled (1 cup)

½ cup coarsely chopped fresh cilantro

12 (8-inch) flour tortillas, warmed

Why This Recipe Works *Arrachera en adobo* is pretty remarkable: This chili-like dish of steak stewed in a pungent adobo sauce is a gem of Mexican American cuisine, virtually unknown outside Texas. Spicy, garlicky, sweet, sour, meaty, fruity, rich—this complex dish, at once comforting and invigorating, is astonishingly good. For a simple adobo sauce that still had the characteristic deep, earthy flavor, we used two kinds of dried chile—ancho chiles (dried poblanos) for their fruitiness and pasilla chiles for their bitter earthiness. Seeding the chiles tamed their heat, while toasting them gave them more complex flavor. Blending the rehydrated chiles with lime juice, chicken broth, oregano, and salsa verde—a green salsa made from tomatillos—created a rich yet tangy adobo sauce. Flank steak proved to be the ideal cut for this dish since it's leaner than a typical stewing cut and thus didn't add flavor-muting greasiness to the sauce. We used jarred salsa verde for ease; our favorite brand is Frontera Tomatillo Salsa. You can substitute skirt steak for flank steak here, if desired. If queso fresco is unavailable, you can substitute farmer's cheese or a mild feta. This dish is also great served over rice.

1 **For the adobo** Adjust oven rack to lower-middle position and heat oven to 350 degrees. Arrange anchos and pasillas on rimmed baking sheet and bake until fragrant, about 5 minutes. Immediately transfer chiles to bowl and cover with hot tap water. Let stand until chiles are softened and pliable, about 5 minutes; drain.

2 Process salsa verde, broth, orange juice, sugar, lime juice, oregano, salt, pepper, and drained chiles in blender until smooth, 1 to 2 minutes; set aside.

3 **For the flank steak** Reduce oven temperature to 300 degrees. Pat beef dry with paper towels and sprinkle with ½ teaspoon salt and ½ teaspoon pepper. Heat 1 tablespoon oil in Dutch oven over medium-high heat until just smoking. Add half of beef and cook, stirring occasionally, until well browned on all sides, 6 to 9 minutes. (Adjust heat, if necessary, to keep bottom of pot from scorching.) Using slotted spoon, transfer beef to large bowl. Repeat with remaining 1 tablespoon oil and remaining beef.

4 Add onion and ½ teaspoon salt to now-empty pot. Reduce heat to medium and cook, stirring occasionally, until golden brown, 3 to 5 minutes, scraping up any browned bits. Add garlic and cumin and cook until fragrant, about 30 seconds. Stir in adobo, beef, and any accumulated juices until well incorporated and bring mixture to simmer.

5 Cover pot; transfer to oven. Cook until beef is tender and sauce has thickened, about 1½ hours. Season with salt and pepper to taste. Sprinkle with queso fresco and cilantro and serve with tortillas.

ULTIMATE CHILI

serves 6 to 8

8 ounces (1¼ cups) dried pinto beans, picked over and rinsed

Salt

6 dried ancho chiles, stemmed, seeded, and torn into 1-inch pieces

2–4 dried arbol chiles, stemmed, seeded, and halved

3 tablespoons cornmeal

2 teaspoons dried oregano

2 teaspoons ground cumin

2 teaspoons unsweetened cocoa powder

2½ cups chicken broth

2 onions, cut into ¾-inch pieces

3 small jalapeño chiles, stemmed, seeded, and cut into ½-inch pieces

3 tablespoons vegetable oil

4 garlic cloves, minced

1 (14.5-ounce) can diced tomatoes

2 teaspoons molasses

3½ pounds blade steak, ¾ inch thick, trimmed and cut into ¾-inch pieces

1½ cups mild lager, such as Budweiser

Why This Recipe Works Our goal in creating an ultimate beef chili was to determine which of the "secret ingredients" recommended by chili experts around the world were spot-on—and which were expendable. We started with the beef. Most recipes call for ground beef, but we preferred meaty blade steaks, which don't require much trimming and stayed in big chunks in our finished chili. For complex chile flavor, we traded in the commercial chili powder in favor of ground dried ancho and arbol chiles; for a grassy heat, we added fresh jalapeños. Dried beans, brined before cooking, stayed creamy for the duration of cooking. Beer and chicken broth outperformed red wine, coffee, and beef broth as the liquid components. For balancing sweetness, light molasses was better than offbeat ingredients we'd seen (including prunes and Coca-Cola). And finally, for thickness, flour and peanut butter didn't perform as promised; instead, a small amount of cornmeal provided just the right consistency in our ultimate beef chili. Because much of the chili flavor is held in the fat of this dish, refrain from skimming fat from the surface. Dried New Mexican or guajillo chiles make a good substitute for the anchos; each dried arbol may be replaced with ⅛ teaspoon cayenne pepper. If you prefer not to work with any whole dried chiles, the anchos and arbols can be replaced with ½ cup commercial chili powder and ¼ to ½ teaspoon cayenne pepper, though the texture of the chili will be slightly compromised. Good choices for condiments include diced avocado, finely chopped red onion, chopped cilantro leaves, lime wedges, sour cream, and shredded Monterey Jack or cheddar cheese.

1 Combine 4 quarts water, beans, and 3 tablespoons salt in Dutch oven and bring to boil over high heat. Remove pot from heat, cover, and let stand for 1 hour. Drain and rinse well.

2 Adjust oven rack to lower-middle position and heat oven to 300 degrees. Place anchos in 12-inch skillet set over medium-high heat; toast, stirring frequently, until flesh is fragrant, 4 to 6 minutes, reducing heat if chiles begin to smoke. Transfer to food processor and let cool (do not clean skillet).

3 Add arbols, cornmeal, oregano, cumin, cocoa, and ½ teaspoon salt to processor with toasted anchos; process until finely ground, about 2 minutes. With processor running, slowly add ½ cup broth until smooth paste forms, about

45 seconds, scraping down sides of bowl as needed. Transfer paste to small bowl. Pulse onions in now-empty processor until coarsely chopped, about 4 pulses. Add jalapeños and pulse until consistency of chunky salsa, about 4 pulses, scraping down sides of bowl as needed.

4 Heat 1 tablespoon oil in Dutch oven over medium-high heat. Add onion mixture and cook, stirring occasionally, until moisture has evaporated and vegetables are softened, 7 to 9 minutes. Add garlic and cook until fragrant, about 1 minute. Add tomatoes and their juice, molasses, and chile paste; stir until thoroughly combined. Add beans and remaining 2 cups broth; bring to boil, then reduce heat to low and simmer.

5 Meanwhile, heat 1 tablespoon oil in now-empty skillet over medium-high heat until shimmering. Pat beef dry with paper towels and sprinkle with 1 teaspoon salt. Brown half of beef on all sides, about 10 minutes; transfer to pot. Add ¾ cup beer to skillet, scraping up any browned bits, and bring to simmer. Transfer beer to pot. Repeat with remaining 1 tablespoon oil, remaining beef, and remaining ¾ cup beer; transfer to pot. Stir to combine and return mixture to simmer.

6 Cover pot; transfer to oven. Cook until meat and beans are fully tender, 1½ to 2 hours. Let chili stand, uncovered, for 10 minutes. Stir well, season with salt to taste, and serve.

BEEF SHORT RIB RAGU

serves 4 to 6

1½ cups beef broth

½ ounce dried porcini mushrooms, rinsed

1 tablespoon extra-virgin olive oil

1 onion, chopped fine

2 garlic cloves, minced

1 tablespoon tomato paste

3 anchovy fillets, rinsed, patted dry, and minced

½ teaspoon five-spice powder

½ cup dry red wine

1 (14.5-ounce) can whole peeled tomatoes, drained with juice reserved, chopped fine

2 pounds boneless beef short ribs, trimmed

Salt and pepper

Why This Recipe Works A typical Sunday gravy is an all-day affair and calls for multiple meats. We wanted a rich sauce using one cut of beef that would be done in about 2 hours. For beefy flavor in a reasonable amount of time, we started with the most obvious source: the meat itself. Boneless beef short ribs were a rich, intensely beefy cut that also gave the sauce a velvety texture. For more impact, we paired the ribs with porcini mushrooms, tomato paste, and anchovy fillets—all umami-rich ingredients that gave the quick sauce deep savor without the all-day simmer. Braising in the oven was a largely hands-off proposition, and removing the lid partway through cooking browned the meat, enhancing its flavor. Finally, many Italian beef ragus call for a touch of warm spices, a nod to the importance of the spice route that passed through Italy from the 15th to the 17th century and introduced Europe to Asian flavors. Instead of using a bunch of separate spices, we turned to a single blend: five-spice powder. Just ½ teaspoon of this mix of cinnamon, cloves, fennel, white pepper, and star anise contributed sweet and warm flavors without tasting identifiably Asian. If you can't find boneless short ribs, don't substitute bone-in short ribs. Instead, use a 2½-pound chuck-eye roast, trimmed and cut into 1-inch chunks. This recipe yields enough to sauce 1 pound of pasta or a batch of Creamy Parmesan Polenta (page 29) (our favorite way to serve it). This recipe can be doubled.

1 Adjust oven rack to middle position and heat oven to 350 degrees. Microwave ½ cup broth and mushrooms in covered bowl until steaming, about 1 minute. Let sit until softened, about 5 minutes. Drain mushrooms in fine-mesh strainer lined with coffee filter, pressing to extract all liquid; reserve liquid and chop mushrooms fine.

2 Heat oil in Dutch oven over medium heat until shimmering. Add onion and cook, stirring occasionally, until softened, about 5 minutes. Add garlic and cook until fragrant, about 1 minute. Add tomato paste, anchovies, and five-spice powder and cook, stirring frequently, until mixture has darkened and fond forms on pot bottom, 3 to 4 minutes. Add wine, increase heat to medium-high, and bring to simmer, scraping up any browned bits. Continue to cook, stirring frequently, until wine is reduced and pot is almost dry, 2 to 4 minutes. Add tomatoes and reserved juice, remaining 1 cup broth, reserved mushroom soaking liquid, and mushrooms and bring to simmer.

3 Toss beef with ¾ teaspoon salt and season with pepper. Add beef to pot and cover; transfer pot to oven. Cook for 1 hour.

4 Uncover and continue to cook until beef is tender, 1 to 1¼ hours longer.

5 Remove pot from oven; using slotted spoon, transfer beef to cutting board and let cool for 5 minutes. Using 2 forks, shred beef into bite-size pieces, discarding any large pieces of fat or connective tissue. Using large spoon, skim off any excess fat that has risen to surface of sauce. Return beef to sauce and season with salt and pepper to taste.

LAMB AND VEAL

Leg of Lamb en Cocotte with Garlic and Rosemary

108 **Braised Lamb Shoulder Chops with Tomatoes and Red Wine**
Braised Lamb Shoulder Chops with Capers, Balsamic Vinegar, and Red Pepper
Braised Lamb Shoulder Chops with Figs and North African Spices
Braised Lamb Shoulder Chops with Tomatoes, Rosemary, and Olives

111 **Braised Lamb Shanks with Lemon and Mint**
Braised Lamb Shanks with North African Spices
Braised Lamb Shanks with Red Wine and Herbes de Provence

112 **Leg of Lamb en Cocotte with Garlic and Rosemary**

114 **Moroccan Braised White Beans with Lamb**

117 **Irish Stew**
with Carrots and Turnips

118 **Italian-Style Lamb Stew with Green Beans, Tomatoes, and Basil**

121 **Lamb Curry with Whole Spices**
Lamb Curry with Figs and Fenugreek

123 **Lamb Tagine with Apricots and Olives**

124 **Lamb Vindaloo**

127 **Osso Buco**

128 **Veal Stew with Fennel, Tarragon, and Cream (Blanquette de Veau)**

BRAISED LAMB SHOULDER CHOPS WITH TOMATOES AND RED WINE

serves 4

4 (8- to 12-ounce) lamb shoulder chops (blade or round bone), about ¾ inch thick, trimmed

Salt and pepper

2 tablespoons olive oil

1 small onion, chopped fine

2 small garlic cloves, minced

⅓ cup dry red wine

1 cup canned whole peeled tomatoes, chopped

2 tablespoons minced fresh parsley

Why This Recipe Works A great thing about braising is that it encourages the use of cuts of meat different than the norm, ones that don't take well to simple searing or roasting. When it comes to lamb, many people turn to the tried-and-true—and expensive—rib or loin chop. The oddly shaped, much less expensive shoulder chops rarely get a second look. Their assertive flavor and somewhat chewy texture make them great for braising. Although shoulder chops have chew, they're not particularly tough; this meant they didn't require a long time in the pot before becoming tender; a relatively quick stovetop braise of just 15 to 20 minutes was all it took. The robust flavor of shoulder chops called for an equally bold sauce. After sautéing some onion and garlic, we deglazed the pan with red wine. Tomatoes balanced out the acidity of the wine, and parsley added a hit of fresh ness. Variations also embrace brash flavors to bring out the best in this weekday-friendly braise.

1 Pat chops dry with paper towels and season with salt and pepper. Heat 1 tablespoon oil in 12-inch skillet over medium-high heat until just smoking. Brown chops, in batches if necessary, 4 to 5 minutes per side; transfer to plate. Pour off fat from skillet.

2 Heat remaining 1 tablespoon oil in now-empty skillet over medium heat until shimmering. Add onion and cook until softened, about 5 minutes. Stir in garlic and cook until fragrant, about 30 seconds. Stir in wine, scraping up any browned bits. Bring to simmer and cook until reduced by half, 2 to 3 minutes. Stir in tomatoes.

3 Nestle chops into skillet along with any accumulated juices and return to simmer. Reduce heat to low, cover, and simmer gently until chops are tender and fork slips easily in and out of meat, 15 to 20 minutes. Transfer chops to serving platter and tent with aluminum foil.

4 Stir parsley into sauce and simmer until sauce thickens, 2 to 3 minutes. Season with salt and pepper to taste. Spoon sauce over chops and serve.

Braised Lamb Shoulder Chops with Capers, Balsamic Vinegar, and Red Pepper

Add 1 diced red bell pepper with onion and stir in 2 tablespoons rinsed capers and 2 tablespoons balsamic vinegar with parsley.

Braised Lamb Shoulder Chops with Figs and North African Spices

Soak ⅓ cup dried figs in ⅓ cup warm water for 30 minutes. Drain, reserving liquid, and cut figs into quarters. Add 1 teaspoon ground coriander, ½ teaspoon ground cumin, ½ teaspoon cinnamon, and ⅛ teaspoon cayenne pepper to skillet with garlic. Omit red wine and replace with ⅓ cup fig soaking water. Add 2 tablespoons honey with tomatoes. Stir in figs with parsley.

Braised Lamb Shoulder Chops with Tomatoes, Rosemary, and Olives

Add 1 tablespoon minced fresh rosemary with garlic and stir in ⅓ cup pitted and sliced kalamata olives with tomatoes.

BRAISED LAMB SHANKS WITH LEMON AND MINT

serves 6

6 (12- to 16-ounce) lamb shanks, trimmed

Salt and pepper

2 tablespoons vegetable oil

3 carrots, peeled and cut into 2-inch pieces

2 onions, sliced thick

2 celery ribs, cut into 2-inch pieces

2 tablespoons tomato paste

2 tablespoons minced fresh mint

4 garlic cloves, minced

2 cups dry white wine

3 cups chicken broth

1 tablespoon grated lemon zest, plus 1 lemon, quartered

Why This Recipe Works Among the most richly flavored cuts of meat is lamb shank and there's so much beauty to braising it; each diner is presented with an impressive shank of meat, once tough, turned meltingly tender. Long, slow cooking in a moisture-rich environment causes the connective tissue to disintegrate and renders the fat without drying out the meat. But lamb shanks have a high fat content, and all too often the result is a greasy sauce. We used a three-prong approach to trim the fat without sacrificing flavor: trimming the shanks well, browning the shanks before cooking to render extra exterior fat and browning them further by cooking them uncovered in the last phase of braising, and defatting the braising liquid after the shanks had cooked. We used more liquid than is called for in many braises; it guaranteed that plenty would remain in the pot despite uncovered cooking, resulting in moist, tender meat. For appropriately robust flavor, we created recipes featuring bright lemon and mint, brassy red wine and herbes de Provence, and bold North African spices. If you're using smaller shanks than the ones called for in this recipe, you'll need to reduce the braising time. Côtes du Rhône works particularly well here.

1 Adjust oven rack to middle position and heat oven to 350 degrees. Pat lamb shanks dry with paper towels and season with salt. Heat 1 tablespoon oil in Dutch oven over medium-high heat until just smoking. Brown 3 shanks on all sides, 7 to 10 minutes. Transfer shanks to large plate and repeat with remaining 1 tablespoon oil and remaining 3 shanks.

2 Pour off all but 2 tablespoons fat from pot. Add carrots, onions, celery, tomato paste, 1 tablespoon mint, garlic, and pinch of salt and cook until vegetables just begin to soften, 3 to 4 minutes. Stir in wine, then broth, scraping up browned bits; add lemon quarters and bring to simmer. Nestle shanks, along with any accumulated juices, into pot.

3 Return to simmer and cover; transfer pot to oven. Cook for 1½ hours. Uncover and continue to cook until tops of shanks are browned, about 30 minutes. Flip shanks and continue to cook until remaining sides are browned and fork slips easily in and out of shanks, 15 to 30 minutes longer.

4 Remove pot from oven and let rest for 15 minutes. Using tongs, transfer shanks and vegetables to large plate and tent with aluminum foil. Skim fat from braising liquid and season with salt and pepper to taste. Stir in lemon zest and remaining 1 tablespoon mint. Return shanks to braising liquid to warm through before serving.

Braised Lamb Shanks with North African Spices

Serve with couscous and one or more of the following: sautéed onion, lemon zest, parsley, mint, toasted almonds, and additional *ras el hanout*.

Add 2 minced ancho chile peppers (or 2 or 3 minced jalapeños) to onions, carrots, and celery in step 2. Substitute 2 tablespoons ras el hanout (page 63) for mint in step 2. Omit lemon in step 2 and lemon zest and mint in step 4.

Braised Lamb Shanks with Red Wine and Herbes de Provence

Substitute dry red wine for white wine. Omit lemon in step 2 and lemon zest in step 4. Substitute 1 tablespoon herbes de Provence for mint in step 2. Omit mint in step 4.

LEG OF LAMB EN COCOTTE WITH GARLIC AND ROSEMARY

serves 6 to 8

1 (4- to 5-pound) boneless leg of lamb shank end, trimmed and tied

Salt and pepper

2 tablespoons olive oil

8 garlic cloves, peeled and sliced thin

2 sprigs fresh rosemary

Why This Recipe Works Cooking *en cocotte* isn't just for beef (see our recipe for Beef en Cocotte with Caramelized Onions on page 56); in fact, we use the technique for just about any protein, including leg of lamb. Since lamb's gamy flavor comes mostly from the fat, we trimmed as much as possible before cooking to give the finished roast a milder flavor that we appreciated for this simply presented application. Garlic and rosemary are traditional flavorings for lamb; we added sprigs of rosemary and a handful of sliced garlic cloves to the pot with the lamb before it went into the oven. In just an hour, we had a simple, beautifully flavored dish to add to our en cocotte repertoire. We prefer the shank end of the boneless leg of lamb here (rather than the sirloin end). There are two methods butchers use to remove the bone, referred to as corkscrewed and butterflied; we find the corkscrewed type much easier to work with but a butterflied leg of lamb will also work.

1 Adjust oven rack to lowest position and heat oven to 250 degrees. Pat lamb dry with paper towels and season with salt and pepper.

2 Heat oil in Dutch oven over medium-high heat until just smoking. Brown lamb well on all sides, 7 to 10 minutes, reducing heat if pot begins to scorch. Transfer lamb to large plate.

3 Pour off fat from pot. Add garlic and rosemary and nestle lamb, with any accumulated juices, into pot. Place large piece of aluminum foil over pot and cover tightly with lid; transfer pot to oven. Cook until lamb registers 120 to 125 degrees (for medium-rare), 45 minutes to 1 hour.

4 Transfer lamb to carving board, tent with foil, and let rest for 20 minutes. Remove rosemary from pot, then cover to keep jus warm.

5 Remove twine, slice lamb against grain into ¼-inch-thick slices, and transfer to serving platter. Spoon jus over lamb and serve.

MOROCCAN BRAISED WHITE BEANS WITH LAMB

serves 6 to 8

Salt and pepper

1 pound (2½ cups) dried great Northern beans, picked over and rinsed

1 (12- to 16-ounce) lamb shank

1 tablespoon extra-virgin olive oil, plus extra for serving

1 onion, chopped

1 red bell pepper, stemmed, seeded, and chopped fine

2 tablespoons tomato paste

3 garlic cloves, minced

2 teaspoons paprika

2 teaspoons ground cumin

1½ teaspoons ground ginger

¼ teaspoon cayenne pepper

½ cup dry white wine

4 cups chicken broth

2 tablespoons minced fresh parsley

Why This Recipe Works A dish of stewed white beans, *loubia* is well loved in Morocco—and for good reason as the beans are cooked in a warm-spiced, tomatoey base with lamb. We like it because it's a warm, comforting, cozy weekend meal. *Khlii*, a Moroccan preserved meat, is often used, but khlii is difficult to find in the United States; we decided to use more easily accessible lamb shank to infuse meaty flavor into the dish. We seared and then slowly braised the lamb in the oven with the beans. A healthy dose of Moroccan-inspired spices gave the dish a deeply flavorful backbone, and some white wine provided welcome acidity. A combination of mostly chicken broth and a little water gave the cooking medium savory depth without making it too salty. We chose dried beans over canned so that the beans would cook at the same rate as the lamb shank, leaving us with creamy, richly flavored beans and melt-in-your-mouth tender pieces of lamb. You can substitute 1 pound of lamb shoulder chops (blade or round bone), 1 to 1½ inches thick, trimmed and halved, for the lamb shank; reduce the browning time in step 2 to 8 minutes.

1 Dissolve 3 tablespoons salt in 4 quarts cold water in large container. Add beans and soak at room temperature for at least 8 hours or up to 24 hours. Drain and rinse well.

2 Adjust oven rack to lower-middle position and heat oven to 350 degrees. Pat lamb dry with paper towels and season with salt and pepper. Heat oil in Dutch oven over medium-high heat until just smoking. Brown lamb on all sides, 10 to 15 minutes; transfer to plate. Pour off all but 2 tablespoons fat from pot.

3 Add onion and bell pepper and cook over medium heat until softened and lightly browned, 5 to 7 minutes. Stir in tomato paste, garlic, paprika, cumin, ginger, cayenne, and ⅛ teaspoon pepper and cook until fragrant, about 30 seconds. Stir in wine, scraping up any browned bits. Stir in broth, 1 cup water, and beans and bring to boil.

4 Nestle lamb into beans along with any accumulated juices and cover; transfer pot to oven. Cook until fork slips easily in and out of lamb and beans are tender, 1½ to 1¾ hours, stirring every 30 minutes.

5 Transfer lamb to cutting board, let cool slightly, then shred into bite-size pieces using 2 forks; discard excess fat and bone. Stir shredded lamb and parsley into beans and season with salt and pepper to taste. Adjust consistency with extra hot water as needed. Serve, drizzling individual portions with extra oil.

IRISH STEW

serves 6

4½ pounds lamb shoulder chops (blade or round bone), 1 to 1½ inches thick, trimmed, meat removed from bones and cut into 1½-inch pieces, bones reserved

Salt and pepper

3 tablespoons vegetable oil

2½ pounds onions, chopped coarse

¼ cup all-purpose flour

3 cups water

1 teaspoon dried thyme

2 pounds Yukon Gold potatoes, peeled and cut into 1-inch pieces

¼ cup minced fresh parsley

Why This Recipe Works At its most traditional, Irish stew is made with just lamb, onions, potatoes, and water. The raw ingredients are layered in the pot and cooked until tender. Nutritious and sustaining, perhaps, but satisfying and memorable? Only if you like bland food. We wanted a rich, deeply flavored stew as delicious as it was filling—the sort of dish for cold winter nights and snowbound days. Chops had a more robust flavor than leg of lamb that gave the stew character and an unmistakable lamb flavor. For a traditional stew, we would cut the meat off the bone into pieces, but we found it essential, although a bit unusual, to add the bones to the pot as well; it gave the stew richness and a velvety texture. We stuck with tradition for one element: the cooking liquid. The stew got deeply flavored back notes from caramelized onion, so all we needed was water in addition as chicken broth muted the flavor of the lamb. Broken-down potatoes (along with some flour for assistance) thickened the stew and gave it heft, so we went with starchier Yukon Golds rather than with our usual choice for stews, red potatoes, which maintain their integrity. All our homey stew needed was a side of Irish soda bread. Though we prefer lamb chops cut 1½ inches thick, 1-inch-thick chops will suffice.

1 Adjust oven rack to lower-middle position and heat oven to 300 degrees. Season lamb with salt and pepper.

2 Heat 1 tablespoon oil in Dutch oven over medium-high heat until shimmering. Add half of lamb to pot so that individual pieces are close together but not touching. Cook, without moving lamb, until well browned, 2 to 3 minutes. Using tongs, flip lamb pieces and continue to cook until most sides are well browned, about 5 minutes longer; transfer to bowl. Add 1 tablespoon oil to pot, swirl to coat pot, and repeat with remaining lamb; transfer to bowl and set aside.

3 Reduce heat to medium, add remaining 1 tablespoon oil, and swirl to coat pot. Add onions and ¼ teaspoon salt and cook, stirring frequently and scraping up any browned bits, until onions have browned, about 8 minutes. Add flour and stir until onions are evenly coated, 1 to 2 minutes.

4 Stir in 1½ cups water, scraping up any remaining browned bits. Gradually add remaining 1½ cups water, stirring constantly and scraping pan edges to dissolve flour. Add thyme and 1 teaspoon salt and bring to simmer. Add reserved bones, then meat and accumulated juices. Return to simmer and cover; transfer pot to oven. Cook for 1 hour.

5 Remove pot from oven and place potatoes on top of meat and bones. Cover and return pot to oven. Cook until lamb is tender, about 1 hour. Stir potatoes into liquid, wait 5 minutes, then skim off any fat that rises to top. Stir in parsley and season with salt and pepper to taste. Discard bones and serve.

Irish Stew with Carrots and Turnips

Substitute 3 carrots, peeled and sliced ¼ inch thick, and 8 ounces turnips, peeled and cut into 1-inch-thick pieces, for half of potatoes.

ITALIAN-STYLE LAMB STEW WITH GREEN BEANS, TOMATOES, AND BASIL

serves 6

4½ pounds lamb shoulder chops (blade or round bone), 1 to 1½ inches thick, trimmed, meat removed from bones and cut into 1½-inch pieces, bones reserved

Salt and pepper

3 tablespoons vegetable oil

2½ pounds onions, chopped coarse

3 garlic cloves, minced

¼ cup all-purpose flour

1¾ cups water

½ cup dry white wine

1 (14.5-ounce) can diced tomatoes

1 tablespoon minced fresh rosemary

2 pounds Yukon Gold potatoes, peeled and cut into 1-inch pieces

¾ pound green beans, trimmed and halved

¼ cup chopped fresh basil

Why This Recipe Works The recipes in this book show that braising is a universal cooking technique that, once mastered, is adaptable to a number of flavor profiles. This lamb stew is a prime example. When developing our Irish Stew (page 117), we learned the principles of a good lamb stew and how it differs from other meat stews; that allowed us to use essentially the same techniques for this very different lamb stew with Italian flavors. We cut the water with a bit of wine and added diced tomatoes. Our choice of herbs moved the flavor profile to Italy as well: complementary rosemary cooked with the stew and infused it with flavor, and basil was stirred in at the end for a fresh hit. For more freshness, we added green beans to this stew. Adding the green beans halfway through cooking kept them from completely breaking down or becoming mushy. With our tested techniques, we easily achieved a hearty all-weather stew with freshness and brightness.

1 Adjust oven rack to lower-middle position and heat oven to 300 degrees. Season lamb with salt and pepper.

2 Heat 1 tablespoon oil in Dutch oven over medium-high heat until shimmering. Add half of lamb to pot so that individual pieces are close together but not touching. Cook without moving lamb, until well browned, 2 to 3 minutes. Using tongs, flip lamb pieces and continue to cook until most sides are well browned, about 5 minutes longer; transfer to bowl. Add 1 tablespoon oil to pot, swirl to coat pot, and repeat with remaining lamb; transfer to bowl and set aside.

3 Reduce heat to medium, add remaining 1 tablespoon oil, and swirl to coat pot. Add onions and ¼ teaspoon salt and cook, stirring frequently and scraping up any browned bits, until onions have softened, about 5 minutes. Add garlic and cook until fragrant, about 30 seconds. Add flour and stir until onions are evenly coated, 1 to 2 minutes.

4 Stir in 1 cup water and wine, scraping up any remaining browned bits. Gradually add remaining ¾ cup water, stirring constantly and scraping pot edges to dissolve flour. Add tomatoes and their juice, rosemary, and 1 teaspoon salt and bring to simmer. Add reserved bones, then lamb and any accumulated juices. Return to simmer and cover; transfer pot to oven. Cook for 1 hour.

5 Remove pot from oven and place potatoes and green beans on top of lamb and bones. Cover pot and return to oven. Cook until lamb is tender, about 1 hour. Stir potatoes and green beans into liquid, wait 5 minutes, then skim off any fat that rises to top. Stir in basil and season with salt and pepper to taste. Discard bones, if desired, and serve.

LAMB CURRY WITH WHOLE SPICES

serves 4 to 6

Whole Spice Blend

1½ cinnamon sticks

4 whole cloves

4 green cardamom pods

8 black peppercorns

1 bay leaf

Curry

¼ cup vegetable oil

1 onion, sliced thin

1½ pounds boneless leg of lamb, trimmed and cut into ¾-inch cubes

⅔ cup canned crushed tomatoes

4 large garlic cloves, minced

1 tablespoon grated fresh ginger

2 teaspoons ground cumin

2 teaspoons ground coriander

1 teaspoon ground turmeric

Salt

2 cups water

1 jalapeño chile, stemmed, halved, and seeded

4 red potatoes, peeled and cut into ¾-inch cubes

¼ cup chopped fresh cilantro

Why This Recipe Works Indian curries can be intimidating to make at home, with complicated processes and unfamiliar ingredients. And too often, all that work produces overly heavy curries with dull, murky flavors. We wanted a complex but not heavy-flavored Indian curry that wouldn't take all day to prepare. Settling the spices—what make curries special—was an important task. We toasted a fragrant combination of whole spices in oil, which infused the cooking oil and provided the authentic, intense flavor we were after. We added ground spices later to provide an aromatic backbone to the dish. Garlic, onion, and ginger further deepened the flavor, while jalapeño offered fresh, subtle spice. Instead of browning the meat, like in European braises and stews, we simply stirred it into the pot along with crushed tomatoes and cooked the mixture until the liquid evaporated and the oil separated. This classic Indian technique allowed the spice flavor to further release in the oil, which was then absorbed by the meat. We then added water and simmered the mixture until the meat was tender. You may substitute a scant ½ teaspoon of cayenne pepper for the jalapeño, adding it to the skillet with the other ground dried spices. Feel free to increase the aromatics (garlic, ginger, jalapeños, and onions) or dry spice quantities. For a creamier curry, substitute ⅔ cup of plain yogurt for the tomatoes.

1 For the spice blend Combine ingredients in small bowl.

2 For the curry Heat oil in Dutch oven over medium-high heat until shimmering. Add spice blend and cook, stirring with wooden spoon until cinnamon sticks unfurl and cloves pop, about 5 seconds. Add onion and cook until softened, 3 to 4 minutes.

3 Stir in lamb, tomatoes, garlic, ginger, cumin, coriander, turmeric, and ½ teaspoon salt and cook, stirring frequently, until liquid evaporates, oil separates and turns orange, and spices begin to fry, 5 to 7 minutes. Continue to cook, stirring constantly, until spices are very fragrant, about 30 seconds longer.

4 Add water and jalapeño. Bring to simmer, then reduce heat to low, cover, and simmer until meat is tender, 30 to 40 minutes.

5 Add potatoes and cook until tender, about 15 minutes. Stir in cilantro, simmer for 3 minutes, season with salt to taste, and serve.

Lamb Curry with Figs and Fenugreek

Omit whole spice blend and potatoes. Add ½ teaspoon fenugreek along with cumin, coriander, and turmeric in step 3 and ¼ cup dried figs, chopped coarse, along with water in step 4.

LAMB TAGINE WITH APRICOTS AND OLIVES

serves 6

1 (3½- to 4-pound) boneless lamb shoulder roast, trimmed and cut into 1½-inch pieces

Salt and pepper

3 tablespoons olive oil

3 onions, halved and sliced through root end into ¼-inch-thick pieces

4 (2-inch) strips lemon zest, plus ½ teaspoon grated zest plus ¼ cup juice (2 lemons)

10 garlic cloves (8 minced, 2 minced to paste)

2½ teaspoons paprika

1 teaspoon ground cumin

½ teaspoon ground ginger

½ teaspoon ground coriander

½ teaspoon ground cinnamon

¼ teaspoon cayenne pepper

¼ cup all-purpose flour

4 cups chicken broth

2 tablespoons honey

1 pound carrots, peeled and sliced 1 inch thick

2 cups pitted Greek green olives, halved

1 cup dried apricots, chopped

¼ cup minced fresh cilantro

Why This Recipe Works Tagines—generously spiced, assertively flavored stews slow-cooked in earthenware vessels of the same name—are a North African specialty. They can include all manner of meats, vegetables, and fruit, so we set our sights on a popular version: fork-tender lamb, sweet dried fruit (we liked apricots), and briny olives. The combination, which is spiked with a number of spices, sounds unlikely, but the ingredients blended harmoniously—if added in the right ratios and prepared well. We started with a boneless lamb shoulder roast, which is well-marbled with flavorful fat. Our spice list was short in terms of ingredients but big on flavor. Cumin and ginger lent depth, cinnamon brought warmth that tempered a little cayenne heat, and coriander enhanced the stew's fruity apricot flavor. Paprika added subtle sweetness and, perhaps more importantly, colored the broth a deep, attractive red. Whole apricots remained leathery in the stew; chopping them into small bits and adding them toward the end softened them and maintained their flavor. Tagines typically get lemon notes from preserved lemon, but we wanted to avoid uncommon ingredients. Two broad ribbons of lemon zest did the trick, and the high heat drew out the zest's oils and mellowed them. Adding grated zest and lemon juice just before serving reinforced the bright flavor. Greek olives are not traditional, but they're easier to find than Moroccan olives. If the olives are particularly salty, rinse them.

1 Adjust oven rack to lower-middle position and heat oven to 325 degrees. Pat lamb dry with paper towels and season with salt and pepper. Heat 1 tablespoon oil in Dutch oven over medium-high heat until just smoking. Brown half of lamb on all sides, 7 to 10 minutes; transfer to bowl. Repeat with 1 tablespoon oil and remaining lamb; transfer to bowl.

2 Add remaining 1 tablespoon oil to pot and heat over medium heat until shimmering. Add onions, lemon zest strips, and ¼ teaspoon salt and cook until onions are softened, 5 to 7 minutes. Stir in minced garlic, paprika, cumin, ginger, coriander, cinnamon, and cayenne and cook until fragrant, about 30 seconds. Stir in flour and cook for 1 minute.

3 Slowly whisk in broth, scraping up any browned bits and smoothing out any lumps. Stir in honey and browned lamb with any accumulated juices, bring to simmer, and cover; transfer pot to oven. Cook for 1 hour. Stir in carrots and continue to cook in oven until lamb is tender, 1 to 1½ hours longer.

4 Remove tagine from oven and discard lemon zest strips. Stir in olives and apricots, cover, and let stand off heat for 5 minutes. Stir in cilantro, lemon zest and juice, and garlic paste. Season with salt and pepper to taste, and serve.

LAMB VINDALOO

serves 6 to 8

1 (3½ - to 4-pound) boneless lamb shoulder roast, trimmed and cut into 1½ -inch pieces

Salt and pepper

3 tablespoons vegetable oil

3 onions, chopped

8 medium garlic cloves, minced

1 tablespoon sweet paprika

¾ teaspoon ground cumin

½ teaspoon ground cardamom

¼ teaspoon cayenne pepper

¼ teaspoon ground cloves

3 tablespoons all-purpose flour

1½ cups chicken broth

1 (14.5-ounce) can diced tomatoes

2 tablespoons red wine vinegar

1 tablespoon mustard seeds

2 bay leaves

1 teaspoon sugar

¼ cup minced fresh cilantro

Why This Recipe Works Vindaloo is a complex, spicy dish that originated in Goa, a region on India's western coast. Because Goa was once a Portuguese colony, much of the local cuisine incorporates Indian and Portuguese ingredients and techniques. In fact, the word vindaloo comes from the Portuguese words for wine vinegar (*vinho*) and garlic (*alhos*). It's no surprise, then, that the sauce is much about the interplay of sweet, sour, and pungent flavors—the pungency provided by the garlic, along with spices and chiles. For the cooking liquid we didn't go with tradition. Most vindaloo recipes simply call for water. The theory is that water is a neutral medium that allows the flavors of the meat and spices to come through as clearly as possible. However, we found that chicken broth added richness and body to the stewing liquid. Two tablespoons of red wine vinegar and 1 teaspoon of sugar provided the right sweet-sour balance. In order to give it time to soften and mix with the other flavors, we added the vinegar at the beginning of cooking. The diced tomatoes provided further acidity.

1 Adjust oven rack to lower-middle position and heat oven to 325 degrees. Pat lamb dry with paper towels and season with salt and pepper. Heat 1 tablespoon oil in Dutch oven over medium-high heat until just smoking. Brown half of lamb on all sides, 7 to 10 minutes; transfer to bowl. Repeat with 1 tablespoon oil and remaining lamb; transfer to bowl.

2 Add remaining 1 tablespoon oil to pot and return to medium heat until shimmering. Add onions and ¼ teaspoon salt and cook, stirring occasionally, until softened, 5 to 7 minutes. Stir in garlic, paprika, cumin, cardamom, cayenne, and cloves and cook until fragrant, about 30 seconds. Stir in flour and cook for 1 minute.

3 Gradually whisk in broth, scraping up browned bits and smoothing out any lumps. Stir in tomatoes and their juice, vinegar, mustard seeds, bay leaves, sugar, and browned lamb and any accumulated juices, bring to simmer, and cover; transfer pot to oven. Cook until meat is tender, about 2 hours. Remove bay leaves. Stir in cilantro, season with salt and pepper to taste, and serve.

OSSO BUCO

Veal Shanks

6 (14- to 16-ounce) veal shanks, 1½ inches thick

Salt and pepper

6 tablespoons olive oil

2½ cups dry white wine

2 onions, chopped

2 carrots, peeled and chopped

2 celery ribs, chopped

6 garlic cloves, minced

2 cups chicken broth

1 (14.5-ounce) can diced tomatoes, drained

2 bay leaves

Gremolata

¼ cup minced fresh parsley

3 garlic cloves, minced

2 teaspoons grated lemon zest

Why This Recipe Works Osso buco is a magical dish that's a trademark of Italy, Milan specifically. Slow, steady cooking renders tough (but gelatin-rich) veal shanks remarkably tender and turns a simple broth of carrots, onion, celery, wine, and stock into a velvety sauce. Each diner gets an individual shank; for some, the best part is the luscious bone marrow, which diners use a small spoon to extract. We sought to create a flavorful, foolproof braising liquid and cooking technique that produced a rich sauce true to this venerable recipe. We deepened the flavor of store-bought stock with lots of aromatics. We oven-braised the shanks, which was the easiest cooking method, and the natural reduction that took place left just the right amount of liquid in the pot. Tying the shanks around the equator kept the meat attached to the bone for an attractive presentation. Many recipes suggest flouring the veal before browning it, but we got better flavor when we simply seared the meat, liberally seasoned with salt and pepper. Browning in two batches enabled us to deglaze the pan twice, thus enriching the sauce. We stirred a traditional accompaniment, gremolata, a mixture of minced garlic, parsley, and lemon zest, into the sauce to brighten the hearty dish.

1 For the veal shanks Adjust oven rack to lower-middle position and heat oven to 325 degrees. Pat shanks dry with paper towels and season with salt and pepper. Tie piece of twine around thickest portion of each shank to keep meat attached to bone while cooking. Heat 2 tablespoons oil in Dutch oven over medium-high heat until just smoking. Brown half of shanks on all sides, 8 to 10 minutes; transfer to large bowl. Repeat with 2 tablespoons oil and remaining shanks; transfer to bowl. Off heat, add 1½ cups wine to now-empty pot and scrape up any browned bits. Pour liquid into bowl with shanks.

2 Heat remaining 2 tablespoons oil in again-empty pot until shimmering. Add onions, carrots, and celery and cook until vegetables are softened and lightly browned, 8 to 10 minutes. Stir in garlic and cook until lightly browned, about 1 minute. Stir in broth, tomatoes, bay leaves, and remaining 1 cup wine and bring to simmer.

3 Nestle shanks into pot along with deglazing liquid. Cover pot, leaving lid slightly ajar, transfer pot to oven. Cook until veal is tender and fork slips easily in and out of meat, but meat is not falling off bone, about 2 hours.

4 For the gremolata Combine all ingredients in small bowl. Remove pot from oven and discard bay leaves. Stir half of gremolata into braising liquid and season with salt and pepper to taste. Let sit for 5 minutes.

5 Transfer shanks to individual bowls and discard twine. Ladle braising liquid over shanks and sprinkle with remaining gremolata. Serve.

VEAL STEW WITH FENNEL, TARRAGON, AND CREAM (BLANQUETTE DE VEAU)

serves 6

2 pounds boneless veal shoulder roast, trimmed and cut into 1-inch pieces

3 tablespoons unsalted butter

4 large shallots, minced

Salt and pepper

2 garlic cloves, minced

2 tablespoons all-purpose flour

¾ cup dry white wine or dry vermouth

1½ cups chicken broth

2 bay leaves

1 large fennel bulb, stalks discarded, bulb halved, cored, and cut into ¼-inch-thick strips

3 carrots, peeled and sliced ¼ inch thick

1 cup frozen peas

½ cup heavy cream

1 tablespoon minced fresh parsley

2 teaspoons minced fresh tarragon

2 teaspoons lemon juice

Why This Recipe Works Veal's subtle, delicate nature is a welcome change of pace from other meats at dinnertime, but this quality also makes it tricky to cook as it's easily overwhelmed by other ingredients. The French have solved this problem with a family of lightly flavored—and lightly colored—cream-enriched stews called *blanquettes de veau*. They are unusual in that browning isn't a goal; in fact, coloring is considered a defect. Sounds bland, right? Far from it: The flavors are refreshingly clear. To maintain the intended pristineness of the dish we started with a traditional and simple step: blanching the veal. This removes any gray "scum"—proteins released by the meat when it's heated. Although simple, this was an extra step, so we streamlined the rest of the recipe: To finish cooking the blanched veal, we stirred it into a sauce we had made of chicken broth, shallots, and white wine, and then just placed the whole thing in a moderate oven and cooked until the meat was tender. And what about the vegetables? They turned to mush if they were included for the full extent of simmering. Adding them soon after the midpoint was just about right, producing vegetables that were cooked through but still crisp. We finished the stew with fresh tarragon, parsley, and a pour of rich cream.

1 Adjust oven rack to middle position and heat oven to 300 degrees.

2 Bring veal and 8 cups water to simmer in Dutch oven over high heat. Reduce heat to medium-low and simmer for 5 minutes. Skim foam from surface, then drain veal in colander, discarding cooking liquid. Rinse veal briefly, then set aside to drain.

3 Rinse and dry pot and return to stove. Melt butter in pot over medium heat. Add shallots and ¼ teaspoon salt and cook until shallots have softened, 3 to 5 minutes. Stir in garlic and cook until fragrant, 30 seconds. Stir in flour and cook for 30 seconds. Add wine, scraping up any browned bits; simmer until thickened. Increase heat to high and add broth, stirring constantly and scraping pan edges. Add bay leaves and veal, bring to simmer, and cover; transfer pot to oven. Cook for 1 hour.

4 Remove pot from oven and stir in fennel and carrots. Continue to cook until meat and vegetables are just tender, 30 to 45 minutes longer.

5 Remove pot from oven. Stir in peas, cream, parsley, and tarragon. Cover and let stand for 5 minutes. Discard bay leaves and stir in lemon juice. Season with salt and pepper to taste, and serve immediately.

PORK

Mexican Pulled Pork (Carnitas)

132 **Pork with Red Cabbage, Apples, and Juniper**

134 **Milk-Braised Pork Loin**

137 **Cider-Braised Pork Roast**

138 **Philadelphia Pork Sandwiches**

140 **Braised Pork Loin with Black Mole Sauce**

142 **French-Style Pot-Roasted Pork Loin**
with Port and Figs

145 **Braised Country-Style Ribs with Black-Eyed Peas
and Collard Greens**

147 **Sweet-and-Sour Pork Ribs**

148 **Pork Grillades**

150 **Red Wine–Braised Pork Chops**

152 **Smothered Pork Chops with Onions and Bacon**
with Cider and Apples
with Spicy Collard Greens

155 **Pork Chops with Vinegar Peppers**

156 **Pork Chops with Tomato Gravy**

159 **Mexican Pulled Pork (Carnitas)**

161 **French-Style Pork Stew**

163 **New Mexican Pork Stew (Posole)**

164 **Colorado Green Chili**

166 **Spicy Mexican Pork Tinga and Rice**

169 **Carne Adovado**

171 **Braised Greek Sausages with Peppers**

172 **Stuffed Cabbage Rolls**

175 **Pork Ragu**

PORK WITH RED CABBAGE, APPLES, AND JUNIPER

serves 4

1 (2¼- to 2½-pound) boneless center-cut pork loin roast, trimmed and tied at 1-inch intervals

Salt and pepper

1 tablespoon vegetable oil

1 large onion, halved and sliced thin

2 bay leaves

4 sprigs fresh thyme

10 juniper berries

10 allspice berries

2 Granny Smith apples, peeled, cored, and chopped coarse

1 small head red cabbage, quartered, cored, and sliced ¼ inch thick

½ cup apple cider

1 teaspoon packed brown sugar

2 teaspoons apple cider vinegar

Why This Recipe Works Alsace's *choucroute garnie*—pork and sauerkraut braised in white wine with juniper berries, allspice, and apples—is a dish in perfect harmony; each ingredient balances the other perfectly in both flavor and texture. We wanted to develop a braise modeled loosely on this dish that was no-fuss and one-pot. Braising the lean roast in lots of liquid at a low temperature, like we might with a beef roast, didn't work; pork loin lacks collagen-rich connective tissue and so it turned out dry and the cabbage dull. We'd need to lower the liquid—the less we used, the better the pork and cabbage came out. Juniper berries lent a woodsy, penetrating bite of pine—a perfect foil to the sweet-tart flavor of the apples. And the thyme and bay leaves rounded out the juniper's bite. Added early on as the vegetables sautéed, the whole spices softened enough in flavor and texture so we didn't have to remove them. As the apples broke down, they lost much of their fruity tartness. Using apple cider as the small amount of braising liquid provided a fruity base we couldn't achieve using only fresh fruit. A finishing splash of vinegar upped the acidity more and revitalized the cabbage's color. If you can find blade-end pork loin, use it in the dish. If you can't find juniper berries, a tablespoon of gin, stirred into the cabbage in step 2, is a suitable substitution. Make sure to add the gin off the heat so that it does not ignite.

1 Adjust oven rack to lower-middle position and heat oven to 300 degrees. Dry roast thoroughly with paper towels, then season with salt and pepper. Heat oil in Dutch oven over medium-high heat until just smoking. Brown roast thoroughly on all sides, reducing heat if fat begins to smoke, about 10 minutes. Transfer roast to large plate.

2 Reduce heat to medium and heat until fat remaining in pot is shimmering. Add onion, bay leaves, thyme sprigs, juniper berries, allspice berries, and ¾ teaspoon salt; cook, scraping up browned bits until onion is soft and beginning to brown, about 6 minutes. Add apples and cabbage; cook until cabbage has softened and reduced in volume, about 8 minutes. Stir in

cider and sugar. Lay roast, fat-side down, on top of cabbage and cover; transfer pot to oven. Cook until pork registers 135 degrees, 45 to 50 minutes (temperature of roast will rise to 145 degrees as it rests).

3 Transfer roast to carving board and tent with aluminum foil. Continue to cook cabbage mixture over medium-high heat, stirring frequently, until excess liquid has evaporated, 5 to 10 minutes. Add vinegar and season with salt and pepper to taste. Remove bay leaves and thyme, as well as juniper and allspice berries, if desired. Remove twine from roast, slice into ½-inch-thick pieces, and serve immediately with cabbage.

MILK-BRAISED PORK LOIN

serves 4 to 6

Salt and pepper

½ cup sugar

1 (2- to 2½-pound) boneless pork loin roast, trimmed

2 ounces salt pork, chopped coarse

3 cups whole milk

5 garlic cloves, peeled

1 teaspoon minced fresh sage

½ teaspoon baking soda

½ cup dry white wine

3 tablespoons chopped fresh parsley

1 teaspoon Dijon mustard

Why This Recipe Works Cooking meat in milk is a classic braising treatment for pork loin in Italy—and for good reason. The milk tenderizes the pork and the meat soaks up the flavors of the resulting sweet, nutty sauce. Bolognese families often prepare this hearty dish on Sundays in the winter. As you'd expect, the milk curdles; Italians don't mind, but we wanted to make the sauce more attractive. We minimized curdling (and amped up flavor) by adding a touch of fat from rendered salt pork; the fat coats the casein proteins in milk and prevents them from bonding. A small amount of baking soda raised the pH of the sauce to create conditions more favorable for Maillard browning, a series of reactions that create flavorful aromatic compounds. The milk will bubble up when added to the pot. If necessary, remove the pot from the heat and stir to break up the foam before returning it to the heat. We prefer natural pork, but if your pork is enhanced (injected with a salt solution), do not brine.

1 Dissolve ¼ cup salt and sugar in 2 quarts cold water in large container. Submerge roast in brine, cover, and refrigerate for at least 1½ hours or up to 2 hours. Remove roast from brine and pat dry with paper towels.

2 Adjust oven rack to middle position and heat oven to 275 degrees. Bring salt pork and ½ cup water to simmer in Dutch oven over medium heat. Simmer until water evaporates and salt pork begins to sizzle, 5 to 6 minutes. Continue to cook, stirring frequently, until salt pork is lightly browned and fat has rendered, 2 to 3 minutes. Using slotted spoon, discard salt pork, leaving fat in pot.

3 Increase heat to medium-high, add roast to pot, and brown on all sides, 8 to 10 minutes. Transfer roast to large plate. Add milk, garlic, sage, and baking soda to pot and bring to simmer, scraping up any browned bits. Cook, stirring frequently, until milk is lightly browned and has consistency of heavy cream, 14 to 16 minutes. Reduce heat to medium-low and continue to cook, stirring and scraping bottom of pot constantly, until milk thickens to consistency of thin batter, 1 to 3 minutes. Remove pot from heat.

4 Return roast to pot and cover; transfer pot to oven. Cook until pork registers 140 degrees, 40 to 50 minutes, flipping roast halfway through cooking. Transfer roast to carving board, tent with aluminum foil, and let rest for 20 to 25 minutes.

5 Once roast has rested, pour any accumulated juices into pot. Add wine and return sauce to simmer over medium-high heat, whisking vigorously to smooth out sauce. Simmer until sauce has consistency of thin gravy, 2 to 3 minutes. Off heat, stir in 2 tablespoons parsley and mustard and season with salt and pepper to taste. Slice roast into ¼-inch-thick slices and transfer to serving dish. Spoon sauce over pork, sprinkle with remaining 1 tablespoon parsley, and serve.

CIDER-BRAISED PORK ROAST

serves 8

1 (5- to 6-pound) bone-in pork butt roast

¼ cup packed brown sugar

Kosher salt and pepper

3 tablespoons vegetable oil

1 onion, halved and sliced thin

6 garlic cloves, smashed and peeled

2 cups apple cider

6 sprigs fresh thyme

2 bay leaves

1 cinnamon stick

2 Braeburn apples, cored and cut into 8 wedges each

¼ cup apple butter

1 tablespoon cornstarch

1 tablespoon cider vinegar

Why This Recipe Works We pair pork and apples relatively often as they're a classic, and we thought braising pork right in cider would be a great way to infuse the meat with flavor. Boston butt was a good candidate—its plentiful fat and connective tissue break down over long cooking times, resulting in tender, silky meat. Rubbing the roast with a brown sugar–salt mixture and refrigerating it overnight seasoned the meat, helped keep it juicy, and picked up on the sweetness of the cider. Onions, garlic, bay leaves, cinnamon, and thyme were welcome additions to the braising liquid that didn't distract from the clean, sweet-tart taste of cider. Apple butter and cider vinegar added more fruity punch. Apple wedges seared in flavorful pork fat united the flavor elements of this hearty roast. Pork butt roast is often labeled Boston butt in the supermarket. This roast needs to cure for 18 to 24 hours before cooking. If you can't find Braeburn apples, substitute Jonagold. If you don't have a fat separator, strain the braising liquid through a fine-mesh strainer into a bowl in step 4 and wait for it to settle.

1 Using sharp knife, trim fat cap on roast to ¼ inch. Cut 1-inch crosshatch pattern in fat cap. Place roast on large sheet of plastic wrap. Combine sugar and ¼ cup salt in bowl and rub mixture over entire roast and into slits. Wrap roast tightly in double layer of plastic, place on plate, and refrigerate for at least 18 hours or up to 24 hours.

2 Adjust oven rack to middle position and heat oven to 275 degrees. Unwrap roast and pat dry with paper towels, brushing away any excess salt mixture from surface. Season roast with pepper.

3 Heat oil in Dutch oven over medium-high heat until just smoking. Brown roast well on all sides, 8 to 12 minutes. Turn roast fat side up. Scatter onion and garlic around roast and cook until fragrant and beginning to brown, about 2 minutes. Add 1¾ cups cider, thyme sprigs, bay leaves, and cinnamon stick and bring to simmer. Cover; transfer pot to oven. Cook until fork slips easily in and out of meat and meat registers 190 degrees, 2¼ to 2¾ hours.

4 Transfer roast to carving board, tent with aluminum foil, and let rest for 30 minutes. Strain braising liquid through fine-mesh strainer into fat separator; discard solids and let liquid settle for at least 5 minutes.

5 About 10 minutes before roast is done resting, wipe pot clean with paper towels. Spoon 1½ tablespoons fat from top of fat separator into pot and heat over medium-high heat until shimmering. Season apples with salt and pepper. Evenly space apples, 1 cut side down, in pot and cook until well browned on both cut sides, about 3 minutes per side. Transfer to platter and tent with foil.

6 Wipe pot clean with paper towels. Return 2 cups defatted liquid to pot and bring to boil over high heat. Whisk in apple butter until incorporated. Whisk cornstarch and remaining ¼ cup cider together in bowl and add to pot. Return to boil and cook until thickened, about 1 minute. Off heat, add vinegar and season with salt and pepper to taste. Cover sauce and keep warm.

7 To carve roast, cut around inverted T-shaped bone until it can be pulled free from roast (use clean dish towel to grasp bone if necessary). Slice pork and transfer to platter with apples. Pour 1 cup sauce over pork and apples. Serve, passing remaining sauce separately.

PHILADELPHIA PORK SANDWICHES

serves 8

Pork and Jus

1 tablespoon kosher salt

2 teaspoons minced fresh rosemary

2 teaspoons dried thyme

2 teaspoons dried oregano

2 teaspoons fennel seeds

1 teaspoon red pepper flakes

1 (4-pound) boneless pork butt roast, trimmed

2 cups chicken broth, plus extra as needed

8 garlic cloves, peeled and smashed

Broccoli Rabe

2 tablespoons extra-virgin olive oil

3 garlic cloves, sliced thin

1 pound broccoli rabe, trimmed and cut into ½-inch pieces

2 teaspoons kosher salt

Pinch red pepper flakes

Sandwiches

8 (8-inch) Italian sub rolls, split lengthwise

12 ounces sliced sharp provolone cheese

Why This Recipe Works You hear Philadelphia, you think cheesesteak. But there's a pork counterpoint, and it's glorious: thinly sliced seasoned pork; bitter, garlicky greens; a rich, herby jus; and a fluffy roll topped with sharp provolone cheese (and optional hot peppers). It's not a shy sandwich, boasting a bold personality full of different flavors. It's a local triumph and a point of pride. To re-create these famous Philly sandwiches at home, we opted for a boneless pork butt roast and braised it in chicken broth. This made tender and flavorful pork, and the juices from the pork mingled with the chicken broth during cooking to create an ultrasavory jus. Thin slices of pork are essential. Letting the roast cool—completely, in the refrigerator—and cutting it in half made it easier to slice paper-thin. We then rewarmed the pork before shingling the thin slices on warm Italian rolls with garlicky broccoli rabe and sharp provolone cheese. You need to let the pork cool for 1 hour and then refrigerate it for at least 1 hour or up to 2 days to make slicing easier. Sharp provolone is often labeled "Provolone Picante," but you can use standard deli provolone, too. If you're using table salt, cut the amounts in half. Serve with jarred hot cherry peppers, if desired.

1 For the pork and jus Adjust oven rack to lower-middle position and heat oven to 300 degrees. Combine salt, rosemary, thyme, oregano, fennel seeds, and pepper flakes in bowl. Tie roast with kitchen twine at 1-inch intervals. Sprinkle roast with salt mixture and transfer to Dutch oven. Pour broth around roast, add garlic to pot, and cover; transfer pot to oven. Cook until pork registers 190 degrees, 2½ to 3 hours.

2 Transfer roast to large plate. Transfer braising liquid to 4-cup liquid measuring cup; add extra broth, if necessary, to equal 3 cups. Let roast and liquid cool completely, about 1 hour. Cover and refrigerate both for at least 1 hour or up to 2 days.

3 For the broccoli rabe Heat oil and garlic in Dutch oven over medium heat until garlic is golden brown, 3 to 5 minutes. Add broccoli rabe, salt, and pepper flakes and cook, stirring occasionally, until tender, 4 to 6 minutes. Transfer to bowl.

4 About 20 minutes before serving, adjust oven rack to middle position and heat oven to 450 degrees. Remove twine and cut cooled roast in half lengthwise to make 2 even-size roasts. Position roasts cut side down and slice each crosswise as thin as possible.

5 Spoon solidified fat off cooled jus and discard. Transfer jus to Dutch oven and bring to boil over high heat. Reduce heat to low, add pork, cover, and cook until pork is heated through, about 3 minutes, tossing occasionally. Cover and keep warm.

6 For the sandwiches Arrange rolls on 2 rimmed baking sheets (4 rolls per sheet). Divide provolone evenly among rolls. Bake, 1 sheet at a time, until cheese is melted and rolls are warmed, about 3 minutes. Using tongs, divide pork and broccoli rabe evenly among rolls (about 1 cup pork and ⅓ cup broccoli rabe per roll). Serve, passing any remaining jus separately.

BRAISED PORK LOIN WITH BLACK MOLE SAUCE

serves 6

4 pasilla chiles, stemmed, seeded, and torn into ½-inch pieces (1 cup)

1 (2½- to 3-pound) boneless pork loin roast, fat trimmed to ¼ inch, tied at 1½-inch intervals

Salt and pepper

2 tablespoons vegetable oil

1 onion, chopped

2 garlic cloves, peeled

2 teaspoons minced fresh oregano or ½ teaspoon dried

⅛ teaspoon ground cloves

⅛ teaspoon ground cinnamon

2 tomatillos, husks and stems removed, rinsed well, dried, and cut into 1-inch pieces

1 tomato, cored and cut into 1-inch pieces

2 cups chicken broth

¼ cup unsalted dry-roasted peanuts

3 tablespoons black or Dutch-processed cocoa powder

3 tablespoons sesame seeds, toasted

2 tablespoons raisins

Why This Recipe Works Hailing from the Mexican state of Oaxaca, black mole is also known as *mole negro*. This thick, complexly flavored sauce consists of dried chiles, spices, tomatillos, tomatoes, cocoa, dried or fresh fruit, nuts, and seeds. Its intense, subtly bitter flavor and deep brown, almost black, color sets it apart from other moles. Usually paired with meat or poultry, it functions as both a sauce and a cooking medium. For our version, we chose to pair the mole with pork, which is one of the most commonly used proteins of the Oaxaca region. After browning the pork loin, we sautéed onion until it was a very deep brown, which contributed to the color and complex flavor of the mole. We then added garlic, oregano, cloves, and cinnamon for aromatic, warm spice notes. Next, the tomato and tomatillos went into the pot to concentrate their flavors. Adding chicken broth allowed us to scrape up the flavorful browned bits on the bottom of the pot. We then finished the sauce with toasted pasilla chiles, peanuts, sesame seeds, raisins, and cocoa powder; black cocoa powder (cocoa powder that has been heavily Dutched) worked especially well for its intense flavor and deep, dark color. Cooking the nuts, seeds, and cocoa along with the pork gave them plenty of time to hydrate and soften, making it easier to blend them into a smooth sauce later. You can find black cocoa powder in specialty stores or online. While we prefer the deeper flavor of black cocoa powder in this recipe, Dutch-processed cocoa powder also works well.

1 Adjust oven rack to lowest position and heat oven to 250 degrees. Toast pasilla chiles in Dutch oven over medium-high heat, stirring frequently, until fragrant, 2 to 6 minutes; transfer to bowl.

2 Pat roast dry with paper towels and season with salt and pepper. Heat oil in now-empty pot over medium-high heat until just smoking. Brown roast well on all sides, 8 to 10 minutes; transfer to plate.

3 Add onion to fat left in pot and cook over medium heat until softened and well browned, about 5 minutes. Stir in garlic, oregano, cloves, and cinnamon and cook until fragrant, about 30 seconds. Stir in tomatillos and tomato and cook until softened, about 5 minutes. Stir in broth, scraping up any browned bits. Stir in peanuts, cocoa, 2 tablespoons sesame seeds, raisins, toasted pasillas, 1 teaspoon salt, and ½ teaspoon pepper and bring to simmer.

4 Nestle browned roast fat side up into pot along with any accumulated juices and cover; transfer pot to oven. Cook until pork registers 140 degrees, 40 minutes to 1 hour.

5 Transfer roast to carving board, tent with aluminum foil, and let rest for 15 to 20 minutes. Meanwhile, process cooking liquid in blender until smooth, 1 to 2 minutes. Season sauce with salt and pepper to taste.

6 Remove twine from roast. Slice pork into ¼-inch-thick slices. Transfer pork to serving platter and spoon 1 cup sauce over pork. Sprinkle with remaining 1 tablespoon sesame seeds, and serve with remaining sauce.

FRENCH-STYLE POT-ROASTED PORK LOIN

serves 4 to 6

2 tablespoons unsalted butter, cut into 2 pieces

6 garlic cloves, sliced thin

1 (2½-pound) boneless center-cut pork loin roast, trimmed

Kosher salt and pepper

1 teaspoon sugar

2 teaspoons herbes de Provence

2 tablespoons vegetable oil

1 Granny Smith apple, peeled, cored, halved, and cut into ¼-inch pieces

1 onion, chopped fine

⅓ cup dry white wine

2 sprigs fresh thyme

1 bay leaf

1 tablespoon unflavored gelatin

¼–¾ cup chicken broth

1 tablespoon chopped fresh parsley

Why This Recipe Works *Enchaud Périgordine* is a fancy name for what's actually a relatively simple French dish: slow-cooked pork loin. Cooked in the oven in a covered casserole dish, the roast turns out incredibly moist and flavorful, with a rich jus to accompany it. At least it does when it's prepared in France where pigs are bred to have plenty of fat. American counterparts are lean, which translates to a bland and stringy roast. To improve the flavor and texture of our center-cut loin, we lowered the oven temperature (to 225 degrees) and removed the roast from the oven when it was medium-rare. Searing just three sides of the roast prevented the bottom from overcooking from direct contact with the pot. Butterflying the pork allowed us to salt a maximum amount of surface area for a roast that was thoroughly seasoned throughout. We eliminated the hard-to-find trotter (or pig's foot) that's traditional and added butter for richness, and a sprinkling of gelatin lent the missing body to our flavorful sauce. We strongly prefer the flavor of natural pork in this recipe, but enhanced pork (injected with a salt solution) can be used. If using enhanced pork, reduce the salt to 2 teaspoons (1 teaspoon per side) in step 3. The pork can be prepared through step 3, wrapped in plastic wrap, and refrigerated for up to two days.

1 Adjust oven rack to lower-middle position and heat oven to 225 degrees. Melt 1 tablespoon butter in 8-inch skillet over medium-low heat. Add half of garlic and cook, stirring frequently, until golden, 5 to 7 minutes. Transfer mixture to bowl and refrigerate.

2 Position roast fat side up. Insert knife one-third of way up from bottom of roast along 1 long side and cut horizontally, stopping ½ inch before edge. Open up flap. Keeping knife parallel to cutting board, cut through thicker portion of roast about ½ inch from bottom of roast, keeping knife level with first cut and stopping about ½ inch before edge. Open up this flap. If uneven, cover with plastic wrap and use meat pounder to even out.

3 Sprinkle 1 tablespoon salt evenly over both sides of roast (½ tablespoon per side) and rub into meat until slightly tacky. Sprinkle sugar over inside of roast, then spread with garlic mixture. Starting from short side, fold roast back together like business letter (keeping fat on outside) and tie crosswise with kitchen twine at 1-inch intervals. Sprinkle roast evenly with herbes de Provence; season with pepper.

4 Heat 1 tablespoon oil in Dutch oven over medium heat until just smoking. Add roast fat side down and brown on fat side and sides (do not brown bottom of roast), 5 to 8 minutes. Transfer roast to large plate. Add remaining 1 tablespoon oil, apple, and onion; cook, stirring frequently, until onion is softened and browned, 5 to 7 minutes. Stir in remaining garlic and cook until fragrant, about 30 seconds. Stir in wine, thyme, and bay leaf; cook for 30 seconds. Return roast, fat side up, to pot. Place large sheet of aluminum foil over pot and cover tightly with lid; transfer pot to oven. Cook until pork registers 140 degrees, 50 minutes to 1½ hours (short, thick roasts will take longer than long, thin ones).

5 Transfer roast to carving board, tent with foil, and let rest for 20 minutes. While roast rests, sprinkle gelatin over ¼ cup broth in bowl and let sit until gelatin softens, about 5 minutes. Discard thyme sprigs and bay leaf. Pour jus into 2-cup liquid measuring cup and add broth as needed to equal 1¼ cups. Return jus to pot and bring to simmer over medium heat. Whisk softened gelatin mixture, parsley, and remaining 1 tablespoon butter into jus and season with salt and pepper to taste; remove from heat and cover to keep warm.

Remove twine from roast. Slice pork into ½-inch-thick slices, adding any accumulated juices to sauce. Serve, passing sauce separately.

French-Style Pot-Roasted Pork Loin with Port and Figs
Substitute ¾ cup chopped dried figs for apple and port for white wine. Add 1 tablespoon balsamic vinegar to sauce with butter in step 5.

double-butterflying a roast

1 Holding chef's knife parallel to cutting board, insert knife one-third of way up from bottom of roast and cut horizontally, stopping ½ inch before edge. Open up flap.

2 Make another horizontal cut into thicker portion of roast. Open up this flap, smoothing out butterflied rectangle of meat.

BRAISED COUNTRY-STYLE RIBS WITH BLACK-EYED PEAS AND COLLARD GREENS

serves 6 to 8

2 pounds country-style pork ribs, trimmed of excess fat

Salt and pepper

1 teaspoon vegetable oil

4 ounces bacon, sliced crosswise into ¼-inch strips

1 red onion, chopped

1 large celery rib, chopped fine

6 garlic cloves, minced

1 pound dried black-eyed peas, picked through and rinsed

3½ cups chicken broth

1 cup water

2 bay leaves

1 pound collard greens, stemmed and sliced thin

1 recipe Spicy Pickled Onion (recipe follows)

Why This Recipe Works There's a simple Southern side dish in which black-eyed peas, collard greens, and a smoked ham hock are stewed together for hours until the beans are creamy, the greens are velvety soft, and the broth is suffused with the smoky sweetness of the ham. Our goal was to capitalize on the flavors and basic technique of the recipe, but expand the dish into a full-blown meal with the addition of a heftier cut of meat. Ham hocks may be flavorful, but they yield a scant amount of edible meat. Country-style ribs, taken from the backbone of the pig, at the juncture of the shoulder and the loin, are very flavorful and resilient because of the relatively high amount of fat and connective tissue between the bones. Stewed from start to finish with the beans and ribs, the collards became soggy and took on an unappealing drab green color. While this is common, we prefer a bit more color and bite, so we sliced the greens thin and simmered them at the end of cooking for just a few minutes. The dish was flavorful and porky, but we missed the smokiness provided by ham hocks, so we added some bacon. Pickled red onion was a brilliant finish, cutting through the richness and enlivening the dish.

1 Adjust oven rack to lower-middle position and heat oven to 300 degrees. Dry ribs thoroughly with paper towels and season with salt and pepper. Heat oil in Dutch oven over medium-high heat until just smoking. Place ribs in single layer and cook, without moving them, until well browned, about 5 minutes. Flip ribs and continue to cook until brown on second side, about 4 minutes longer; transfer ribs to plate.

2 Pour off fat in pot and return to medium heat. Add bacon and cook, stirring frequently, until most of fat has rendered, about 3 minutes. Add onion and celery; cook, stirring occasionally, until softened and beginning to brown, about 6 minutes. Add garlic and cook until fragrant, about 30 seconds. Add beans, broth, water, bay leaves, and browned ribs, bring to simmer, and cover; transfer pot to oven. Cook until beans are tender and sharp knife slips easily in and out of meat, about 1 hour.

3 Transfer ribs to carving board and tent with aluminum foil. Return pot to medium-high heat and stir in collard greens; cook until wilted and tender, 4 to 8 minutes. Discard bay leaves and season with salt and pepper to taste. Serve immediately with ribs and pickled onion.

SPICY PICKLED ONION
makes about 2 cups

¾ cup red wine vinegar

2 tablespoons sugar

½ teaspoon salt

¼ teaspoon red pepper flakes

2 bay leaves

1 red onion, halved and sliced thin

Bring vinegar, sugar, salt, pepper flakes, and bay leaves to a boil over medium-high heat in a small saucepan. Add onion, return to boil, and cook for 1 minute. Transfer to shallow bowl and refrigerate until cooled.

SWEET-AND-SOUR PORK RIBS

serves 4

2 tablespoons vegetable oil

2 racks loin back or baby back ribs (about 4 pounds total), cut into individual ribs

3 garlic cloves, minced

1 tablespoon grated fresh ginger

½ cup plus 1 tablespoon red wine vinegar

½ cup soy sauce

½ cup water

⅓ cup packed brown sugar

3 tablespoons Chinese rice cooking wine or dry sherry

Why This Recipe Works Order ribs in sweet-and-sour sauce at a Chinese restaurant in the United States, and you're often met with ribs covered in a sticky-sweet glaze more akin to candy than dinner fare. We wanted a balanced sauce to both cook and gently flavor the ribs, not coat them with a sticky shellac. The best way to cook loin back or baby back ribs is to slow-cook them with moist heat. This allows time for the meat to become meltingly tender and for a generous amount of fat to melt away from the meat and bone (we removed the fat from the sauce after cooking by transferring it to a fat separator). Browning the ribs first in the Dutch oven added substantial flavor to the braising liquid and resulting sauce. And to keep it from being cloying, we backed off on the sugar from many recipes, switched from white to brown to deepen the flavor, and added a little garlic and ginger. Poured over the tender, flavorful ribs, the bright sweet-and-sour sauce enlivened dinner. Note that baby back and loin back ribs are the same type of rib—although loin back ribs come from larger pigs and are thus a bit meatier. Either works well in this recipe. We usually braise meats in the oven, but because these ribs are stirred frequently during cooking, we prefer to cook them on top of the stove.

1 Heat oil in Dutch oven over medium-high heat until just smoking. Brown one-third of the ribs on several sides, about 6 minutes, reducing heat if the pot begins to scorch. Transfer ribs to plate and repeat twice more with remaining ribs using fat left in pot.

2 Add garlic and ginger to fat in pot and cook over medium heat until fragrant, about 30 seconds. Stir in vinegar, soy sauce, water, sugar, and rice wine, scraping up browned bits. Bring to simmer, stirring to dissolve sugar.

3 Return ribs to pot. Cover, reduce heat to medium-low, and cook until ribs are tender and meat easily pulls away from bone, 1¾ to 2¼ hours, using tongs to rearrange ribs every 30 minutes, so that they're moistened with braising liquid. (Liquid should simmer very gently; adjust heat as necessary.)

4 Transfer ribs to serving platter and tent with aluminum foil. Strain juices from pot into fat separator. Let liquid settle for 5 minutes (you should have about 1½ cups of defatted sauce). Gently pour defatted sauce over ribs and serve.

PORK GRILLADES

serves 6 to 8

1 cup all-purpose flour

8 (6- to 8-ounce) bone-in blade-cut pork chops, ½ inch thick, bones discarded, and trimmed

2 tablespoons Louisiana Seasoning (recipe follows)

Salt and pepper

½ cup vegetable oil

1 onion, chopped

1 green bell pepper, stemmed, seeded, and chopped

1 celery rib, chopped

2 garlic cloves, minced

2 cups chicken broth

1 (14.5-ounce) can whole peeled tomatoes, crushed by hand

2 slices bacon

1 tablespoon Worcestershire sauce

1 bay leaf

1 teaspoon Tabasco sauce, plus extra for serving

2 scallions, sliced thin

Why This Recipe Works Despite their name, grillades are not grilled; this flavorful New Orleans dish instead consists of thinly sliced cuts of meat browned and stewed in a supersavory tomato-based gravy that gets soaked up by a bed of rice. To skip the tedious slicing, we found that center-cut pork blade chops (with the bones cut off) worked well; they cooked evenly and held up to stewing. We cut down the traditional time it takes to make a roux for the base of our gravy by dry-toasting flour in advance in a skillet. Using our own Cajun seasoning spice blend and the traditional mix of bell peppers, celery, and onion provided a strong flavor base. Finally, finishing with a dash of Louisiana-native Tabasco sauce gave the dish just the right amount of spice and acidity. We prefer pork blade chops because they hold up to stewing better than loin chops. Blade chops aren't typically available boneless; ask your butcher to bone them for you. Use our Louisiana Seasoning or your favorite store-bought variety. Serve over rice.

1 Adjust oven rack to lower-middle position and heat oven to 350 degrees. Toast ¼ cup flour in small skillet over medium heat, stirring constantly, until just beginning to brown, about 3 minutes; set aside.

2 Season chops with 1½ teaspoons Louisiana seasoning, salt, and pepper. Whisk remaining ¾ cup flour and remaining 1½ tablespoons Louisiana Seasoning together in shallow dish. Working with 1 chop at a time, dredge in seasoned flour, shaking off excess; transfer chops to plate.

3 Heat oil in Dutch oven over medium heat until shimmering. Add 4 chops and cook until browned, 3 to 5 minutes per side; transfer to plate. Repeat with remaining 4 chops.

4 Pour off all but ¼ cup oil from Dutch oven and return to medium heat. Add toasted flour to pot and cook, whisking constantly, until deep brown, about 2 minutes. Add onion, bell pepper, celery, and 1 teaspoon salt and cook, stirring often, until vegetables are just softened, about 3 minutes. Add garlic and cook until fragrant, about 30 seconds.

5 Stir in broth, tomatoes and their juice, bacon, Worcestershire, and bay leaf, scraping up any browned bits. Nestle chops into liquid along with any accumulated pork juices. Bring to simmer and cover; transfer pot to oven. Cook until fork slips easily in and out of pork, about 1 hour.

6 Remove grillades from oven. Discard bacon and bay leaf; stir in Tabasco sauce. Season with salt and pepper to taste. Serve, sprinkled with scallions and passing extra Tabasco sauce.

LOUISIANA SEASONING

makes about ¾ cup

While you can buy Cajun or Creole Louisiana seasoning blends in the grocery store, they're often harsh and stale-tasting. We prefer to make our own. You'll need just 2 tablespoons of this Cajun seasoning for our Pork Grillades; try the leftover seasoning on scrambled eggs, boiled potatoes, or roast chicken.

5 tablespoons paprika
2 tablespoons garlic powder
1 tablespoon dried thyme
1 tablespoon cayenne pepper
1 tablespoon celery salt
1 tablespoon salt
1 tablespoon pepper

Combine all ingredients in bowl.

RED WINE–BRAISED PORK CHOPS

serves 4

Salt and pepper

4 (10- to 12-ounce) bone-in blade-cut
pork chops, 1 inch thick

2 teaspoons vegetable oil

2 onions, halved and sliced thin

5 sprigs fresh thyme,
plus ¼ teaspoon minced

2 garlic cloves, peeled

2 bay leaves

1 (½-inch) piece ginger, peeled
and crushed

⅛ teaspoon ground allspice

½ cup red wine

¼ cup ruby port

2 tablespoons plus ½ teaspoon
red wine vinegar

1 cup chicken broth

2 tablespoons unsalted butter

1 tablespoon minced fresh parsley

Why This Recipe Works Braising pork chops is less cumbersome than a roast and should be an easy route to a flavorful dinner. We started with blade-cut pork chops; their large amount of fat and connective tissue made them well suited to a longer braise that developed deep flavor. We trimmed them of excess fat and connective tissue to prevent the chops from buckling during braising, which would result in an unattractive appearance and uneven cooking. Although the move was at first utilitarian, there was an added benefit: We used those trimmings to build a rich and flavorful braising liquid with the perfect amount of depth and sweetness and a bit of tang from a combination of red wine and ruby port. Fresh ginger and allspice infused the braising liquid with warm backnotes, while fresh thyme complemented the wine with a bit of woodsiness. When the chops were done braising, we quickly reduced the braising liquid to a tasty sauce, enriched with a swirl of butter. Look for chops with a small eye and a large amount of marbling, as these are the best suited to braising. The pork scraps can be removed when straining the sauce in step 4 and served alongside the chops. (They taste great.)

1 Dissolve 3 tablespoons salt in 1½ quarts cold water in large container. Submerge chops in brine, cover, and refrigerate for 1 hour.

2 Adjust oven rack to lower-middle position and heat oven to 275 degrees. Remove chops from brine and pat dry with paper towels. Trim off cartilage, meat cap, and fat opposite rib bones. Cut trimmings into 1-inch pieces. Heat oil in Dutch oven over medium-high heat until shimmering. Add trimmings and brown on all sides, 6 to 9 minutes.

3 Reduce heat to medium and add onions, thyme sprigs, garlic, bay leaves, ginger, and allspice. Cook, stirring occasionally, until onions are golden brown, 5 to 10 minutes. Stir in wine, port, and 2 tablespoons vinegar and cook until reduced to thin syrup, 5 to 7 minutes. Add broth, spread pork trimmings mixture into even layer, and bring to simmer. Arrange chops on top of pork trimmings mixture and cover; transfer pot to oven.

4 Cook until meat is tender, 1¼ to 1½ hours. Remove from oven and let chops rest in pot, covered, for 30 minutes. Transfer chops to serving platter and tent with aluminum foil. Strain braising liquid through fine-mesh strainer set over large bowl; discard solids. Transfer braising liquid to fat separator. Let liquid settle for 5 minutes.

5 Wipe now-empty pot clean with paper towels. Return defatted braising liquid to pot and cook over medium-high heat until reduced to 1 cup, 3 to 7 minutes. Off heat, whisk in butter, minced thyme, and remaining ½ teaspoon vinegar. Season with salt and pepper to taste. Pour sauce over chops, sprinkle with parsley, and serve.

SMOTHERED PORK CHOPS

serves 4

3 slices bacon, cut into ¼-inch pieces

2 tablespoons vegetable oil, plus extra as needed

2 tablespoons all-purpose flour

1¾ cups chicken broth

4 (6- to 8-ounce) bone-in pork rib chops, ½ to ¾ inch thick, trimmed

Salt and pepper

2 onions, halved and sliced thin

2 tablespoons water

2 garlic cloves, minced

1 teaspoon minced fresh thyme

2 bay leaves

1 tablespoon minced fresh parsley

Why This Recipe Works Tender, flavorful pork chops stand up well to rich, hearty gravies. But most of the time, the gravy misses the mark: It's either so thick you can't find the chop, or so thin and watery that the meat seems to float on the plate. We wanted a foolproof recipe for juicy chops smothered in thick, satiny gravy. Thin, not thick, rib chops were best for absorbing the gravy's flavors. Browning the chops well left meaty browned bits in the pan, essential for making a flavorful gravy. To build further flavor, we made a nut-brown, bacony roux. Thinly sliced yellow onions contributed a significant amount of moisture to the gravy, bringing it to just the right consistency. Garlic, thyme, and bay leaves rounded out the flavorful gravy. A lengthy braise of the chops in the gravy resulted in moist, tender meat; it also allowed the gravy to thicken and its flavors to meld, so the chops had a rich, velvety coating when served. We prefer natural to enhanced pork (pork that has been injected with a salt solution to increase moistness and flavor) for this recipe, though either will work here.

1 Cook bacon in small saucepan over medium heat, stirring occasionally, until lightly browned, 8 to 10 minutes. Using slotted spoon, transfer bacon to paper towel–lined plate, leaving fat in saucepan (you should have 2 tablespoons bacon fat; if not, supplement with oil). Reduce heat to medium-low and gradually whisk flour into fat until smooth. Cook, whisking frequently, until mixture is light brown (about the color of peanut butter), about 5 minutes. Whisk in broth in slow, steady stream; increase heat to medium-high and bring to boil, stirring occasionally; cover and set aside off heat.

2 Pat chops dry with paper towels and sprinkle with ½ teaspoon pepper. Heat 1 tablespoon oil in 12-inch skillet over high heat until just smoking, 2 to 3 minutes. Cook chops until deep golden brown, about 3 minutes. Flip chops and cook until browned on second side, about 3 minutes longer. Transfer chops to large plate; set aside.

3 Reduce heat to medium and add onions, water, remaining 1 tablespoon oil, and ¼ teaspoon salt to now-empty skillet, scraping up any browned bits. Cook, stirring frequently, until onions are softened and browned around edges, about 5 minutes. Stir in garlic and thyme and cook until fragrant, about 30 seconds. Arrange chops in skillet in single layer, covering chops with onions. Pour in warm sauce and any

accumulated juices from pork; add bay leaves. Cover, reduce heat to low, and simmer until fork slips easily in and out of pork, about 30 minutes.

4 Transfer chops to warmed serving platter and tent with aluminum foil. Increase heat to medium-high and simmer sauce rapidly, stirring frequently, until thickened to gravy-like consistency, 5 to 7 minutes. Remove bay leaves, stir in parsley, and season with salt and pepper to taste. Spoon sauce over chops, sprinkle with reserved bacon, and serve.

Smothered Pork Chops with Cider and Apples

Substitute apple cider for chicken broth and 1 large Granny Smith apple, peeled, cored, and cut into ⅜-inch wedges, for 1 onion. Increase salt added with onions to ½ teaspoon.

Smothered Pork Chops with Spicy Collard Greens

Increase oil in step 3 to 2 tablespoons, omit 1 onion, and increase garlic to 4 cloves. Just before returning browned chops to pan in step 3, add 4 cups stemmed and thinly sliced collard greens and ½ teaspoon red pepper flakes.

PORK CHOPS WITH VINEGAR PEPPERS

serves 4

3 tablespoons sugar

Salt and pepper

4 (8- to 10-ounce) bone-in pork rib chops, 1 inch thick, trimmed

⅓ cup all-purpose flour

2 tablespoons olive oil

1 onion, halved and sliced thin

8 garlic cloves, lightly crushed and peeled

2 anchovy fillets, rinsed, patted dry, and minced

2 cups thinly sliced sweet green vinegar peppers

1 sprig fresh rosemary

1 cup chicken broth

½ cup red wine vinegar

1 tablespoon unsalted butter

Why This Recipe Works Thick, meaty chops braised with tangy vinegar peppers has been an Italian American restaurant favorite for decades. But, as we learned with our other pork chop recipes, slow braising, while creating lots of flavor, also dries out lean center-cut pork chops—what's typically called for in this recipe. So we strayed from the classic, choosing thick, bone-in pork rib chops. We brined them for 30 minutes before cooking for extra insurance against drying and browned them on only one side to prevent overcooking. Then we covered the skillet and braised them for just 10 minutes: browned, juicy, perfect. Jarred sweet vinegar peppers held up to braising and had a mild tang that we liked. But our sauce left after braising lacked a bit of depth because of the short cooking time. We added a secret ingredient to remedy this: anchovy fillets, which lent savoriness without imparting a fishy flavor. We thickened the sauce in two ways: by flouring the chops (which also aided in forming their browned crust) and by reducing the sauce slightly after the pork was done. Arrange the pork chops in a pinwheel pattern so they fit easily in the skillet.

1 Dissolve sugar and 3 tablespoons salt in 1½ quarts cold water in large container. Add chops, cover, and refrigerate for 30 minutes to 1 hour.

2 Place flour in shallow dish. Remove chops from brine. Pat chops dry with paper towels and season with pepper. Working with 1 chop at a time, dredge both sides in flour, shaking off excess. Heat 1 tablespoon oil in 12-inch skillet over medium-high heat until just smoking. Cook chops until well browned, 5 to 7 minutes. Flip chops and cook for 1 minute; transfer to plate browned side up.

3 Reduce heat to medium and add remaining 1 tablespoon oil, onion, garlic, and anchovies to now-empty skillet. Cook, stirring frequently, until onion is softened and golden brown, 6 to 8 minutes. Add peppers and rosemary and cook until peppers begin to caramelize, about 5 minutes. Add broth and vinegar and bring to boil.

4 Transfer chops browned side up from plate to skillet and add any accumulated juices. Reduce heat to low, cover, and simmer until chops register 145 degrees, 6 to 10 minutes. Transfer chops to serving platter and tent with aluminum foil.

5 Increase heat to high and boil sauce until slightly thickened, about 3 minutes. Off heat, stir in butter and season with salt and pepper to taste. Stir any accumulated juices from platter into sauce. Discard rosemary and spoon sauce over chops. Serve.

PORK CHOPS WITH TOMATO GRAVY

serves 4

Salt and pepper

½ teaspoon paprika

½ teaspoon sugar

¼ teaspoon cayenne pepper

4 (8- to 10-ounce) bone-in pork rib chops, 1 inch thick, trimmed

4 slices bacon, chopped fine

2 tablespoons vegetable oil

1 onion, chopped fine

1 celery rib, minced

1 garlic clove, minced

3 tablespoons all-purpose flour

1 tablespoon tomato paste

1 cup chicken broth

1 (8-ounce) can tomato sauce

1 teaspoon minced fresh thyme

1 bay leaf

Why This Recipe Works This Louisiana dish, like many of our favorites from the state, carries the bold flavor that results from long, slow cooking; could we capture the meaty flavors we loved without the wait? We rubbed the chops with Cajun spices and turned to finely chopped bacon to develop a salty, smoky flavor base. After cooking the bacon bits in a skillet, we removed the bacon and used its rendered fat to brown the pork chops on one side to develop fond. With the browned chops set aside, we cooked oil, onion, celery, and garlic in the same skillet. To establish our gravy's flavorful roux, we added flour and tomato paste, allowing them to brown and bloom before also whisking in broth, tomato sauce, thyme, bay leaf, and the reserved bacon. Our sauce was now thick, smoky, and rich. We arranged the chops in the skillet brow-ned side up and let them braise in the simmering sauce until done. The finished chops boasted a crisp, tasty crust and a deep, full-flavored tomato gravy to match—and with time to spare. Arrange the pork chops in a pinwheel pattern so they fit easily in the skillet.

1 Combine 1 teaspoon salt, 1 teaspoon pepper, paprika, sugar, and cayenne in small bowl. Pat chops dry with paper towels and sprinkle evenly with spice mixture.

2 Cook bacon in 12-inch nonstick skillet over medium heat until crisp, 5 to 7 minutes. Using slotted spoon, transfer bacon to paper towel–lined plate. Pour off all but 1 tablespoon fat from skillet. Increase heat to medium-high, add chops, and cook until well browned on 1 side, 5 to 7 minutes. Transfer to plate browned side up.

3 Reduce heat to medium, add oil, and heat until shimmering. Add onion, celery, and garlic and cook until softened, 5 to 7 minutes. Add flour and tomato paste and cook, stirring constantly, for 2 minutes. Whisk in broth, tomato sauce, thyme, bay leaf, and reserved bacon and bring to boil.

4 Transfer chops browned side up and any accumulated juices to skillet. Reduce heat to low, cover, and simmer until chops register 145 degrees, 8 to 12 minutes. Transfer chops to serving platter, tent with aluminum foil, and let rest for 5 to 10 minutes. Season gravy with salt and pepper to taste, discard bay leaf, cover, and keep warm. Stir any accumulated juices from platter into gravy and pour over chops. Serve.

MEXICAN PULLED PORK (CARNITAS)

serves 6

1 (3½- to 4-pound) boneless pork butt roast, fat trimmed to ⅛ inch, cut into 2-inch pieces

2 cups water

1 onion, peeled and halved

2 tablespoons lime juice

1 teaspoon dried oregano

1 teaspoon ground cumin

2 bay leaves

Salt and pepper

1 orange, halved

18 (6-inch) corn tortillas, warmed

Why This Recipe Works Spanish for "little meats," carnitas offer fall-apart-tender hunks of pork with lightly crisped, caramelized exteriors. Traditionally, the flavor of the pork takes center stage, subtly accented by earthy oregano and sour orange. The chunks of meat are often deep-fried in lard or oil, but this method is impractical and messy at home. We were able to replicate deep-fried taste and texture by braising the pork in a small amount of liquid, then reducing the liquid into a syrupy glaze and incorporating it back into the meat. Broiling the glazed pork pieces on a rack not only crisped the exterior, but also allowed the excess fat to drip off, preventing a greasy final dish. For the finishing touch, we refined our cooking liquid's flavors with a mixture of lime and orange juices (which emulated the flavor of sour oranges), along with bay leaves, cumin, and oregano. Adding the spent orange halves to the braising liquid deepened the orange flavor and offered subtle floral notes. Boneless pork butt roast is often labeled Boston butt in the supermarket. We like serving carnitas spooned into small corn tortillas, with chopped onion, diced avocado, thinly sliced radish, and/or cilantro leaves, but it can also be used as a filling for tamales, enchiladas, and burritos.

1 Adjust oven rack to lower-middle position and heat oven to 300 degrees. Combine pork, water, onion, lime juice, oregano, cumin, bay leaves, 1 teaspoon salt, and ½ teaspoon pepper in Dutch oven (liquid should just barely cover meat). Juice orange into bowl and remove any seeds (you should have about ⅓ cup juice). Add juice and spent orange halves to pot.

2 Bring mixture to simmer over medium-high heat, stirring occasionally, and cover; transfer pot to oven. Cook until meat is soft and falls apart when prodded with fork, about 2 hours, flipping pieces of meat once during cooking.

3 Remove pot from oven and heat broiler. Using slotted spoon, transfer pork to bowl; discard onion, orange halves, and bay leaves from cooking liquid (do not skim fat from liquid). Carefully place pot over high heat (handles will be hot) and simmer liquid, stirring frequently, until thick and syrupy (spatula should leave wide trail when dragged through glaze), 8 to 12 minutes. (You should have about 1 cup reduced liquid.)

4 Using 2 forks, pull each piece of pork in half. Fold in reduced liquid; season with salt and pepper to taste. Spread pork in even layer on wire rack set in rimmed baking sheet or on broiler pan (meat should cover almost entire surface of rack or pan). Place sheet on lower-middle rack and broil until top of meat is well browned (but not charred) and edges are slightly crispy, 5 to 8 minutes. Using wide metal spatula, flip meat and continue to broil until top is well browned and edges are slightly crispy, 5 to 8 minutes longer. Serve with tortillas.

FRENCH-STYLE PORK STEW

serves 8

2 tablespoons vegetable oil

1 onion, chopped

Salt and pepper

3 garlic cloves, minced

2 teaspoons herbes de Provence

1 (3-pound) boneless pork butt roast, pulled apart at seams, trimmed, and cut into 1½-inch pieces

1¼ pounds smoked ham hocks

5 cups water

4 cups chicken broth

1 pound Yukon Gold potatoes, unpeeled, cut into ¾-inch pieces

4 carrots, peeled and cut into ½-inch pieces

12 ounces kielbasa sausage, halved lengthwise and sliced ½ inch thick

½ head savoy cabbage, cored and shredded (8 cups)

¼ cup minced fresh parsley

Why This Recipe Works In the realm of stews, pork is either overlooked in favor of other proteins or, when used, overpowered by more assertive ingredients. We wanted a robust and satisfying (but not heavy) stew that put pork in the forefront. We took inspiration from a classic French dish, *potée*, a stew that uses multiple parts of the pig, at least one of which is always smoked, to yield a deep, meaty flavor. For our version, we chose a mix of pork butt for a base of tasty, succulent meat; collagen-rich smoked ham hocks, which would impart smokiness and a silky consistency to the broth; and kielbasa for a firm bite and additional smoky flavor. For our vegetables, we stuck with the traditional potatoes, carrots, and cabbage. We started to build a flavorful backbone by cooking onion, garlic, and herbs de Provence. We then added our liquid (mostly water, to keep the stew from becoming heavy, plus chicken broth to prevent the flavors from becoming washed out), and added the pork and ham hocks. Because the pork would take 2 hours to become perfectly tender, we added our other ingredients in stages to prevent them from becoming mushy or overcooked. About halfway through, we removed the ham hocks to shred the meat, which we added back to the stew. Pork butt roast is often labeled Boston butt in the supermarket.

1 Adjust oven rack to middle position and heat oven to 325 degrees. Heat oil in Dutch oven over medium heat until shimmering. Add onion, ½ teaspoon salt, and ¼ teaspoon pepper and cook until onion is softened and lightly browned, 5 to 7 minutes. Stir in garlic and herbes de Provence and cook until fragrant, about 30 seconds. Add pork butt, ham hocks, water, and broth; bring to simmer and cover; transfer pot to oven. Cook until pork is tender, 1¼ to 1½ hours.

2 Remove pot from oven. Transfer ham hocks to cutting board, let cool slightly, then shred into bite-size pieces using 2 forks, discarding skin and bones. While ham hocks cool, stir potatoes and carrots into stew, return covered pot to oven, and cook until vegetables are almost tender, 20 to 25 minutes.

3 Remove pot from oven and stir in shredded ham, kielbasa, and cabbage. Return covered pot to oven and cook until kielbasa is heated through and cabbage is wilted and tender, 15 to 20 minutes. Stir in parsley and season with salt and pepper to taste before serving.

NEW MEXICAN PORK STEW (POSOLE)

serves 6

¾ ounce (about 3) dried ancho chiles

8 cups chicken broth

2 pounds boneless country-style pork ribs

Salt and pepper

3 tablespoons vegetable oil

3 (15-ounce) cans white hominy, rinsed

2 onions, chopped

5 garlic cloves, minced

1 tablespoon minced fresh oregano

1 tablespoon lime juice

Why This Recipe Works New Mexican posole is one of those wonderful Southwestern stews that emerged when Mexican and European cooking traditions collided in the New World. Recipes for this warming, mildly spicy stew range from oversimplified to overcomplicated; we wanted posole with a streamlined method but complex flavor. Baking dried ancho chiles deepened their flavor, and steeping them in chicken broth produced an extra boost. Browning boneless country-style pork ribs before adding them to the pot built flavor easily. *Posole* is Spanish for "hominy," so using this canned dried corn was a must. Browning hominy in the ribs' rendered fat turned it sweet, toasty, and chewy, and reserving the cooked hominy until the end preserved these qualities. Sautéed onions and garlic pureed with the chiles created a gentle, caramelized sweetness. We combined the chile puree, broth, and pork, cooking the ribs to tenderness in about an hour. We shredded the pork and added it back to the stew just before serving. Serve this posole with sliced radishes and green cabbage, chopped avocado, hot sauce, and lime wedges.

1 Adjust oven rack to middle position and heat oven to 350 degrees. Place chiles on baking sheet and bake until puffed and fragrant, about 6 minutes. When chiles are cool enough to handle, remove stems and seeds. Combine chiles and 1 cup broth in medium bowl. Cover and microwave until bubbling, about 2 minutes. Let stand until softened, 10 to 15 minutes.

2 Pat ribs dry with paper towels and season with salt and pepper. Heat 2 tablespoons oil in Dutch oven over medium-high heat until just smoking. Cook ribs until well browned all over, about 10 minutes; transfer pork to plate. Add hominy to now-empty pot and cook, stirring frequently, until fragrant and hominy begins to darken, 2 to 3 minutes; transfer hominy to bowl.

3 Heat remaining 1 tablespoon oil in now-empty pot over medium heat until shimmering. Add onions and cook until softened, about 5 minutes. Stir in garlic and cook until fragrant, about 30 seconds. Puree onion mixture with softened chile mixture in blender. Combine remaining 7 cups broth, pureed onion-chile mixture, pork, oregano, ½ teaspoon salt, and ½ teaspoon pepper in now-empty pot and bring to boil. Reduce heat to low and simmer, covered, until meat is tender, 1 to 1½ hours.

4 Transfer pork to clean plate. Add hominy to pot and simmer, covered, until tender, about 30 minutes. Using wide spoon, skim fat from broth. When meat is cool enough to handle, shred into bite-size pieces, discarding fat. Return pork to pot and cook until heated through, about 1 minute. Off heat, add lime juice. Season with salt and pepper to taste, and serve.

COLORADO GREEN CHILI

serves 6

1 (3-pound) boneless pork butt roast, pulled apart at seams, trimmed, and cut into 1-inch pieces

Salt

2 pounds (10 to 12) Anaheim chiles, stemmed, halved lengthwise, and seeded

3 jalapeño chiles

1 (14.5-ounce) can diced tomatoes

1 tablespoon vegetable oil

2 onions, chopped fine

8 garlic cloves, minced

1 tablespoon ground cumin

¼ cup all-purpose flour

4 cups chicken broth

Cayenne pepper

Lime wedges

Why This Recipe Works Unlike Texas chili, this mildly spicy Colorado stew is based on pork and lots of green Hatch chiles—more than 2 pounds of them to be exact. In fact, it's just as much about the chiles as the pork. Since real Hatch chiles need to be mail-ordered, we approximated their flavor with Anaheims and jalapeños. Halving the Anaheims before roasting meant no tedious flipping or post-roast seeding, and pureeing half of the chiles (along with a can of diced tomatoes) while chopping the other half by hand gave the stew some texture. Since we had the chile roasting to deal with, we wanted to avoid browning the pork in batches. Starting all of the pork pieces in the Dutch oven with water allowed its fat to render evenly; after several minutes, we uncovered the pot and let the pork brown in its own fat. Using the oven to cook the chili provides gentle heat—and hands-off cooking—and finishing the stew with the chopped, roasted jalapeños added a fresh hit of heat. Pork butt roast is often labeled Boston butt in the supermarket. The chiles can be roasted and refrigerated up to 24 hours in advance. Serve with flour tortillas.

1 Combine pork, ½ cup water, and ½ teaspoon salt in Dutch oven over medium heat. Cover and cook for 20 minutes, stirring occasionally. Uncover, increase heat to medium-high, and continue to cook, stirring frequently, until liquid evaporates and pork browns in its own fat, 15 to 20 minutes. Transfer pork to bowl; set aside.

2 Meanwhile, adjust 1 oven rack to lowest position and second rack 6 inches from broiler element. Heat broiler. Line rimmed baking sheet with aluminum foil and spray with vegetable oil spray. Arrange Anaheims skin side up and jalapeños in single layer on prepared sheet. Place sheet on upper rack and broil until chiles are mostly blackened and soft, 15 to 20 minutes, rotating sheet and flipping only jalapeños halfway through broiling. Place Anaheims in large bowl and cover with plastic wrap; let cool for 5 minutes. Set aside jalapeños. Heat oven to 325 degrees.

3 Remove skins from Anaheims. Chop half of Anaheims into ½-inch pieces and transfer to bowl. Process remaining Anaheims in food processor until smooth, about 10 seconds; transfer to bowl with chopped Anaheims. Pulse tomatoes and their juice in now-empty food processor until coarsely ground, about 4 pulses.

4 Heat oil in now-empty Dutch oven over medium heat until shimmering. Add onions and cook until lightly browned, 5 to 7 minutes. Stir in garlic and cumin and cook until fragrant, about 30 seconds. Stir in flour and cook for 1 minute. Stir in broth, Anaheims, tomatoes, and pork with any accumulated juices and bring to simmer, scraping up any browned bits. Cover pot, transfer to lower oven rack, and cook until pork is tender, 1 to 1¼ hours.

5 Without peeling, stem and seed jalapeños and reserve seeds. Finely chop jalapeños and stir into chili. Season chili with salt, cayenne, and reserved jalapeño seeds to taste. Serve with lime wedges.

SPICY MEXICAN PORK TINGA AND RICE

serves 4 to 6

2 pounds boneless pork butt roast, trimmed and cut into 1-inch pieces

Salt and pepper

2 tablespoons extra-virgin olive oil

2 onions, chopped fine

5 garlic cloves, minced

1–2 tablespoons minced canned chipotle chile in adobo sauce

2 teaspoons minced fresh oregano or ½ teaspoon dried

1 teaspoon minced fresh thyme or ¼ teaspoon dried

2 cups chicken broth

1 (8-ounce) can tomato sauce

1½ cups long-grain white rice, rinsed

½ cup minced fresh cilantro

3 scallions, sliced thin

1 tablespoon lime juice

Why This Recipe Works Spiced with chipotle chiles and bathed in a tomatoey sauce, pork tinga is a rich stew-like dish from Mexico. Rather than spooning it onto crispy tostadas, we used rice to absorb the sauce's flavors in this simple one-pot version. The challenge was in maintaining the dish's bold essence while achieving perfectly tender pork and well-cooked rice, all in the same pot. Early attempts were lackluster in flavor, so we browned the pork in batches to develop a golden-brown crust. The technique worked, imparting a meaty richness to the rice as it simmered away. We built upon our rich fond by adding onions, garlic, herbs, and chipotle chile in adobo sauce. The chipotles lent a subtle heat, as well as smokiness and depth. To provide a more substantial, meaty bite with the rice, we again veered away from many recipes that shred the pork and instead chose to leave the tender cooked pork in chunks. Finally, we finished our dish with a sprinkling of fresh chopped scallions and cilantro, along with a splash of lime juice. You can vary the spice level of this dish by adjusting the amount of chipotle chiles. Pork butt roast is often labeled Boston butt in the supermarket.

1 Adjust oven rack to lower-middle position and heat to 300 degrees. Pat pork dry with paper towels and season with salt and pepper. Heat 1 tablespoon oil in Dutch oven over medium-high heat until just smoking. Add half of pork and brown on all sides, 7 to 10 minutes; transfer to large bowl. Repeat with remaining 1 tablespoon oil and remaining pork.

2 Add onions and ½ teaspoon salt to fat left in pot and cook over medium heat until onions are softened, about 5 minutes. Stir in garlic, chipotle, oregano, and thyme and cook until fragrant, about 30 seconds. Stir in broth and tomato sauce, scraping up any browned bits.

3 Add pork and any accumulated juices, bring to simmer, and cover; transfer pot to oven. Cook until pork is tender, 1¼ to 1½ hours.

4 Remove pot from oven and increase oven temperature to 350 degrees. Using wide spoon, skim any fat from surface of broth. Stir in rice and cover pot; return to oven. Cook, gently stirring every 10 minutes, until rice is tender and liquid has been absorbed, 20 to 30 minutes.

5 Remove pot from oven and stir in cilantro, scallions, and lime juice. Season with salt and pepper to taste. Cover and let stand for 5 minutes before serving.

CARNE ADOVADA

serves 6

1 (3½- to 4-pound) boneless pork butt roast, pulled apart at seams, trimmed, and cut into 1½-inch pieces

Kosher salt

4 ounces dried New Mexican chiles, wiped clean, stemmed, seeded, and torn into 1-inch pieces

4 cups boiling water

2 tablespoons honey

2 tablespoons distilled white vinegar

5 garlic cloves, peeled

2 teaspoons dried Mexican oregano

2 teaspoons ground cumin

½ teaspoon cayenne pepper

⅛ teaspoon ground cloves

Lime wedges

Why This Recipe Works Carne adovada is one of New Mexico's most celebrated dishes and quite possibly the easiest braise you'll ever make. It includes fall-apart tender pork, yes, but more importantly it's a way to feature New Mexican chiles—an enormous pride of the state. The pork cooks in a thick chile sauce. We started by cutting boneless pork butt into large chunks and salting them (so that they would be well seasoned and retain moisture during cooking) while we prepared the sauce. We used a generous 4 ounces of dried red New Mexican chiles, which are fruity and relatively mild. But rather than toast them, as we often do with dried chiles, we simply steeped them in water to preserve their bright trademark flavor. When they were pliable, we blended them with aromatics and spices (including garlic, oregano, cumin, cayenne, and cloves), as well as honey, white vinegar, and some of the soaking water to form a puree to toss the pork with before braising. For an accurate measurement of boiling water, bring a full kettle of water to a boil and then measure out the desired amount. If you can't find New Mexican chiles, substitute dried California chiles. Dried chiles should be pliable and smell slightly fruity. You can use kitchen shears to cut them. If you can't find Mexican oregano, substitute Mediterranean oregano. Letting the stew rest for 10 minutes before serving allows the sauce to thicken and better coat the meat. Pork butt roast is often labeled Boston butt in the supermarket. Serve with rice and beans, crispy potatoes, or flour tortillas with shredded lettuce and chopped tomato, or shred the pork as a filling for tacos and burritos.

1 Toss pork and 1 tablespoon salt together in bowl; refrigerate for 1 hour.

2 Place chiles in medium bowl. Pour boiling water over chiles, making sure they are completely submerged, and let stand until softened, 30 minutes. Adjust oven rack to lower-middle position and heat oven to 325 degrees.

3 Drain chiles and reserve 2 cups soaking liquid (discard remaining liquid). Process chiles, honey, vinegar, garlic, oregano, cumin, cayenne, cloves, and 1 teaspoon salt in blender until chiles are finely ground and thick paste forms, about 30 seconds. With blender running, add 1 cup reserved liquid and process until smooth, 1½ to 2 minutes, adding up to ¼ cup additional reserved liquid to maintain vortex. Add remaining reserved liquid and continue to blend sauce at high speed, 1 minute longer.

4 Combine pork and chile sauce in Dutch oven, stirring to make sure pork is evenly coated. Bring to boil over high heat. Cover pot, transfer to oven, and cook until pork is tender and fork inserted into pork meets little to no resistance, 2 to 2½ hours.

5 Using wooden spoon, scrape any browned bits from sides of pot and stir until pork and sauce are recombined and sauce is smooth and homogeneous. Let stand, uncovered, for 10 minutes. Season with salt to taste. Serve with lime wedges.

BRAISED GREEK SAUSAGES WITH PEPPERS

serves 4 to 6

1½ pounds loukaniko sausage

2 tablespoons extra-virgin olive oil

4 bell peppers (red, yellow, and/or green), stemmed, seeded, and cut into 1½-inch pieces

1 onion, chopped

2 jalapeño chiles, stemmed, seeded, and minced

Salt and pepper

3 garlic cloves, minced

1 tablespoon tomato paste

2 teaspoons grated orange zest

1 teaspoon ground fennel

½ cup dry white wine

1 (14.5-ounce) can diced tomatoes

¾ cup chicken broth

1 tablespoon minced fresh oregano

Why This Recipe Works In Greece, *spetsofai* is a classic dish of savory sausages braised with wine and peppers. A traditional Greek pork sausage with fennel and orange called *loukaniko* is often used in it. For our version, we started by searing whole loukaniko to create flavorful browning. We then sautéed a colorful assortment of sweet bell peppers, spicy jalapeños, and bold onion. For our aromatics, we quickly cooked garlic, tomato paste, grated orange zest, and ground fennel to bring out their flavors before adding the tomatoes, white wine, and chicken broth. We cut our sausages into pieces and added them to the skillet. Once the sausages were completely cooked and the flavors were beginning to meld, we uncovered the skillet and let the peppers finish cooking through while also reducing our sauce, concentrating its flavor. A final sprinkle of fresh oregano rounded out this flavorful braise. Loukaniko sausage can be found in specialty markets; if you cannot find it, you can substitute hot or sweet Italian sausage.

1 Prick sausages with fork in several places. Heat 1 tablespoon oil in 12-inch nonstick skillet over medium-high heat until just smoking. Brown sausages well on all sides, about 8 minutes. Transfer sausages to cutting board, let cool slightly, then cut into quarters.

2 Heat remaining 1 tablespoon oil in now-empty skillet over medium heat until shimmering. Add bell peppers, onion, jalapeños, ½ teaspoon salt, and ½ teaspoon pepper and cook until peppers are beginning to soften, about 5 minutes. Stir in garlic, tomato paste, orange zest, and fennel and cook until fragrant, about 1 minute. Stir in wine, scraping up any browned bits.

3 Stir in tomatoes and their juice, broth, and sausages and any accumulated juices and bring to simmer. Cover, reduce heat to low, and simmer gently until sausages are cooked through, about 5 minutes.

4 Uncover, increase heat to medium, and cook until sauce has thickened slightly, about 10 minutes. Stir in oregano and season with salt and pepper to taste. Serve.

loukaniko

Loukaniko is a traditional Greek sausage typically made of pork and flavored with orange peel, fennel, and spices; it is not very spicy. It is most often found fresh and must be cooked before eating. Loukaniko can be bought in specialty markets; if you cannot find it, you can substitute hot or sweet Italian sausage.

STUFFED CABBAGE ROLLS

serves 4

1 head green cabbage (2 pounds), cored

1 tablespoon vegetable oil

1 onion, chopped fine

3 garlic cloves, minced

1 teaspoon ground ginger

½ teaspoon ground cinnamon

¼ teaspoon ground nutmeg

1 (28-ounce) can tomato sauce

¼ cup packed light brown sugar

3 tablespoons red wine vinegar

Salt and pepper

2 slices hearty white sandwich bread, torn into 1-inch pieces

½ cup milk

12 ounces 85 percent lean ground beef

12 ounces bratwurst, casings removed

Why This Recipe Works When done right, softened cabbage leaves filled with ground meat and simmered in a smooth tomato sauce flavored with warm spices, sugar, and vinegar are comfort food at its finest. Many times, however, blown-out rolls are filled with chewy, flavorless meat and bland rice swimming in a sugary sauce. For our cabbage rolls, canned tomato sauce had a smooth texture tasters liked and was thin enough to properly coat the rolls without becoming pasty. Sautéed onions and garlic provided a savory foundation, and ground ginger, cinnamon, and nutmeg added the requisite warm spice flavor to the sauce. Tasters preferred brown sugar to white for its more complex flavor, and red wine vinegar to white for its bite. We supplemented the beef filling with bratwurst, a mild German sausage, to boost the meaty flavor. A panade (paste) of milk and bread helped keep the filling soft and moist. If the baked cabbage rolls appear dry after the foil is removed, spoon some sauce over them.

1 Adjust oven rack to middle position and heat oven to 375 degrees. Place cabbage in large bowl, cover tightly with plastic wrap, and microwave until outer leaves are pliable and translucent, 3 to 6 minutes. Using tongs, carefully remove wilted outer leaves; set aside. Repeat until you have 15 to 17 large, intact leaves.

2 Heat oil in Dutch oven over medium-high heat until shimmering. Add onion and cook until golden, about 5 minutes. Add garlic, ginger, cinnamon, and nutmeg and cook until fragrant, about 30 seconds. Transfer half of onion mixture to small bowl and set aside. Off heat, add tomato sauce, sugar, vinegar, ½ teaspoon salt, and ¼ teaspoon pepper to pot with remaining onion mixture and stir until sugar dissolves. (Cooled sauce can be refrigerated for up to 24 hours.)

3 Pulse bread and milk in food processor until smooth paste forms, 8 to 10 pulses. Add beef, bratwurst, reserved onion mixture, ½ teaspoon salt, and ¼ teaspoon pepper and pulse until well combined, about 10 pulses.

4 Working with 1 cabbage leaf at a time, cut along both sides of rib at base of leaf to form narrow triangle; remove rib. Continue cutting up center of leaf about 1 inch above triangle, then slightly overlap cut ends of cabbage. Place 2 heaping tablespoons of meat mixture on each leaf about ½ inch from bottom of where cut ends overlap. Fold bottom of leaf over filling and fold in sides. Roll leaf tightly around filling. Repeat with remaining leaves and remaining filling. Arrange rolls seam side down in 13 by 9-inch baking dish. (Unbaked rolls can be refrigerated for up to 24 hours.)

5 Pour sauce over rolls, cover dish tightly with aluminum foil, and bake until sauce is bubbling and rolls are heated through, about 45 minutes. Remove foil and bake until sauce is slightly thickened and cabbage is tender, about 15 minutes. Serve.

keeping cabbage rolls intact

1 Remove thick rib from base of cabbage leaves by cutting along both sides of rib to form narrow triangle. Continue cutting up center about 1 inch above triangle.

2 Overlap cut ends of cabbage to prevent any filling from spilling out.

3 Place 2 tablespoons of filling ½ inch from bottom of leaf where cut ends overlap. Fold bottom of leaf over filling and fold in sides. Roll leaf tightly around filling to create tidy roll.

PORK RAGU

serves 8

2 (2¼- to 2½-pound) racks baby back ribs, trimmed and each rack cut into quarters

2 teaspoons ground fennel

Kosher salt and pepper

3 tablespoons olive oil

1 large onion, chopped fine

1 large fennel bulb, stalks discarded, bulb halved, cored, and chopped fine

2 large carrots, peeled and chopped fine

¼ cup minced fresh sage

1½ teaspoons minced fresh rosemary

1 cup plus 2 tablespoons dry red wine

1 (28-ounce) can whole peeled tomatoes, drained and crushed coarse

3 cups chicken broth

1 garlic head, outer papery skins removed and top quarter of head cut off and discarded

Why This Recipe Works Ragu can be made from any meat or combination of meats, but the earthiness of a pure pork ragu is undeniably attractive—and great comfort food. Most recipes for traditional pork ragu use pork shoulder and a hard-to-find, bony cut like neck, shank, or feet to give the sauce great body. We were determined to use just one: Quick-cooking pork sausage or lean pork loin were parched after braising. We needed a collagen-rich cut of pork, which would have deep flavor and a melting texture after long cooking—and the bones included. Baby back ribs fit the bill perfectly. We tried using all baby back ribs and found the resulting ragu rich and meaty with perfect silkiness. For a classic Italian flavor profile, fennel took the place of celery in the ragu's base and ground fennel rubbed into the ribs echoed the anise flavor. Simmering the garlic head whole right in the sauce yielded sweeter softened cloves that we squeezed back into the sauce when tender. With fresh herbs and red wine, our ragu tasted balanced and far more complex than its simple preparation would suggest. This recipe makes enough sauce to coat 2 pounds of pasta. Serve with grated Parmesan cheese.

1 Adjust oven rack to middle position and heat oven to 300 degrees. Sprinkle ribs with ground fennel and generously season with salt and pepper, pressing on spices to adhere. Heat oil in Dutch oven over medium-high heat until just smoking. Add half of ribs, meat side down, and cook, without moving them, until meat is well browned, 6 to 8 minutes; transfer to plate. Repeat with remaining ribs; set aside.

2 Reduce heat to medium and add onion, fennel, carrots, 2 tablespoons sage, rosemary, and ½ teaspoon salt to now-empty pot. Cook, stirring occasionally and scraping up any browned bits, until vegetables are well browned and beginning to stick to pot bottom, 12 to 15 minutes.

3 Add 1 cup wine and cook until evaporated, about 5 minutes. Stir in tomatoes and broth and bring to simmer. Submerge garlic and ribs, meat side down, in liquid; add any accumulated juices from plate. Cover and transfer to oven. Cook until ribs are fork-tender, about 2 hours.

4 Remove pot from oven and transfer ribs and garlic to rimmed baking sheet. Using large spoon, skim any fat from surface of sauce. Once cool enough to handle, shred meat from bones; discard bones and gristle. Return meat to pot. Squeeze garlic from its skin into pot. Stir in remaining 2 tablespoons sage and remaining 2 tablespoons wine. Season with salt and pepper to taste.

POULTRY

Chicken Vesuvio

178 **Coq au Vin**

180 **Chicken Provençal**
with Saffron, Orange, and Basil

182 **Chicken with 40 Cloves of Garlic**

185 **Chicken Cacciatore**

186 **Chicken Paprikash**

189 **Filipino Chicken Adobo**

191 **Quick Chicken Fricassee**

192 **Chicken Florentine**

195 **Chicken Scarpariello**

196 **Chicken Vesuvio**

198 **Mahogany Chicken Thighs**

200 **Chicken with Pumpkin Seed Sauce**

202 **Chicken in a Pot with Red Potatoes, Carrots, and Shallots**

204 **Chicken Bouillabaisse**

207 **Spanish Braised Chicken with Sherry and Saffron (Pollo en Pepitoria)**

209 **Lemon-Braised Chicken Thighs with Chickpeas and Fennel**

210 **Chicken Curry**
with Sweet Potato and Cauliflower

212 **Chicken Tagine with Olives and Lemon**

214 **Southern-Style Smothered Chicken**

216 **Braised Chicken Thighs with Chard and Mustard**
Braised Chicken Thighs with Spinach and Garlic

219 **Brunswick Stew**

220 **Chicken Stew**

223 **Cajun Chicken, Sausage, and Corn Stew**

224 **Ethiopian-Style Spicy Chicken Stew (Doro Wat)**

226 **Chicken and Dumplings**

229 **White Chicken Chili**

230 **Indoor Pulled Chicken**

232 **Turkey Breast en Cocotte with Pan Gravy**
Turkey Breast en Cocotte with Mole Sauce
Turkey Breast en Cocotte with Orange-Chipotle Sauce

COQ AU VIN

serves 4

6 ounces thick-cut bacon
(about 5 slices), chopped

Vegetable oil

4 pounds bone-in, skin-on chicken
pieces (split breasts cut in half,
drumsticks, and/or thighs)

Salt and pepper

2 cups frozen pearl onions

10 ounces white mushrooms,
trimmed and quartered

2 garlic cloves, minced

1 tablespoon tomato paste

3 tablespoons all-purpose flour

1 (750-milliliter) bottle
medium-bodied red wine

2½ cups chicken broth

1 teaspoon minced fresh thyme
leaves or ¼ teaspoon dried

2 bay leaves

2 tablespoons unsalted butter,
cut into 2 pieces, chilled

2 tablespoons minced fresh parsley

Why This Recipe Works Coq au vin—the luscious wine- and pork-enhanced French chicken braise—is supposed to be a rustic dish, but conventional recipes take upwards of 3 hours to prepare. So why should it take so much effort? We wanted to create a dish with tender, juicy chicken infused with the flavors of red wine, onions, mushrooms, and bacon in less than 2 hours. We leave it to the cook to choose what chicken parts to use; if using a mix of dark and white meat chicken, we started the dark before the white, so that all the meat finished cooking at the same time and nothing was overcooked or undercooked. To thicken the stewing liquid, we sprinkled flour over the sautéed vegetables and whisked in butter toward the end of cooking. Chicken broth added a savory note to the sauce and an entire bottle of red wine provided a great base of flavor. Tomato paste was a fuss-free way to add extra depth and body to the sauce, while a sprinkling of crisp, salty bacon rounded out the acidity of the wine. This combination of wise ingredient choices and cooking procedures resulted in coq au vin with all of the homey richness and little of the fuss. Use a medium-bodied red wine, such as Pinot Noir, Côtes du Rhône, or Zinfandel, for this recipe.

1 Cook bacon in Dutch oven over medium heat until crispy, 5 to 7 minutes. Using slotted spoon, transfer bacon to paper towel–lined plate. (You should have about 2 tablespoons bacon fat in pot; if not, supplement with vegetable oil.) Set bacon aside.

2 Pat chicken dry with paper towels and season with salt and pepper. Return pot to medium-high heat and heat fat until shimmering. Brown half of chicken, 5 to 8 minutes per side, reducing heat if pan begins to scorch. Transfer chicken to large plate, leaving fat in pot. Return pot to medium-high heat and repeat with remaining chicken; transfer chicken to plate.

3 Pour off all but 1 tablespoon fat from pot (or add vegetable oil if needed to make this amount). Add onions and mushrooms and cook over medium heat, stirring occasionally, until lightly browned, about 10 minutes. Stir in garlic and tomato paste and cook until fragrant, about 30 seconds. Stir in flour and cook for 1 minute. Stir in wine, broth, thyme, and bay leaves, scraping up any browned bits.

4 Nestle chicken, along with any accumulated juices, into pot and bring to simmer. Cover pot, reduce heat to medium-low, and simmer until chicken is tender and breasts register 160 degrees, about 20 minutes, and/or thighs and drumsticks register 175, about 1 hour. (If using both types of chicken, simmer thighs and drumsticks for 40 minutes before adding breasts.)

5 Transfer chicken to serving dish and tent with aluminum foil. Using wide spoon, skim as much fat as possible from surface and return to simmer until sauce is thickened and measures about 2 cups, about 20 minutes. Off heat, remove bay leaves, whisk in butter, and season with salt and pepper to taste. Pour sauce over chicken, sprinkle with parsley and reserved bacon, and serve.

CHICKEN PROVENÇAL

serves 4

8 (5- to 7-ounce) bone-in chicken thighs, trimmed

Salt

1 tablespoon extra-virgin olive oil

1 small onion, chopped fine

6 garlic cloves, minced

1 anchovy fillet, rinsed and minced

⅛ teaspoon cayenne pepper

1 cup dry white wine

1 (14.5-ounce) can diced tomatoes, drained

1 cup chicken broth

2½ tablespoons tomato paste

1½ tablespoons chopped fresh thyme

1 teaspoon chopped fresh oregano

1 teaspoon herbes de Provence (optional)

1 bay leaf

1½ teaspoons grated lemon zest

½ cup pitted niçoise olives

1 tablespoon chopped fresh parsley

Why This Recipe Works Chicken Provençal represents the best of historical rustic peasant food, now enjoyed by the masses. Bone-in chicken is traditionally simmered all day in a tomatoey, garlicky herb broth. But all too often, this formula results in dry, rubbery chicken, watery or overly thick sauce, and dulled or muddied flavors—and a whole lot of wasted time. We wanted to rejuvenate chicken Provençal. For the best flavor and most tender texture, we used bone-in chicken thighs. Skinless thighs stuck to the pan when we browned them, and skin-on thighs developed a flabby texture when braised later on. So we browned the thighs with the skin on (to develop rich flavor and leave browned bits in the pan) and then ditched the skins prior to the braising (to avoid flabby skin). We spooned off the excess fat left behind from browning the chicken, but kept enough to sauté our garlic and onion. Diced tomatoes, white wine, and chicken broth also went into the sauce. As for flavor enhancers, a small amount of niçoise olives added an essential brininess to the dish, and some minced anchovy made the sauce taste richer and fuller. We prefer niçoise olives here; the flavor of kalamatas and other types of brined or oil-cured olives is too potent.

1 Adjust oven rack to lower-middle position and heat oven to 300 degrees. Season chicken thighs with salt. Heat 1 teaspoon oil in Dutch oven over medium-high heat until shimmering. Add 4 thighs skin side down and cook without moving them until skin is well browned, about 5 minutes. Using tongs, flip chicken and brown on second side, about 5 minutes longer; transfer to large plate. Repeat with remaining 4 thighs and transfer to plate; set aside. Pour off all but 1 tablespoon fat from pot.

2 Add onion to pot and cook over medium heat, stirring occasionally, until browned, about 4 minutes. Add garlic, anchovy, and cayenne and cook, stirring constantly, until fragrant, about 1 minute. Add wine, scraping up any browned bits. Stir in tomatoes; broth; tomato paste; thyme; oregano; herbes de Provence, if using; and bay leaf. Remove and discard skin from chicken, then submerge chicken in liquid and add any accumulated chicken juices to pot. Increase heat to high, bring to simmer, and cover; transfer pot to oven. Cook until chicken registers 195 degrees, about 1¼ hours.

3 Using slotted spoon, transfer chicken to platter and tent with aluminum foil. Discard bay leaf. Set pot over high heat, stir in 1 teaspoon lemon zest, bring to boil, and cook, stirring occasionally, until slightly thickened and reduced to 2 cups, about 5 minutes. Stir in olives and cook until heated through, about 1 minute. Meanwhile, mix parsley and remaining ½ teaspoon lemon zest together. Spoon sauce over chicken, drizzle chicken with remaining 2 teaspoons oil, sprinkle with parsley mixture, and serve.

Chicken Provençal with Saffron, Orange, and Basil

Add ⅛ teaspoon saffron threads with wine in step 2. Substitute orange zest for lemon zest and 2 tablespoons chopped fresh basil for parsley.

CHICKEN WITH 40 CLOVES OF GARLIC

serves 4

3 large garlic heads, cloves separated and unpeeled

2 shallots, peeled and quartered lengthwise

5 teaspoons olive oil

Salt and pepper

2 sprigs fresh thyme

1 sprig fresh rosemary

1 bay leaf

4 pounds bone-in chicken pieces (2 split breasts cut in half crosswise, 2 drumsticks, and 2 thighs)

¾ cup dry vermouth or dry white wine

¾ cup chicken broth

2 tablespoons unsalted butter, cut into 2 pieces and chilled

Why This Recipe Works Perhaps an arbitrary number of cloves, the 40 in this French dish are iconic; while the chicken braises, the generous cloves become appealingly soft and spreadable. But their flavor is often spiritless. Another offense: The chicken is tender, but the breast meat dries out and tastes wan. We wanted to revisit this classic dish to make it faster and better, so it would boast well-browned, full-flavored chicken, sweet and nutty garlic, and a savory sauce. Using chicken pieces rather than a whole bird ensured that the meat cooked evenly—and quickly. We roasted the garlic cloves first to caramelize them and develop their flavor and then added them to the braising liquid with the chicken. Finishing the braised chicken under the broiler made the skin crispy. Some shallots and herbs added flavor to the sauce, and several roasted garlic cloves, smashed into a paste, thickened and flavored the sauce. If using a kosher chicken, skip the brining process and begin with step 2. Avoid heads of garlic that have begun to sprout (the green shoots will make the sauce taste bitter). Tie the rosemary and thyme sprigs together with kitchen twine so they will be easy to retrieve from the pan. Serve the dish with slices of crusty baguette; you can spread them with the roasted garlic cloves.

1 Adjust oven rack to middle position and heat oven to 400 degrees. Toss garlic and shallots with 2 teaspoons oil, ¼ teaspoon salt, and ¼ teaspoon pepper in pie plate; cover tightly with aluminum foil and roast until softened and beginning to brown, about 30 minutes, shaking pie plate once after 15 minutes to toss contents (foil can be left on during tossing). Uncover, stir, and continue to roast, uncovered, until garlic is browned and fully tender, about 10 minutes longer, stirring halfway through roasting. Remove pie plate from oven and increase oven temperature to 450 degrees.

2 Using kitchen twine, tie together thyme sprigs, rosemary sprig, and bay leaf; set aside.

3 Season chicken with salt and pepper. Heat remaining 1 tablespoon oil in 12-inch ovensafe skillet over medium-high heat until just smoking. Add chicken skin side down and cook until well browned, 5 to 8 minutes, reducing heat if pan begins to scorch. Using tongs, flip chicken and lightly brown second side, about 3 minutes; transfer to large plate. Pour off fat from skillet. Off heat, add vermouth, broth, and herb bundle to now-empty skillet, scraping up any browned bits. Place skillet over medium heat, add garlic mixture, then nestle chicken skin side up on top of and between garlic cloves.

4 Transfer skillet to oven and cook chicken until breasts register 160 degrees and drumsticks/thighs register 175 degrees, 10 to 12 minutes. If desired, heat broiler element and broil chicken to crisp skin, 3 to 5 minutes.

5 Remove skillet from oven (skillet handle will be hot) and transfer chicken to platter. Using slotted spoon, remove 10 to 12 garlic cloves and set aside. Transfer remaining garlic cloves and shallots to platter with chicken. Discard herb bundle. Place reserved garlic cloves in fine-mesh strainer set over bowl. Using rubber spatula, push garlic cloves through strainer; discard skins. Add garlic paste to sauce in skillet and bring to simmer, whisking occasionally to incorporate garlic. Season with salt and pepper to taste. Off heat, whisk in butter. Serve chicken, passing sauce separately.

CHICKEN CACCIATORE

serves 4 to 6

4 pounds bone-in chicken pieces
(2 split breasts cut in half crosswise,
2 drumsticks, and 2 thighs)

Salt and pepper

2 tablespoons extra-virgin olive oil

1 onion, chopped

1 carrot, peeled and chopped

1 celery rib, chopped

2 garlic cloves, minced

1½ teaspoons minced fresh rosemary

½ cup dry white wine

½ cup chicken broth

1 (14.5-ounce) can diced tomatoes,
drained

1 tablespoon minced fresh parsley

Why This Recipe Works In Italy, anything cooked *alla cacciatora* is cooked "the hunter's way." Hunters would braise their fresh-killed game simply, until supertender and enveloped in a savory sauce. Given the dish's throw-together nature, there isn't one recipe. What is always standard: The meat (typically rabbit or poultry) is first sautéed and then cooked slowly with a selection of vegetables, which are often foraged. Many know only of the Italian American version, which features chicken in a thick marinara-like sauce. We wanted something you'd find in central Italy, with a sauce that is just substantial enough to cling to the chicken. Tomatoes were in, as we liked their sweetness and acidity, and our wine of choice was white for its lighter profile. To keep this mix from being too harsh we cut it with chicken broth, which buffered the presence of the wine and rounded the savory flavors. The flavors of garlic and rosemary complemented the poultry. For even cooking, we sautéed the chicken on the stove and then transferred it to the oven to finish cooking through gently. As the chicken rested, we reduced the infused broth to form a flavorful sauce.

1 Adjust oven rack to middle position and heat oven to 325 degrees. Pat chicken dry with paper towels and season with salt and pepper. Heat oil in Dutch oven over medium-high heat until just smoking. Brown half of chicken on all sides, 8 to 10 minutes; transfer to plate. Repeat with remaining chicken; transfer to plate.

2 Add onion, carrot, and celery to fat left in pot and cook over medium heat until softened and lightly browned, 6 to 8 minutes. Stir in garlic and rosemary and cook until fragrant, about 30 seconds. Stir in wine, scraping up any browned bits, and cook until almost completely evaporated, about 2 minutes. Stir in broth and tomatoes and bring to simmer.

3 Return chicken to pot along with any accumulated juices and cover; transfer pot to oven. Cook until breasts register 160 degrees and drumsticks/thighs register 175 degrees, 35 to 40 minutes, turning chicken halfway through cooking.

4 Remove pot from oven. Transfer chicken to serving dish and tent with aluminum foil. Bring sauce to simmer over medium-high heat and cook until reduced to about 2 cups, 5 to 8 minutes. Season with salt and pepper to taste. Spoon sauce over chicken and sprinkle with parsley. Serve.

CHICKEN PAPRIKASH

serves 4

8 (5- to 7-ounce) bone-in chicken thighs, trimmed

Salt and pepper

1 teaspoon vegetable oil

1 large onion, halved and sliced thin

1 large red bell pepper, stemmed, seeded, halved widthwise, and cut into ¼-inch-wide strips

1 large green bell pepper, stemmed, seeded, halved widthwise, and cut into ¼-inch-wide strips

3½ tablespoons paprika

1 tablespoon all-purpose flour

¼ teaspoon dried marjoram

½ cup dry white wine

1 (14.5-ounce) can diced tomatoes, drained

⅓ cup sour cream

2 tablespoons chopped fresh parsley

Why This Recipe Works Of Hungarian origin, chicken paprikash should be an easy-to-make braise with succulent chicken; a balance of heat, spice, and aromatics; and a rich, flavorful sauce with paprika taking center stage. Our goal was to pare down the usual mile-long ingredient list. First we had to pick our paprika from the many different varieties. We found that Hungarian sweet paprika was the best. (Other sweet paprikas can deliver good results, but don't use hot paprika in this dish.) For bold flavor, we added the paprika to our recipe twice: once while sautéing the vegetables to let its flavor bloom and then once again when adding sour cream to finish the dish with a bold hit. Adding sour cream directly to the pot caused it to curdle, so we found it essential to temper the sour cream by stirring a few tablespoons of the hot liquid from the stew pot together with the sour cream in a small bowl and then adding the warmed mixture to the pot. Removing the skin after browning the chicken prevented the accumulation of excess fat and a greasy sauce.

1 Adjust oven rack to lower-middle position and heat oven to 300 degrees. Season both sides of chicken thighs with salt and pepper. Heat oil in Dutch oven over medium-high heat until shimmering. Add 4 thighs skin side down and cook without moving them until skin is well browned, about 5 minutes. Using tongs, flip chicken and brown on second side, about 5 minutes longer; transfer to large plate. Repeat with remaining 4 thighs and transfer to plate; set aside. Pour off all but 1 tablespoon fat from pot.

2 Add onion to pot and cook, stirring occasionally, over medium heat until softened, 5 to 7 minutes. Add bell peppers and cook, stirring occasionally, until onion is browned and peppers are softened, about 3 minutes. Stir in 3 tablespoons paprika, flour, and marjoram and cook, stirring constantly, until fragrant, about 1 minute. Add wine, scraping up browned bits. Stir in tomatoes and 1 teaspoon salt. Remove and discard skin from chicken, then submerge chicken in vegetables and add any accumulated chicken juices. Bring to a simmer, then cover tightly with lid; transfer pot to oven. Cook until chicken registers 175 degrees, about 30 minutes.

3 Combine sour cream and remaining 1½ teaspoons paprika in small bowl. Transfer chicken to individual plates. Stir a few tablespoons of hot sauce into sour cream to temper, then stir mixture back into sauce in pot. Spoon sauce and peppers over chicken, sprinkle with parsley, and serve immediately.

FILIPINO CHICKEN ADOBO

serves 4

8 (5- to 7-ounce) bone-in chicken thighs, trimmed

⅓ cup soy sauce

1 (13.5-ounce) can coconut milk

¾ cup cider vinegar

8 garlic cloves, peeled

4 bay leaves

2 teaspoons pepper

1 scallion, sliced thin

Why This Recipe Works Many braised chicken recipes rely on lots of ingredients and prep—mincing garlic, chopping onions, and slicing myriad vegetables. With chicken adobo, the national dish of the Philippines, the approach is quite different. The ingredient list is very short and nothing—other than the chicken—requires prep time. This formula works because the key ingredients that go into this braise—soy sauce, vinegar, garlic, bay leaves, and black pepper—are each so potent. The end result is a pantry-friendly braise with bold, tangy flavors. Keeping the skin on our bone-in chicken breasts allowed us to crisp it into a craggy crust that the sauce could grab onto. A brief marinade in soy sauce tenderized and flavored the meat. We also added a can of coconut milk; the thick, rich milk mellowed the sharp saltiness of the traditional vinegar and soy sauce braising liquid—and it added body to the sauce. To render the gummy fat layer in the chicken skin and crisp its surface, we started the meat in a room-temperature nonstick skillet and then turned up the heat, allowing the fat to melt before the exterior burned. We started the browned chicken pieces skin side down in the braising liquid and then, to preserve as much crispness as possible in the finished dish, we turned the chicken pieces skin side up, giving the skin a chance to dry out a little before serving.

1 Toss chicken thighs with soy sauce in large bowl. Refrigerate for at least 30 minutes or up to 1 hour.

2 Remove chicken from soy sauce, allowing excess to drip back into bowl. Transfer chicken skin side down to 12-inch nonstick skillet; set aside soy sauce.

3 Place skillet over medium-high heat and cook until chicken skin is browned, 7 to 10 minutes. While chicken is browning, whisk coconut milk, vinegar, garlic, bay leaves, and pepper into soy sauce.

4 Transfer chicken to plate and pour off fat from skillet. Return chicken to skillet skin side down, add coconut milk mixture, and bring to boil. Reduce heat to medium-low and simmer, uncovered, for 20 minutes. Flip chicken skin side up and continue to cook, uncovered, until chicken registers 175 degrees, about 15 minutes. Transfer chicken to platter and tent with aluminum foil.

5 Remove bay leaves and skim any fat from surface of sauce. Return skillet to medium-high heat and cook until sauce is thickened, 5 to 7 minutes. Pour sauce over chicken, sprinkle with scallion, and serve.

QUICK CHICKEN FRICASSEE

serves 4 to 6

2 pounds boneless, skinless chicken breasts and/or thighs, trimmed

Salt and pepper

1 tablespoon unsalted butter

1 tablespoon olive oil

1 pound cremini mushrooms, trimmed and sliced ¼ inch thick

1 onion, chopped fine

¼ cup dry white wine

1 tablespoon all-purpose flour

1 garlic clove, minced

1½ cups chicken broth

⅓ cup sour cream

1 large egg yolk

2 teaspoons lemon juice

2 teaspoons minced fresh tarragon

½ teaspoon ground nutmeg

Why This Recipe Works Chicken fricassee is a classic French braise that has a lot going for it: tender chicken with clean flavor, earthy mushrooms and onions, and rich cream sauce. But the dish is time-consuming and many recipes taste heavy and bland. In search of a streamlined week-night-friendly chicken fricassee with a brighter, more complex sauce, we replaced the bone-in chicken parts with boneless, skinless breasts and thighs. Boneless chicken breasts aren't commonly found in braises, but we knew that with just 5 to 10 minutes of gentle simmering in liquid after browning, the lean meat would be much more impervious to over-cooking than it would be with simple searing in a dry pan. Then we found two ways to reintroduce the richness we'd lost by omitting the skin and bones: We browned the meat in a combination of butter (for extra browning) and oil (to tame the richness), and we browned the vegetables until they developed their own fond to serve as the base of the sauce. Increasing the amount of mushrooms boosted the fricassee's meaty flavor, while finishing the sauce with sour cream added missing body and pleasant tang. Finally, whisking an egg yolk into the sour cream thickened the sauce and made it incredibly silky. Two tablespoons of chopped fresh parsley leaves may be substituted for the tarragon.

1 Pat chicken dry with paper towels and sprinkle with 1 teaspoon salt and ½ teaspoon pepper. Heat butter and oil in 12-inch skillet over medium-high heat until butter is melted. Brown chicken well, about 4 minutes per side; transfer to large plate.

2 Add mushrooms, onion, and wine to now-empty skillet and cook, stirring occasionally, until liquid has evaporated and mushrooms are browned, 8 to 10 minutes. Add flour and garlic; cook, stirring constantly, for 1 minute. Add broth and bring mixture to boil, scraping up any browned bits. Add chicken, along with any accumulated juices, to skillet. Reduce heat to medium-low, cover, and simmer until breasts register 160 degrees and thighs register 175 degrees, 5 to 10 minutes.

3 Transfer chicken to clean platter and tent with aluminum foil. Whisk sour cream and egg yolk together in bowl. Whisking constantly, slowly stir ½ cup heated sauce into sour cream mixture to temper. Stirring constantly, slowly pour sour cream mixture into simmering sauce. Stir in lemon juice, tarragon, and nutmeg; return to simmer. Season with salt and pepper to taste, pour sauce over chicken, and serve.

CHICKEN FLORENTINE

serves 4 to 6

2 tablespoons vegetable oil

12 ounces (12 cups) baby spinach

4 (6-ounce) boneless, skinless chicken breasts, trimmed

Salt and pepper

1 shallot, minced

2 garlic cloves, minced

1¼ cups chicken broth

1¼ cups water

1 cup heavy cream

6 tablespoons grated Parmesan cheese

1 teaspoon grated lemon zest plus 1 teaspoon juice

Why This Recipe Works Chicken Florentine is a buffet-line favorite featuring chicken breast and spinach in a mild cream-and-Parmesan sauce—sometimes stuffed inside, sometimes stacked on top. All of these components are good, but this dish can often be stodgy (think old-fashioned casserole) or fussy (involving dredging chicken in flour and sautéeing). We wanted a simplified recipe for an elegant dish with clearer, brighter flavors. Braising was the perfect technique to achieve this: For flavor, we seared the chicken breasts first, cooked aromatics and added our cooking liquid (a balanced mix of water and chicken broth enriched with a modest amount of cream), and then simmered the chicken in the reducing sauce until perfectly cooked. After we topped the tender chicken with some sautéed spinach and the cream sauce, it needed just a quick run under the broiler to become appealingly golden on top. We like tender, quick-cooking bagged baby spinach here; if using curly-leaf spinach, chop it before cooking.

1 Adjust oven rack to upper-middle position and heat broiler. Heat 1 tablespoon oil in 12-inch skillet over medium-high heat until shimmering. Add spinach and cook, stirring occasionally, until wilted, 1 to 2 minutes. Transfer spinach to colander set over bowl and press with spoon to release excess liquid; discard liquid.

2 Pat chicken breasts dry with paper towels and season with salt and pepper. Wipe out pan with paper towels and heat remaining 1 tablespoon oil over medium-high heat until just smoking. Cook chicken on both sides until golden, about 4 minutes. Add shallot and garlic to skillet and cook until fragrant, about 30 seconds. Stir in broth, water, and cream and bring to boil.

3 Reduce heat to medium-low and simmer until chicken is cooked through, about 10 minutes; transfer chicken to large plate and tent with aluminum foil. Continue to simmer sauce until reduced to 1 cup, about 10 minutes. Off heat, stir in ¼ cup Parmesan and lemon zest and juice.

4 Cut breasts crosswise into ½-inch-thick slices and arrange on broiler-safe platter. Scatter spinach over chicken and pour sauce over spinach. Sprinkle with remaining 2 tablespoons Parmesan and broil until golden brown, 3 to 5 minutes. Serve.

CHICKEN SCARPARIELLO

serves 4 to 6

3 pounds bone-in chicken pieces
(2 split breasts cut in half crosswise,
2 drumsticks, and 2 thighs), trimmed

Salt and pepper

1 tablespoon vegetable oil

8 ounces sweet Italian sausage,
casings removed

1 onion, halved and sliced thin

1 red bell pepper, stemmed, seeded,
and sliced thin

5 jarred hot cherry peppers, seeded,
rinsed, and sliced thin (½ cup),
plus 2 tablespoons brine

5 garlic cloves, minced

1 teaspoon dried oregano

1 tablespoon all-purpose flour

¾ cup chicken broth

2 tablespoons chopped fresh parsley

Why This Recipe Works Chicken scarpariello is an Italian American dish of browned chicken and sausage bathed in a spicy, garlicky sauce chock-full of bell peppers, onions, and pickled cherry peppers. When done right, it's a hearty weeknight supper with bold flavors. We wanted our version to be bright and punchy but balanced, not too briny and certainly not too spicy. We started by tempering the heat of the cherry peppers by removing their seeds. We wanted some extra flavor, so we added just a couple of tablespoons of the vinegary cherry pepper brine. After browning the sausage and chicken, we sautéed the vegetables and then nestled the chicken and sausage in the vegetables to finish cooking in the oven, which kept the chicken skin crispy. Three-quarters of a cup of chicken broth and a tablespoon of flour resulted in a sauce with the perfect consistency—thick enough to coat the chicken and sausage without being gloppy. We used sweet Italian sausage to balance the spiciness of the cherry peppers. For a spicier dish, substitute hot Italian sausage for sweet.

1 Adjust oven rack to middle position and heat oven to 350 degrees. Pat chicken dry with paper towels and season with salt and pepper. Heat oil in 12-inch skillet over medium-high heat until just smoking. Add chicken to skillet skin side down and cook without moving it until well browned, about 5 minutes. Flip chicken and continue to cook until browned on second side, about 3 minutes; transfer to plate.

2 Add sausage to fat left in skillet and cook, breaking up with spoon, until browned, about 3 minutes. Transfer sausage to paper towel–lined plate.

3 Pour off all but 1 tablespoon fat from skillet and return to medium-high heat. Add onion and bell pepper and cook until vegetables are softened and lightly browned, about 5 minutes. Add cherry peppers, garlic, and oregano and cook until fragrant, about 1 minute. Stir in flour and cook for 30 seconds. Add broth and cherry pepper brine and bring to simmer, scraping up any browned bits.

4 Remove skillet from heat and stir in sausage. Arrange chicken pieces, skin side up, in single layer in skillet and add any accumulated juices; transfer skillet to oven. Cook until breasts register 160 degrees and drumsticks/thighs register 175 degrees, 20 to 25 minutes.

5 Carefully remove skillet from oven. Transfer chicken to serving platter. Season onion mixture with salt and pepper to taste, then spoon over chicken. Sprinkle with parsley. Serve.

CHICKEN VESUVIO

serves 4

4 (6-ounce) boneless, skinless chicken breasts, trimmed

Salt and pepper

2 tablespoons olive oil

1½ pounds small red potatoes, unpeeled, halved

2 garlic cloves, minced

1 teaspoon minced fresh rosemary

½ teaspoon dried oregano

1½ cups chicken broth

½ cup white wine

1 cup frozen peas, thawed

2 tablespoons unsalted butter

2 teaspoons lemon juice

Why This Recipe Works The list of Chicago restaurants serving great chicken Vesuvio—chicken and potatoes napped in an assertive garlic sauce—is long, and everyone has a favorite. To enjoy this meal at home, we made it a one-skillet supper. Streamlining this dish meant starting with boneless, skinless chicken breasts. After browning the chicken in a skillet, we set it aside and added potatoes. Since we had broken a few traditions already, we went with baby red potatoes instead of the standard russets, because the waxy, firm potatoes would maintain their shape and texture during cooking. We added the spuds to the skillet cut side down and built the sauce around them as they browned. Garlic, oregano, and white wine reflected the dish's Italian American roots, fresh rosemary gave our sauce its assertive herbal flavor, and chicken broth added a meaty boost. While the potatoes finished browning, we returned the chicken to the skillet to continue cooking in the simmering sauce. Once the chicken and potatoes were cooked, we finished the sauce with some butter, a squeeze of lemon, and peas. We prefer to use small red potatoes measuring 1 to 1½ inches in diameter. If you can't find small red potatoes, you can substitute larger red potatoes that have been quartered. For a spicier dish, stir in ¼ teaspoon red pepper flakes with the garlic in step 2.

1 Pat chicken breasts dry with paper towels and season with salt and pepper. Heat 1 tablespoon oil in 12-inch nonstick skillet over medium-high heat until just smoking. Brown chicken well, about 4 minutes per side; transfer to plate.

2 Add remaining 1 tablespoon oil to skillet and heat until shimmering. Add potatoes, cut side down, and cook until golden brown, about 7 minutes. Stir in garlic, rosemary, oregano, and ½ teaspoon salt and cook until fragrant, about 30 seconds. Add broth and wine, scraping up any browned bits, and bring to boil. Return chicken to skillet on top of potatoes. Reduce heat to medium-low and simmer, covered, until potatoes are tender and chicken registers 160 degrees, about 12 minutes. Using slotted spoon, transfer chicken and potatoes to serving platter and tent with aluminum foil.

3 Increase heat to medium-high and cook, uncovered, until sauce is reduced to 1 cup, about 5 minutes. Stir in peas and cook until heated through, about 1 minute. Off heat, whisk in butter and lemon juice and season with salt and pepper to taste. Pour sauce over chicken and potatoes and serve.

MAHOGANY CHICKEN THIGHS

serves 4 to 6

1½ cups water

1 cup soy sauce

¼ cup dry sherry

2 tablespoons sugar

2 tablespoons molasses

1 tablespoon distilled white vinegar

8 (5- to 7-ounce) bone-in chicken thighs, trimmed

1 (2-inch) piece ginger, peeled, halved, and smashed

6 garlic cloves, peeled and smashed

1 tablespoon cornstarch

Why This Recipe Works Braising is an ideal cooking method for chicken thighs; it does an excellent job of rendering sneaky pockets of fat and producing luxurious, flavorful meat. But there is one drawback: While we often achieve crisp skin on our braised dishes, we were missing the cracklingly crisp skin of great roasted chicken. For this dish, we wanted the best of both worlds. We took a hybrid approach: Braise for tenderness and then broil for crispy skin. We oven-braised the thighs in a flavor-infusing combination of soy sauce, sherry, white vinegar, a big piece of smashed ginger, smashed garlic, and sugar and molasses for sweetness (both would also caramelize and boost the mahogany hue). After braising for an hour, the fat was fully rendered, and although the meat was overcooked according to our usual standards, the melted connective tissue had converted to gelatin, which resulted in meat that was supple and juicy. Turning the chicken skin side up halfway through braising allowed the rendered skin to dry before broiling, which helped it crisp a little more. For a simple, streamlined finish, we used a portion of the braising liquid to make a quick sauce (thickened with a little cornstarch for body). For best results, trim all visible fat and skin from the underside of the thighs.

1 Adjust oven rack to middle position and heat oven to 300 degrees. Whisk 1 cup water, soy sauce, sherry, sugar, molasses, and vinegar in 12-inch ovensafe skillet until sugar is dissolved. Arrange chicken thighs skin side down in soy mixture and nestle ginger and garlic between thighs.

2 Bring soy sauce mixture to simmer over medium heat and simmer for 5 minutes. Transfer skillet to oven and cook, uncovered, for 30 minutes.

3 Flip chicken skin side up and continue to cook, uncovered, until chicken registers 195 degrees, 20 to 30 minutes longer. Transfer chicken to platter, taking care not to tear skin. Pour cooking liquid through fine-mesh strainer into fat separator and let settle for 5 minutes. Heat broiler.

4 Whisk cornstarch and remaining ½ cup water together in bowl. Pour 1 cup defatted cooking liquid into now-empty skillet and bring to simmer over medium heat. Whisk cornstarch mixture into cooking liquid and simmer until thickened, about 1 minute. Pour sauce into bowl and set aside.

5 Return chicken skin side up to now-empty skillet and broil until well browned, about 4 minutes. Return chicken to platter and let rest for 5 minutes. Serve, passing reserved sauce separately.

CHICKEN WITH PUMPKIN SEED SAUCE

serves 4

⅓ cup pepitas

¼ cup sesame seeds

2 tablespoons vegetable oil

1 onion, chopped fine

Salt and pepper

1 jalapeño chile, stemmed, seeded, and chopped

3 garlic cloves, minced

1 teaspoon minced fresh thyme or ¼ teaspoon dried

6 ounces tomatillos, husks and stems removed, rinsed well, dried, and chopped

1½ cups chicken broth

4 (6- to 8-ounce) boneless, skinless chicken breasts, trimmed

1 cup fresh cilantro leaves

1 tablespoon lime juice

Pinch sugar

Why This Recipe Works *Pipian verde* is a traditional Pueblan sauce made with tangy, fresh tomatillos and nutty toasted seeds that can be served with just about any protein. We particularly like how it dramatically boosted the flavor of plain chicken breasts. The beauty of this recipe is that we could braise the chicken right in the sauce ingredients; this ensured moist, flavorful meat and a streamlined dish that didn't use the multiple pans, hours of time, and synchronized cooking often required for dishes featuring complex Mexican sauces. Our first move was to toast sesame seeds and pumpkin seeds (we chose pepitas over unhulled pumpkin seeds, which made a smoother sauce) in a skillet, which we then used to build our sauce. Onion, garlic, and thyme gave the sauce an aromatic base, while a fresh jalapeño provided lively spice. We chopped the tomatillos so they would soften nicely in the allotted amount of time. Once the chicken was done, we pureed the sauce in the blender; lime juice, cilantro, and a pinch of sugar added at this point gave the sauce just the right brightness and rounded out the flavors. We spooned the vibrant sauce over our moist, flavorful chicken and sprinkled it with more seeds to serve.

1 Toast pepitas and sesame seeds in 12-inch nonstick skillet over medium heat until seeds are golden and fragrant, about 15 minutes; transfer to bowl. Reserve 1 tablespoon seeds for garnish.

2 Add oil, onion, and ½ teaspoon salt to now-empty skillet and cook over medium-high heat until softened, 5 to 7 minutes. Stir in jalapeño, garlic, and thyme and cook until fragrant, about 30 seconds. Stir in tomatillos, broth, and toasted seeds; cover; and cook until tomatillos begin to soften, about 10 minutes.

3 Season chicken breasts with salt and pepper, then nestle into mixture in skillet. Cover, reduce heat to medium-low, and cook until chicken registers 160 degrees, 10 to 15 minutes, flipping chicken halfway through cooking. Transfer chicken to platter, tent with aluminum foil, and let rest for 5 to 10 minutes.

4 Carefully transfer mixture left in skillet to blender. Add cilantro, lime juice, and sugar to blender and process until mostly smooth, about 1 minute. Season with salt and pepper to taste. Spoon some of sauce over chicken and sprinkle with reserved seeds. Serve with remaining sauce.

toasting seeds

Toast pepitas and sesame seeds in dry 12-inch nonstick skillet over medium heat until seeds are golden and fragrant, about 15 minutes.

CHICKEN IN A POT WITH RED POTATOES, CARROTS, AND SHALLOTS

serves 4

1 (3½- to 4-pound) whole chicken, giblets discarded

Salt and pepper

1 tablespoon vegetable oil

1½ pounds red potatoes, unpeeled, cut into 1-inch pieces

1 pound carrots, peeled and cut into 1-inch pieces

4 shallots, peeled and halved

3 garlic cloves, minced

1 teaspoon minced fresh thyme or ¼ teaspoon dried

½ cup dry white wine

½ cup chicken broth, plus extra as needed

1 bay leaf

2 tablespoons unsalted butter

1 tablespoon lemon juice

1 tablespoon minced fresh parsley

Why This Recipe Works It sounded simple: Add root vegetables to classic *poulet en cocotte*, where a whole chicken cooks in a covered pot, yielding unbelievably tender meat and a sauce of the chicken's own concentrated juices. We gave it a try, but after an hour of baking, the vegetables were still underdone. Including jus-weakening liquid is a faux pas in classic recipes, yet we forged ahead, adding chicken broth and wine for acidity and mild sweetness. Now we had tender vegetables, but the jus had lost its intensity. To recover the flavor, we browned the chicken to build fond, which deepened the jus, and we sautéed our potatoes, carrots, and shallots. With some browning on our bird, we were reluctant to put on the lid, and we had to wonder: Was this step still critical? The increased amount of liquid in the Dutch oven's confined space meant that uncovered roasting might intensify the sauce without evaporating too much while also bathing our vegetables in flavor. As it turned out, the domino effect we'd started by adding vegetables paid off, and we were left with succulent meat, crisped skin, and superflavorful vegetables—not to mention an incredible sauce.

1 Adjust oven rack to lower-middle position and heat oven to 350 degrees. Pat chicken dry with paper towels, tuck wingtips behind back, and season with salt and pepper.

2 Heat oil in Dutch oven over medium-high heat until just smoking. Add chicken breast side down and cook until lightly browned, about 5 minutes. Carefully flip chicken breast side up and cook until back is well browned, 6 to 8 minutes; transfer to large plate.

3 Pour off all but 1 tablespoon fat from pot. Add potatoes, carrots, shallots, and ½ teaspoon salt and cook over medium heat until vegetables are just beginning to brown, 5 to 7 minutes. Stir in garlic and thyme and cook until fragrant, about 30 seconds. Stir in wine, broth, and bay leaf, scraping up any browned bits.

4 Off heat, return chicken, breast side up, and any accumulated juices to pot, placing chicken on top of vegetables. Transfer pot to oven and cook, uncovered, until breast registers 160 degrees and thighs register 175 degrees, 55 minutes to 1 hour 5 minutes. Remove pot from oven. Transfer chicken to carving board and let rest for 20 minutes.

5 Using slotted spoon, transfer vegetables to platter and tent with aluminum foil to keep warm. Discard bay leaf. Pour liquid left in pot into fat separator and let settle for 5 minutes. (You should have ¾ cup defatted liquid; if not, add extra broth as needed to equal ¾ cup.) Return defatted liquid to now-empty pot and simmer until it measures ½ cup, 5 to 7 minutes.

6 Off heat, whisk in butter and lemon juice and season with salt and pepper to taste. Sprinkle vegetables with parsley, carve chicken, and serve with sauce.

CHICKEN BOUILLABAISSE

serves 4 to 6

3 pounds bone-in chicken pieces (split breasts cut in half, drumsticks, and/or thighs), trimmed

Salt and pepper

2 tablespoons extra-virgin olive oil

1 large leek, white and light green parts only, halved lengthwise, sliced thin, and washed thoroughly

1 small fennel bulb, stalks discarded, bulb halved, cored, and sliced thin

4 garlic cloves, minced

1 tablespoon tomato paste

1 tablespoon all-purpose flour

¼ teaspoon saffron threads, crumbled

¼ teaspoon cayenne pepper

3 cups chicken broth

1 (14.5-ounce) can diced tomatoes, drained

12 ounces Yukon Gold potatoes, unpeeled, cut into ¾-inch pieces

½ cup dry white wine

¼ cup pastis or Pernod

1 (3-inch) strip orange zest

1 tablespoon chopped fresh tarragon or parsley

1 recipe Rouille (recipe follows)

Why This Recipe Works Bouillabaisse is a traditional French stew bursting with flavors used in Provençal cooking: tomatoes, fennel, saffron, garlic, and orange. A dollop of thick, creamy rouille finishes the light stew with a hit of richness. Bouillabaisse is usually made with numerous varieties of seafood, but in this update, we swapped in readily available bone-in chicken pieces. To adapt the recipe to accommodate chicken, we substituted chicken broth for fish stock for the braising base and added flour and tomato paste to the saffron and cayenne before adding the broth to give the sauce extra body that was more appropriate with chicken. Pouring in the pastis—an anise liquor that enhances the flavor of the fennel—earlier than usual gave the alcohol time to cook off to avoid harshness. For the oven braise, we rested the chicken on the potatoes so the skin stayed out of the liquid and was crisp. To brighten the traditional saffron rouille for our chicken bouillabaisse recipe, we added lemon juice and Dijon mustard.

1 Adjust oven rack to middle position and heat oven to 375 degrees. Pat chicken dry with paper towels and season with salt and pepper. Heat oil in Dutch oven over medium-high heat until just smoking. Brown chicken well, 5 to 8 minutes per side; transfer to plate.

2 Add leek and fennel to fat left in pot and cook, stirring often, until beginning to soften, about 4 minutes. Stir in garlic, tomato paste, flour, saffron, and cayenne and cook until fragrant, about 30 seconds. Slowly whisk in broth, scraping up any browned bits and smoothing out any lumps. Stir in tomatoes, potatoes, wine, pastis, and orange zest. Bring to simmer and cook for 10 minutes.

3 Nestle chicken thighs and drumsticks into pot with skin above surface of liquid. Cook, uncovered, for 5 minutes. Nestle breast pieces into pot, adjusting pieces to ensure that skin stays above surface of liquid. Transfer pot to oven and cook, uncovered, until breasts register 145 degrees and/or thighs/drumsticks register 160 degrees, 10 to 20 minutes.

4 Remove pot from oven and heat broiler. Return pot to oven and broil until chicken skin is crisp and breasts register 160 degrees and/or thighs/drumsticks register 175 degrees, 5 to 10 minutes. Discard orange zest. Skim excess fat from surface of stew, stir in tarragon, and season with salt and pepper to taste. Serve with rouille.

ROUILLE

makes about 1 cup

Rouille is a traditional accompaniment to bouillabaisse but
is also great with a variety of chicken and seafood soups and
stews. For an accurate measurement of boiling water, bring
a full kettle of water to a boil and then measure out the
desired amount. The egg yolk in this recipe is not cooked.
If you prefer, you can substitute 2 tablespoons Egg Beaters.

3 tablespoons boiling water
¼ teaspoon saffron threads, crumbled
1 (3-inch) piece baguette, crusts removed,
torn into 1-inch pieces (1 cup)
4 teaspoons lemon juice
1 large egg yolk
2 teaspoons Dijon mustard

2 garlic cloves, minced
¼ teaspoon cayenne pepper
½ cup vegetable oil
½ cup extra-virgin olive oil
Salt and pepper

Combine boiling water and saffron in bowl and let steep for
5 minutes. Stir bread pieces and lemon juice into saffron-
infused water and let soak for 5 minutes. Using whisk, mash
soaked bread mixture until uniform paste forms, 1 to 2 minutes. Whisk in egg yolk, mustard, garlic, and cayenne until
smooth, about 15 seconds. Whisking constantly, slowly drizzle
in vegetable oil until smooth mayonnaise-like consistency is
reached, scraping down bowl as necessary. Slowly whisk in
olive oil in steady stream until smooth. Season with salt and
pepper to taste.

SPANISH BRAISED CHICKEN WITH SHERRY AND SAFFRON (POLLO EN PEPITORIA)

serves 8

8 (5- to 7-ounce) bone-in chicken thighs, trimmed

Salt and pepper

1 tablespoon extra-virgin olive oil

1 onion, chopped fine

3 garlic cloves, minced

1 bay leaf

¼ teaspoon ground cinnamon

⅔ cup dry sherry

1 cup chicken broth

1 (14.5-ounce) can whole peeled tomatoes, drained and chopped fine

2 hard-cooked large eggs, yolks and whites separated, whites chopped fine

½ cup slivered almonds, toasted

Pinch saffron threads, crumbled

2 tablespoons chopped fresh parsley

1½ teaspoons lemon juice

Why This Recipe Works *Pollo en pepitoria* is a classic chicken dish from Spain's saffron-producing Castilla–La Mancha region, with a color to match, that has a sherry-based sauce thickened not with dulling cream or starch but with ground almonds and hard-cooked egg yolks. To balance the richness of the nuts and yolks in our version, we brightened the lush sauce with canned tomatoes and a little lemon juice. Adding some of the braising liquid to the nut mixture when we blended it to make the sauce helped it puree thoroughly but still retain a pleasantly coarse consistency. Chicken thighs are fully cooked when they reach 175 degrees, but we purposely overcooked them—and did it slowly— which allowed collagen in the meat to break down into gelatin, making the meat ultratender. We finished our dish with a sprinkle of chopped egg white left from the hard-cooked eggs. Any dry sherry, such as fino or Manzanilla, will work in this dish.

1 Adjust oven rack to middle position and heat oven to 300 degrees. Pat chicken thighs dry with paper towels and season with salt and pepper. Heat oil in 12-inch skillet over medium-high heat until just smoking. Brown chicken well, about 5 minutes per side; transfer to plate. Pour off all but 2 teaspoons fat from skillet.

2 Add onion and ¼ teaspoon salt to fat left in skillet and cook over medium heat until just softened, about 3 minutes. Stir in two-thirds of garlic, bay leaf, and cinnamon and cook until fragrant, about 1 minute. Stir in sherry and cook, scraping up any browned bits, until sherry starts to thicken, about 2 minutes. Stir in broth and tomatoes and bring to simmer. Nestle chicken into skillet and cover; transfer skillet to oven. Cook until chicken registers 195 degrees, 45 to 50 minutes.

3 Remove skillet from oven and carefully transfer chicken to serving platter, discard skin, and tent with aluminum foil.

4 Discard bay leaf. Transfer ¾ cup cooking liquid, egg yolks, almonds, saffron, and remaining garlic to blender. Process until smooth, about 2 minutes, scraping down sides of jar as needed. Return almond mixture to skillet along with 1 tablespoon parsley and lemon juice. Bring to simmer over medium heat and cook, whisking frequently, until sauce has thickened, 3 to 5 minutes. Season with salt and pepper to taste. Spoon sauce over chicken and sprinkle with remaining 1 tablespoon parsley and egg whites. Serve.

LEMON-BRAISED CHICKEN THIGHS WITH CHICKPEAS AND FENNEL

serves 4

2 (15-ounce) cans chickpeas, rinsed

6 (5- to 7-ounce) bone-in chicken thighs, trimmed

Salt and pepper

1 tablespoon olive oil

1 large fennel bulb, stalks discarded, bulb halved and cut into ½-inch-thick wedges through core

4 garlic cloves, minced

2 teaspoons grated lemon zest plus 1½ tablespoons juice

1 teaspoon ground coriander

½ teaspoon red pepper flakes

½ cup dry white wine

1 cup pitted large brine-cured green olives, halved

¾ cup chicken broth

1 tablespoon honey

2 tablespoons chopped fresh parsley

1 baguette, sliced

Why This Recipe Works This skillet meal-in-one is a great example of a dish that builds flavor in little time. We focused on building flavor fast: We first browned meaty bone-in chicken thighs to build a savory base. Next, we layered in aromatics like sweet fennel, garlic, lemon zest, and citrusy coriander for brightness and complexity. Chickpeas pulled double duty here: Whole chickpeas added heft to the dish, while mashed chickpeas helped thicken the sauce. To keep the chicken skin crispy, we nestled the browned chicken thighs on top of the aromatics and braised the mixture uncovered on the oven's upper-middle rack. Keeping the skillet uncovered allowed the sauce to reduce as the chicken braised, and placing the skillet on the upper rack took advantage of the reflected heat from the oven ceiling, ensuring crispy skin. Cooking the chicken to an internal temperature of 195 degrees rendered the fat and melted the tough connective tissues into rich gelatin. We prefer briny green olives like Manzanilla, Picholine, or Cerignola in this recipe; look for them in your grocery store's salad bar section or in the pickle aisle.

1 Adjust oven rack to upper-middle position and heat oven to 350 degrees. Place ½ cup chickpeas in bowl and mash to coarse puree with potato masher; set aside. Pat chicken thighs dry with paper towels and season with salt and pepper.

2 Heat oil in ovensafe 12-inch skillet over medium-high heat until just smoking. Add chicken skin side down and cook until skin is crisped and well browned, 8 to 10 minutes. Transfer chicken to plate skin side up.

3 Pour off all but 2 tablespoons fat from skillet, then heat fat left in skillet over medium heat until shimmering. Add fennel, cut side down, and sprinkle with ¼ teaspoon salt. Cook, covered, until lightly browned, 3 to 5 minutes per side. Add garlic, lemon zest, coriander, and pepper flakes and cook, uncovered, until fragrant, about 30 seconds. Stir in wine, scraping up any browned bits, and cook until almost evaporated, about 2 minutes.

4 Stir in olives, broth, honey, lemon juice, mashed chickpeas, and remaining whole chickpeas and bring to simmer. Nestle chicken into liquid, keeping skin above surface; transfer skillet to oven. Cook, uncovered, until fennel is tender and chicken registers 195 degrees, 35 to 40 minutes. Sprinkle with parsley and serve with baguette slices.

CHICKEN CURRY

serves 4 to 6

4 pounds bone-in chicken pieces (split breasts cut in half, drumsticks, and/or thighs), trimmed

Salt and pepper

2 tablespoons vegetable oil

2 tablespoons curry powder

1 teaspoon garam masala

2 onions, chopped fine

1 jalapeño chile, stemmed, seeded, and minced

6 garlic cloves, minced

1 tablespoon grated fresh ginger

1 tablespoon tomato paste

1 cup water

2 plum tomatoes, cored, seeded, and chopped fine

½ cup frozen peas

½ cup canned coconut milk

2 tablespoons unsalted butter

¼ cup minced fresh cilantro

Why This Recipe Works We wanted to serve up a bold curry that avoided the esoteric and relied on supermarket staples. Working with bone-in, skin-on chicken parts meant we could count on some flavorful renderings to enrich the curry sauce. After browning the meat in our Dutch oven, we softened chopped onion and bloomed curry powder and garam masala right in the juices for a complex base without much effort. Garlic, a minced jalapeño, fresh ginger, and tomato paste backed up that base for a superfragrant, richly spiced curry. Finishing off the curry sauce with canned coconut milk and butter added richness and body, while chopped tomatoes and frozen peas offered color and freshness, with convenience. This sauce was plenty thick, so we cooked it just enough to warm the vegetables before spooning it over the tender chicken. For a spicier curry, reserve, mince, and add the ribs and seeds from the jalapeño chile. We prefer the richer flavor of regular coconut milk here; however, light coconut milk can be substituted. Serve with Cilantro-Mint Chutney and/or Onion Relish (recipes follow).

1 Pat chicken dry with paper towels and season with salt and pepper. Heat 1 tablespoon oil in Dutch oven over medium-high heat until just smoking. Brown half of chicken, 3 to 5 minutes per side; transfer to large plate. Repeat with remaining 1 tablespoon oil and remaining chicken. Remove and discard skin from drumsticks and thighs, if using.

2 Pour off all but 2 tablespoons fat from pot. Reduce heat to medium, add curry powder and garam masala, and cook until fragrant, about 10 seconds. Add onions and ¼ teaspoon salt and cook until softened, 5 to 7 minutes. Add jalapeño, garlic, ginger, and tomato paste and cook until fragrant, about 30 seconds. Add water, scraping up any browned bits. Nestle chicken and any juices into pot and bring to simmer.

3 Cover, reduce heat to medium-low, and simmer until breasts register 160 degrees, about 20 minutes, and/or drumsticks/thighs register 175 degrees, about 1 hour, flipping chicken halfway through cooking. (If using both types of chicken, simmer thighs and drumsticks for 40 minutes before adding breasts.)

4 Transfer chicken to platter, tent with aluminum foil, and let rest while finishing sauce. Using wide spoon, skim as much fat as possible from surface of braising liquid.

5 Add tomatoes, peas, coconut milk, and butter to pot and continue to simmer until butter is melted and vegetables are heated through, 1 to 2 minutes. Off heat, stir in cilantro and season with salt and pepper to taste. Spoon sauce over chicken and serve.

Chicken Curry with Sweet Potato and Cauliflower

Omit tomatoes and peas. Add 1 sweet potato, peeled and cut into 1-inch chunks, to pot during last 20 minutes of cooking in step 3 (with breast pieces, if using). Stir ½ head cauliflower, cored and cut into 1-inch florets, into pot with coconut milk in step 5; cover and simmer until cauliflower is tender, 10 to 12 minutes.

CILANTRO-MINT CHUTNEY
makes about 1 cup

2 cups fresh cilantro leaves
1 cup fresh mint leaves
⅓ cup plain whole-milk yogurt
¼ cup finely chopped onion
1 tablespoon lime juice
1½ teaspoons sugar
½ teaspoon ground cumin
¼ teaspoon salt

Process all ingredients in food processor until smooth, about 20 seconds, scraping down sides of bowl halfway through processing. (Chutney can be refrigerated for up to 24 hours.)

ONION RELISH
makes about 1 cup
If using a yellow onion instead of a Vidalia, increase the sugar to 1 teaspoon.

1 Vidalia onion, chopped fine
1 tablespoon lime juice
½ teaspoon paprika
½ teaspoon sugar
⅛ teaspoon salt
Pinch cayenne pepper

Combine all ingredients in bowl. (Relish can be refrigerated for up to 24 hours.)

CHICKEN TAGINE WITH OLIVES AND LEMON

serves 4

1¼ teaspoons paprika

½ teaspoon ground cumin

½ teaspoon ground ginger

¼ teaspoon cayenne pepper

¼ teaspoon ground coriander

¼ teaspoon ground cinnamon

3 (2-inch) strips lemon zest
plus 3 tablespoons juice

5 garlic cloves, minced

4 pounds bone-in, skin-on chicken
pieces, trimmed

Salt and pepper

1 tablespoon olive oil

1 large onion, halved and sliced
¼ inch thick

1¾ cups chicken broth

1 tablespoon honey

2 carrots, peeled and cut crosswise
into ½-inch-thick rounds, very large
pieces cut into half-moons

2 cups pitted Greek green olives, halved

2 tablespoons chopped fresh cilantro

Why This Recipe Works We love the way the liberal warm spices, sweetness, and tart brininess of a tagine enliven workaday chicken, so we set to develop a chicken tagine with depth of flavor—in about an hour. We followed our standard for braised chicken recipes: We browned the skin-on chicken pieces to give the braising liquid deep flavor, removed the chicken from the pot and sautéed the aromatics (onion, garlic, and lemon zest strips) along with a blend of spices (paprika, cumin, cayenne, ginger, coriander, and cinnamon), and added chicken broth for braising and honey for sweetness. With the flavorful base built, we returned the chicken to the pot, starting the longer-cooking thighs and drumsticks before the breasts. Along with green olives, we finished and brightened the dish with a mixture of minced lemon zest strips and garlic, lemon juice, and fresh cilantro. For best results, use four chicken thighs and two chicken breasts, each breast split in half; the dark meat contributes valuable flavor to the broth and should not be omitted. Make sure to trim any white pith from the zest, as it can impart bitter flavor. If the olives are particularly salty, give them a rinse.

1 Combine paprika, cumin, ginger, cayenne, coriander, and cinnamon in small bowl; set aside. Mince 1 lemon zest strip and combine with 1 teaspoon garlic; mince together until reduced to fine paste and set aside.

2 Season chicken with salt and pepper. Heat oil in Dutch oven over medium-high heat until just smoking. Add chicken, skin side down, and cook until well browned, about 5 minutes. Using tongs, flip chicken and brown second side, about 4 minutes longer; transfer to large plate. When cool enough to handle, discard skin. Pour off all but 1 tablespoon fat from pot.

3 Add onion and remaining 2 lemon zest strips to pot and cook, stirring occasionally, until onion slices have browned at edges but still retain their shape, 5 to 7 minutes (add 1 tablespoon water as needed if pot begins to scorch). Add remaining garlic and cook, stirring frequently, until

fragrant, about 30 seconds. Add reserved spice mixture and cook, stirring constantly, until darkened and very fragrant, 45 seconds to 1 minute. Stir in broth and honey, scraping up any browned bits. Add drumsticks and thighs, reduce heat to medium, and simmer for 5 minutes.

4 Add carrots to pot, then arrange breast pieces in single layer on top of carrots. Cover, reduce heat to medium-low, and simmer until breast pieces register 160 degrees and drumsticks/thighs register 175 degrees, 10 to 15 minutes.

5 Transfer chicken to plate and tent with aluminum foil. Add olives to pot; increase heat to medium-high and simmer until liquid has thickened slightly and carrots are tender, 4 to 6 minutes. Return chicken to pot and stir in cilantro, lemon juice, and reserved garlic mixture. Season with salt and pepper to taste, and serve.

SOUTHERN-STYLE SMOTHERED CHICKEN

serves 4

3 pounds bone-in chicken pieces
(split breasts cut in half crosswise,
drumsticks, and/or thighs), trimmed

Salt and pepper

½ cup plus 2 tablespoons
all-purpose flour

¼ cup vegetable oil

2 onions, chopped fine

2 celery ribs, chopped fine

3 garlic cloves, minced

1 teaspoon dried sage leaves

2 cups chicken broth

1 tablespoon cider vinegar

2 tablespoons minced fresh parsley

Why This Recipe Works As chicken is relatively mild, chicken dishes often taste like whatever else is in the dish rather than the chicken itself. But smothered chicken is designed to coax out as much chicken flavor as possible and then bolster it with supporting—not distracting— ingredients. After browning floured chicken pieces, we sautéed a simple mix of onions and celery, plus some garlic and dried sage, in the chicken fat to provide a clean, savory base that enhanced, rather than challenged, the rich flavor of chicken. We found that we needed just 2 tablespoons of flour to thicken the gravy to a rich—but not stodgy—consistency. A splash of cider vinegar brightened and clarified the sauce so the chicken's flavor would shine. You can substitute ¼ teaspoon ground sage for the dried sage leaves.

1 Pat chicken dry with paper towels and season with salt and pepper. Spread ½ cup flour in shallow dish. Working with 1 piece at a time, dredge chicken in flour, shaking off excess, and transfer to plate.

2 Heat oil in Dutch oven over medium-high heat. Add half of chicken to pot skin side down and cook until deep golden brown, 4 to 6 minutes per side; transfer to plate. Repeat with remaining chicken, adjusting heat if flour begins to burn.

3 Pour off all but 2 tablespoons fat and return pot to medium heat. Add onions, celery, 1 teaspoon salt, and ½ teaspoon pepper and cook until softened, 6 to 8 minutes. Stir in garlic, sage, and remaining 2 tablespoons flour and cook until vegetables are well coated with flour and garlic is fragrant, about 1 minute. Whisk in broth, scraping up any browned bits.

4 Nestle chicken into sauce, along with any accumulated juices from plate, and bring to boil. Reduce heat to low, cover, and simmer until breasts register 160 degrees and drumsticks/thighs register 175 degrees, 30 to 40 minutes.

5 Transfer chicken to serving dish. Stir vinegar into sauce and season with salt and pepper to taste. Pour sauce over chicken, sprinkle with parsley, and serve.

BRAISED CHICKEN THIGHS WITH CHARD AND MUSTARD

serves 4

8 (6-ounce) bone-in chicken thighs, trimmed

Salt and pepper

1 tablespoon extra-virgin olive oil

1 pound Swiss chard, stems chopped fine, leaves sliced thin

1 onion, chopped fine

6 garlic cloves, minced

1 tablespoon minced fresh thyme or 2 teaspoons dried

1 anchovy fillet, rinsed and minced

2 tablespoons all-purpose flour

1½ cups chicken broth

½ cup dry white wine

2 bay leaves

1 teaspoon grated lemon zest

1 tablespoon whole-grain mustard

Why This Recipe Works Hearty and rustic, braised bone-in chicken thighs become juicy and tender after a long braise in a covered pot and lend their rich flavor to the surrounding sauce. The only question is what to do about the skin: Browning it brings rich flavor, but it would still become flabby after a long simmer, and we weren't excited to eat flabby skin. So, after searing skin-on thighs to develop lots of flavorful fond, we discarded the skin. Then we built our braise with bold ingredients: sturdy chard for earthiness and heft; garlic, thyme, and an umami-packed anchovy fillet for flavor; lemon zest for brightness; and bay leaves for subtle aromatic depth. Cooking the chicken thighs for a full hour (to 195 degrees rather than the standard 175) allowed the collagen to melt almost completely into rich gelatin, adding body and depth to the sauce. At the end, a dollop of mustard added sharp contrast to the sauce's richness. We like to use green or white Swiss chard here; if using red chard, note that the sauce will take on a reddish hue.

1 Adjust oven rack to lower-middle position and heat oven to 300 degrees. Pat chicken thighs dry with paper towels and season with salt and pepper. Heat oil in Dutch oven over medium-high heat until just smoking. Add 4 thighs and brown on both sides, 7 to 10 minutes; transfer to plate. Repeat with remaining 4 thighs. When chicken is cool enough to handle, remove and discard skin.

2 Pour off all but 2 tablespoons fat left in pot and heat over medium-high heat until shimmering. Add chard stems and onion and cook until softened and lightly browned, 5 to 7 minutes. Stir in garlic, thyme, and anchovy and cook until fragrant, about 30 seconds. Stir in flour and cook for 30 seconds. Whisk in broth and wine, scraping up any browned bits and smoothing out any lumps.

3 Add bay leaves and chicken along with any accumulated juices, bring to simmer, and cover; transfer pot to oven. Cook until chicken is very tender, almost falling off bone, and registers 195 degrees, about 1 hour.

4 Remove pot from oven. Transfer chicken to platter, tent with aluminum foil, and let rest while finishing sauce. Let liquid in pot settle for 5 minutes, then use wide spoon to skim any fat from surface. Stir in chard leaves and lemon zest, bring to simmer, and cook until sauce is thickened, about 10 minutes.

5 Off heat, discard bay leaves, stir in mustard, and season with salt and pepper to taste. Pour sauce over chicken and serve.

Braised Chicken Thighs with Spinach and Garlic

Omit chard and mustard. Add 10 ounces chopped curly-leaf spinach and 2 additional minced garlic cloves to pot with lemon zest in step 4.

BRUNSWICK STEW

serves 4 to 6

1 tablespoon vegetable oil

1 onion, chopped fine

¾ cup ketchup

4 cups water

2 pounds boneless, skinless chicken thighs, trimmed

1 pound russet potatoes, peeled and cut into ½-inch chunks

8 ounces kielbasa sausage, sliced ¼ inch thick

6–8 tablespoons cider vinegar

2 tablespoons Worcestershire sauce

1 tablespoon yellow mustard

1 teaspoon garlic powder

Salt and pepper

¼ teaspoon red pepper flakes

1 cup canned crushed tomatoes

½ cup frozen lima beans

½ cup frozen corn

Why This Recipe Works There's one thing about rich, tomato-based Brunswick stew that's for certain: It's of Southern origin, found simmering near the smoking pits at barbecues. The consensus ends there. Everything else—the type of meat (rabbit, squirrel, chicken, pork, or some combination thereof) the vegetables (okra or no okra, the variety of beans, and corn), and the specific origin (does the honor go to Brunswick, Georgia, or Brunswick County, Virginia?)—is up for grabs. Because there is no definitive Brunswick stew, many cooks use it as a kitchen sink dump-all, and it becomes bogged down by too many additions. Our aim was to make a simple yet complexly flavored version. To start, we built our stew around a homemade barbecue sauce; browning the ketchup we were adding to the sauce caramelized its sugars and gave it depth. Lean chicken breasts dried out, but chicken thighs, which contain more collagen, yielded more-tender meat. Adding kielbasa sausage gave our stew its smokiness, and staggering the addition of a streamlined list of vegetables—potatoes (for bulk and stew-thickening starch) and then tomatoes and frozen lima beans and corn (for ease of preparation and cooking)—to the pot ensured that all the vegetables finished cooking at the same time. Our favorite kielbasa is Wellshire Farms Smoked Polska Kielbasa.

1 Heat oil in Dutch oven over medium-high heat until shimmering. Add onion and cook until softened, 3 to 5 minutes. Add ketchup and ¼ cup water and cook, stirring frequently, until fond begins to form on bottom of pot and mixture has thickened, about 6 minutes.

2 Add chicken thighs, potatoes, kielbasa, 6 tablespoons vinegar, 1½ tablespoons Worcestershire, mustard, garlic powder, 1 teaspoon salt, 1 teaspoon pepper, pepper flakes, and remaining 3¾ cups water and bring to boil. Reduce heat to low, cover, and simmer until potatoes are tender, 30 to 35 minutes, stirring frequently.

3 Transfer chicken to plate and let cool for 5 minutes; using 2 forks, shred chicken into bite-size pieces. While chicken cools, stir tomatoes, lima beans, and corn into stew and continue to simmer, uncovered, for 15 minutes. Stir in shredded chicken and remaining 1½ teaspoons Worcestershire and cook until warmed through, about 2 minutes. Season with salt, pepper, and remaining vinegar (up to 2 tablespoons) to taste. Serve.

CHICKEN STEW

serves 6 to 8

2 pounds boneless, skinless chicken thighs, halved crosswise and trimmed

Kosher salt and pepper

3 slices bacon, chopped

1 pound chicken wings, cut at joints

1 onion, chopped fine

1 celery rib, minced

2 garlic cloves, minced

2 teaspoons anchovy paste

1 teaspoon minced fresh thyme

5 cups chicken broth

1 cup dry white wine, plus extra for seasoning

1 tablespoon soy sauce

3 tablespoons unsalted butter, cut into 3 pieces

⅓ cup all-purpose flour

1 pound small red potatoes, unpeeled, quartered

4 carrots, peeled and cut into ½-inch pieces

2 tablespoons chopped fresh parsley

Why This Recipe Works Beef stew is an American supper standard. So why not chicken stew? Recipes that do exist are either too fussy or too fancy, or seem more soup than stew—too thin and wan to qualify as the latter. We wanted a rich recipe for chicken stew that could stand up to its beef brethren—one with succulent bites of chicken, tender vegetables, and a truly robust gravy. To do this, we looked to two different chicken parts: We seared and simmered wings to provide rich chicken flavor and plenty of thickening gelatin, and then we gently simmered bite-size pieces of boneless chicken thighs for tender bites throughout the stew. Some bacon, crisped in the pot before we browned the wings in the rendered fat, added pork flavor and a hint of smoke. Soy sauce and anchovy paste may sound like strange additions to an all-American chicken stew, but they added meatiness, without making the stew taste salty or fishy. Finally, we took full advantage of the concentrating effect of reduction by cooking down wine, broth, and aromatics at the start and simmering the stew uncovered during its stay in the oven.

1 Adjust oven rack to lower-middle position and heat oven to 325 degrees. Arrange chicken thighs on baking sheet and lightly season both sides with salt and pepper; cover with plastic wrap and set aside.

2 Cook bacon in Dutch oven over medium-low heat, stirring occasionally, until fat is rendered and bacon is browned, 6 to 8 minutes. Using slotted spoon, transfer bacon to bowl. Add chicken wings to pot, increase heat to medium, and cook until well browned on both sides, 10 to 12 minutes; transfer wings to bowl with bacon.

3 Add onion, celery, garlic, anchovy paste, and thyme to fat left in pot; cook, stirring occasionally, until dark fond forms on bottom of pot, 2 to 4 minutes. Increase heat to high; stir in 1 cup broth, wine, and soy sauce, scraping up any browned bits; and bring to boil. Cook, stirring occasionally, until liquid evaporates and vegetables begin to sizzle, 12 to 15 minutes.

Add butter and stir to melt; sprinkle flour over vegetables and stir to combine. Gradually whisk in remaining 4 cups broth until smooth. Stir in potatoes, carrots, and wings and bacon; bring to simmer. Transfer to oven and cook, uncovered, for 30 minutes, stirring once halfway through cooking.

4 Remove pot from oven. Use wooden spoon to draw gravy up sides of pot and scrape browned fond into stew. Place over high heat, add thighs, and bring to simmer. Return pot to oven, uncovered, and continue to cook, stirring occasionally, until fork slips easily in and out of chicken and vegetables are tender, about 45 minutes longer.

5 Discard wings and season stew with up to 2 tablespoons extra wine. Season with salt and pepper to taste, sprinkle with parsley, and serve.

CAJUN CHICKEN, SAUSAGE, AND CORN STEW

serves 6 to 8

6 ears corn, husks and silk removed

3 pounds bone-in, skin-on chicken thighs, trimmed

Salt and pepper

2 tablespoons vegetable oil

1 pound kielbasa sausage, sliced ¼ inch thick

2 red bell peppers, stemmed, seeded, and cut into ½-inch pieces

2 onions, minced

2 celery ribs, minced

¼ teaspoon cayenne pepper

4 garlic cloves, minced

1 teaspoon minced fresh thyme leaves, or ¼ teaspoon dried

3½ cups chicken broth

2 bay leaves

¼ cup minced fresh cilantro leaves

Hot sauce

Why This Recipe Works Louisiana's Cajun-style cooking is rustic and satisfying, and we thought it ideal for a spicy, chunky chicken stew. We pictured a highly seasoned, heady stew with chicken, sausage, fresh corn, and the classic Cajun trio of green peppers, onions, and celery. We were concerned, however, that the sausage's flavor might overshadow the more subtle-tasting chicken and corn. Andouille sausage is commonly used in Cajun cooking, but its intense dry-spice flavor dominated the stew as predicted, and we couldn't taste the chicken. Kielbasa lent a similar meatiness and a hint of smokiness to the stew, but ensured that it maintained its identity as a chicken stew. Six ears of corn provided bites of corn in each spoonful. To extract as much corn flavor as possible from all those cobs, after removing the kernels, we scraped the cobs with the back of a butter knife to release the corn milk and pulp. As an added bonus, the starch from the corn helped thicken the stew. A final sprinkling of fresh cilantro and a few dashes of hot sauce countered the dish's richness, bringing our Cajun-style stew into balance.

1 Adjust oven rack to lower-middle position and heat oven to 300 degrees. Working with 1 ear of corn at a time, stand corn on end inside large bowl. Use paring knife to cut kernels off cob. Using back of butter knife, scrape any remaining pulp off cob and into bowl. Discard cobs.

2 Pat chicken thighs dry with paper towels and season with salt and pepper. Heat 1 tablespoon oil in Dutch oven over medium-high heat until just smoking. Add half of chicken and brown on both sides, 5 to 8 minutes, reducing heat if pot begins to scorch. Transfer chicken to bowl. Repeat with remaining 1 tablespoon oil and remaining chicken; transfer to bowl. When chicken is cool enough to handle, remove and discard skin.

3 Pour off all but 1 tablespoon of fat left in pot. Add kielbasa and cook over medium heat until it begins to brown, about 2 minutes. Stir in bell peppers, onions, celery, cayenne, and ¼ teaspoon salt and cook until vegetables are softened, 8 to 10 minutes. Stir in garlic and thyme and cook until fragrant, about 30 seconds. Stir in corn, scraping up any browned bits. Stir in broth and bring to simmer.

4 Add chicken along with any accumulated juices and bay leaves, bring to simmer, and cover pot; transfer pot to oven. Cook until chicken registers 195 degrees, about 1¼ hours.

5 Remove pot from oven, transfer chicken to cutting board, and remove bay leaves. Using 2 forks, shred chicken into bite-size pieces; discard bones.

6 If sauce is too thin, continue to simmer stew over medium-high heat as needed to thicken. Off heat, stir in shredded chicken, cover, and let stand for 5 minutes. Stir in cilantro and season with salt, pepper, and hot sauce to taste before serving.

ETHIOPIAN-STYLE SPICY CHICKEN STEW (DORO WAT)

serves 4

4 pounds bone-in, skin-on chicken pieces (split breasts cut in half, drumsticks, and/or thighs)

Salt and pepper

2 tablespoons vegetable oil

1 onion, chopped fine

2 tablespoons tomato paste

3 garlic cloves, minced

1 tablespoon grated fresh ginger

1 tablespoon chili powder

½ teaspoon ground cardamom

½ teaspoon ground nutmeg

½ teaspoon ground fenugreek

3 tablespoons all-purpose flour

2 cups low-sodium chicken broth

2 cups dry red wine

1½ cups water

4 hard-cooked eggs

2 tablespoons unsalted butter, cut into 2 pieces and chilled

Why This Recipe Works Stews in Ethiopia are deeply flavored with warm spices and are traditionally served with injera, a type of flatbread that is made from teff and is used as a utensil to eat the stew. Our favorite is *doro wat*, a hearty chicken stew garnished with hard-cooked eggs. The meat is cooked in a cardamom, garlic, ginger, and cinnamon-spiced butter called *niter kibbeh* and seasoned with *berbere*, a spice blend typically consisting of hot red chiles, paprika, cloves, nutmeg, fenugreek, and cumin. These require extra steps, however, so we wanted to trim the fussy components. The method for doro wat is not unlike a chicken stew from any other country: brown the chicken, sauté the aromatics, then add liquid and cook. It's just the seasonings and garnishes that differ. A combination of chicken broth and wine is more modern than just water but it gave the stew nice acidity and depth. We found that cooking the spices along with the aromatics—onion, ginger, and garlic—heightened their flavors. Cooking tomato paste (another modern addition) with the aromatics promoted the dark color of the stew and added another layer of flavor. A spiced butter seemed superfluous in the highly seasoned stew, but finishing the dish with plain butter gave it a rich lift. Fenugreek, a slightly bitter herb, can be found in the spice aisle of well-stocked supermarkets and specialty markets. Serve with the Ethiopian flatbread injera if you can find it. The stew can alternatively be served with white rice or noodles.

1 Pat chicken dry with paper towels and season with salt and pepper. Heat oil in Dutch oven over medium-high heat until just smoking. Brown half of chicken, 5 to 8 minutes per side, reducing heat if pan begins to scorch. Transfer chicken to plate, leaving fat in pot. Return pot with fat to medium-high heat and repeat with remaining chicken; transfer chicken to plate.

2 Pour off all but 1 tablespoon fat left in pot. Add onion and cook over medium heat, stirring occasionally, until softened, 5 to 7 minutes. Stir in tomato paste, garlic, ginger, chili powder, cardamom, nutmeg, and fenugreek and cook until fragrant, about 30 seconds. Stir in flour and cook for 1 minute. Stir in broth, wine, and water, scraping up any browned bits.

3 Nestle chicken, along with any accumulated juices, into pot and bring to simmer. Cover, turn heat to medium-low, and simmer until chicken is fully cooked and tender, about 20 minutes for the breasts (160 degrees on an instant-read thermometer) or 1 hour for the thighs and drumsticks. (If using both types of chicken, simmer thighs and drumsticks for 40 minutes before adding breasts.)

4 Transfer chicken to serving dish, tent loosely with foil, and let rest while finishing sauce. Skim as much fat as possible off surface of sauce and return to simmer until sauce is thickened and measures about 3 cups, about 20 minutes. Stir in eggs and cook until warmed through, about 1 minute. Off heat, stir in butter and season with salt and pepper to taste. Pour sauce over chicken.

CHICKEN AND DUMPLINGS

serves 6 to 8

Stew

2½ pounds bone-in chicken thighs, trimmed

Salt and pepper

2 teaspoons vegetable oil

2 small onions, chopped fine

2 carrots, peeled and cut into ¾-inch pieces

1 celery rib, chopped fine

¼ cup dry sherry

1 pound chicken wings

6 cups chicken broth

1 teaspoon minced fresh thyme

¼ cup minced fresh parsley

Dumplings

2 cups (10 ounces) all-purpose flour

1 teaspoon sugar

1 teaspoon salt

½ teaspoon baking soda

¾ cup buttermilk, chilled

4 tablespoons unsalted butter, melted and hot

1 large egg white

Why This Recipe Works The best chicken and dumplings boast dumplings as airy as drop biscuits in a broth full of clean, concentrated chicken flavor. We found that browning chicken thighs and then adding store-bought chicken broth produced the most flavorful stew base. To give our broth body, we added chicken wings to the pot—they readily gave up their collagen, providing the stew with a velvety consistency. For a light but sturdy dumpling recipe with good flavor, we came up with a formula that employed buttermilk for flavor and swapped in baking soda for baking powder. Wrapping the lid of the Dutch oven in a dish towel prevented moisture from saturating our light-as-air dumplings. We strongly recommend buttermilk for the dumplings, but it's acceptable to substitute ½ cup plain yogurt thinned with ¼ cup milk. If you want to include white meat (and don't mind losing a bit of flavor in the process), replace two chicken thighs with two 8-ounce boneless, skinless chicken breasts; brown the chicken breasts along with the thighs and remove them from the stew once they register 160 degrees, 20 to 30 minutes. Since the wings yield only about 1 cup of meat, using their meat is optional.

1 For the stew Pat chicken thighs dry with paper towels and season with salt and pepper. Heat oil in Dutch oven over medium-high heat until shimmering. Brown chicken well, about 5 minutes per side; transfer to plate.

2 Pour off all but 1 teaspoon fat from pot and add onions, carrots, and celery. Cook vegetables, stirring often, until well browned, 7 to 9 minutes. Stir in sherry, scraping up any browned bits; add chicken wings, broth, thyme, and chicken thighs along with any accumulated juices. Bring to simmer and cover pot. Cook until fork slips easily in and out of chicken thighs but chicken still clings to bones, 45 to 55 minutes.

3 Remove pot from heat. Transfer chicken to cutting board. Using 2 forks, shred chicken into 1-inch pieces; discard skin and bones. Let liquid settle for about 5 minutes, then use wide spoon to skim fat from surface. Stir shredded chicken into pot.

4 For the dumplings Whisk flour, sugar, salt, and baking soda together in large bowl. Stir chilled buttermilk and melted butter together in second large bowl until butter forms small clumps, then whisk in egg white. Stir buttermilk mixture into flour mixture with rubber spatula until just incorporated.

5 Return stew to simmer over medium-low heat, stir in parsley, and season with salt and pepper to taste. Using greased 1-tablespoon measure or #60 scoop, scoop level amount of dumpling batter over top of stew, spacing about ¼ inch apart (about 24 dumplings). Wrap lid of Dutch oven with clean dish towel (keep towel away from heat source), and cover pot. Simmer gently until dumplings have doubled in size and toothpick inserted into center comes out clean, 13 to 16 minutes. Serve.

making chicken and dumplings

1 After adding shredded meat, return stew to simmer and then portion dumplings over top. If stew is not simmering, dumplings may break apart and not cook through evenly.

2 Wrap lid of Dutch oven with clean dish towel and simmer gently until dumplings are cooked through. Towel will prevent condensation from making dumplings soggy.

WHITE CHICKEN CHILI

serves 6 to 8

3 pounds bone-in split chicken breasts, trimmed

Salt and pepper

1 tablespoon vegetable oil, plus extra as needed

3 jalapeño chiles, stemmed

3 poblano chiles, stemmed, seeded, and cut into large pieces

3 Anaheim chiles, stemmed, seeded, and cut into large pieces

2 onions, cut into large pieces

6 garlic cloves, minced

1 tablespoon ground cumin

1½ teaspoons ground coriander

2 (15.5-ounce) cans cannellini beans, rinsed

3 cups chicken broth

¼ cup minced fresh cilantro

4 scallions, sliced thin

3 tablespoons lime juice (2 limes)

Why This Recipe Works A big pot of white chicken chili with all the fixings is a great change from typical, heavier beef-and-bean chilis. But it can often be, well, plain bland, which is probably why it hasn't achieved the same favored status. We found three solutions that make this chili just as worthy: To fix the often watery sauce, we pureed some of our sautéed chile-onion mixture and beans with the broth to thicken the base. To avoid floating bits of rubbery chicken, we browned, poached, and shredded bone-in, skin-on chicken breasts, which gave our chicken pieces a hearty texture and full flavor. And to solve the problem of insufficient chile flavor, we used a trio of fresh chiles: jalapeño, poblano, and Anaheim. The food processor kept most of this prep easy; we chopped the chiles with it and used it later for the pureeing. You can use chicken thighs for the chicken breasts in this recipe. If using thighs, increase the cooking time in step 4 to about 40 minutes. Serve with sour cream, tortilla chips, and lime wedges.

1 Season chicken breasts with 1 teaspoon salt and ¼ teaspoon pepper. Heat oil in Dutch oven over medium-high heat until just smoking. Add chicken skin side down and cook until golden brown, about 4 minutes. Using tongs, flip chicken and lightly brown second side, about 2 minutes; transfer to plate. When cool enough to handle, remove and discard skin.

2 Discard ribs and seeds from 2 jalapeños, then mince; set aside. Pulse half of poblanos, half of Anaheims, and half of onions in food processor until consistency of chunky salsa, 10 to 12 pulses, scraping down sides of bowl as needed. Transfer mixture to bowl. Repeat with remaining poblanos, Anaheims, and onions. Add mixture to bowl with first batch (do not clean processor bowl).

3 Pour off all but 1 tablespoon fat from pot (add extra oil as needed) and set heat to medium. Add garlic, cumin, coriander, minced jalapeños, chile mixture, and ¼ teaspoon salt. Cover and cook, stirring occasionally, until vegetables have softened, about 10 minutes. Remove pot from heat.

4 Transfer 1 cup cooked vegetable mixture to now-empty processor. Add 1 cup beans and 1 cup broth and process until smooth, about 20 seconds. Add vegetable-bean mixture, remaining 2 cups broth, and chicken to pot and bring to boil over medium-high heat. Reduce heat to medium-low and simmer, covered, stirring occasionally, until chicken registers 160 degrees, 15 to 20 minutes.

5 Transfer chicken to large plate. Stir in remaining beans and continue to simmer, uncovered, until beans are heated through and chili has thickened slightly, about 10 minutes.

6 Mince remaining 1 jalapeño, mincing and reserving ribs and seeds if desired, and set aside. When cool enough to handle, use 2 forks to shred chicken into bite-size pieces; discard bones. Stir cilantro, scallions, lime juice, chicken, remaining minced jalapeño, and ribs and seeds, if using, into chili and return to simmer. Season with salt and pepper to taste, and serve.

INDOOR PULLED CHICKEN

serves 6 to 8

1 cup chicken broth

2 tablespoons molasses

1 tablespoon sugar

1 tablespoon liquid smoke

1 teaspoon unflavored gelatin

Salt and pepper

2 pounds boneless, skinless chicken thighs, halved crosswise

1 recipe barbecue sauce (recipes follow)

Hot sauce

Why This Recipe Works Pulled chicken isn't just an outdoor project—and it doesn't have to be a huge event, taking a day's worth of time. Our Indoor Pulled Chicken mimics the texture and flavor of outdoor slow-smoked pulled chicken in just a fraction of the time. We started by braising boneless, skinless chicken thighs in a mixture of chicken broth, salt, sugar, molasses, gelatin, and liquid smoke, which simulated the flavor of traditional smoked chicken. The gelatin and broth helped mimic the unctuous texture and intense chicken flavor of whole chicken parts. To mimic the richness of skin-on chicken, we skipped trimming the fat from the thighs and added the rendered fat back to the finished pulled chicken. Finally, we mixed the shredded meat with some of the barbecue sauce and cooked it briefly to drive off excess moisture. Do not trim the fat from the chicken thighs. If you don't have 3 tablespoons of fat to add back to the pot in step 3, add melted butter to make up the difference. We like mild molasses in this recipe; do not use blackstrap. Serve the pulled chicken on white bread or hamburger buns with pickles and coleslaw.

1 Bring broth, molasses, sugar, 2 teaspoons liquid smoke, gelatin, and 1 teaspoon salt to boil in Dutch oven over high heat, stirring to dissolve sugar. Add chicken and return to simmer. Reduce heat to medium-low, cover, and cook, stirring occasionally, until chicken is easily shredded with fork, about 25 minutes.

2 Transfer chicken to medium bowl and set aside. Strain cooking liquid through fine-mesh strainer set over bowl (do not wash pot). Let liquid settle for 5 minutes; skim fat from surface. Set aside fat and defatted liquid.

3 Using tongs, squeeze chicken until shredded into bite-size pieces. Transfer chicken, 1 cup barbecue sauce, ½ cup reserved defatted liquid, 3 tablespoons reserved fat, and remaining 1 teaspoon liquid smoke to now-empty pot. Cook mixture over medium heat, stirring frequently, until liquid has been absorbed and exterior of meat appears dry, about 5 minutes. Season with salt, pepper, and hot sauce to taste. Serve, passing remaining barbecue sauce separately.

LEXINGTON VINEGAR BARBECUE SAUCE
makes about 2 cups
For a spicier sauce, add hot sauce to taste.

1 cup cider vinegar
½ cup ketchup
½ cup water
1 tablespoon sugar
¾ teaspoon salt
¾ teaspoon red pepper flakes
½ teaspoon pepper

Whisk all ingredients together in bowl.

SOUTH CAROLINA MUSTARD BARBECUE SAUCE

makes about 2 cups

You can use either light or dark brown sugar in this recipe.

1 cup yellow mustard
½ cup distilled white vinegar
¼ cup packed brown sugar
¼ cup Worcestershire sauce
2 tablespoons hot sauce
1 teaspoon salt
1 teaspoon pepper

Whisk all ingredients together in bowl.

SWEET AND TANGY BARBECUE SAUCE

makes about 2 cups

We like mild molasses in this recipe.

1½ cups ketchup
¼ cup molasses
2 tablespoons Worcestershire sauce
1 tablespoon hot sauce
½ teaspoon salt
½ teaspoon pepper

Whisk all ingredients together in bowl.

TURKEY BREAST EN COCOTTE WITH PAN GRAVY

serves 6 to 8

1 (6- to 7-pound) whole bone-in turkey breast, trimmed

Salt and pepper

2 tablespoons olive oil

1 onion, chopped

1 carrot, peeled and chopped

1 celery rib, chopped

6 garlic cloves, lightly crushed and peeled

2 sprigs fresh thyme

1 bay leaf

2 tablespoons all-purpose flour

2 cups chicken broth

Why This Recipe Works Roasting an entire turkey can be tedious. After all, the whole bird has to be turned or flipped, and then there's the complicated carving to deal with. But we didn't want to relegate turkey to holiday-only status. So we could enjoy our turkey year-round, we opted for a bone-in breast, which was easier to maneuver and required no fancy carving, and we set out to cook it en cocotte so the meat would be moist and tender—a difficult feat when simply roasting a turkey breast. We started by browning the turkey in our Dutch oven to build flavor. After setting the cooked turkey aside for a brief rest, we used the drippings left behind in the pot to build a rich gravy. The recipe worked so well that, in addition to the more-traditional gravy, we developed recipes with two different flavor profiles so they were good for any time of year. Use a Dutch oven that holds 7 quarts or more. Don't buy a turkey breast larger than 7 pounds; it won't fit in the pot.

1 Adjust oven rack to lowest position and heat oven to 250 degrees. Pat turkey dry with paper towels and season with salt and pepper. Heat oil in Dutch oven over medium-high heat until just smoking. Brown turkey on all sides, about 12 minutes; transfer to large plate.

2 Pour off all but 2 tablespoons fat from pot and heat over medium heat until shimmering. Add onion, carrot, and celery and cook, stirring occasionally, until softened, about 5 minutes. Stir in garlic, thyme sprigs, and bay leaf and cook until fragrant, about 30 seconds. Off heat, return turkey skin side up to pot along with any accumulated juices.

3 Place large piece of aluminum foil over pot and cover tightly with lid; transfer pot to oven. Cook until turkey registers 160 degrees, about 2 hours.

4 Carefully remove pot from oven. Transfer turkey to carving board, tent with foil, and let rest while making gravy.

5 Being careful of hot pot handles, bring remaining juices and vegetables to simmer over medium-high heat and cook until nearly all liquid has evaporated, about 15 minutes. Add flour and cook, stirring constantly, until browned, 1 to 3 minutes. Slowly add broth, whisking constantly to smooth out any lumps. Bring to simmer and cook, stirring often, until gravy is thickened and measures about 1½ cups, about 10 minutes. Strain gravy through fine-mesh strainer and season with salt and pepper to taste. Discard solids.

6 Remove and discard turkey skin, carve turkey, and serve, passing gravy separately.

Turkey Breast en Cocotte with Mole Sauce

Omit flour and chicken broth. After tenting turkey with foil, strain juices from pot into fat separator, reserving strained vegetables. Let liquid settle for 5 minutes, then return defatted liquid to now-empty pot. Meanwhile, add remaining 3 tablespoons oil, 3 minced garlic cloves, 2 tablespoons chili powder, 2 tablespoons cocoa powder, ½ teaspoon ground cinnamon, and ⅛ teaspoon cloves to pot and cook over medium heat until fragrant, about 1 minute. Stir in defatted juices, strained vegetables, any accumulated juices from turkey, 1 (14.5-ounce) can diced tomatoes, drained, ¼ cup raisins, and 2 tablespoons creamy peanut butter and simmer over medium-high heat, stirring occasionally, until slightly thickened, 8 to 10 minutes. Discard thyme and bay leaf, then puree sauce in blender until smooth, about 20 seconds. Season with salt and pepper to taste. Serve sauce with carved turkey.

Turkey Breast en Cocotte with Orange-Chipotle Sauce

For a spicier sauce, use the larger amount of chipotle in adobo.

Omit flour and chicken broth. After tenting turkey with foil, strain juices from pot into fat separator, discarding strained vegetables. Let liquid settle for 5 minutes, then return defatted liquid to now-empty pot. Stir in 2 cups orange juice, ½ cup sugar, ¼ cup white wine vinegar, and any accumulated juices from turkey. Simmer sauce over medium-high heat until it is thickened and measures 1 cup, 10 to 12 minutes. Stir in 2 tablespoons cilantro, 1 to 2 teaspoons minced canned chipotle chile in adobo sauce, and 1 minced clove of garlic. Season with salt and pepper to taste. Serve sauce with carved turkey.

SEAFOOD

Calamari Stew with Garlic and Tomatoes

236 **Braised Cod with Leeks and Cherry Tomatoes**

238 **Braised Cod Provençal**
Braised Cod with Peperonata
Braised Cod Veracruz

241 **Braised Halibut with Leeks and Mustard**
Braised Halibut with Carrots and Coriander
Braised Halibut with Fennel and Tarragon

242 **Hake in Saffron Broth with Chorizo and Potatoes**

245 **Catfish in Salty Caramel (Ca Kho To)**

246 **Salmon en Cocotte with Leeks and White Wine**
Salmon en Cocotte with Celery and Orange

248 **Halibut en Cocotte with Roasted Garlic and Cherry Tomatoes**
Halibut en Cocotte with Fennel and Saffron

251 **Swordfish en Cocotte with Carrots and Chermoula**
Swordfish en Cocotte with Shallots, Cucumber, and Mint

252 **Red Wine—Braised Octopus**

254 **Cioppino**

256 **Bouillabaisse**

258 **Spanish Shellfish Stew**
with Lobster

260 **Monkfish Tagine**

262 **Brazilian Shrimp and Fish Stew (Moqueca)**

265 **Calamari Stew with Garlic and Tomatoes**

BRAISED COD WITH LEEKS AND CHERRY TOMATOES

serves 4

3 tablespoons unsalted butter

1 pound leeks, white and light green parts only, halved lengthwise, sliced thin, and washed thoroughly

Salt and pepper

4 garlic cloves, minced

12 ounces cherry tomatoes, halved

½ cup dry white wine or dry vermouth

4 (6- to 8-ounce) skinless cod fillets, 1 to 1½ inches thick

Why This Recipe Works You may be used to pan-searing thick-cut white fish fillets any time you take them home from the market and want a quick dinner, but it's worth it to try a different technique. Braising is a great way to add flavor to mild-tasting fish, it's a mess-free alternative to cooking in oil in a skillet, and it doesn't take much longer to execute with fish. Using cherry tomatoes and making a white wine sauce in the pan made the dish fresh and bright—perfect for pristine white fish. Cooking the fillets among sautéed leeks imparted a subtle sweet flavor to the fish. To ensure the fish cooked through gently and evenly, we turned down the heat and covered the skillet so the fish both simmered and steamed. A pat of butter swirled into the resulting sauce contributed richness. Haddock, snapper, tilapia, bluefish, monkfish, and sea bass fillets are good substitutes for the cod.

1 Melt 2 tablespoons butter in 12-inch nonstick skillet over medium-high heat. Add leeks and ¼ teaspoon salt and cook until softened, about 5 minutes. Stir in garlic and cook until fragrant, about 30 seconds. Stir in tomatoes, wine, and ¼ teaspoon pepper and bring to simmer.

2 Pat cod dry with paper towels and season with salt and pepper. Nestle cod into skillet and spoon some vegetables and sauce over top. Cover and reduce heat to medium-low. Cook until fish flakes apart when gently prodded with paring knife and registers 140 degrees, 10 to 12 minutes.

3 Carefully transfer cod to platter. Stir remaining 1 tablespoon butter into vegetables, season with salt and pepper to taste, and spoon vegetables and sauce over cod. Serve.

tucking the tail

For fish with a thinner tail end, simply tuck the thinner end under itself before cooking so that it cooks at the same rate.

BRAISED COD PROVENÇAL

serves 4

2 tablespoons extra-virgin olive oil, plus extra for drizzling

1 onion, halved and sliced thin

1 fennel bulb, stalks discarded, bulb halved, cored, and sliced thin

Salt and pepper

4 garlic cloves, minced

1 (14.5-ounce) can diced tomatoes, drained

½ cup dry white wine

1 teaspoon minced fresh thyme

4 (6- to 8-ounce) skinless cod fillets, 1 to 1½ inches thick

2 tablespoons minced fresh parsley

Why This Recipe Works Bread crumbs, batter, and/or a side of chips are common cod accompaniments, but they can detract from the fish itself. We turned to the fragrant flavors of Provence—fennel, tomatoes, and fresh herbs—for a cod recipe that was robust enough to capture interest but delicate enough to let the fish shine. For the canned tomatoes, we found that crushed and pureed produced thick, sweet, sauces, more like Italian American red sauces, that were overbearing in this application. Canned diced tomatoes, though more promising, presented the opposite problem: They contain a fair amount of liquid and the resulting sauce was too thin. Draining them was the simple way to sauce with just the right texture. Sliced fennel, with its subtle anise flavor, was a great pick for accompanying the fish. All this dish needed to round it out was a loaf of crusty bread to sop up the extra sauce. Halibut, snapper, bluefish, monkfish, and sea bass fillets are good substitutes for the cod fillets.

1 Heat oil in 12-inch nonstick skillet over medium-high heat until shimmering. Add onion, fennel, and ½ teaspoon salt and cook until vegetables are softened, about 5 minutes. Stir in garlic and cook until fragrant, about 30 seconds. Stir in tomatoes, wine, and thyme and bring to simmer.

2 Season cod with salt and pepper. Nestle cod into skillet and spoon some of sauce over top. Cover, reduce heat to medium-low, and cook until fish flakes apart when gently prodded with paring knife and registers 140 degrees, about 10 minutes.

3 Transfer cod to individual plates. Stir parsley into sauce and season with salt and pepper to taste. Spoon sauce over cod and drizzle with extra oil. Serve.

Braised Cod with Peperonata

Substitute 2 red bell peppers, stemmed, seeded, and cut into thin strips, for fennel. Add 2 teaspoons paprika to skillet with garlic in step 1. Substitute chopped fresh basil for parsley. After drizzling fillets with oil, lightly season with balsamic or sherry vinegar to taste before serving.

Braised Cod Veracruz

Omit fennel. Add 1 teaspoon chili powder and ½ teaspoon cumin to skillet with garlic step 1.

BRAISED HALIBUT WITH LEEKS AND MUSTARD

serves 4

4 (4- to 6-ounce) skinless halibut fillets, ¾ to 1 inch thick

Salt and pepper

¼ cup extra-virgin olive oil, plus extra for serving

1 pound leeks, white and light green parts only, halved lengthwise, sliced thin, and washed thoroughly

1 teaspoon Dijon mustard

¾ cup dry white wine

1 tablespoon minced fresh parsley

Lemon wedges

Why This Recipe Works In addition to being a forgiving cooking method for fish, all but guaranteeing moist, succulent fish, braising is also a convenient route to a one-pan meal as you can easily add vegetables to the mix as we do in this elegant dish. Meaty halibut is the filet mignon of white fish, and its sweet, delicate flavor was an excellent pair for classic French ingredients: leeks, white wine, and Dijon mustard. Because the portion of the firm fillets submerged in liquid cooks more quickly than the upper half that cooks through in the steam, we seared the fillets in oil for a few minutes on one side (their firm texture made them easy to handle) and then braised them parcooked side up to even things out. For the cooking liquid, wine supplemented by the juices released by the fish and vegetables during cooking delivered a sauce with balanced, nuanced flavor and just the right amount of brightness. Options with varying vegetables and flavor profiles made this elegant and deceptively simple meal a seafood go-to. If halibut isn't available, you can substitute sea bass.

1 Pat halibut dry with paper towels and sprinkle with ½ teaspoon salt. Heat oil in 12-inch skillet over medium heat until warm, about 15 seconds. Place halibut skinned side up in skillet and cook until bottom half of halibut begins to turn opaque (halibut should not brown), about 4 minutes. Carefully transfer halibut raw side down to large plate.

2 Add leeks, mustard, and ¼ teaspoon salt to oil left in skillet and cook over medium heat, stirring frequently, until softened, 10 to 12 minutes. Stir in wine and bring to simmer. Place halibut raw side down on top of leeks. Reduce heat to medium-low, cover, and simmer gently until fish flakes apart when gently prodded with paring knife and registers 140 degrees, 6 to 10 minutes. Carefully transfer halibut to platter, tent with aluminum foil, and let rest while finishing leeks.

3 Return leeks to high heat and simmer briskly until mixture is thickened slightly, 2 to 4 minutes. Season with salt and pepper to taste. Arrange leek mixture around halibut, drizzle with extra oil, and sprinkle with parsley. Serve with lemon wedges.

Braised Halibut with Carrots and Coriander

Substitute 1 pound carrots, peeled and shaved with vegetable peeler into ribbons, and 4 shallots, halved and sliced thin, for leeks. Substitute ½ teaspoon ground coriander for Dijon mustard and stir 1½ teaspoons lemon juice into carrot mixture before seasoning with salt and pepper in step 3. Substitute 1 tablespoon minced fresh cilantro for parsley.

Braised Halibut with Fennel and Tarragon

Substitute 2 fennel bulbs, halved, cored, and sliced thin, and 4 shallots, halved and sliced thin, for leeks. Omit Dijon mustard and stir 1 teaspoon lemon juice into fennel mixture before seasoning with salt and pepper in step 3. Substitute 1 tablespoon minced fresh tarragon for parsley.

HAKE IN SAFFRON BROTH WITH CHORIZO AND POTATOES

serves 4

1 tablespoon extra-virgin olive oil, plus extra for serving

1 onion, chopped fine

3 ounces Spanish-style chorizo sausage, sliced ¼ inch thick

4 garlic cloves, minced

¼ teaspoon saffron threads, crumbled

1 (8-ounce) bottle clam juice

¾ cup water

½ cup dry white wine

4 ounces small red potatoes, unpeeled, sliced ¼ inch thick

1 bay leaf

4 (4- to 6-ounce) skinless hake fillets, 1 to 1½ inches thick

Salt and pepper

1 teaspoon lemon juice

2 tablespoons minced fresh parsley

Why This Recipe Works Saffron's distinctive aroma and bright yellow-orange color pair particularly well with delicate seafood; we wanted to utilize the exquisite spice in a Spanish-inspired seafood dish. Versatile hake is a favorite white fish in Spain, and its mild flavor was the perfect stage for the saffron. We created a flavorful saffron broth with aromatics, white wine, and clam juice in which we braised the fish, and then we ladled the broth over the fillets before serving. For additional flavor, we added spicy Spanish-style chorizo to the pan with the onions and sautéed the sausage until browned; this lent a subtle but not overwhelming heat—more of a smoky flavor—to the broth. Then we looked for a starchy element to round out the meal. Waxy red potatoes, sliced into coins to mirror the slices of chorizo, brought in just the right creaminess to soak up the flavorful broth. A hit of lemon added brightness to the broth at the end of cooking, and a sprinkle of parsley and drizzle of olive oil on the flaky fish, swimming in the fragrant saffron liquid, brought it all together. Haddock and cod are good substitutes for the hake. Use small red potatoes measuring 1 to 2 inches in diameter. Serve with crusty bread.

1 Heat oil in 12-inch skillet over medium heat until shimmering. Add onion and chorizo and cook until onion is softened and lightly browned, 5 to 7 minutes. Stir in garlic and saffron and cook until fragrant, about 30 seconds. Stir in clam juice, water, wine, potatoes, and bay leaf and bring to simmer. Reduce heat to medium-low, cover, and cook until potatoes are almost tender, about 10 minutes.

2 Pat hake dry with paper towels and season with salt and pepper. Nestle hake skinned side down into skillet and spoon some broth over top. Bring to simmer, cover, and cook until potatoes are fully tender and fish flakes apart when gently prodded with paring knife and registers 140 degrees, 10 to 12 minutes.

3 Carefully transfer hake to individual shallow bowls. Using slotted spoon, divide potatoes and chorizo evenly among bowls. Discard bay leaf. Stir lemon juice into broth and season with salt and pepper to taste. Spoon broth over hake, sprinkle with parsley, and drizzle with extra oil. Serve.

CATFISH IN SALTY CARAMEL (CA KHO TO)

serves 4 to 6

¼ cup vegetable oil

5 garlic cloves, minced

¼ cup cold water plus 2 cups boiling water

⅓ cup sugar

¼ cup fish sauce

1½ teaspoons pepper

2 pounds boneless, skinless catfish fillets, sliced crosswise into 2-inch-wide pieces

1 cup fresh cilantro leaves

4 scallions, green parts only, sliced thin on bias

Why This Recipe Works One of the most popular southern Vietnamese homestyle dishes is catfish simmered in a caramel sauce (*ca kho to*), a uniquely satisfying combination. Vietnamese caramel sauce is a simple caramel made from a mixture of sugar and water that cooks just until it becomes slightly bitter, at which point more water is added to create a thin, caramel-flavored liquid—just the right consistency to serve as a cooking medium for the fish. For ease, we made the sauce right in the pan we'd use to cook the fish rather than cook the caramel in a separate saucepan. White sugar, rather than molasses-y brown, gave the sauce a clean flavor that complemented the fish. Garlic is a typical addition to the sauce, and we liked a generous five cloves to add complexity. We balanced the sweet sauce with a quarter-cup of fish sauce and a good dose of black pepper for a spicy dimension. Cooking the catfish in the sauce at medium-low for 25 minutes was enough time for it to absorb the sauce's flavor without overcooking. We particularly like the flavor of catfish here; however, any thin, medium-firm white fish fillets can be substituted. For an accurate measurement of boiling water, bring a full kettle of water to boil, then measure out the desired amount.

1 Mix oil and garlic in small bowl; set aside. Pour cold water into 12-inch nonstick skillet, then sprinkle sugar evenly into water. Cook sugar mixture over medium heat, gently swirling pan occasionally (do not stir), until sugar melts and mixture turns color of maple syrup, about 10 minutes.

2 Stir in garlic mixture and cook until fragrant, about 30 seconds. Off heat, slowly whisk in boiling water (sauce may bubble and sizzle slightly). Return skillet to medium heat and stir in fish sauce and pepper.

3 Lay catfish fillets in skillet (without overlapping), and turn to coat evenly with sauce. Bring to simmer, then reduce heat to medium-low and cook, uncovered, until fish flakes apart when gently prodded with paring knife and sauce has thickened to thick, syrupy consistency, about 25 minutes. Transfer catfish to platter and pour sauce over the top. Sprinkle with cilantro and scallions and serve.

SALMON EN COCOTTE WITH LEEKS AND WHITE WINE

serves 4

1 (1¾- to 2-pound) skinless salmon fillet, about 1½ inches at thickest part

Salt and pepper

2 tablespoons extra-virgin olive oil

2 leeks, white and light green parts only, halved lengthwise, sliced thin, and washed thoroughly

2 sprigs fresh thyme

2 garlic cloves, minced

½ cup dry white wine

2 tablespoons unsalted butter, cut into 2 pieces

Why This Recipe Works As we learned with recipes for beef, lamb, pork, and poultry, cooking *en cocotte*—cooking a protein in a covered pot with little to no liquid—concentrates flavor. We were skeptical that the technique would successfully translate to fish. Fish cooks quickly; would the fish dry out in the dry pot? We gave the technique a shot with fatty salmon fillets, however, and we were more than pleasantly surprised. By passing on searing the salmon fillets, we found that we got just what we wanted: perfectly cooked, moist salmon, basted in its own jus, that flaked apart in large buttery chunks. Leeks sautéed and then layered first in the pot contributed their onion-like sweetness and protected the fish from the heat of the pan bottom. A quick sauce made with white wine and butter added some more dimension and richness. To ensure uniform pieces of fish that cook at the same rate, we prefer to buy a whole center-cut fillet and cut it into evenly sized individual fillets ourselves. If buying individual fillets, make sure they are the same size and thickness. If the fillets are thicker or thinner than 1½ inches, you may need to adjust the cooking time slightly. If you can find only skin-on fillets, remove the skin before cooking or the sauce will be greasy.

1 Adjust oven rack to lowest position and heat oven to 250 degrees. Trim any whitish fat from belly of fillet, then cut fish into 4 equal pieces. Pat salmon dry with paper towels and season with salt and pepper.

2 Heat oil in Dutch oven over medium-low heat until shimmering. Add leeks, thyme, and pinch salt, cover, and cook until softened, 8 to 10 minutes. Stir in garlic and cook until fragrant, about 30 seconds. Remove pot from heat.

3 Lay salmon, skinned side down, on top of leeks. Place large piece of aluminum foil over pot and cover tightly with lid; transfer pot to oven. Cook until salmon is opaque and flakes apart when gently prodded with paring knife, 25 to 30 minutes.

4 Transfer fish to serving platter and tent with foil. Stir wine into leeks in pot and simmer over medium-high heat until slightly thickened, about 2 minutes. Off heat, whisk in butter and season with salt and pepper to taste. Spoon sauce over salmon and serve.

Salmon en Cocotte with Celery and Orange
Add 2 thinly sliced celery ribs and 1 teaspoon minced orange zest along with garlic in step 2. Substitute ½ cup orange juice for wine, and add 1 orange, peeled and segmented, when thickening sauce in step 4.

HALIBUT EN COCOTTE WITH ROASTED GARLIC AND CHERRY TOMATOES

serves 4

¼ cup extra-virgin olive oil

2 garlic cloves, sliced thin

⅛ teaspoon red pepper flakes

Salt and pepper

12 ounces cherry tomatoes, quartered

1 tablespoon capers, rinsed

1 teaspoon minced fresh thyme

2 (1¼-pound) skin-on full halibut steaks, each about 1¼ inches thick and 10 to 12 inches long, and trimmed of cartilage at both ends

Why This Recipe Works After the success of our Salmon en Cocotte with Leeks and White Wine (page 246), we wondered if we could get similarly successful results with a popular lean fish: halibut. The halibut took a little longer to cook through than the fatty salmon (about 10 minutes longer), but the results were just as satisfying since the low-temperature oven and sealed pot kept in moisture for succulent fish. A combination of olive oil, garlic, thyme, capers, red pepper flakes, and tomatoes formed a sauce that was a bright, briny counterpoint to the mild halibut. Cooking sliced garlic in olive oil drew out its flavor, and once the garlic was golden brown, we stirred in the cherry tomatoes and placed the halibut on top. As the fish cooked, the tomatoes began to break down, releasing their juices and helping to build a sauce. Finishing with another splash of extra-virgin olive oil rounded out the flavors and gave the dish a lush feel. Make sure your halibut steaks are of equal size to ensure even cooking; if your steaks are thicker or thinner than 1¼ inches, you may need to adjust the cooking time slightly.

1 Adjust oven rack to lowest position and heat oven to 250 degrees. Cook 2 tablespoons oil, garlic, red pepper flakes, and pinch of salt in Dutch oven over medium-low heat until garlic is light golden, 2 to 4 minutes. Off heat, stir in tomatoes, capers, and thyme.

2 Pat halibut dry with paper towels and season with salt and pepper. Lay halibut on top of tomatoes. Place large piece of aluminum foil over pot and cover tightly with lid; transfer pot to oven. Cook until fish flakes apart when gently prodded with paring knife and registers 140 degrees, 35 to 40 minutes.

3 Transfer halibut to platter and tent with foil. Bring tomato mixture to simmer over medium-high heat until slightly thickened, about 2 minutes. Off heat, stir in remaining 2 tablespoons olive oil and season with salt and pepper to taste. Spoon sauce over halibut and serve.

Halibut en Cocotte with Fennel and Saffron

Pernod is a French anise-flavored liqueur available at most liquor stores. You can substitute dry sherry for the Pernod; however, the flavor of the sauce will be quite different.

Add 1 fennel bulb, halved, cored, and cut into ½-inch-thick strips, and a pinch of saffron to pot after garlic has lightly browned in step 1; cover and cook over medium-low heat until fennel is tender, 8 to 10 minutes, then continue with the recipe as directed. Stir 1 tablespoon Pernod into pot when thickening the tomato mixture in step 3.

serving halibut steaks

Remove skin from cooked steaks and separate each quadrant of meat from bones by slipping spatula or knife gently between them.

SWORDFISH EN COCOTTE WITH CARROTS AND CHERMOULA

serves 4

¾ cup fresh cilantro leaves

5 tablespoons extra-virgin olive oil

2 tablespoons lemon juice

4 garlic cloves, minced

1 teaspoon ground cumin

1 teaspoon paprika

¼ teaspoon cayenne pepper

Salt and pepper

2 carrots, peeled and grated

4 (6- to 8-ounce) swordfish steaks, about 1¼ inches thick

Why This Recipe Works Swordfish is meaty and mild in flavor, so when we developed a recipe for it cooked *en cocotte*, we knew it would stand up to and benefit from a boldly flavored sauce. Chermoula, a traditional Moroccan sauce, was a perfectly lively pairing. This paste is usually used as a marinade for fish and typically consists of generous amounts of cilantro, lemon, garlic, and olive oil. Sweet carrots are a nice complement to heady chermoula, so we incorporated them into our dish. We grated the carrots (for quicker cooking), and after sautéing them we added the chermoula and nestled the swordfish on top. The combination of flavors and the moist, tender fish made this our new favorite way to cook satisfying swordfish steaks. Make sure your swordfish steaks are of equal size to ensure even cooking; if your steaks are thicker or thinner than 1¼ inches, the cooking time may vary slightly.

1 Adjust oven rack to lowest position and heat oven to 250 degrees. Process cilantro, 3 tablespoons oil, lemon juice, garlic, cumin, paprika, cayenne, and ¼ teaspoon salt in food processor until smooth, about 20 seconds.

2 Heat remaining 2 tablespoons oil in Dutch oven over medium-low heat until shimmering. Add carrots, cover, and cook, stirring occasionally, until softened, 4 to 6 minutes. Off heat, stir in cilantro mixture.

3 Pat swordfish dry with paper towels and season with salt and pepper. Lay swordfish on top of carrot-cilantro mixture. Place large piece of aluminum foil over pot and cover tightly with lid; transfer pot to oven. Cook until fish flakes apart when gently prodded with paring knife and registers 140 degrees, 35 to 40 minutes.

4 Transfer swordfish to platter. Season carrot-chermoula mixture with salt and pepper to taste, then spoon over swordfish and serve.

Swordfish en Cocotte with Shallots, Cucumber, and Mint

Substitute 3 shallots, sliced thin, for carrots. Substitute ¾ cup fresh mint leaves and ¼ cup fresh parsley leaves for cilantro and omit paprika. Add 1 cucumber, peeled, seeded, and sliced thin, to pot with pureed herb mixture in step 2.

RED WINE–BRAISED OCTOPUS

serves 4

1 (4-pound) octopus, rinsed

1 tablespoon extra-virgin olive oil

2 tablespoons tomato paste

4 garlic cloves, peeled and smashed

1 sprig fresh rosemary

2 bay leaves

Pepper

Pinch ground cinnamon

Pinch ground nutmeg

1 cup dry red wine

2 tablespoons red wine vinegar

2 tablespoons unflavored gelatin

2 teaspoons chopped fresh parsley

Why This Recipe Works Working with octopus may seem intimidating, but in Greek cuisine, it's more than typical to braise octopus, often in an intense, silky red wine sauce. Octopus flesh is a dense array of thin muscle fibers reinforced by a network of collagen and connective tissue, so it can be tough and chewy. Most of the octopus you can buy in the United States is frozen, and we found that simply defrosting it helped lead to tender octopus; the ice crystals tore through the tough muscle fibers and helped them break down during cooking. Thinking the octopus collagen and connective tissue would break down with gentle, low-heat cooking as meat does, we cooked the octopus in red wine over low heat. But because octopus is made up of almost half salt water by weight, it released its salty juices into the sauce, making it unpalatable. We found that the best way to desalinate our braise was to cook the octopus in water first; however, since octopus contains a lot of collagen, which transforms into gelatin as it cooks, we also lost the viscosity and velvety texture provided by the collagen. To counteract this, we added powdered gelatin to our wine sauce. Octopus can be found cleaned and frozen in the seafood section of specialty grocery stores and Asian markets. Be sure to rinse the defrosted octopus well, as sand can collect in the suckers. Be sure to peel the octopus' membrane-like skin as soon as it's cool enough to handle. You can thaw frozen octopus in a large container under cold running water; it will be ready in about 2 hours.

1 Using sharp knife, separate octopus mantle (large sac) and body (lower section with tentacles) from head (midsection containing eyes); discard head. Place octopus in large pot, cover with water by 2 inches, and bring to simmer over high heat. Reduce heat to low, cover, and simmer gently, flipping octopus occasionally, until skin between tentacle joints tears easily when pulled, 45 minutes to 1¼ hours.

2 Transfer octopus to cutting board and let cool slightly. Measure out and reserve 3 cups octopus cooking liquid; discard remaining liquid and wipe pot dry with paper towels.

3 While octopus is still warm, use paring knife to cut mantle into quarters, then trim and scrape away skin and interior fibers; transfer to bowl. Using your fingers, remove skin from body, being careful not to remove suction cups from tentacles. Cut tentacles from around core of body in three sections; discard core. Separate tentacles and cut into 2-inch lengths; transfer to bowl.

4 Heat oil in now-empty pot over medium-high heat until shimmering. Add tomato paste and cook, stirring constantly, until beginning to darken, about 1 minute. Stir in garlic, rosemary sprig, bay leaves, ½ teaspoon pepper, cinnamon, and nutmeg and cook until fragrant, about 30 seconds. Stir in reserved octopus cooking liquid, wine, vinegar, and gelatin, scraping up any browned bits. Bring to boil and cook, stirring occasionally, for 20 minutes.

5 Stir in octopus and any accumulated juices and bring to simmer. Cook, stirring occasionally, until octopus is tender and sauce has thickened slightly and coats back of spoon, 20 to 25 minutes. Off heat, discard rosemary sprig and bay leaves. Stir in parsley and season with pepper to taste. Serve.

CIOPPINO

serves 4 to 6

¼ cup vegetable oil

2 large onions, chopped fine

Salt and pepper

¼ cup water

4 garlic cloves, minced

2 bay leaves

1 teaspoon dried oregano

⅛–¼ teaspoon red pepper flakes

1 (28-ounce) can whole peeled tomatoes, drained with juice reserved, chopped coarse

1 (8-ounce) bottle clam juice

1 (1½-pound) skinless halibut fillet, ¾ to 1 inch thick, cut into 6 pieces

1 pound littleneck clams, scrubbed

1¼ cups dry white wine

4 tablespoons unsalted butter

1 pound mussels, scrubbed and debearded

¼ cup chopped fresh parsley

Extra-virgin olive oil

Why This Recipe Works Brought to San Francisco by Italian immigrants, the earliest versions of cioppino were uncomplicated affairs made by fishermen with the day's catch. Today's restaurant versions showcase a variety of fish and shellfish piled high in a bright, complex broth and anointed with fruity olive oil. We wanted a restaurant-worthy cioppino in which every component was perfectly cooked but which could be on the table quickly and with minimal fuss. First, we scaled down the seafood to create a good mix of textures and flavors. For the fish, halibut fillets were tender and had just enough heft. As for the shellfish, a combination of briny littleneck clams and savory-sweet mussels was perfectly balanced. The only way to perfectly cook three varieties of seafood was to cook each one separately and bring them together in a pot of hot broth. We poached the halibut in the broth while the clams and mussels steamed in a separate pan. Removing the shellfish as they opened ensured ideal doneness for each one, and using a shallow skillet made the task easy. We used white wine to steam the mussels and clams and then added the briny cooking liquid to the stew for a boost of intense seafood flavor. Replacing the water in the broth with bottled clam juice improved the broth further. Cod or sea bass are good substitutes for the halibut. Discard clams or mussels with unpleasant odors, cracked shells, or shells that won't close. If littlenecks are not available, substitute Manila or mahogany clams, or use 2 pounds of mussels. If using only mussels, skip step 3 and cook them all at once with the butter and wine for 3 to 5 minutes.

1 Heat vegetable oil in Dutch oven over medium-high heat until shimmering. Add onions, ½ teaspoon salt, and ½ teaspoon pepper; cook, stirring frequently, until onions begin to brown, 7 to 9 minutes. Add water and cook, stirring frequently, until onions are soft, 2 to 4 minutes. Stir in garlic, bay leaves, oregano, and pepper flakes and cook for 1 minute. Stir in tomatoes and reserved juice and clam juice and bring to simmer. Reduce heat to low, cover, and simmer for 5 minutes.

2 Submerge halibut in broth, cover, and gently simmer until fish is cooked through, 12 to 15 minutes. Remove pot from heat and, using slotted spoon, transfer halibut to plate; cover with aluminum foil and set aside.

3 Bring clams, wine, and butter to boil in 12-inch skillet, covered, over high heat. Steam until clams just open, 5 to 8 minutes, transferring them to pot with tomato broth as they open.

4 Once all clams have been transferred to pot, add mussels to skillet, cover, and cook over high heat until mussels have opened, 2 to 4 minutes, transferring them to pot with tomato broth as they open. Pour cooking liquid from skillet into pot, being careful not to pour any grit from skillet into pot. Return broth to simmer.

5 Stir parsley into broth and season with salt and pepper to taste. Divide halibut among serving bowls. Ladle broth over halibut, making sure each portion contains both clams and mussels. Drizzle with olive oil and serve immediately.

BOUILLABAISSE

serves 6 to 8

¼ cup extra-virgin olive oil

1 small fennel bulb, stalks discarded, bulb halved, cored, and chopped fine

1 onion, chopped fine

8 garlic cloves, minced

1 teaspoon minced fresh thyme or ¼ teaspoon dried

¼ teaspoon saffron threads, crumbled

⅛ teaspoon red pepper flakes

¾ cup dry white wine or dry vermouth

2 (8-ounce) bottles clam juice

1 (14.5-ounce) can whole peeled tomatoes, drained with juice reserved, chopped

2 bay leaves

1 pound skinless halibut fillets, ¾ to 1 inch thick, cut into 3- to 4-inch pieces

Salt and pepper

12 ounces mussels, scrubbed and debearded

1 pound large sea scallops, tendons removed

8 ounces medium-large shrimp (31 to 40 per pound), peeled and deveined

2 tablespoons minced fresh tarragon

Why This Recipe Works Bouillabaisse is a classic Provençal dish with humble origins—a fisherman's cost-effective family meal turned upscale seafood stew that brings the flavors and aroma of the French seaside into your kitchen. It relies on a deeply flavored homemade fish stock (or *fumet*). After the broth has simmered for hours, a variety of fish and shellfish is poached in the complex broth. Our goal was to create a simpler adaptation of this French classic that was still authentic in flavor. In the interest of time and expense, we limited our variety of seafood to diverse but widely available shrimp, scallops, mussels, and halibut. While we loved the idea of using homemade fish stock, we wondered if with everything going on in the pot we could get away with using bottled clam juice. Fortified with sautéed aromatics, fennel, white wine, and a generous amount of garlic, we created a solidly flavorful broth on which to build the rest of our dish. Additionally, diced tomatoes, fresh thyme, bay leaves and just enough saffron to perfume the broth provided flavor, color, and an exquisite aroma. As the shrimp, scallops, halibut, and mussels cooked, their juices combined with the saffron-infused tomato base to produce the ideal amount of cooking liquid with plenty left to ladle into the bowl and dip into with crusty bread. Serve with Rouille (page 205).

1 Heat oil in Dutch oven over medium-high heat until shimmering. Add fennel and onion and cook until softened, about 5 minutes. Stir in garlic, thyme, saffron, and pepper flakes and cook until fragrant, about 30 seconds. Stir in wine and cook until slightly reduced, about 30 seconds.

2 Stir in clam juice, tomatoes with their juice, and bay leaves. Bring to simmer and cook until liquid has reduced by about half, 7 to 9 minutes.

3 Pat halibut dry with paper towels and season with salt and pepper. Nestle halibut into pot, spoon some cooking liquid over top, and bring to simmer. Reduce heat to medium-low, cover, and simmer gently for 2 minutes. Nestle mussels and scallops into pot, cover, and continue to cook until halibut is almost cooked through, about 3 minutes.

4 Arrange shrimp evenly over stew, cover, and continue to cook until halibut flakes apart when gently prodded with paring knife, shrimp and scallops are firm and opaque in center, and mussels have opened, about 2 minutes.

5 Off heat, discard bay leaves and any mussels that refuse to open. Gently stir in tarragon and season with salt and pepper to taste. Serve.

SPANISH SHELLFISH STEW

serves 4 to 6

¼ cup extra-virgin olive oil

8 ounces medium-large shrimp (31 to 40 per pound), peeled and deveined, shells reserved

1½ cups dry white wine or dry vermouth

1 onion, chopped fine

1 red bell pepper, stemmed, seeded, and chopped fine

3 garlic cloves, minced

1 teaspoon paprika

¼ teaspoon saffron threads, crumbled

⅛ teaspoon red pepper flakes

2 tablespoons brandy

1 (28-ounce) can whole peeled tomatoes, drained with juice reserved, chopped

2 bay leaves

1½ pounds littleneck clams, scrubbed

8 ounces mussels, scrubbed and debearded

12 ounces large sea scallops, tendons removed

1 recipe Picada (recipe follows)

1 tablespoon minced fresh parsley

Salt and pepper

Lemon wedges

Why This Recipe Works Less well-known than France's bouillabaisse is Spain's version of shellfish stew, *zarzuela*. Chock-full of shellfish like lobsters, clams, and mussels, this tomato-based stew is seasoned with saffron and paprika and thickened with a *picada*, a flavorful mixture of ground almonds, bread crumbs, and olive oil. Unlike many seafood stews, this one contains no fish stock or clam juice—instead, the shellfish release their rich liquors into the pot as they cook to provide the broth with clean, fresh seafood flavor. To create our version, we followed Spanish tradition and began with a *sofrito* of onion, red bell pepper, and garlic and next added paprika, saffron, red pepper flakes, and bay leaves to create a rich foundation. Canned tomatoes and dry white wine formed the liquid base of our broth, and a little brandy lent depth of flavor. Knowing that shells contribute significant flavor to dishes, we enriched the broth by steeping the shrimp shells in wine while we prepared the other ingredients. After stirring in the picada, all that was left to do was sprinkle the dish with fresh parsley and a squeeze of lemon for a bright, fresh finish. Be sure to buy shrimp with their shells on and reserve the shells when cleaning the shrimp; they add important flavor to the cooking liquid in step 1.

1 Heat 1 tablespoon oil in medium saucepan over medium heat until shimmering. Add shrimp shells and cook, stirring frequently, until they begin to turn spotty brown and pot starts to brown, 2 to 4 minutes. Off heat, stir in wine, cover, and let steep until ready to use.

2 Heat remaining 3 tablespoons oil in Dutch oven over medium-high heat until shimmering. Add onion and bell pepper and cook until softened and lightly browned, 5 to 7 minutes. Stir in garlic, paprika, saffron, and pepper flakes and cook until fragrant, about 30 seconds. Stir in brandy, scraping up any browned bits. Stir in tomatoes and their juice and bay leaves and cook until slightly thickened, 5 to 7 minutes.

3 Strain wine mixture into Dutch oven, pressing on solids to extract as much liquid as possible; discard solids. Bring to simmer and cook until flavors meld, 3 to 5 minutes.

4 Nestle clams into pot, cover, and cook for 4 minutes. Nestle mussels and scallops into pot, cover, and continue to cook until most clams have opened, about 3 minutes. Arrange shrimp evenly over stew, cover, and continue to cook until shrimp are opaque throughout, scallops are firm and opaque in center, and clams and mussels have opened, 1 to 2 minutes.

5 Off heat, discard bay leaves and any clams and mussels that refuse to open. Stir in picada and parsley and season with salt and pepper to taste. Serve with lemon wedges.

Spanish Shellfish Stew with Lobster

In Spain, this stew is often made with *langostinos*, or prawns. Fresh prawns are difficult to find stateside, so we chose to use lobster instead.

Reduce number of clams and mussels to 12 each. Stir 8 ounces cooked lobster meat, cut into ½-inch pieces, into stew with picada in step 5; cover and let sit until heated through, about 1 minute, before serving.

PICADA
makes about 1 cup

¼ cup slivered almonds
2 slices hearty white sandwich bread, torn into quarters
2 tablespoons extra-virgin olive oil
⅛ teaspoon salt
Pinch pepper

Adjust oven rack to middle position and heat oven to 375 degrees. Pulse almonds in food processor to fine crumbs, about 20 pulses. Add bread, oil, salt, and pepper and pulse bread to coarse crumbs, about 10 pulses. Spread mixture evenly in rimmed baking sheet and bake, stirring often, until golden brown, about 10 minutes. Set aside to cool. (Picada can be stored at room temperature for up to 2 days.)

MONKFISH TAGINE

serves 4 to 6

3 (2-inch) strips orange zest

5 garlic cloves, minced

2 tablespoons extra-virgin olive oil

1 large onion, halved and sliced ¼ inch thick

3 carrots, peeled, halved lengthwise, and sliced ¼ inch thick

Salt and pepper

1 tablespoon tomato paste

1¼ teaspoons paprika

1 teaspoon ground cumin

½ teaspoon dried mint

¼ teaspoon saffron threads, crumbled

1 (8-ounce) bottle clam juice

1½ pounds skinless monkfish fillets, 1 to 1½ inches thick, trimmed and cut into 3-inch pieces

¼ cup pitted oil-cured black olives, quartered

2 tablespoons minced fresh mint

1 teaspoon sherry vinegar

Why This Recipe Works We loved the idea of creating a Moroccan-style tagine with the signature sweet and sour flavors of the region that utilized fish. Meaty monkfish fillets were our choice for this dish, as their firm texture helped them keep their shape while simmering in the pot. For sweetness, we turned to orange zest, onion, carrots, and tomato paste, which, along with fragrant paprika, cumin, dried mint, and saffron, built the base for the tagine's broth. Deglazing the sautéed aromatics with a bottle of clam juice brought in a salty, briny element and created a rich broth in which to braise the fish. Nestling the fillets into the broth, covering the pot, and turning down the heat allowed all of the flavors to meld while the fish and carrots cooked through. For a salty, sour punch, we finished the sauce by stirring in pungent Moroccan oil-cured olives and a teaspoon of sherry vinegar. Fresh mint completed the dish with bright flavor. Sweet, tangy, vibrantly colored, and perfectly moist, our monkfish tagine offered intense Moroccan flavors in just half an hour. Monkfish fillets are surrounded by a thin membrane that needs to be removed before cooking. Your fishmonger can do this for you, or you can remove it yourself.

1 Mince 1 strip orange zest and combine with 1 teaspoon garlic in bowl; set aside.

2 Heat oil in Dutch oven over medium heat until shimmering. Add onion, carrots, ¼ teaspoon salt, and remaining 2 strips orange zest and cook until vegetables are softened and lightly browned, 10 to 12 minutes. Stir in remaining garlic, tomato paste, paprika, cumin, dried mint, and saffron and cook until fragrant, about 30 seconds. Stir in clam juice, scraping up any browned bits.

3 Pat monkfish dry with paper towels and season with salt and pepper. Nestle monkfish into pot, spoon some cooking liquid over top, and bring to simmer. Reduce heat to medium-low, cover, and simmer gently until monkfish is opaque in center and registers 160 degrees, 8 to 12 minutes.

4 Discard orange zest. Gently stir in olives, fresh mint, vinegar, and garlic–orange zest mixture. Season with salt and pepper to taste. Serve.

trimming monkfish

Slip knife under membrane, angle knife slightly upward, and use back-and-forth motion to cut it away from fish.

BRAZILIAN SHRIMP AND FISH STEW (MOQUECA)

Pepper Sauce

4 pickled hot cherry peppers (3 ounces)

½ onion, chopped coarse

¼ cup extra-virgin olive oil

⅛ teaspoon sugar

Salt

Stew

1 pound large shrimp (26 to 30 per pound), peeled, deveined, and tails removed

1 pound skinless cod fillets, ¾ to 1 inch thick, cut into 1½-inch pieces

3 garlic cloves, minced

Salt and pepper

1 onion, chopped coarse

1 (14.5-ounce) can whole peeled tomatoes

¾ cup chopped fresh cilantro

2 tablespoons extra-virgin olive oil

1 red bell pepper, stemmed, seeded, and cut into ½-inch pieces

1 green bell pepper, stemmed, seeded, and cut into ½-inch pieces

1 (14-ounce) can coconut milk

2 tablespoons lime juice

Why This Recipe Works Almost every region with a coastline boasts its own version of seafood stew. Brazilian *moqueca* is a standout: A combination of rich coconut milk, briny seafood, bright citrus, and savory vegetables produces a broth that's full-bodied, lush, and vibrant—a particularly complex concoction compared with stews based solely on dairy, tomatoes, or broth. For a bright, fresh, and filling version, we started with the seafood. Cod and shrimp are both easy to find and provided two different flavors and textures of seafood. To balance the richness and sweetness of the coconut milk with the bright, fresh flavor of the aromatics, we blended the onion, the tomatoes, and a portion of the cilantro in the food processor until they had the texture of a slightly chunky salsa, which added body to the stew. We kept the bell peppers diced for contrasting texture and bite. To ensure the seafood was properly cooked, we brought the broth to a boil to make sure the pot was superhot, added the seafood and lime juice, covered the pot, and removed it from the heat, allowing the seafood to gently cook in the residual heat. To finish our moqueca, we added more cilantro and a couple tablespoons of homemade pepper sauce, which elevated the stew with its bright, vinegary tang. Haddock is a good substitute for the cod. We prefer untreated shrimp, but if your shrimp are treated with sodium, do not add salt to the shrimp in step 2. Our favorite coconut milk is made by Aroy-D.

1 For the pepper sauce Process all ingredients in food processor until smooth, about 30 seconds, scraping down sides of bowl as needed. Season with salt to taste and transfer to bowl. Rinse out processor bowl.

2 For the stew Toss shrimp and cod with garlic, ½ teaspoon salt, and ¼ teaspoon pepper in bowl. Set aside.

3 Process onion, tomatoes and their juice, and ¼ cup cilantro in food processor until finely chopped and mixture has texture of pureed salsa, about 30 seconds.

4 Heat oil in Dutch oven over medium-high heat until shimmering. Add red and green bell peppers and ½ teaspoon salt and cook, stirring frequently, until softened, 5 to 7 minutes. Add onion-tomato mixture and ½ teaspoon salt. Reduce heat to medium and cook, stirring frequently, until puree has reduced and thickened slightly, 3 to 5 minutes (pot should not be dry).

5 Increase heat to high, stir in coconut milk, and bring to boil (mixture should be bubbling across entire surface). Add seafood mixture and lime juice and stir to evenly distribute seafood, making sure all pieces are submerged in liquid. Cover pot and remove from heat. Let stand until shrimp and cod are opaque and just cooked through, about 15 minutes.

6 Gently stir in 2 tablespoons pepper sauce and remaining ½ cup cilantro, being careful not to break up cod too much. Season with salt and pepper to taste. Serve, passing remaining pepper sauce separately.

CALAMARI STEW WITH GARLIC AND TOMATOES

serves 4 to 6

¼ cup extra-virgin olive oil,
plus extra for drizzling

2 onions, chopped fine

2 celery ribs, sliced thin

8 garlic cloves, minced

¼ teaspoon red pepper flakes

½ cup dry white wine or dry vermouth

2 pounds small squid, bodies sliced
crosswise into 1-inch-thick rings,
tentacles halved

Salt and pepper

3 (28-ounce) cans whole peeled
tomatoes, drained and chopped coarse

⅓ cup pitted brine-cured green olives,
chopped coarse

1 tablespoon capers, rinsed

3 tablespoons minced fresh parsley

Why This Recipe Works Stewed calamari with tomatoes, garlic, and white wine is a classic Mediterranean dish. This preparation puts the sweet, subtle flavor of the squid front and center. We started building our stew's flavor with onions, a generous amount (eight whole cloves) of garlic, and fresh, vegetal celery; then we added white wine to these aromatics. After much testing, we found that around the 45-minute mark was when the squid became tender enough for our liking; any longer and they became tough and rubbery. As for the tomatoes, we had the best luck with canned whole tomatoes, which not only gave the stew a fresh tomato flavor but broke down just enough to thicken the stew while remaining a distinct component. We wanted a hearty, substantial stew, so we combined 2 pounds of squid with three 28-ounce cans of tomatoes. Because the tomatoes tended to lose their fresh flavor the longer they cooked, we added them to the pot after the squid had simmered for 15 minutes. Green olives and capers lent a welcome briny element, and red pepper flakes provided just the right amount of heat. Finished with fresh parsley and a drizzle of extra-virgin olive oil, our stew was a grand stage for calamari. Be sure to use small squid (with bodies 3 to 4 inches in length) because they cook more quickly and are more tender than larger squid.

1 Heat oil in Dutch oven over medium-high heat until shimmering. Add onions and celery and cook until softened, about 5 minutes. Stir in garlic and pepper flakes and cook until fragrant, about 30 seconds. Stir in wine, scraping up any browned bits, and cook until nearly evaporated, about 1 minute.

2 Pat squid dry with paper towels and season with salt and pepper. Stir squid into pot. Reduce heat to medium-low, cover, and simmer gently until squid has released its liquid, about 15 minutes. Stir in tomatoes, olives, and capers, cover, and continue to cook until squid is very tender, 30 to 35 minutes.

3 Off heat, stir in parsley and season with salt and pepper to taste. Drizzle individual portions with extra oil and serve.

VEGETARIAN MAINS

Quinoa and Vegetable Stew

268 **Ratatouille**

271 **Wild Mushroom Ragu**

272 **Hearty Ten-Vegetable Stew**

275 **Ultimate Vegetarian Chili**

276 **Quinoa and Vegetable Stew**
with Eggs

279 **Artichoke, Pepper, and Chickpea Tagine**

280 **Indian-Style Vegetable Curry with Potatoes and Cauliflower**
Indian-Style Vegetable Curry with Sweet Potato and Eggplant

282 **Potato Vindaloo**

285 **Braised Squash and Winter Greens with Coconut Curry**

287 **Caribbean-Style Swiss Chard and Butternut Squash Stew**

289 **Chile-Braised Tofu**

290 **Asian Braised Tofu with Squash and Coconut Milk**

293 **Braised Fennel with Radicchio and Parmesan**

RATATOUILLE

serves 4

⅓ cup plus 1 tablespoon extra-virgin olive oil

2 large onions, cut into 1-inch pieces

8 large garlic cloves, peeled and smashed

Salt and pepper

1½ teaspoons herbes de Provence

¼ teaspoon red pepper flakes

1 bay leaf

1½ pounds eggplant, peeled and cut into 1-inch pieces

2 pounds plum tomatoes, peeled, cored, and chopped coarse

2 small zucchini, halved lengthwise and cut into 1-inch pieces

1 red bell pepper, stemmed, seeded, and cut into 1-inch pieces

1 yellow bell pepper, stemmed, seeded, and cut into 1-inch pieces

2 tablespoons chopped fresh basil

1 tablespoon minced fresh parsley

1 tablespoon sherry vinegar

Why This Recipe Works Braising isn't just for meat and fish, and the Provençal dish ratatouille is an iconic example of that. In it, vegetables both delicate and meaty become tender and even silky through braising, for a garden-fresh mélange of simple but extraordinary flavors. We wanted a recipe that could stand on its own, with some crusty bread and maybe a side, as a satisfying summer supper. We started by sautéing our aromatics; once we added the eggplant and tomatoes, which broke down to thicken the stew, we moved the cooking to the ambient heat of the oven to concentrate the stew's flavor. Zucchini and bell peppers went into the pot last so they retained some texture. Finishing the dish with fresh herbs and sherry vinegar brightened the braise, and a final drizzle of extra-virgin olive oil added richness. This dish is best prepared using ripe, in-season tomatoes. If good tomatoes are not available, substitute one 28-ounce can of whole peeled tomatoes that have been drained and chopped coarse. Serve ratatouille with crusty bread, topped with an egg, or over pasta or rice. This dish can be served warm, at room temperature, or chilled.

1 Adjust oven rack to middle position and heat oven to 400 degrees. Heat ⅓ cup oil in Dutch oven over medium-high heat until shimmering. Add onions, garlic, 1 teaspoon salt, and ¼ teaspoon pepper and cook, stirring occasionally, until onions are translucent and starting to soften, about 10 minutes. Add herbes de Provence, pepper flakes, and bay leaf and cook, stirring frequently, for 1 minute. Stir in eggplant and tomatoes. Sprinkle with ½ teaspoon salt and ¼ teaspoon pepper and stir to combine. Transfer pot to oven and cook, uncovered, until vegetables are very tender and spotty brown, 40 to 45 minutes.

2 Remove pot from oven and, using potato masher or heavy wooden spoon, smash and stir eggplant mixture until broken down to sauce-like consistency. Stir in zucchini, bell peppers, ¼ teaspoon salt, and ¼ teaspoon pepper and return to oven. Cook, uncovered, until zucchini and bell peppers are just tender, 20 to 25 minutes.

3 Remove pot from oven, cover, and let sit until zucchini is translucent and easily pierced with tip of paring knife, 10 to 15 minutes. Using wooden spoon, scrape any browned bits from sides of pot and stir back into ratatouille. Discard bay leaf. Stir in 1 tablespoon basil, parsley, and vinegar. Season with salt and pepper to taste. Transfer ratatouille to serving platter, drizzle with remaining 1 tablespoon oil, and sprinkle with remaining 1 tablespoon basil. Serve.

WILD MUSHROOM RAGU

serves 4

1 pound portobello mushroom caps, gills removed, halved and sliced ½ inch thick

18 ounces chanterelle mushrooms, trimmed and halved if small or quartered if large

2 tablespoons unsalted butter

1 onion, chopped fine

½ ounce dried porcini mushrooms, rinsed and minced

Salt and pepper

3 garlic cloves, minced

1 teaspoon minced fresh thyme or ¼ teaspoon dried

½ cup dry red wine

1 (14.5-ounce) can diced tomatoes, drained with juice reserved, chopped

2 tablespoons minced fresh parsley

Why This Recipe Works The wooded north of Italy is a treasure trove of mushrooms, and residents often braise the bounty with wine and serve it over polenta. To re-create this hearty, luxurious combination in our kitchen, we started with a mix of dried and fresh mushrooms available stateside. Dried porcini delivered depth of flavor, while a combination of splurge-worthy, flavorsome chanterelle mushrooms and meaty portobellos provided deep, nutty flavor and great texture, respectively. Developing fond with 2 pounds of moisture-rich mushrooms took quite a lot of time, so we jump-started the cooking process in the microwave. After 6 minutes the mushrooms were tender and had released a fair amount of their juice (which we added to our deglazing liquid so we didn't lose its flavor), so they browned faster in the pot. Red wine, garlic, thyme, and canned diced tomatoes rounded out the flavors of our stew. You can substitute any wild mushrooms for the chanterelles in this recipe. Serve with polenta or over pasta.

1 Microwave portobello mushrooms and chanterelle mushrooms in covered bowl, stirring occasionally, until tender and mushrooms have released their liquid, 6 to 8 minutes. Transfer mushrooms to colander set in bowl and let drain, reserving liquid.

2 Melt butter in Dutch oven over medium heat. Add onion, porcini, and ½ teaspoon salt and cook until softened and lightly browned, 5 to 7 minutes. Add mushrooms and cook, stirring often, until dry and lightly browned, about 5 minutes. Stir in garlic and thyme and cook until fragrant, about 30 seconds.

3 Stir in wine and reserved mushroom liquid, scraping up any browned bits. Stir in tomatoes and their juice, bring to simmer, and cook until ragu is slightly thickened, about 8 minutes. Off heat, stir in parsley and season with salt and pepper to taste. Serve.

HEARTY TEN-VEGETABLE STEW

serves 6 to 8

2 tablespoons vegetable oil

1 pound white mushrooms, trimmed and sliced thin

Salt and pepper

8 ounces Swiss chard, stems chopped fine, leaves sliced ½ inch thick

2 onions, chopped fine

1 celery rib, cut into ½-inch pieces

1 carrot, peeled and cut into 1-inch pieces

1 red bell pepper, stemmed, seeded, and cut into ½-inch pieces

6 garlic cloves, minced

2 teaspoons minced fresh thyme or ¾ teaspoon dried

2 tablespoons all-purpose flour

1 tablespoon tomato paste

½ cup dry white wine

3 cups vegetable broth

2½ cups water

8 ounces red potatoes, cut into 1-inch pieces

2 parsnips, peeled and cut into 1-inch pieces

8 ounces celery root, peeled and cut into 1-inch pieces

2 bay leaves

1 zucchini, halved lengthwise, seeded, and cut into ½-inch pieces

¼ cup minced fresh parsley leaves

1 tablespoon lemon juice

Why This Recipe Works Great vegetable stews marry hearty vegetables with a richly flavored broth and herbs or spices that complement the vegetables. But too often, they're little more than a jumble of soggy produce devoid of color and flavor. We wanted a fresh, flavorful vegetable stew that could be as soul-satisfying in the dead of winter as a beef stew. Sautéing a number of aromatics until they were well browned and then deglazing the pot with wine created a rich base for our 10 vegetables. A variety of starchier root vegetables—carrots, potatoes, parsnips, and celery root—provided our stew with an earthy flavor and thickened broth. The size we cut the vegetables proved key: too small, and they disappeared into the stew; too large, and they didn't cook through. Swiss chard gave us our greens, and we added thestems earlier in the process since the leaves needed just 5 minutes to simmer. To give our vegetable stew meatiness without meat, we browned white button mushrooms. Finally, zucchini gave the stew freshness (we added it near the end so it had some bite), and a splash of lemon juice perked up the flavors. Kale greens or curly-leaf spinach, stemmed and sliced ½ inch thick, can be substituted for the chard leaves (omit the stems); the kale may require up to 5 minutes of additional simmering time in step 5 to become tender.

1 Heat 1 tablespoon oil in Dutch oven over medium heat until shimmering. Add mushrooms and ¼ teaspoon salt, cover, and cook until mushrooms have released their liquid, about 5 minutes. Uncover and continue to cook until mushrooms are dry and browned, 5 to 10 minutes.

2 Stir in remaining 1 tablespoon oil, chard stems, onions, celery, carrot, and bell pepper and cook until vegetables are well browned, 7 to 10 minutes.

3 Stir in garlic and thyme and cook until fragrant, about 30 seconds. Stir in flour and tomato paste and cook for 1 minute. Stir in wine, scraping up browned bits, and cook until nearly evaporated, about 1 minute.

4 Stir in broth, water, potatoes, parsnips, celery root, and bay leaves and bring to boil. Reduce to gentle simmer, cover pot partially (leaving about 1 inch of the pot open), and cook until stew is thickened and vegetables are tender, about 1 hour.

5 Stir in zucchini and chard leaves and continue to simmer until just tender, 5 to 10 minutes. Off heat, remove bay leaves and stir in parsley and lemon juice. Season with salt and pepper to taste, and serve.

ULTIMATE VEGETARIAN CHILI

serves 6 to 8

Salt

1 pound (2½ cups) assorted dried beans, picked over and rinsed

2 dried ancho chiles

2 dried New Mexican chiles

½ ounce dried shiitake mushrooms, chopped coarse

4 teaspoons dried oregano

½ cup walnuts, toasted

1 (28-ounce) can diced tomatoes, drained with juice reserved

3 tablespoons tomato paste

1–2 jalapeño chiles, stemmed and chopped coarse

6 garlic cloves, minced

3 tablespoons soy sauce

¼ cup vegetable oil

2 pounds onions, chopped fine

1 tablespoon ground cumin

⅔ cup medium-grind bulgur

¼ cup minced fresh cilantro

Why This Recipe Works We wanted to develop a vegetarian version of classic chili so flavorful, savory, and satisfying that even meat lovers would enjoy it on its own merits. We'd need to find replacements for the different ways that meat adds depth and flavor to chili. Along with two kinds of beans, bulgur bulked up the chili, giving it a substantial texture. A combination of umami-rich ingredients—soy sauce, dried shiitake mushrooms, and tomatoes—added deep, savory flavor. Walnuts are also high in flavor-boosting glutamates; when we ground some and stirred them in, they contributed even more savoriness plus richness and body. To capitalize on the ability of the fat in the chili to create body in the sauce, we gave the chili a vigorous stir and a 20-minute rest after we took it out of the oven. Stirring helped to release starch from the beans and the bulgur. The starch then clustered around the fat droplets in the chili, preventing them from coalescing and helping to create a thick, velvety emulsion. To substitute chili powder for the dried chiles, grind the shiitakes and oregano and add them to the pot with ¼ cup of chili powder in step 4. We recommend a mix of at least two types of beans, one creamy (such as cannellini or navy) and one earthy (such as pinto, black, or red kidney). For a spicier chili, use both jalapeños. Serve with lime wedges, sour cream, diced avocado, chopped red onion, and/or shredded Monterey Jack or cheddar cheese, if desired.

1 Dissolve 3 tablespoons salt in 4 quarts cold water in large container. Add beans and soak at room temperature for at least 8 hours or up to 24 hours. Drain and rinse well.

2 Adjust oven rack to middle position and heat oven to 300 degrees. Arrange anchos and New Mexican chiles on rimmed baking sheet and toast until fragrant and puffed, about 8 minutes. Transfer to plate, let cool for 5 minutes, then remove stems and seeds. Working in batches, grind toasted chiles, mushrooms, and oregano in spice grinder (or with mortar and pestle) until finely ground.

3 Process walnuts in food processor until finely ground, about 30 seconds; transfer to bowl. Process drained tomatoes, tomato paste, jalapeño(s), garlic, and soy sauce in food processor until tomatoes are finely chopped, about 45 seconds.

4 Heat oil in Dutch oven over medium-high heat until shimmering. Add onions and 1¼ teaspoons salt and cook, stirring occasionally, until onions begin to brown, 8 to 10 minutes. Reduce heat to medium, add ground chile mixture and cumin, and cook, stirring constantly, until fragrant, about 1 minute. Stir in rinsed beans and 7 cups water, bring to boil, and cover; transfer pot to oven, and cook for 45 minutes.

5 Stir in bulgur, ground walnuts, tomato mixture, and reserved tomato juice and continue to cook in oven, covered, until beans are fully tender, about 2 hours.

6 Remove pot from oven, stir well, and let stand, uncovered, for 20 minutes. Stir in cilantro before serving.

QUINOA AND VEGETABLE STEW

serves 6 to 8

2 tablespoons vegetable oil

1 onion, chopped

1 red bell pepper, stemmed, seeded, and cut into ½-inch pieces

5 garlic cloves, minced

1 tablespoon paprika

2 teaspoons ground coriander

1½ teaspoons ground cumin

6 cups vegetable broth

1 pound red potatoes, unpeeled, cut into ½-inch pieces

1 cup prewashed white quinoa

1 cup fresh or frozen corn

2 tomatoes, cored and chopped coarse

1 cup frozen peas

Salt and pepper

8 ounces queso fresco or feta cheese, crumbled (2 cups) (optional)

1 avocado, halved, pitted, and diced

½ cup minced fresh cilantro

Why This Recipe Works Quinoa stews are common in South American regions, where the seed is abundant. The quinoa thickens the stew but also retains its unique texture through braising. Authentic recipes call for obscure ingredients from the region, however. We set out to make a traditional quinoa stew with an easy-to-navigate ingredient list. For spice, we found that paprika has a similar flavor profile to traditional annatto powder; we rounded it out with cumin and coriander. As for the vegetables, we chose red bell pepper, tomatoes, red potatoes, sweet corn, and frozen peas. We added the quinoa after the potatoes had softened and cooked it until it released starch to give the stew body. Finally, we added the traditional garnishes: avocado and cilantro. We like the convenience of prewashed quinoa. If you buy unwashed quinoa (or if you are unsure whether it's washed), be sure to rinse it before cooking to remove its bitter protective coating (called saponin). This stew tends to thicken as it sits; add additional warm vegetable broth as needed before serving to loosen. Do not omit the garnishes; they are important to the flavor of the stew.

1 Heat oil in Dutch oven over medium heat until shimmering. Add onion and bell pepper and cook until softened, 5 to 7 minutes. Stir in garlic, paprika, coriander, and cumin and cook until fragrant, about 30 seconds. Stir in broth and potatoes and bring to boil over high heat. Reduce heat to medium-low and simmer gently for 10 minutes.

2 Stir in quinoa and simmer for 8 minutes. Stir in corn and simmer until potatoes and quinoa are just tender, 5 to 7 minutes. Stir in tomatoes and peas and let heat through, about 2 minutes.

3 Off heat, season with salt and pepper to taste. Sprinkle individual portions with queso fresco, if using; avocado; and cilantro before serving.

Quinoa and Vegetable Stew with Eggs
Serving this stew with a cooked egg on top is a common practice in Peru.

Crack 6 large eggs evenly over top of stew after removing from heat and seasoning with salt and pepper in step 3; cover and let eggs poach off heat until whites have set but yolks are still soft, about 4 minutes. To serve, carefully scoop cooked egg and stew from pot with large spoon.

ARTICHOKE, PEPPER, AND CHICKPEA TAGINE

¼ cup extra-virgin olive oil,
plus extra for serving

3 cups jarred whole baby artichoke
hearts packed in water, quartered,
rinsed, and patted dry

2 yellow or red bell peppers, stemmed,
seeded, and cut into ½-inch-wide strips

1 onion, halved and sliced ¼-inch thick

4 (2-inch) strips lemon zest plus
1 teaspoon grated zest (2 lemons)

8 garlic cloves, minced

1 tablespoon paprika

½ teaspoon ground cumin

¼ teaspoon ground ginger

¼ teaspoon ground coriander

¼ teaspoon ground cinnamon

⅛ teaspoon cayenne pepper

2 tablespoons all-purpose flour

3 cups vegetable broth

2 (15-ounce) cans chickpeas, rinsed

½ cup pitted kalamata olives, halved

½ cup golden raisins

2 tablespoons honey

½ cup plain whole-milk Greek yogurt

½ cup minced fresh cilantro

Salt and pepper

Why This Recipe Works North African tagines traditionally boast a range of meats and vegetables. We wanted to turn out a satisfying meatless version, so we packed it with big bites of artichokes and peppers and tender chickpeas, and flavored it with pungent garlic, lots of warm spices, briny olives, and tangy lemon. Using quick-cooking vegetables kept the time it took to make this dish far shorter than our other tagines—slow-cooked flavor in a little more than 30 minutes. First we drained and rinsed jarred artichokes and then we sautéed them to drive off any remaining moisture. Next we lightly browned bell peppers and onion. Canned chickpeas needed only a 15-minute simmer in the flavorful broth. Lots of lemon zest gave us the required tang. Finally, we enriched the broth of this naturally leaner stew by stirring in Greek yogurt just before serving. While we prefer the richer, fuller flavor of whole-milk Greek yogurt, regular plain whole-milk yogurt can be substituted; the sauce will be slightly thinner. A rasp-style grater makes quick work of turning the garlic into a paste. While we prefer the flavor and texture of jarred whole baby artichoke hearts, you can substitute 18 ounces frozen artichoke hearts, thawed and patted dry, for the jarred.

1 Heat 1 tablespoon oil in Dutch oven over medium heat until shimmering. Add artichokes and cook until golden brown, 5 to 7 minutes; transfer to bowl.

2 Add 1 tablespoon oil, bell peppers, onion, and lemon zest strips to now-empty pot and cook over medium heat until vegetables are softened and lightly browned, 5 to 7 minutes. Stir in two-thirds of garlic, paprika, cumin, ginger, coriander, cinnamon, and cayenne and cook until fragrant, about 30 seconds. Stir in flour and cook for 1 minute.

3 Slowly whisk in broth, scraping up any browned bits and smoothing out any lumps. Stir in artichoke hearts, chickpeas, olives, raisins, and honey and bring to simmer. Reduce heat to low, cover, and simmer gently until vegetables are tender, about 15 minutes.

4 Off heat, discard lemon zest strips. Combine ¼ cup hot liquid and yogurt in bowl to temper, then stir yogurt mixture into pot. Stir in cilantro, remaining 2 tablespoons oil, grated lemon zest, and remaining garlic. Season with salt and pepper to taste. Serve, drizzling individual portions with extra oil.

INDIAN-STYLE VEGETABLE CURRY WITH POTATOES AND CAULIFLOWER

serves 4 to 6

1 (14.5-ounce) can diced tomatoes

3 tablespoons vegetable oil

4 teaspoons curry powder

1½ teaspoons garam masala

2 onions, chopped fine

12 ounces red potatoes, unpeeled, cut into ½-inch pieces

Salt and pepper

3 garlic cloves, minced

1 serrano chile, stemmed, seeded, and minced

1 tablespoon grated fresh ginger

1 tablespoon tomato paste

½ head cauliflower (1 pound), cored and cut into 1-inch florets

1½ cups water

1 (15-ounce) can chickpeas, rinsed

1½ cups frozen peas

½ cup coconut milk

¼ cup minced fresh cilantro

Why This Recipe Works We wanted a recipe for the ultimate vegetable curry, one with a wide variety of perfectly cooked vegetables and a deeply flavorful (but weeknight-friendly) red curry sauce. We started with the sauce. Blooming store-bought curry powder in a bit of oil brought out incredible dimension, turning it into a flavor powerhouse, and garam masala added even more spice flavor. To build the rest of our flavor base, we incorporated a generous amount of sautéed onion, garlic, ginger, and fresh chile, as well as tomato paste for sweetness. For the vegetables, we chose hearty potatoes, cauliflower, and peas, plus convenient canned chickpeas. We found that sautéing the spices with the main ingredients enhanced and melded their collective flavors. Finally, we rounded out our sauce with a combination of water, pureed canned tomatoes, and coconut milk. For a spicier curry, include the chile seeds and ribs when mincing the serrano. We prefer the richer flavor of regular coconut milk here; however, light coconut milk can be substituted. Serve with Cilantro-Mint Chutney (page 211), if desired.

1 Pulse diced tomatoes with their juice in food processor until nearly smooth with some ¼-inch pieces visible, about 3 pulses.

2 Heat oil in Dutch oven over medium-high heat until shimmering. Add curry powder and garam masala and cook until fragrant, about 10 seconds. Stir in onions, potatoes, and ¼ teaspoon salt and cook, stirring occasionally, until onions are browned and potatoes are golden brown at edges, about 10 minutes.

3 Reduce heat to medium. Stir in garlic, serrano, ginger, and tomato paste and cook until fragrant, about 30 seconds. Add cauliflower florets and cook, stirring constantly, until florets are coated with spices, about 2 minutes.

4 Gradually stir in water, scraping up any browned bits. Stir in chickpeas and processed tomatoes and bring to simmer. Cover, reduce to gentle simmer, and cook until vegetables are tender, 20 to 25 minutes.

5 Stir in peas and coconut milk. Cook, uncovered, over medium-low heat until peas are heated through, 1 to 2 minutes. Off heat, stir in cilantro, season with salt and pepper to taste, and serve.

Indian-Style Vegetable Curry with Sweet Potato and Eggplant

Omit peas and substitute 12 ounces sweet potato (about 1 medium), peeled and cut into 1-inch chunks, for red potatoes. Substitute 8 ounces green beans, trimmed and cut into 1-inch lengths, and 1 medium eggplant (about 1 pound), cut into ½-inch pieces, for cauliflower.

POTATO VINDALOO

2 tablespoons vegetable oil

2 onions, chopped fine

1 pound red potatoes, unpeeled and cut into ½-inch pieces

1 pound sweet potatoes, peeled and cut into ½-inch pieces

Salt and pepper

10 garlic cloves, minced

4 teaspoons paprika

1 teaspoon ground cumin

¾ teaspoon ground cardamom

½ teaspoon cayenne pepper

¼ teaspoon ground cloves

2½ cups water

2 bay leaves

1 tablespoon mustard seeds

1 (28-ounce) can diced tomatoes

2½ tablespoons red wine vinegar

¼ cup minced fresh cilantro

Why This Recipe Works Complex, spicy vindaloo is often associated with lamb. But with its warm spices, spicy chiles, vibrant wine vinegar, rich tomatoes, and aromatic onions, garlic, and mustard seeds we knew vindaloo could be transformed into a hearty vegetarian version with the same comfort-food appeal. Vindaloo requires some time to develop complex flavors, so we centered our dish around a longer-cooking vegetable: potatoes. A combination of red and sweet potatoes elevated our stew's flavor. However, after 45 minutes of simmering—more than enough time to build flavor—the potatoes still weren't fully cooked. A second look at our ingredients showed us why: The acidic environment created by the tomatoes and vinegar was preventing our potatoes from becoming tender. To test our theory, we whipped up another batch, this time leaving out the tomatoes and vinegar until the end, cooking them just enough to mellow their flavors. Sure enough, after just 15 minutes, our potatoes were perfectly tender and had soaked up the flavors as they cooked. Serve with a dollop of yogurt.

1 Heat oil in Dutch oven over medium heat until shimmering. Add onions, red potatoes, sweet potatoes, and ½ teaspoon salt and cook, stirring occasionally, until onions are softened and potatoes begin to soften at edges, 10 to 12 minutes.

2 Stir in garlic, paprika, cumin, cardamom, cayenne, and cloves and cook until fragrant and vegetables are well coated, about 2 minutes. Gradually stir in water, scraping up any browned bits. Stir in bay leaves, mustard seeds, and 1 teaspoon salt and bring to simmer. Cover, reduce heat to medium-low, and cook until potatoes are tender, 15 to 20 minutes.

3 Stir in tomatoes and their juice and vinegar and continue to simmer, uncovered, until flavors are blended and sauce has thickened slightly, about 15 minutes. Discard bay leaves, stir in cilantro, and season with salt and pepper to taste. Serve.

BRAISED SQUASH AND WINTER GREENS WITH COCONUT CURRY

serves 4

3 tablespoons extra-virgin olive oil

1 onion, chopped fine

2 pounds butternut squash, peeled, seeded, and cut into ½-inch pieces (6 cups)

5 garlic cloves, minced

2 teaspoons grated fresh ginger

1 teaspoon curry powder

2 pounds kale, stemmed and chopped

1 cup vegetable broth

1 (13.5-ounce) can coconut milk

Salt and pepper

1 tablespoon lime juice

⅓ cup roasted pepitas

Why This Recipe Works Butternut squash is a sweet, tender counterpart to earthy, filling kale in this braise, and it's one of the best braising vegetables, becoming creamy and deep in flavor with time. At first, when paired with the sweet squash, the kale seemed a bit bitter. To balance it, we flavored our vegetable dish with spice and coconut milk, transforming it into an appealing curry. A mere teaspoon of curry powder was all we needed for its flavor to carry through. It was important to bloom the curry powder in oil to bring out and deepen its flavor before adding the braising liquid—otherwise, it tasted raw and the dish was bland. We cooked the curry in a combination of creamy coconut milk and vegetable broth for balanced richness, reserving a half-cup of the coconut milk to stir in at the end of cooking to reinforce the creaminess before serving. To brighten the flavor of our hearty winter dish, we finished it with a squeeze of lime juice. A sprinkle of crunchy roasted pepitas provided a light crunch.

1 Heat 2 tablespoons oil in Dutch oven over medium heat until shimmering. Add onion and cook, stirring frequently, until softened, about 5 minutes. Add squash and cook, stirring occasionally, until just beginning to brown, about 5 minutes; transfer to bowl.

2 Add garlic, ginger, and curry powder to oil in pot and cook over medium-high heat until fragrant, about 30 seconds. Add half of kale and stir until beginning to wilt, about 1 minute. Stir in remaining kale, broth, all but ½ cup coconut milk, and ½ teaspoon salt. Cover pot, reduce heat to medium-low, and cook, stirring occasionally, until kale is wilted, about 15 minutes.

3 Stir in squash and any accumulated juices, cover, and continue to cook until kale and squash are tender, 10 to 20 minutes.

4 Uncover, increase heat to medium-high, and cook, stirring occasionally, until most of liquid has evaporated and sauce has thickened, 2 to 5 minutes. Off heat, stir in lime juice, remaining 1 tablespoon oil, and remaining ½ cup coconut milk. Season with salt and pepper to taste, sprinkle with pepitas, and serve.

CARIBBEAN-STYLE SWISS CHARD AND BUTTERNUT SQUASH STEW

serves 4

2 tablespoons vegetable oil

2 onions, chopped fine

4 scallions, minced

Salt

4 garlic cloves, minced

1 habanero or Scotch bonnet chile, stemmed, seeded, and minced

1 teaspoon minced fresh thyme or ¼ teaspoon dried

Pinch cayenne pepper

3½ cups vegetable broth

2 pounds butternut squash, peeled, seeded, and cut into ½-inch pieces (6 cups)

1 pound Swiss chard, stemmed and cut into 1-inch pieces

1 cup canned coconut milk

Angostura bitters (optional)

Why This Recipe Works For a vegetarian stew that was warm and comforting for winter but with bright, vegetal flavors appropriate for when the sun's out, too, we were inspired by an earthy, spicy island stew that pairs Caribbean callaloo leaves with squash in a rich, coconut-infused broth. We found that Swiss chard was a good alternative to replicate the earthy, slightly citrusy notes of the callaloo leaves. A combination of fresh chile and cayenne pepper gave the stew a robust heat that balanced the sweetness of the butternut squash. A handful of recipes called for a few dashes of angostura bitters, an aromatic alcohol infused with herbs and citrus. While not a must, the bitters gave the stew a uniquely authentic flavor. We pureed a small portion of the stew to give it a thick consistency and bright green color, while leaving most of the greens and squash in large bites. For a spicier stew, include the chile seeds and ribs when mincing.

1 Heat oil in Dutch oven over medium heat until shimmering. Stir in onions, scallions, and ½ teaspoon salt and cook until vegetables are softened, 5 to 7 minutes. Stir in garlic, habanero, thyme, and cayenne and cook until fragrant, about 30 seconds.

2 Stir in broth and squash, scraping up any browned bits, and bring to boil. Reduce to gentle simmer and cook for 15 minutes. Stir in chard and continue to simmer until squash and chard are tender, 10 to 15 minutes. Stir in coconut milk and bring to brief simmer.

3 Process 2 cups stew in blender until smooth, about 45 seconds; return to pot. Season with salt and bitters, if using, to taste, and serve.

CHILE-BRAISED TOFU

serves 4

3 dried ancho chiles, stemmed, seeded, and torn into 1-inch pieces

1 onion, chopped

1 tablespoon tomato paste

2 garlic cloves, crushed and peeled

1 teaspoon ground cumin

1 teaspoon sugar

Salt

3 tablespoons unsalted butter

21 ounces extra-firm tofu, sliced crosswise into ¾-inch-thick slabs

1 tablespoon lime juice, plus lime wedges for serving

2 tablespoons minced fresh cilantro

Why This Recipe Works It may seem counterintuitive to braise already-tender, delicate tofu. But we found that the longer cooking time was perfect for infusing tofu with flavor as it cooked gently in a highly seasoned sauce, turning mild tofu into a bold dish. For the sauce, we didn't go with a predictable Asian profile; instead, we used dried ancho chiles to make a potent, Tex-Mex-inspired sauce. Soaking the dried chiles in boiling water for 15 minutes softened them so they easily broke down to a paste in the blender. The chiles alone, however, were too bitter and one-dimensional. Adding aromatic onion, garlic, and cumin made our sauce taste more well rounded, while a teaspoon of sugar helped soften the slightly bitter ancho flavor without making our sauce taste sweet. Tomato paste thickened the sauce and gave it more savory depth. Finishing the sauce with some butter gave it a silky richness, and a little lime juice brightened the overall flavor of our dish. You can use either firm or extra-firm tofu in this recipe.

1 Pour 2 cups boiling water over anchos in bowl and let sit until very soft, about 15 minutes; drain anchos, discarding liquid. Process softened anchos, onion, ¼ cup water, tomato paste, garlic, cumin, sugar, and 1 teaspoon salt in blender until mixture forms thick but smooth puree, about 1 minute, stopping to scrape down sides of blender jar as needed,

2 Melt 1 tablespoon butter in 12-inch skillet over medium heat. Add ancho puree and cook, stirring often, until mixture is fragrant and thickens slightly, about 3 minutes. Whisk in 1¾ cups water until smooth.

3 Lay tofu in skillet in even layer and bring to simmer. Reduce heat to low and simmer gently until tofu is warmed through and flavors have melded, about 30 minutes.

4 Transfer tofu to platter. Stir remaining 2 tablespoons butter and lime juice into sauce and season with salt and pepper to taste. Pour sauce over tofu, sprinkle with cilantro, and serve with lime wedges.

ASIAN BRAISED TOFU WITH SQUASH AND COCONUT MILK

serves 4

14 ounces extra-firm tofu, cut into ¾-inch cubes

Salt and pepper

3 tablespoons vegetable oil

1½ pounds butternut squash, peeled, seeded, and cut into ½-inch pieces (4½ cups)

1 pound eggplant, cut into ½-inch pieces

1 onion, chopped fine

8 garlic cloves, minced

2 tablespoons grated fresh ginger

1 lemon grass stalk, trimmed to bottom 6 inches and bruised with back of chef's knife

1 (13.5-ounce) can coconut milk

½ cup vegetable broth

½ cup minced fresh cilantro

4 teaspoons lime juice

Soy sauce

2 scallions, sliced thin

Why This Recipe Works This satisfying vegetarian braised dish has many layers of flavor including sweet butternut squash; meaty, creamy eggplant; fragrant Asian aromatics; and rich coconut milk. In addition to the vegetables, we added tofu for bulk, and we browned it, as well as the squash and eggplant, in a skillet. To build a flavorful base for our braise, we sautéed onion, garlic, ginger, and lemon grass until they softened and their fragrance was released. For the braising liquid, we combined vegetable broth with coconut milk, which added a creamy texture without making the sauce too heavy. The vegetables needed only 20 minutes to cook through and lend their flavors to the sauce, which we finished with some cilantro and lime juice for freshness and soy sauce for depth and salinity. You can use either firm or extra-firm tofu in this recipe.

1 Spread tofu over paper towel–lined baking sheet, let drain for 20 minutes, then gently press dry with paper towels. Season with salt and pepper.

2 Meanwhile, heat 1 tablespoon oil in 12-inch nonstick skillet over medium-high heat until shimmering. Add squash and cook until golden brown, 8 to 10 minutes; transfer to large bowl.

3 Add 1 tablespoon oil to now-empty skillet and heat over medium-high heat until shimmering. Add eggplant and cook until golden brown, 5 to 7 minutes; transfer to bowl with squash.

4 Add remaining 1 tablespoon oil to skillet and heat over medium heat until shimmering. Add onion and cook until softened and lightly browned, 5 to 7 minutes. Stir in garlic, ginger, and lemon grass and cook until fragrant, about 30 seconds. Stir in coconut milk, broth, browned squash-eggplant mixture, and drained tofu. Bring to simmer, reduce heat to medium-low, and cook until vegetables are softened and sauce is slightly thickened, 15 to 20 minutes.

5 Off heat, discard lemon grass. Stir in cilantro and lime juice. Season with soy sauce and pepper to taste. Sprinkle with scallions and serve.

BRAISED FENNEL WITH RADICCHIO AND PARMESAN

serves 6

3 tablespoons olive oil

3 fennel bulbs (12 ounces each), 2 tablespoons fronds minced, stalks discarded, bulbs cut vertically into ½-inch-thick slabs

½ teaspoon grated lemon zest plus 2 teaspoons juice

Salt and pepper

½ cup dry white wine

1 head radicchio (10 ounces), cored and sliced thin

¼ cup water

2 teaspoons honey

2 tablespoons chopped toasted pine nuts

Shaved Parmesan cheese

Why This Recipe Works Slow-cooked fennel becomes richly aromatic and meaty in texture, so it's a great accompaniment to just about anything—from richer meats to delicate fish—but it can even stand alone for supper, served with polenta. We cut the fennel into thick, satisfying slabs and braised them with wine and aromatics. Keeping the core intact allowed us to flip the slabs for this special dish without them falling apart. For deeper flavor, we opted to leave the fennel in the skillet even after the braising liquid had evaporated to achieve a deeply golden, caramelized crust. To take advantage of the fond left in the pan from browning and to balance the sweetness of the fennel, we stirred in sliced radicchio, cooking it briefly with water and honey to tame its bitter edge and create a complex pan sauce. A sprinkle of Parmesan cheese and toasted pine nuts added salt, richness, and crunch, and some minced fennel fronds provided freshness.

1 Heat oil in 12-inch skillet over medium heat until shimmering. Add fennel pieces, lemon zest, ½ teaspoon salt, and ¼ teaspoon pepper, then pour wine over fennel. (Skillet will be slightly crowded at first, but fennel will fit into single layer as it cooks.) Cover, reduce heat to medium-low, and cook until fennel is just tender, about 20 minutes.

2 Increase heat to medium, flip fennel pieces, and continue to cook, uncovered, until fennel is well browned on first side and liquid is almost completely evaporated, 5 to 8 minutes. Flip fennel pieces and continue to cook until well browned on second side, 2 to 4 minutes. Transfer fennel to serving platter and tent with aluminum foil.

3 Add radicchio, water, honey, and pinch salt to now-empty skillet and cook over low heat, scraping up any browned bits, until radicchio is wilted, 3 to 5 minutes. Off heat, stir in lemon juice and season with salt and pepper to taste. Arrange radicchio over fennel and sprinkle with pine nuts, minced fennel fronds, and shaved Parmesan. Serve.

BEANS

Drunken Beans

297 **Hearty Tuscan White Bean Stew**

298 **Cranberry Beans with Warm Spices**

301 **Drunken Beans**

302 **Baked Navy Beans**

304 **Red Beans and Rice**

306 **Sicilian White Beans and Escarole**

309 **Stewed Chickpeas with Eggplant and Tomatoes**

311 **Chickpeas with Spinach, Chorizo, and Smoked Paprika**

312 **Black-Eyed Peas and Greens**

314 **Cuban-Style Black Beans and Rice**

317 **Black Bean Chili**

319 **North African Vegetable and Bean Stew**

321 **Lentils with Spinach and Garlic Chips**

322 **French Lentils with Carrots and Parsley**
   Curried French Lentils with Golden Raisins
   French Lentils with Swiss Chard

325 **Spiced Red Lentils (Masoor Dal)**
   Red Lentils with Coconut Milk

326 **French Pork and White Bean Casserole**

328 **Brazilian Black Bean and Pork Stew**

331 **Texas-Style Pinto Beans**

HEARTY TUSCAN WHITE BEAN STEW

serves 8

Salt and pepper

1 pound (2½ cups) dried cannellini beans, picked over and rinsed

6 ounces pancetta, cut into ¼-inch pieces

1 tablespoon extra-virgin olive oil, plus extra for serving

1 onion, chopped

2 carrots, peeled and cut into ½-inch pieces

2 celery ribs, cut into ½-inch pieces

8 garlic cloves, peeled and smashed

4 cups chicken broth

2 bay leaves

1 pound kale or collard greens, stemmed and chopped

1 (14.5-ounce) can diced tomatoes, drained

1 sprig fresh rosemary

Why This Recipe Works The people of Tuscany are known as *mangiafagioli*, or "bean eaters," a nod to the prominent role beans play in their cuisine. Cannellini (white kidney) beans are the region's most famous legume, and Tuscan cooks go to extremes to ensure these beans are cooked perfectly, from simmering them in rainwater to slow-cooking them overnight in a wine bottle in a fire's dying embers. This quintessential bean stew features an aromatic base, hearty greens, tomatoes, pancetta and, of course, creamy, buttery beans—the hardest part to nail. Soaking the beans overnight was essential to soften them so their interiors cooked up creamy. And salting the soaking water—essentially brining the beans—softened the skins until they were barely perceptible for ultratender beans. After experimenting with cooking times and temperatures, we found that a vigorous stovetop simmer caused some beans to explode, so we gently cooked them in a 250-degree oven for even results. Adding the tomatoes toward the end of cooking ensured their acidity wouldn't toughen the beans.

1 Dissolve 3 tablespoons salt in 4 quarts cold water in large container. Add beans and soak at room temperature for at least 8 hours or up to 24 hours. Drain and rinse well.

2 Adjust oven rack to lower-middle position and heat oven to 250 degrees. Cook pancetta and oil in Dutch oven over medium heat, stirring occasionally, until pancetta is lightly browned and fat is rendered, 6 to 10 minutes. Stir in onion, carrots, and celery and cook until softened and lightly browned, 10 to 16 minutes. Stir in garlic and cook until fragrant, about 1 minute. Stir in broth, 3 cups water, bay leaves, and beans; bring to boil; and cover. Transfer pot to oven. Cook until beans are almost tender (very center of beans will still be firm), 45 minutes to 1 hour.

3 Stir in kale and tomatoes, cover, and cook until beans and greens are fully tender, 30 to 40 minutes.

4 Remove pot from oven and submerge rosemary sprig in stew. Cover and let sit for 15 minutes. Discard bay leaves and rosemary sprig and season stew with salt and pepper to taste. If desired, use back of spoon to mash some beans against side of pot to thicken stew. Drizzle individual portions with extra oil before serving.

CRANBERRY BEANS WITH WARM SPICES

serves 6 to 8

Salt and pepper

1 pound (2½ cups) dried cranberry beans, picked over and rinsed

¼ cup extra-virgin olive oil

1 onion, chopped fine

2 carrots, peeled and chopped fine

4 garlic cloves, sliced thin

1 tablespoon tomato paste

½ teaspoon ground cinnamon

½ cup dry white wine

4 cups chicken or vegetable broth

2 tablespoons lemon juice, plus extra for seasoning

2 tablespoons minced fresh mint

Why This Recipe Works Cranberry beans have a delicate flavor and a creamy texture similar to that of pinto or cannellini beans. We wanted to create a dish that would highlight these beans, and since they're common in Turkey, we took inspiration from the region to create a spiced flavor profile. Since cranberry beans are rarely canned, we knew we'd have to start with dried beans. To help the beans cook up creamy and tender, we soaked them overnight in salt water before thoroughly rinsing them to remove any excess salt. We sautéed aromatic vegetables along with tomato paste for depth of flavor; just a touch of cinnamon imparted a subtle yet distinctly Turkish flavor. White wine offered acidity, and broth gave the dish a hearty backbone. Letting the beans cook through in the gentle heat of the oven ensured that they were perfectly cooked without the need for constant monitoring. We completed our comforting side dish with lemon juice and fresh mint, which nicely balanced the warm, rich flavors of the beans. If cranberry beans are unavailable, you can substitute pinto beans.

1 Dissolve 3 tablespoons salt in 4 quarts cold water in large container. Add beans and soak at room temperature for at least 8 hours or up to 24 hours. Drain and rinse well.

2 Adjust oven rack to lower-middle position and heat oven to 350 degrees. Heat oil in Dutch oven over medium heat until shimmering. Add onion and carrots and cook until softened, about 5 minutes. Stir in garlic, tomato paste, cinnamon, and ¼ teaspoon pepper and cook until fragrant, about 1 minute. Stir in wine, scraping up any browned bits. Stir in broth, ½ cup water, and beans; bring to boil; and cover; transfer pot to oven. Cook until beans are tender, about 1½ hours, stirring every 30 minutes.

3 Stir in lemon juice and mint. Season with salt, pepper, and extra lemon juice to taste. Adjust consistency with extra hot water as needed. Serve.

DRUNKEN BEANS

serves 6

Salt

1 pound (2½ cups) dried pinto beans, picked over and rinsed

30 sprigs fresh cilantro (1 bunch)

4 slices bacon, cut into ¼-inch pieces

1 onion, chopped fine

2 poblano chiles, stemmed, seeded, and chopped fine

3 garlic cloves, minced

½ cup tequila

2 bay leaves

1 cup Mexican lager

¼ cup tomato paste

2 limes, quartered

2 ounces Cotija cheese, crumbled (½ cup)

Why This Recipe Works A common dish on Mexican tables, *frijoles borrachos*, or drunken beans, consists of pinto beans that are cooked with beer or tequila, a bit of pork or lard, and herbs and aromatics. Once the flavors meld and the cooking liquid thickens from the beans' starches, the dish is as satisfying as a rich stew. To give our drunken beans complex flavor without imparting booziness or bitterness, we turned to a balanced mixture of both beer and tequila. We used bacon for its smoky, meaty flavor, but to preserve that flavor, we removed the bacon from the pot after crisping it, using it as a garnish, and sautéed onion, garlic, and poblano chiles in the fat for a flavorful base. We pulled the pot off the heat, poured in the tequila, and let it evaporate, cooking off some of the alcohol and leaving behind its smoky sweetness. Cilantro leaves are a classic garnish for drunken beans, but the stems also have a great aromatic quality, so we tied the plucked stems into a bundle and added them to the pot along with the beans and other seasonings; we held back the acidic beer and tomato paste until the beans were tender. A vigorous simmer to finish jostled the beans, causing them to release more starches that gave the cooking liquid pleasant body.

1 Dissolve 3 tablespoons salt in 4 quarts cold water in large bowl or container. Add beans and soak at room temperature for at least 8 hours or up to 24 hours. Drain and rinse well.

2 Adjust oven rack to lower-middle position and heat oven to 275 degrees. Pick leaves from 20 cilantro sprigs (reserve stems), chop fine, and refrigerate until needed. Using kitchen twine, tie remaining 10 cilantro sprigs and reserved stems into bundle.

3 Cook bacon in Dutch oven over medium heat, stirring occasionally, until crispy, 5 to 8 minutes. Using slotted spoon, transfer bacon to paper towel–lined bowl; set aside. Add onion, poblanos, and garlic to fat in pot and cook, stirring frequently, until vegetables are softened, 6 to 7 minutes. Remove from heat. Add tequila and cook until evaporated, 3 to 4 minutes. Return to heat. Increase heat to high; stir in 3½ cups water, bay leaves, 1 teaspoon salt, beans, and cilantro bundle; and bring to boil. Cover and transfer pot to oven. Cook until beans are just soft, 45 minutes to 1 hour.

4 Remove pot from oven. Discard bay leaves and cilantro bundle. Stir in beer and tomato paste and bring to simmer over medium-low heat. Simmer vigorously, stirring frequently, until liquid is thick and beans are fully tender, about 30 minutes. Season with salt to taste. Serve, passing chopped cilantro, lime wedges, Cotija, and reserved bacon separately.

BAKED NAVY BEANS

serves 4 to 6

1 pound (2½ cups) dried navy beans, picked over and rinsed

1 tablespoon baking soda

1 tablespoon vegetable oil

1 onion, chopped fine

¼ cup molasses

2 tablespoons packed dark brown sugar

2 tablespoons soy sauce

4 teaspoons Dijon mustard

2 teaspoons smoked paprika

Salt and pepper

2 teaspoons cider vinegar

Why This Recipe Works Authentic Boston baked beans have "baked" in their name, but they're essentially a braise: Small white beans like navy beans cook slowly in a pot with a mix of ingredients that turns them sweet, tangy, rich, and saucy. They're always a picnic hit, but we don't often have the 5 to 6 hours they traditionally require. We were intrigued to develop a recipe for baked beans that had the same sweet, tangy, and rich flavors but didn't take all the time. An additional challenge: Since we were already shaking things up, we thought we'd make the dish universally enjoyable by developing a vegetarian version (salt pork and bacon are often the first ingredients in the pot). To get creamy-textured beans in a lot less time, first we simmered dried beans with a little baking soda. The alkaline soda weakened the cell structure of the beans, tenderizing them more quickly and allowing us to shave the cooking time down to 2 hours. We added traditional flavorings—molasses, brown sugar, mustard, and cider vinegar—before covering the pot and continuing to braise the beans in the oven, but we needed to find a way to deepen the flavor and amp up the meatiness of the dish. Supplementing with soy sauce and smoked paprika was the solution; the umami-rich soy sauce gave the dish more savory flavor, and the paprika added great smoky depth. Cooking the beans uncovered in the last 30 minutes helped the beans reduce and caramelize a bit, giving them that "baked" quality and a perfect glaze.

1 Adjust oven rack to middle position and heat oven to 350 degrees. Bring 3 quarts water, beans, and baking soda to boil in Dutch oven over high heat. Reduce heat to medium-high and simmer vigorously for 20 minutes. Drain and rinse beans and pot; dry pot.

2 Heat oil in now-empty pot over medium heat until shimmering. Add onion and cook until softened, about 5 minutes. Stir in 4½ cups water, rinsed beans, molasses, sugar, soy sauce, 1 tablespoon mustard, paprika, ¾ teaspoon salt, and ¼ teaspoon pepper and bring to boil. Cover and transfer pot to oven. Cook until beans are nearly tender, about 1½ hours.

3 Uncover and continue to bake until beans are completely tender, about 30 minutes. Stir in remaining 1 teaspoon mustard and vinegar. Season with salt and pepper to taste. Serve.

RED BEANS AND RICE

serves 8 to 10

Salt and pepper

1 pound (about 2 cups) dried small red beans, picked over and rinsed

4 slices bacon, chopped fine

1 onion, chopped fine

1 small green bell pepper, stemmed, seeded and chopped fine

1 celery rib, chopped fine

3 garlic cloves, minced

1 teaspoon minced fresh thyme

1 teaspoon sweet paprika

2 bay leaves

¼ teaspoon cayenne pepper

3 cups chicken broth

6 cups water

8 ounces andouille sausage, halved lengthwise and cut into ¼-inch slices

1 teaspoon red wine vinegar, plus extra for seasoning

3 scallions, sliced thin

Hot sauce (optional)

Why This Recipe Works In many Creole kitchens, red beans and rice was (and is) a Monday night dish. The hambone saved from Sunday dinner would simmer on the back burner, its marrow flavoring the red beans and thickening the broth. Today, however, most home cooks don't have leftover hambones readily available, so we set out to serve an equally flavorful, spicy dish with ingredients we could pick up at the supermarket. For porky, salty flavor, we cooked four strips of bacon and added onion, bell pepper, and celery to the rendered fat, then the garlic and spices. To ensure that our beans turned out tender and tasted meaty without a hambone, we cooked them in both water and chicken broth before adding smoky, spicy andouille sausage. Half an hour was just enough time for the sausage to impart great flavor to the beans without becoming too tough. We would be happy to serve this Louisiana classic, spooned over hot white rice, any night of the week. Andouille sausage is traditional in this recipe. If you can't find andouille at your local market, use kielbasa. In order for the starch from the beans to thicken the cooking liquid, it's important to maintain a vigorous simmer in step 2. Serve over white rice.

1 Dissolve 3 tablespoons salt in 4 quarts cold water in large container. Add beans and soak at room temperature for at least 8 hours or up to 24 hours. Drain and rinse well.

2 Heat bacon in Dutch oven over medium heat, stirring occasionally, until browned and almost fully rendered, 5 to 8 minutes. Add onion, bell pepper, and celery; cook, stirring frequently, until vegetables are softened, 6 to 7 minutes. Stir in garlic, thyme, paprika, bay leaves, cayenne pepper, and ¼ teaspoon black pepper; cook until fragrant, about 30 seconds. Stir in beans, broth, and water, and bring to boil over high heat. Reduce heat and vigorously simmer, stirring occasionally, until beans are just soft and liquid begins to thicken, 45 minutes to 1 hour.

3 Stir in sausage and 1 teaspoon vinegar and cook until liquid is thick and beans are fully tender and creamy, about 30 minutes. Season with salt, pepper, and additional vinegar to taste. Serve over rice, sprinkling with scallions and passing hot sauce separately, if using.

SICILIAN WHITE BEANS AND ESCAROLE

serves 4

1 tablespoon extra-virgin olive oil, plus extra for serving

2 onions, chopped fine

Salt and pepper

4 garlic cloves, minced

⅛ teaspoon red pepper flakes

1 head escarole (1 pound), trimmed and sliced 1 inch thick

1 (15-ounce) can cannellini beans, rinsed

1 cup chicken or vegetable broth

1 cup water

2 teaspoons lemon juice

Why This Recipe Works Braising is often about cooking low and slow, which is part of why bean cookery is a quintessential example of the technique. But bean braises can also be your quickest weekday dinners—if you use canned beans. We love some varieties of beans canned, and since they're already cooked, braising serves to warm them through to perfect creaminess and infuse the starchy specimens with the flavors in the pot for a succulent dish. White beans and escarole are a classic pairing in Italian cooking: Combining the buttery texture of canned cannellini beans with tender, slightly bitter escarole resulted in a well-balanced and simple side dish. Sautéed onions gave the dish a rich, deep flavor base without requiring too much time at the stove. Red pepper flakes lent a slight heat without overwhelming the other ingredients, and a combination of broth and water were a flavorful backbone. We added the escarole and beans along with the liquid, and then we cooked the greens just until the leaves were wilted before cranking up the heat so the liquid would quickly evaporate. This short stint over the heat prevented the beans from breaking down and becoming mushy. Once we took the pot off the heat, we stirred in lemon juice for a bright finish and drizzled on some extra olive oil for richness. Chicory can be substituted for the escarole; however, its flavor is stronger.

1 Heat oil in Dutch oven over medium heat until shimmering. Add onions and ½ teaspoon salt and cook until softened and lightly browned, 5 to 7 minutes. Stir in garlic and pepper flakes and cook until fragrant, about 30 seconds.

2 Stir in escarole, beans, broth, and water and bring to simmer. Cook, stirring occasionally, until escarole is wilted, about 5 minutes. Increase heat to high and cook until liquid is nearly evaporated, 10 to 15 minutes. Stir in lemon juice and season with salt and pepper to taste. Drizzle individual portions with extra oil and serve.

STEWED CHICKPEAS WITH EGGPLANT AND TOMATOES

serves 6

¼ cup extra-virgin olive oil

2 onions, chopped

1 green bell pepper, stemmed, seeded, and chopped fine

Salt and pepper

3 garlic cloves, minced

1 tablespoon minced fresh oregano or 1 teaspoon dried

2 bay leaves

1 pound eggplant, cut into 1-inch pieces

1 (28-ounce) can whole peeled tomatoes, drained with juice reserved, chopped coarse

2 (15-ounce) cans chickpeas, drained with 1 cup liquid reserved

Why This Recipe Works In Greece, fresh eggplant and dried chickpeas are cooked together for hours to create a hearty stew with impressive depth of savory flavor; the silky, luxurious texture of the eggplant is complemented by the firm-tender chickpeas. We found that canned chickpeas held up well, even during the long cooking that the eggplant required, and their surprisingly flavorful liquid was a bonus that we put to good use. We chopped canned whole tomatoes to give the dish a rustic texture and a pleasantly acidic tomatoey backbone. A combination of stovetop and oven cooking created the texture we were after. We added our chickpeas, tomatoes, and eggplant (cut into 1-inch pieces to ensure that it softened but didn't completely break down) to our base of sautéed aromatics and transferred the pot to the oven. Baking the mixture uncovered concentrated the flavors and allowed any unwanted liquid to evaporate, eliminating the need to pretreat the eggplant. Stirring a couple of times during cooking ensured that the top layer didn't dry out. Some fresh oregano, added at the end, gave this savory dish a welcome burst of herbaceous flavor. This versatile dish tastes equally good when served warm or at room temperature.

1 Adjust oven rack to lower-middle position and heat oven to 400 degrees. Heat oil in Dutch oven over medium heat until shimmering. Add onions, bell pepper, ½ teaspoon salt, and ¼ teaspoon pepper and cook until softened, about 5 minutes. Stir in garlic, 1 teaspoon oregano, and bay leaves and cook until fragrant, about 30 seconds.

2 Stir in eggplant, tomatoes and reserved juice, and chickpeas and reserved liquid and bring to boil; transfer pot to oven. Cook, uncovered, until eggplant is very tender, 45 minutes to 1 hour, stirring twice during cooking.

3 Discard bay leaves. Stir in remaining 2 teaspoons oregano and season with salt and pepper to taste. Serve.

CHICKPEAS WITH SPINACH, CHORIZO, AND SMOKED PAPRIKA

serves 4 to 6

2 tablespoons boiling water

Pinch saffron threads, crumbled

2 teaspoons extra-virgin olive oil

8 ounces curly-leaf spinach, stemmed

3 ounces Spanish-style chorizo sausage, chopped fine

5 garlic cloves, sliced thin

1 tablespoon smoked paprika

1 teaspoon ground cumin

Salt and pepper

2 (15-ounce) cans chickpeas

1 recipe Picada (page 259)

1 tablespoon sherry vinegar

Why This Recipe Works *Espinacas* is a traditional tapas dish found in the southern Spanish region of Andalucia consisting of tender stewed chickpeas, delicate wilted spinach, and bold North African–influenced spices. We set out to develop an adaptation of this dish that could work as a larger meal. We stuck with the classic southern Spanish flavors of saffron, garlic, smoked paprika, and cumin. Tasters also liked the traditional addition of chorizo, which added meaty richness. Curly-leaf spinach was the best choice for its sturdy texture in this brothy dish. To keep the recipe streamlined, we opted to wilt the spinach and then set it aside before building the brothy base with canned chickpeas and aromatics. Including the chickpeas' flavorful, starchy canning liquid helped to give the dish more body. Finally, we added a traditional *picada*, which is often used in Spanish cooking as a thickener. The bread crumb–based mixture gave the stewed beans and greens just the right velvety texture and flavor boost. Our finished dish would be equally at home as part of a tapas spread or served as an entrée over rice or with good crusty bread to sop up the flavorful broth. If you can't find curly-leaf spinach, you can substitute flat-leaf spinach; do not substitute baby spinach. For an accurate measurement of boiling water, bring a full kettle of water to a boil and then measure out the desired amount.

1 Combine boiling water and saffron in small bowl and let steep for 5 minutes.

2 Heat 1 teaspoon oil in Dutch oven over medium heat until shimmering. Add spinach and 2 tablespoons water, cover, and cook, stirring occasionally, until spinach is wilted but still bright green, about 1 minute. Transfer spinach to colander and gently press to release liquid. Transfer spinach to cutting board and chop coarse. Return to colander and press again.

3 Heat remaining 1 teaspoon oil in now-empty pot over medium heat until shimmering. Add chorizo and cook until lightly browned, about 5 minutes. Stir in garlic, paprika, cumin, and ¼ teaspoon pepper and cook until fragrant, about 30 seconds. Stir in chickpeas and their liquid, 1 cup water, and saffron mixture and bring to simmer. Cook, stirring occasionally, until chickpeas are tender and liquid has thickened slightly, 10 to 15 minutes.

4 Off heat, stir in picada, spinach, and vinegar and let sit until heated through, about 2 minutes. Adjust sauce consistency with hot water as needed. Season with salt and pepper to taste, and serve.

BLACK-EYED PEAS AND GREENS

serves 6 to 8

6 slices bacon, cut into ½-inch pieces

1 onion, halved and sliced thin

1¼ teaspoons salt

4 garlic cloves, minced

½ teaspoon ground cumin

½ teaspoon pepper

¼ teaspoon red pepper flakes

1 (14.5-ounce) can diced tomatoes

1½ cups chicken broth

1 pound collard greens, stemmed and chopped

2 (15-ounce) cans black-eyed peas, rinsed

1 tablespoon cider vinegar

1 teaspoon sugar

Why This Recipe Works A big pot of black-eyed peas and greens is quintessential Southern food, traditionally served on New Year's, and there are about as many versions as there are Southern cooks. We wanted to spend our holiday celebrating, not cooking, so we created our version with canned beans and the traditional choice of collards; we made sure to add the beans in just the last 15 minutes of cooking and stir them gently so they wouldn't break down too much. With no time to draw flavor out of a hambone—a classic addition—we relied on smoky bacon and savory chicken broth for the appropriate meaty flavor. Canned tomatoes, a handful of aromatics and spices, a tablespoon of vinegar, and a teaspoon of sugar balanced the flavors and rounded out this hearty dish. Once the beans were warm, the greens were silken, and the rustic flavors had melded, we removed the lid and upped the heat to let the liquid reduce and concentrate. Don't crush the black-eyed peas; stir gently.

1 Cook bacon in Dutch oven over medium heat until crispy, 5 to 7 minutes. Using slotted spoon, transfer bacon to paper towel–lined plate; set aside.

2 Pour off all but 2 tablespoons fat from pot. Add onion and salt and cook, stirring frequently, until golden brown, about 10 minutes. Add garlic, cumin, pepper, and pepper flakes and cook until fragrant, about 30 seconds.

3 Add tomatoes and their juice. Stir in broth and bring to boil. Add greens, cover, and reduce heat to medium-low. Simmer until greens are tender, about 15 minutes.

4 Add black-eyed peas to pot, cover, and cook, stirring occasionally, until greens are silky and completely tender, about 15 minutes. Remove lid, increase heat to medium-high, and cook until liquid is reduced by one-quarter, about 5 minutes. Stir in vinegar and sugar. Top with reserved bacon and serve.

CUBAN-STYLE BLACK BEANS AND RICE

serves 6

Salt

1 cup dried black beans, picked over and rinsed

2 cups chicken broth

2 large green bell peppers, halved, stemmed, and seeded

1 large onion, halved at equator and peeled, root end left intact

1 head garlic, 5 cloves minced, rest of head halved at equator with skin left intact

2 bay leaves

1½ cups long-grain white rice

2 tablespoons olive oil

6 ounces lean salt pork, cut into ¼-inch pieces

4 teaspoons ground cumin

1 tablespoon minced fresh oregano

2 tablespoons red wine vinegar

2 scallions, sliced thin

Lime wedges

Why This Recipe Works *Moros y Cristianos*, Cuban black beans and rice, is popular well beyond its island home because of the complex flavors contributed by sautéed vegetables, spices, and pork. The dried beans are traditionally simmered on their own, and then some of the inky bean liquid is used to cook the rice, adding still more depth to this one-dish meal. For our own version, we expanded on this method, simmering a portion of the *sofrito* (the traditional combination of garlic, bell pepper, and onion) with our beans to infuse them with flavor and then using the liquid to cook our rice and beans together. Lightly browning the remaining sofrito vegetables and spices with rendered salt pork added complex, meaty flavor, and finishing the dish in the oven eliminated the crusty bottom that can form when the dish is cooked entirely on the stove. It's important to use lean—not fatty—salt pork. If you can't find it, substitute six slices of bacon. If using bacon, decrease the cooking time in step 4 to 8 minutes.

1 Dissolve 1½ tablespoons salt in 2 quarts cold water in large container. Add beans and soak at room temperature for at least 8 hours or up to 24 hours. Drain and rinse well.

2 Stir beans, 2 cups water, broth, 1 bell pepper half, 1 onion half (with root end), halved garlic head, bay leaves, and 1 teaspoon salt in Dutch oven. Bring to simmer over medium-high heat, cover, and reduce heat to low. Cook until beans are just soft, 30 to 35 minutes. Using tongs, discard bell pepper, onion, garlic, and bay leaves. Drain beans in colander set over large bowl, reserving 2½ cups bean cooking liquid. (If you don't have enough bean cooking liquid, add water to equal 2½ cups.) Do not clean pot.

3 Adjust oven rack to middle position and heat oven to 350 degrees. Place rice in large fine-mesh strainer and rinse under cold running water until water runs clear, about 1½ minutes. Shake strainer vigorously to remove all excess water; set rice aside. Cut remaining bell peppers and

remaining onion half into 2-inch pieces and pulse in food processor until broken into rough ¼-inch pieces, about 8 pulses, scraping down sides of bowl as needed; set aside.

4 Heat 1 tablespoon oil and salt pork in now-empty pot over medium-low heat and cook, stirring frequently, until lightly browned and fat is rendered, 15 to 20 minutes. Add remaining 1 tablespoon oil, chopped bell peppers and onion, cumin, and oregano. Increase heat to medium and continue to cook, stirring frequently, until vegetables are softened and beginning to brown, 10 to 15 minutes longer. Add minced garlic and cook, stirring constantly, until fragrant, about 1 minute. Add rice and stir to coat, about 30 seconds.

5 Stir in beans, reserved bean cooking liquid, vinegar, and ½ teaspoon salt. Increase heat to medium-high, bring to simmer, and cover; transfer pot to oven. Cook until liquid is absorbed and rice is tender, about 30 minutes. Fluff with fork and let rest, uncovered, for 5 minutes. Serve, passing scallions and lime wedges separately.

BLACK BEAN CHILI

serves 6 to 8

1 pound white mushrooms, trimmed and broken into rough pieces

1 tablespoon mustard seeds

2 teaspoons cumin seeds

3 tablespoons vegetable oil

1 onion, chopped fine

9 garlic cloves, minced

1 tablespoon minced canned chipotle chile in adobo sauce

3 tablespoons chili powder

2½ cups vegetable broth

2½ cups water, plus extra as needed

1 pound (2½ cups) dried black beans, picked over and rinsed

1 tablespoon packed light brown sugar

⅛ teaspoon baking soda

2 bay leaves

1 (28-ounce) can crushed tomatoes

2 red bell peppers, stemmed, seeded, and cut into ½-inch pieces

½ cup minced fresh cilantro

Salt and pepper

Why This Recipe Works Black bean chili is an essential bean-only chili but it can be thin and wan—more like soup than a soul-satisfying chili. We wanted a hearty black bean chili that boasted tender, well-seasoned beans. Dried beans were essential here, but since we didn't mind if some beans burst—they thickened the chili and gave it the rustic texture of meat versions—we skipped the lengthy step of salt-soaking. White mushrooms gave the chili meaty flavor without meat. Whole cumin seeds and chipotle added depth and smokiness, and a surprising ingredient, toasted mustard seeds, added a pungency and complexity that tasters loved. A sprinkle of minced cilantro brightened the complex, deeply flavored dish. We strongly prefer the texture and flavor of mustard seeds and cumin seeds in this chili, but you can substitute ½ teaspoon dry mustard and/or ½ teaspoon ground cumin, added to the pot with the chili powder in step 3. Serve with lime wedges, sour cream, shredded cheddar or Monterey Jack cheese, chopped tomatoes, and/or finely chopped onion.

1 Adjust oven rack to lower-middle position and heat oven to 325 degrees. Pulse mushrooms in food processor until coarsely chopped and uniform in size, about 10 pulses.

2 Toast mustard seeds and cumin seeds in Dutch oven over medium heat, stirring constantly, until fragrant, about 1 minute. Stir in oil, onion, and processed mushrooms, cover, and cook until vegetables have released their liquid, about 5 minutes. Uncover and continue to cook until vegetables are browned, 5 to 10 minutes.

3 Stir in garlic and chipotle and cook until fragrant, about 30 seconds. Stir in chili powder and cook, stirring constantly, until fragrant, about 1 minute. Stir in broth, water, beans, sugar, baking soda, and bay leaves and bring to simmer, skimming as needed. Cover; transfer pot to oven. Cook for 1 hour.

4 Stir in crushed tomatoes and bell peppers and continue to cook in oven, covered, until beans are fully tender, about 1 hour. (If chili begins to stick to bottom of pot or is too thick, add water as needed.)

5 Remove pot from oven and discard bay leaves. Stir in cilantro and season with salt and pepper to taste. Serve.

NORTH AFRICAN VEGETABLE AND BEAN STEW

serves 6 to 8

1 tablespoon extra-virgin olive oil

1 onion, chopped fine

8 ounces Swiss chard, stems chopped fine, leaves cut into ½-inch pieces

4 garlic cloves, minced

1 teaspoon ground cumin

½ teaspoon paprika

½ teaspoon ground coriander

¼ teaspoon ground cinnamon

2 tablespoons tomato paste

2 tablespoons all-purpose flour

7 cups vegetable broth

2 carrots, peeled and cut into ½-inch pieces

1 (15-ounce) can chickpeas, rinsed

1 (15-ounce) can butter beans, rinsed

½ cup small pasta, such as ditalini, tubettini, or elbow macaroni

⅓ cup minced fresh parsley

6 tablespoons harissa

Salt and pepper

Why This Recipe Works North African stews combine heady, potent spices with hearty, filling vegetables, pasta, and beans. We set out to create a rich-tasting vegetable stew in the manner of Tunisian and Moroccan cookery. A combination of chickpeas and butter beans gave our stew a balance of earthiness and creaminess. For the vegetables, we chose Swiss chard and chunks of carrot. Tiny dried pasta like ditalini worked nicely in place of the traditional handmade North African noodles; we liked how the pasta was smaller than the beans—the true starchy star of the dish. Harissa, a ubiquitous North African spice paste made with ground chiles, cumin, coriander, garlic, and olive oil, added both heat and depth of flavor to the stew. You can substitute one 10-ounce bag of frozen baby lima beans for the butter beans.

1 Heat oil in Dutch oven over medium heat until shimmering. Add onion and chard stems and cook until softened, about 5 minutes. Stir in garlic, cumin, paprika, coriander, and cinnamon and cook until fragrant, about 30 seconds. Stir in tomato paste and flour and cook for 1 minute.

2 Slowly stir in broth and carrots, scraping up any browned bits and smoothing out any lumps, and bring to boil. Reduce heat to gentle simmer and cook for 10 minutes. Stir in chard leaves, chickpeas, beans, and pasta and simmer until vegetables and pasta are tender, 10 to 15 minutes. Stir in parsley and ¼ cup harissa. Season with salt and pepper to taste. Serve, passing remaining harissa separately.

LENTILS WITH SPINACH AND GARLIC CHIPS

serves 6

2 tablespoons extra-virgin olive oil

4 garlic cloves, sliced thin

Salt and pepper

1 onion, chopped fine

1 teaspoon ground coriander

1 teaspoon ground cumin

2½ cups water

1 cup green or brown lentils, picked over and rinsed

8 ounces curly-leaf spinach, stemmed and chopped coarse

1 tablespoon red wine vinegar

Why This Recipe Works Lentils deserve more than side-dish status. In the eastern Mediterranean, tender-firm lentils are often paired with spinach and garlic to create a simple yet flavorful dish that can serve as an entrée. We started by frying sliced garlic in oil; the crunchy golden garlic chips added a nice textural contrast and infused the cooking oil with garlic flavor. Surprisingly, we preferred the clean flavor of lentils cooked in water to those cooked in broth. Allowing our sturdy curly-leaf spinach to wilt in the pot with the lentils was simple and avoided using extra pans for sautéeing; the mineral-y flavor of the spinach complemented the earthy lentils perfectly. As a finishing touch, we stirred in some red wine vinegar for brightness. It's important to cook the garlic until just golden—if it becomes too dark, it will have an unpleasant bitter taste. If you can't find curly-leaf spinach, you can substitute flat-leaf spinach; do not substitute baby spinach. We prefer green or brown lentils for this recipe, but it will work with any type of lentil except red or yellow (note that cooking times will vary depending on the type of lentil used).

1 Cook oil and garlic in large saucepan over medium-low heat, stirring often, until garlic turns crisp and golden but not brown, about 5 minutes. Using slotted spoon, transfer garlic to paper towel–lined plate and season lightly with salt; set aside.

2 Add onion and ½ teaspoon salt to oil left in saucepan and cook over medium heat until softened and lightly browned, 5 to 7 minutes. Stir in coriander and cumin and cook until fragrant, about 30 seconds.

3 Stir in water and lentils and bring to simmer. Reduce heat to low, cover, and simmer gently, stirring occasionally, until lentils are mostly tender but still intact, 45 to 55 minutes.

4 Stir in spinach, 1 handful at a time. Cook, uncovered, stirring occasionally, until spinach is wilted and lentils are completely tender, about 8 minutes. Stir in vinegar and season with salt and pepper to taste. Transfer to serving dish, sprinkle with toasted garlic, and serve.

FRENCH LENTILS WITH CARROTS AND PARSLEY

serves 4 to 6

2 tablespoons extra-virgin olive oil

2 carrots, peeled and chopped fine

1 onion, chopped fine

1 celery rib, chopped fine

Salt and pepper

2 garlic cloves, minced

1 teaspoon minced fresh thyme or ¼ teaspoon dried

2½ cups water

1 cup lentilles du Puy, picked over and rinsed

2 tablespoons minced fresh parsley

2 teaspoons lemon juice

Why This Recipe Works Smaller and firmer than the more common brown and green varieties, French lentils, or *lentilles du Puy*, boast a rich, complex flavor and tender texture. For a simple side dish that would highlight their sweet, earthy flavors, we took inspiration from their home country and looked to France, slowly cooking the lentils with carrots, onion, and celery (a classic French combination called a *mirepoix*). We found that soaking the lentils before cooking wasn't necessary, since they held their shape nicely through cooking. Garlic and thyme added aromatic flavors that complemented the lentils. Using water rather than broth let the other flavors come through. Lentilles du Puy are also called French green lentils and are our first choice for this recipe, but brown, black, or regular green lentils are fine, too (note that cooking times will vary depending on the type of lentil used).

1 Combine 1 tablespoon oil, carrots, onion, celery, and ½ teaspoon salt in large saucepan. Cover and cook over medium-low heat, stirring occasionally, until vegetables are softened, 8 to 10 minutes. Stir in garlic and thyme and cook until fragrant, about 30 seconds.

2 Stir in water and lentils and bring to simmer. Reduce heat to low, cover, and simmer gently, stirring occasionally, until lentils are mostly tender, 40 to 50 minutes.

3 Uncover and continue to cook, stirring occasionally, until lentils are completely tender, about 8 minutes. Stir in parsley, lemon juice, and remaining 1 tablespoon oil. Season with salt and pepper to taste, and serve.

Curried French Lentils with Golden Raisins

Add 1 teaspoon curry powder to pot with onion in step 1. Stir ½ cup golden raisins into pot after uncovering in step 3. Substitute minced fresh cilantro for parsley.

French Lentils with Swiss Chard

Omit carrots, celery, and parsley. Separate stems and leaves from 12 ounces Swiss chard; chop stems fine and cut leaves into ½-inch pieces. Add chard stems to pot with onion in step 1, and stir chard leaves into pot after uncovering in step 3.

SPICED RED LENTILS (MASOOR DAL)

1 tablespoon vegetable oil

½ teaspoon ground coriander

½ teaspoon ground cumin

½ teaspoon ground cinnamon

½ teaspoon ground turmeric

⅛ teaspoon ground cardamom

⅛ teaspoon red pepper flakes

1 onion, chopped fine

4 garlic cloves, minced

1½ teaspoons grated fresh ginger

4 cups water

8½ ounces (1¼ cups) red lentils, picked over and rinsed

1 pound plum tomatoes, cored, seeded, and chopped

½ cup minced fresh cilantro

2 tablespoons unsalted butter

Salt and pepper

Lemon wedges

Why This Recipe Works Dals are heavily spiced lentil stews common throughout India. Split red lentils give the dish a mild, slightly nutty taste, and as the stew slowly simmers, they break down to a smooth consistency. We wanted our dal to be simple yet still embody the complex flavors of Indian cuisine, so we started with what unlocks that complexity: the spices. We created a balanced blend of warm spices with just a subtle layer of heat. Blooming the spices in oil until they were fragrant boosted and deepened their flavors. Onion, garlic, and ginger rounded out the aromatic flavor. Authentic dal should have a porridge-like consistency, bordering on a puree (without the need for a blender). Getting this consistency required cooking the lentils with just the right amount of water: We finally settled on 4 cups water to 1¼ cups lentils for a dal that was smooth but not thin. Before serving, we added cilantro for color and freshness, diced raw tomato for sweetness and acidity, and a pat of butter for richness. You cannot substitute other types of lentils for the red lentils here; they have a very different texture.

1 Heat oil in large saucepan over medium-high heat until shimmering. Add coriander, cumin, cinnamon, turmeric, cardamom, and pepper flakes and cook until fragrant, about 10 seconds. Stir in onion and cook until softened, about 5 minutes. Stir in garlic and ginger and cook until fragrant, about 30 seconds.

2 Stir in water and lentils and bring to boil. Reduce heat to low and simmer, uncovered, until lentils are tender and resemble coarse puree, 20 to 25 minutes.

3 Stir in tomatoes, cilantro, and butter and season with salt and pepper to taste. Serve with lemon wedges.

Red Lentils with Coconut Milk

The addition of coconut milk provides a lush, creamy texture and rich flavor; do not use light coconut milk here.

Substitute 1 cup coconut milk for 1 cup of water and omit butter.

FRENCH PORK AND WHITE BEAN CASSEROLE

serves 8 to 10

Salt and pepper

1 pound (2½ cups) dried cannellini beans, picked over and rinsed

2 celery ribs

4 sprigs fresh thyme

1 bay leaf

1½ pounds fresh French garlic sausage

4 ounces salt pork, rinsed

¼ cup vegetable oil

1½ pounds pork shoulder, cut into 1-inch chunks

1 large onion, chopped fine

2 carrots, peeled and cut into ¼-inch pieces

4 garlic cloves, minced

1 tablespoon tomato paste

½ cup dry white wine

1 (14.5-ounce) can diced tomatoes

4 cups chicken broth

4 large slices hearty white sandwich bread, torn into rough pieces

½ cup chopped fresh parsley

Why This Recipe Works Though it may look like just a humble peasant stew of white beans and meat, cassoulet is the very definition of French country cooking. It also requires ingredients that can be tough to find, and it demands hours—even more than 24—of effort. We wanted to both streamline our cassoulet and use the even, constant heat of the oven for most of the cooking, so the cook would be off-duty—and so he or she would make it more than once a year. To replace the common addition of duck confit, which can be expensive to buy and time-consuming to make, we used salt pork, which provided all the necessary richness. Pork shoulder fit the bill as the requisite stewing pork. Because we'd taken liberties with the ingredient list thus far, we opted to keep the fresh French garlic sausage. To prevent the tall sides of our pot from trapping moisture and prohibiting us from getting a crisp bread-crumb crust while the cassoulet baked covered, we used half of our crumbs to absorb the excess liquid in the casserole. Then we uncovered the pot, added the remaining crumbs, and let the dish cook until they were crisp. If you can't find fresh French garlic sausage, Irish bangers or bratwurst may be substituted.

1 Dissolve 2 tablespoons salt in 3 quarts cold water in large bowl or container. Add beans and soak at room temperature for 8 to 24 hours. Drain and rinse well.

2 Adjust oven rack to lower-middle position and heat oven to 300 degrees. Using kitchen twine, tie together celery, thyme sprigs, and bay leaf. Place sausage and salt pork in medium saucepan and add cold water to cover by 1 inch; bring to boil over high heat. Reduce heat to simmer and cook for 5 minutes. Transfer sausage to cutting board; let cool slightly, then cut into 1-inch pieces. Remove salt pork from water; set aside.

3 Heat 2 tablespoons oil in Dutch oven over medium-high heat until just smoking. Add sausage and brown on all sides, 8 to 12 minutes; transfer to bowl. Add pork shoulder and brown on all sides, 8 to 12 minutes total. Add onion and carrots; cook, stirring constantly, until onion is translucent, about 2 minutes. Add garlic and tomato paste and cook, stirring constantly, until fragrant, about 30 seconds. Return sausage to pot; add wine, scraping up any browned bits. Cook until slightly reduced, about 30 seconds. Stir in tomatoes, celery bundle, and reserved salt pork.

4 Stir in broth and beans, pressing beans into even layer. If any beans are completely exposed, add up to 1 cup water to submerge (beans may still break surface of liquid). Increase heat to high, bring to simmer, and cover; transfer pot to oven. Cook until beans are tender, about 1½ hours. Discard celery bundle and salt pork. (Alternatively, dice salt pork and return it to casserole.) Using wide spoon, skim fat from surface and discard. Season with salt and pepper to taste. Increase oven temperature to 350 degrees and bake, uncovered, for 20 minutes.

5 Meanwhile, pulse bread and remaining 2 tablespoons oil in food processor until crumbs are no larger than ⅛ inch, 8 to 10 pulses. Transfer to bowl, add parsley, and toss to combine. Season with salt and pepper to taste.

6 Sprinkle ½ cup bread-crumb mixture evenly over casserole; bake, covered, for 15 minutes. Remove lid and bake 15 minutes longer. Sprinkle remaining bread-crumb mixture over casserole and bake until topping is golden brown, about 30 minutes. Let rest for 15 minutes before serving.

BRAZILIAN BLACK BEAN AND PORK STEW

4 slices bacon, chopped fine

1 onion, chopped fine

4 garlic cloves, minced

10½ cups water

2 pounds (5 cups) dried black beans, picked over and rinsed

Salt and pepper

2 bay leaves

⅛ teaspoon baking soda

2 (1-pound) pork tenderloins, trimmed and cut in half crosswise

2 (2½- to 3-pound) racks baby back ribs, trimmed, each rack cut into 3 pieces

¼ cup vegetable oil

1 pound linguiça sausage, cut into 6-inch lengths

Why This Recipe Works Considered one of Brazil's national dishes, *feijoada* is a hearty black bean stew typically loaded with all manner of pork cuts (as well as pig parts such as feet, ears, tail, and snout) and flavored with *molho apimentado*, a fresh, salsa-like hot sauce. We headed into the kitchen with the intention of translating this complex classic into something anyone could make at home. The key would be getting the timing right. We started by cooking the black beans until tender. Next we'd have to layer the meats (ham hock to flavor the beans, pork spareribs, linguiça sausage, and pork tenderloin) in with the beans so the flavors melded and all the elements cooked at the right rate. Knowing that the collagen-rich ribs would cook longer than the lean tenderloin, we added the ribs (and the sausage) to the beans first and cooked them for 40 minutes before adding the tenderloin. Chopped bacon provided a smokiness without taking up as much real estate as ham hocks. Mashing some of the braised beans thickened the liquid a bit, giving it a creamy consistency. Adding a small amount of baking soda to the beans helped preserve their dark hue. If the drippings look as though they're going to burn at any time when browning the meats in steps 2 and 3, simply add some of the water to the skillet, scrape up the browned bits, and transfer them to the simmering beans; wipe the skillet dry between batches and continue to brown the meats as directed. In addition to Brazilian Hot Sauce and Brazilian Toasted Manioc Flour (recipes follow), feijoada is served with steamed white rice, orange segments, and sautéed kale.

1 Cook bacon in 12-quart stockpot over medium heat until fat is partly rendered and bacon is lightly browned, about 5 minutes. Stir in onion and cook until softened, 5 to 7 minutes. Stir in garlic and cook until fragrant, about 30 seconds. Stir in 10 cups water, beans, 1 teaspoon salt, bay leaves, and baking soda and bring to boil over high heat, skimming foam off surface. Reduce heat to low, cover, and cook, stirring occasionally, until beans begin to soften, about 1 hour.

2 While beans are simmering, pat tenderloins and ribs dry with paper towels and season with salt and pepper. Heat 1 tablespoon oil in 12-inch skillet over medium-high heat until just smoking. Brown tenderloins on all sides, 8 to 10 minutes. (Reduce heat if fond begins to burn.) Transfer tenderloins to plate; set aside. Add ¼ cup water to skillet and reduce heat to low, scraping up any browned bits; add water with browned bits to simmering beans.

3 Wipe skillet clean with paper towels, add 1 tablespoon oil, and heat over medium-high heat until just smoking. Brown 2 rib pieces on meat side only, about 5 minutes (reduce heat if fond begins to burn). Transfer browned ribs to plate and repeat twice with remaining 2 tablespoons oil and remaining 4 rib pieces. After all ribs are browned, add remaining ¼ cup water to skillet and reduce heat to low, scraping up any browned bits; add water and browned bits to simmering beans.

4 After beans have softened, nestle linguiça and browned ribs into beans, submerging meat as much as possible. Continue to cook, covered, until beans are soft, about 40 minutes, stirring thoroughly halfway through cooking.

5 Gently place browned tenderloins on top of beans (they may sink slightly) and continue to cook, covered, until beans are tender and tenderloins register 145 degrees, 20 to 30 minutes longer.

6 Using tongs, transfer tenderloins, ribs, and linguiça to carving board and tent with aluminum foil. Discard bay leaves. Measure out and reserve 1½ cups bean cooking liquid. Transfer 2 cups beans and ½ cup reserved cooking liquid to bowl and mash with potato masher or fork until smooth; return to pot. Adjust consistency with remaining reserved cooking liquid as needed; beans should be loose but not soupy.

7 Slice tenderloins ½ inch thick. Cut linguiça into ¾-inch pieces. Slice ribs between bones into single-rib portions. Transfer meats to serving platter. Season beans with salt and pepper to taste; serve with meats.

BRAZILIAN HOT SAUCE (MOLHO APIMENTADO)
makes about 3 cups

Malagueta chiles, small hot Brazilian peppers, are the traditional choice for molho apimentado; however, we found jalapeño chiles to be a suitable (and much easier-to-find) alternative.

2 ripe but firm tomatoes, cored, seeded, and chopped fine
1 large onion, chopped fine
1 small green bell pepper, stemmed, seeded, and chopped fine
1 malagueta or jalapeño chile, stemmed, seeded, and minced
⅓ cup white wine vinegar
3 tablespoons extra-virgin olive oil
1 tablespoon minced fresh cilantro
½ teaspoon salt

Combine all ingredients in bowl and let stand at room temperature until flavors meld, about 30 minutes, before serving. (Hot sauce can be refrigerated for up to 2 days.)

BRAZILIAN TOASTED MANIOC FLOUR (FAROFA)
makes 1 cup

Manioc flour or meal can be found in most Latin American specialty stores in a variety of textures ranging from fine to coarse (much like cornmeal); finely ground is the most common, but any type will work here.

2 tablespoons unsalted butter
1 cup manioc flour

Melt butter in 10-inch skillet over medium heat. Add manioc flour and cook, stirring frequently, until golden brown, 5 to 7 minutes. Transfer to bowl and let cool for about 5 minutes before serving. (Toasted flour can be refrigerated for up to 5 days.)

TEXAS-STYLE PINTO BEANS

serves 8

Salt

1 pound (2½ cups) dried pinto beans, picked over and rinsed

1 (10-ounce) smoked ham hock

Why This Recipe Works Often, lunch at barbecue spots around Texas includes a scoop of brown pinto beans on your plate. Different from mashed or refried versions, these whole beans are long-simmered with pork in a velvety, savory broth and are tender, flavorful, and creamy. To cook the brined beans, we covered them with fresh water, and added a bit more salt to ensure that the bean skins were fully tender and a smoked ham hock to provide rich pork flavor—that's it: Just salt and pork flavors these beans and plenty ably. We then simmered them uncovered for 1½ hours to reduce and concentrate the cooking liquid and give it smoky complexity and meaty, buttery sweetness. If you can't find a ham hock, substitute 4 ounces of salt pork, omit the salt in step 2, and season to taste once finished. Monitor the water level as the beans cook: Don't let it fall below the level of the beans before they're done. If it does, add more water. Serve with finely chopped onion, dill pickles, jalapeños, and/or tomatoes. Use the meat from the ham hock within a few days to flavor another dish.

1 Dissolve 1½ tablespoons salt in 2 quarts cold water in large container. Add beans and soak at room temperature for at least 8 hours or up to 24 hours. Drain and rinse well.

2 Combine 12 cups water, ham hock, beans, and 1 teaspoon salt in Dutch oven. Bring to boil over high heat. Reduce heat to medium-low and simmer, uncovered, stirring occasionally, until beans are tender, about 1½ hours, skimming any foam from surface with spoon. Remove from heat and let stand for 15 minutes. Reserve ham hock for another use. Season with salt to taste. Serve.

VEGETABLE SIDES

Maple-Glazed Brussels Sprouts

334 **Braised Spring Vegetables with Tarragon**

337 **Braised Artichokes with Tomatoes and Thyme**

338 **Beets with Lemon and Almonds**
Beets with Ginger and Cashews
Beets with Lime and Pepitas
Beets with Orange and Walnuts

341 **Braised Bok Choy with Garlic**
Braised Bok Choy with Shiitake Mushrooms

343 **Braised Brussels Sprouts**
Cream-Braised Brussels Sprouts
Curried Brussels Sprouts with Currants

344 **Maple-Glazed Brussels Sprouts**

347 **Braised Red Cabbage**

348 **Beer-Braised Cabbage**

350 **Cream-Braised Cabbage with Lemon and Shallot**
Braised Cabbage with Parsley and Thyme

353 **Slow-Cooked Whole Carrots**
with Green Olive and Raisin Relish
with Onion-Balsamic Relish
with Pine Nut Relish

354 **Glazed Carrots**
Glazed Carrots with Ginger and Rosemary
Glazed Curried Carrots with Currants and Almonds
Honey-Glazed Carrots with Lemon and Thyme

357 **Braised Cauliflower with Garlic and White Wine**
Braised Cauliflower with Capers and Anchovies
Braised Cauliflower with Sumac and Mint

359 **Braised Belgian Endive**
Braised Belgian Endive with Bacon and Cream
Cider-Braised Belgian Endive with Apples

360 **Braised Fennel**

362 **Bacon-Braised Green Beans**

364 **Mediterranean Braised Green Beans**
with Mint and Feta
with Potatoes and Basil

367 **Green Beans and Mushrooms Braised in Cream**

368 **Braised Hearty Greens**
with Chorizo and Pimentos
with Pancetta and Pine Nuts
with Raisins and Almonds
with White Beans

370 **Garlicky Braised Kale**
Braised Kale with Coconut and Curry

373 **Braised Red Potatoes with Lemon and Chives**
Bacon-Braised Red Potatoes
Braised Red Potatoes with Dijon and Tarragon
Braised Red Potatoes with Miso and Scallions

BRAISED SPRING VEGETABLES WITH TARRAGON

serves 4 to 6

¼ cup extra-virgin olive oil

1 shallot, sliced into thin rounds

2 garlic cloves, sliced thin

3 sprigs fresh thyme

Pinch red pepper flakes

10 radishes, trimmed and quartered lengthwise

1¼ cups water

2 teaspoons grated lemon zest

2 teaspoons grated orange zest

1 bay leaf

Salt and pepper

1 pound asparagus, trimmed and cut into 2-inch lengths

2 cups frozen peas

4 teaspoons chopped fresh tarragon

Why This Recipe Works While raw and roasted vegetables certainly have their place, braising is a great technique for cooking even the most delicate vegetables. You may think braising would turn verdant spring vegetables drab and watery but, in fact, braising can maximize their freshness and make them taste more like themselves. To turn early-season produce into a warm side dish, we started by softening a minced shallot in olive oil with additional aromatics for a savory base. To build a flavorful braising liquid, we poured in water and lemon and orange zest and dropped in a bay leaf. Adding the vegetables in stages ensured that each cooked at its own rate and maintained a crisp texture. Peppery radishes, which turned soft and sweet with cooking, were nicely complemented by the more vegetal notes of asparagus and peas (frozen peas were reliably sweet, and adding them off the heat prevented overcooking). In no time at all, we had a simple side of radiant vegetables in an invigorating, complex broth—proof positive that braising can bring out the best in even the most delicate flavors. A toss of chopped fresh tarragon gave a final nod to spring. Look for asparagus spears no thicker than ½ inch.

1 Cook oil, shallot, garlic, thyme sprigs, and pepper flakes in Dutch oven over medium heat until shallot is just softened, about 2 minutes. Stir in radishes, water, lemon zest, orange zest, bay leaf, and 1 teaspoon salt and bring to simmer. Reduce heat to medium-low, cover, and cook until radishes can be easily pierced with tip of paring knife, 3 to 5 minutes. Stir in asparagus, cover, and cook until tender, 3 to 5 minutes.

2 Off heat, stir in peas, cover, and let sit until heated through, about 5 minutes. Discard thyme sprigs and bay leaf. Stir in tarragon and season with salt and pepper to taste. Serve.

BRAISED ARTICHOKES WITH TOMATOES AND THYME

serves 4 to 6

1 lemon

4 artichokes (8 to 10 ounces each)

2 tablespoons extra-virgin olive oil

1 onion, chopped fine

Salt and pepper

3 garlic cloves, minced

2 anchovy fillets, rinsed, patted dry, and minced

1 teaspoon minced fresh thyme or ¼ teaspoon dried

½ cup dry white wine

1 cup chicken broth

6 ounces cherry tomatoes, halved

2 tablespoons chopped fresh parsley

Why This Recipe Works Fresh artichokes are a fleeting pleasure, so we like to cook them as often as possible when they're at their best. We wanted to depart from the obvious presentations of whole artichokes, like steaming them and dipping the leaves in aïoli, and use fresh artichokes to create a simple side in which the seasonal gems shone. Gently braising artichoke wedges, just the most tender inner leaves, to perfect tenderness fit the bill—and allowed us to create a rich, flavorful sauce at the same time. A braising liquid of white wine and chicken broth imparted acidity and depth of flavor. Earthy thyme complemented the artichokes' delicate flavor, and anchovies amplified the savory qualities of the dish. Canned tomatoes are common in braises, but when we used them, tasters detected a metallic note; replacing them with halved cherry tomatoes at the end of cooking made for a clean-tasting dish and added welcome pops of color. If your artichokes are larger than 8 to 10 ounces, strip away another layer or two of the toughest outer leaves.

1 Cut lemon in half, squeeze halves into container filled with 2 quarts water, then add spent halves. Working with 1 artichoke at a time, trim stem to about ¾ inch and cut off top quarter of artichoke. Break off bottom 3 or 4 rows of tough outer leaves by pulling them downward. Using paring knife, trim outer layer of stem and base, removing any dark green parts. Cut artichoke in half lengthwise, remove fuzzy choke and any tiny inner purple-tinged leaves using small spoon, then cut each half into 1-inch-thick wedges. Submerge prepped artichokes in lemon water.

2 Heat oil in 12-inch skillet over medium heat until shimmering. Add onion, ¾ teaspoon salt, and ¼ teaspoon pepper and cook until softened and lightly browned, 5 to 7 minutes. Stir in garlic, anchovies, and thyme and cook until fragrant, about 30 seconds. Stir in wine and cook until almost evaporated, about 1 minute. Stir in broth and bring to simmer.

3 Remove artichokes from lemon water, shaking off excess water, and add to skillet. Cover, reduce heat to medium-low, and simmer until artichokes are tender, 20 to 25 minutes.

4 Stir in tomatoes, bring to simmer, and cook until tomatoes start to break down, 3 to 5 minutes. Off heat, stir in parsley and season with salt and pepper to taste. Serve.

preparing artichokes

1 Using paring knife, trim outer layer of stem and base, removing any dark green parts.

2 Cut artichoke in half lengthwise, remove fuzzy choke and any tiny inner purple-tinged leaves using small spoon.

BEETS WITH LEMON AND ALMONDS

serves 4 to 6

1½ pounds beets, trimmed and halved horizontally

1¼ cups water

Salt and pepper

3 tablespoons distilled white vinegar

1 tablespoon packed light brown sugar

1 shallot, sliced thin

1 teaspoon grated lemon zest

½ cup almonds, toasted and chopped

2 tablespoons chopped fresh mint

1 teaspoon chopped fresh thyme

Why This Recipe Works Beets have a sweet, earthy flavor and are visually stunning, but finding a streamlined way to cook them that maximizes these qualities—with minimal mess—is tough. Roasting the beets took more than an hour, and boiling washed away their flavor, but braising worked perfectly. We partially submerged the beets in just 1¼ cups of water so that they partially simmered and partially steamed. Halving the beets cut down our cooking time even further. In just 45 minutes, the beets were tender and their skins slipped off easily. To further amplify their flavor, we reduced the braising liquid and added brown sugar and vinegar to make a glossy sauce. Shallot, toasted almonds, fresh mint and thyme, and a little lemon zest finished the dish. Look for beets that are roughly 2 to 3 inches in diameter. The beets can be served warm or at room temperature. If serving at room temperature, add the nuts and fresh herbs right before serving.

1 Place beets, cut side down, in single layer in 11-inch straight-sided sauté pan or Dutch oven. Add water and ¼ teaspoon salt and bring to simmer over high heat. Reduce heat to low, cover, and simmer until beets are tender and tip of paring knife inserted into beets meets no resistance, 45 to 50 minutes.

2 Transfer beets to cutting board. Increase heat to medium-high and reduce cooking liquid, stirring occasionally, until pan is almost dry, 5 to 6 minutes. Add vinegar and sugar, return to boil, and cook, stirring constantly with heat-resistant spatula, until spatula leaves wide trail when dragged through glaze, 1 to 2 minutes. Remove pan from heat.

3 When beets are cool enough to handle, rub off skins with paper towel and cut into ½-inch wedges. Add beets, shallot, lemon zest, ½ teaspoon salt, and ¼ teaspoon pepper to glaze and toss to coat. Transfer to platter; sprinkle with almonds, mint, and thyme; and serve.

Beets with Ginger and Cashews
Omit thyme. Slice white parts of 4 scallions thin and green parts thin on bias; substitute scallion whites for shallot and 1 teaspoon fresh grated ginger for lemon zest. Substitute cashews for almonds and scallion greens for mint.

Beets with Lime and Pepitas
Omit thyme. Substitute lime zest for lemon zest, toasted pepitas for almonds, and cilantro for mint.

Beets with Orange and Walnuts
Substitute orange zest for lemon zest, walnuts for almonds, and parsley for mint.

BRAISED BOK CHOY WITH GARLIC

serves 4

2 tablespoons peanut or vegetable oil

1½ pounds bok choy, stalks halved lengthwise then cut crosswise into ½-inch pieces, greens sliced into ½-inch-wide strips

4 garlic cloves, minced

½ cup chicken broth

1 teaspoon rice vinegar

Salt and pepper

Why This Recipe Works Unlike so many leafy greens, bok choy doesn't shrink down to nothing when cooked. The stalks are crisp and fleshy— like celery but not stringy. When fully cooked, they become creamy, with a meaty texture and an underlying sweetness. In contrast, the leaves become tender and soft, with an earthy, robust flavor similar to that of chard or even spinach. For evenly cooked bok choy, we'd have to separate these two components. Blanching and steaming cooked the bok choy through but left them watery and flavorless. Braising with a little chicken broth coaxed out much more flavor and retained bok choy's desirable texture. We first stir-fried the stalks to give them some light browning, and then we added the greens and some stock and let the bok choy simmer away. After about 4 minutes, the stalks were soft but not mushy, their texture creamy and delicious, the leaves completely tender. Best of all, the bok choy's flavor seemed more robust and earthy. This dish is fairly brothy, making it an excellent accompaniment to seared pork chops, sautéed chicken breasts, or a firm fish such as cod.

1 Heat 12-inch nonstick skillet over high heat, add oil, and swirl to coat. Add bok choy stalks and cook, stirring frequently, until edges begin to turn translucent, 4 to 5 minutes. Add garlic and cook, stirring constantly, until fragrant, about 30 seconds. Add broth and bok choy greens. Cover, reduce heat to medium-low, and cook, stirring twice, until bok choy is just tender, 3 to 4 minutes.

2 Remove cover, increase heat to medium-high, and cook for 2 minutes. Stir in vinegar and season with salt and pepper to taste. Serve immediately.

Braised Bok Choy with Shiitake Mushrooms

Microwave 1 cup water and ¼ ounce dried shiitake mushrooms in covered bowl until steaming, about 1 minute. Let sit until softened, about 5 minutes. Drain mushrooms in fine-mesh strainer lined with coffee filter and reserve ½ cup liquid. Trim stems and slice mushrooms ¼ inch thick. Substitute 1 tablespoon grated fresh ginger for 2 garlic cloves and substitute mushroom liquid and sliced mushrooms for chicken broth.

BRAISED BRUSSELS SPROUTS

serves 4

2 tablespoons unsalted butter

1 shallot, minced

Salt and pepper

1 pound Brussels sprouts, trimmed and halved

1 cup vegetable broth

Why This Recipe Works Those who avoid Brussels sprouts usually expect limp, bitter, overcooked specimens from any method other than roasting. That's because braised sprouts are nearly always overcooked. Braising doesn't have to be a slow process, and when done right, braised Brussels sprouts can be crisp, tender, and nutty-flavored. We've found that using a skillet on the stovetop is the best for braising the little cabbages. As for the liquid, a combination of vegetable broth enhanced by a quickly sautéed shallot easily added depth. We started the cooking in a covered skillet to quickly steam the sprouts and then removed the lid to let the broth reduce to a flavorful glaze during the final few minutes of cooking. When trimming the Brussels sprouts, be careful not to cut too much off the stem end or the leaves will fall away from the core.

1 Melt butter in 12-inch nonstick skillet over medium heat. Add shallot and ¼ teaspoon salt and cook until shallot is softened, about 2 minutes. Add Brussels sprouts, broth, and ⅛ teaspoon pepper and bring to simmer. Cover and cook until sprouts are bright green, about 9 minutes.

2 Uncover and continue to cook until sprouts are tender and liquid is slightly thickened, about 2 minutes. Season with salt and pepper to taste, transfer to platter, and serve.

Cream-Braised Brussels Sprouts

Substitute heavy cream for broth. Add pinch nutmeg to pan with sprouts. Sprinkle Brussels sprouts with 2 tablespoons minced fresh parsley or chives before serving.

Curried Brussels Sprouts with Currants

Add 1½ teaspoons curry powder to pan with shallot. Add 3 tablespoons currants to pan with sprouts.

MAPLE-GLAZED BRUSSELS SPROUTS

serves 6 to 8

4 tablespoons unsalted butter

2 pounds Brussels sprouts, trimmed and halved

½ cup chicken broth

2 tablespoons maple syrup

1 teaspoon minced fresh thyme

⅛ teaspoon cayenne pepper

4 teaspoons cider vinegar

Salt and pepper

Why This Recipe Works These Brussels sprouts, with their nicely browned and crisp yet supremely tender buds and sweet, sour, and subtly spicy coating, may become your new favorite winter side. Maple syrup provided welcome sweetness that complemented the assertive vegetable; a little vinegar and cayenne pepper perked it up and kept the dish from being too sweet. To get the best of roasted Brussels sprouts—browned, caramelized edges—in our braised dish, we sautéed the sprouts for a few extra minutes before adding the liquid to ensure deep browning. Just 2 tablespoons of maple syrup, combined with the chicken broth, was enough to sweeten the dish, but it lacked some of the characteristic earthy flavors of maple. To solve this, we added 1 tablespoon with the braising liquid and the rest at the end, so its presence was clear. Choose Brussels sprouts with small, tight heads no more than 1½ inches in diameter. When trimming the Brussels sprouts, be careful not to cut too much off the stem end or the leaves will fall away from the core.

1 Melt 2 tablespoons butter in 12-inch skillet over medium-high heat. Add Brussels sprouts and cook until browned, 6 to 8 minutes. Stir in broth, 1 tablespoon maple syrup, thyme, and cayenne; reduce heat to medium-low; and cook, covered, until Brussels sprouts are nearly tender, 6 to 8 minutes.

2 Uncover and increase heat to medium-high. Continue to cook until liquid is nearly evaporated, about 5 minutes longer. Off heat, stir in vinegar, remaining 2 tablespoons butter, and remaining 1 tablespoon maple syrup. Season with salt and pepper to taste, and serve.

BRAISED RED CABBAGE

serves 4

3 tablespoons unsalted butter

1 onion, halved and sliced thin

1 head red cabbage (2 pounds), cored and sliced ½ inch thick

1 cup dry red wine

½ cup frozen orange juice concentrate

1½ tablespoons packed brown sugar

Salt and pepper

1 Granny Smith apple, peeled, cored, and cut into ¼-inch pieces

3 tablespoons minced fresh parsley

Why This Recipe Works We wanted to transform humble cabbage into a dish that wouldn't be out of place on a dinner party table. This German American dish is all about balancing sweet and sour, turning braised cabbage into something unexpectedly lively. Sometimes the dish turns out mushy and bland and sometimes it's so vinegary it tastes pickled. We got a balanced dish by braising the cabbage in orange juice concentrate (to save time reducing orange juice), red wine, and brown sugar for a fair amount of time to really infuse the hardy vegetable with flavor. Removing the lid partway through cooking allowed the braising liquid to reduce to a thick, syrupy glaze. A Granny Smith apple added for the last 25 minutes of the braise was a nice, tart flavor contrast. Stirring in some butter for richness and parsley for freshness at the end brought everything together. This dish gives the vegetable's reputation a serious promotion. Any dry red wine will work for this recipe. Our favorite frozen orange juice concentrate is Minute Maid Original Frozen Concentrated Orange Juice.

1 Melt 2 tablespoons butter in Dutch oven over medium heat. Add onion and cook until golden, 7 to 9 minutes. Stir in cabbage, wine, orange juice concentrate, sugar, 1¼ teaspoons salt, and ½ teaspoon pepper and bring to boil. Cover, reduce heat to low, and simmer for 45 minutes.

2 Stir in apple. Increase heat to medium-low and continue to simmer, uncovered, until cabbage is tender and liquid is syrupy, 25 to 30 minutes longer.

3 Off heat, stir in parsley and remaining 1 tablespoon butter. Season with salt and pepper to taste. Serve.

BEER-BRAISED CABBAGE

serves 4

2 tablespoons unsalted butter

1 onion, chopped fine

½ cup light-bodied lager

1 tablespoon whole grain mustard

½ teaspoon minced fresh thyme

1 small head green cabbage (about 1 pound), halved, cored, and sliced thin

2 teaspoons cider vinegar

Salt and pepper

Why This Recipe Works Braising in beer is rarely a bad idea and it's an especially swell pairing for cabbage, a vegetable that can stand up to a robust braising liquid. Beer gives the braising liquid a rich, deep flavor with caramel notes and a hint of pleasant alcohol burn. We chose a light-bodied lager and added ingredients that complemented the beer, like sautéed onion for aromatic depth and sweetness, mustard for sharpness, vinegar for tang that enlivened the cabbage, and woodsy, fragrant thyme. We wanted our cabbage to retain a good amount of texture in this dish, so to ensure that it wouldn't become mushy or unappealing from extended cooking, we simmered the braising liquid until slightly thickened before we added the cabbage. This was crisp-tender, flavorful beer-braised cabbage that didn't need juicy sausages alongside to taste good—though they'd certainly be a welcome accompaniment here.

1 Melt butter in 12-inch skillet over medium-high heat. Cook onion until softened, about 5 minutes. Stir in beer, mustard, and thyme and simmer until slightly thickened, about 2 minutes.

2 Add cabbage and vinegar and cook covered, stirring occasionally, until wilted and tender, about 8 minutes. Season with salt and pepper to taste. Serve.

CREAM-BRAISED CABBAGE WITH LEMON AND SHALLOT

serves 4

¼ cup heavy cream

1 shallot, minced

1 teaspoon lemon juice

½ head green cabbage, cored and shredded (4 cups)

Salt and pepper

Why This Recipe Works The French have long cooked cabbage in cream, and when we tried it, we loved the subtle flavors and slight crunch of the cabbage within the sauce that was creamy but not overly heavy and didn't weigh down the cabbage shreds. Sure, cream on its own is rich, but with lemon juice (for its acidity) and shallot (for its subtle, sweet onion flavor) to cut it, the luxurious sauce was perfectly balanced. The cabbage needed only minutes to braise in a covered pan before it was cooked to perfection, napped with sauce, and ready to serve. We loved the technique for producing crisp-tender and flavorful cabbage through braising so much that we also created a simpler variation that was slightly less rich but aromatic and fresh with thyme and parsley.

Heat cream, shallot, and lemon juice in 12-inch skillet over medium heat until just simmering. Add cabbage and toss to coat. Cover and simmer, stirring occasionally, until cabbage is wilted but still bright green, 7 to 9 minutes. Season with salt and pepper to taste, transfer to bowl, and serve.

Braised Cabbage with Parsley and Thyme

Omit cream, shallot, and lemon juice. Melt 1 tablespoon unsalted butter in 12-inch skillet over medium heat. Add 1 tablespoon chicken broth, then cabbage and ¼ teaspoon fresh thyme leaves. Cover and cook as directed. Sprinkle with 1 tablespoon minced fresh parsley before serving.

SLOW-COOKED WHOLE CARROTS

serves 4 to 6

1 tablespoon extra-virgin olive oil

½ teaspoon salt

1½ pounds carrots, peeled

Why This Recipe Works Slow-cooking carrots brings out their sweetness and flavor. We wanted to develop a recipe that would yield sweet carrots that were meltingly tender from one end to the other without becoming waterlogged. Gently steeping the carrots in warm water before cooking them firmed up the vegetable's cell walls so the carrots could be cooked for a long time without falling apart. We also topped the carrots with a cartouche (a circle of parchment that sits on the food) during cooking to ensure that the moisture in the pan cooked the carrots—thick and thin ends—evenly. Finishing cooking at a simmer evaporated the liquid and concentrated the carrots' flavor so that they tasted great when served on their own or with a relish. Use carrots that measure ¾ to 1¼ inches across at the thickest end.

1 Cut parchment paper into 11-inch circle, then cut 1-inch hole in center, folding paper as needed.

2 Bring 3 cups water, oil, and salt to simmer in 12-inch skillet over high heat. Off heat, add carrots, top with parchment, cover skillet, and let sit for 20 minutes.

3 Uncover, leaving parchment in place, and bring to simmer over high heat. Reduce heat to medium-low and cook until most of water has evaporated and carrots are very tender, about 45 minutes.

4 Discard parchment, increase heat to medium-high, and cook carrots, shaking skillet often, until lightly glazed and no water remains, 2 to 4 minutes. Serve.

Slow-Cooked Whole Carrots with Green Olive and Raisin Relish

Microwave ⅓ cup raisins and 1 tablespoon water in medium bowl until hot, about 1 minute; let sit for 5 minutes. Stir in ½ cup chopped green olives, 1 minced shallot, 2 tablespoons extra-virgin olive oil, 1 tablespoon red wine vinegar, 1 tablespoon minced fresh parsley, ½ teaspoon ground fennel, and ¼ teaspoon salt. Spoon relish over carrots before serving.

Slow-Cooked Whole Carrots with Onion-Balsamic Relish

Heat 3 tablespoons extra-virgin olive oil in medium saucepan over medium heat until shimmering. Add 1 finely chopped red onion and ¼ teaspoon salt and cook until soft and well browned, about 15 minutes. Stir in 2 minced garlic cloves and cook until fragrant, about 30 seconds. Stir in 2 tablespoons balsamic vinegar and cook for 1 minute. Let cool for 15 minutes. Stir in 2 tablespoons minced fresh mint. Spoon relish over carrots before serving.

Slow-Cooked Whole Carrots with Pine Nut Relish

Combine ⅓ cup toasted pine nuts, 1 minced shallot, 1 tablespoon sherry vinegar, 1 tablespoon minced fresh parsley, 1 teaspoon honey, ½ teaspoon minced fresh rosemary, ¼ teaspoon smoked paprika, ¼ teaspoon salt, and pinch cayenne pepper in bowl. Spoon relish over carrots before serving.

folding parchment for slow-cooked carrots

1 Cut parchment into 11-inch circle, then cut 1-inch hole in center, folding paper as needed to cut out hole.

2 Lay parchment circle on top of carrots, underneath lid, to help retain and evenly distribute moisture during cooking.

GLAZED CARROTS

serves 4

2 pounds carrots, peeled and
sliced on bias ¼ inch thick

¾ cup chicken broth

6 tablespoons sugar

Salt and pepper

2 tablespoons unsalted butter,
cut into 8 pieces

4 teaspoons lemon juice

Why This Recipe Works Glazing might be the most popular way to prepare carrots, but they often turn out saccharine, with a limp and soggy or undercooked and fibrous texture. We wanted fully tender carrots with a glossy and clingy—yet modest—glaze. Baby carrots are a standard in the dish, but we opted to peel regular carrots and cut them on the bias for uniform ovals that cooked evenly and looked elegant. We cooked and glazed the carrots in one single operation, starting by cooking the sliced carrots in a covered skillet with chicken broth, salt, and a bit of sugar. Once the carrots were almost tender, we removed the lid and turned up the heat to reduce the liquid. Finally, a little butter and some more sugar added to the skillet resulted in a pale amber glaze with light caramel flavor. A sprinkle of fresh lemon juice brightened the dish and lent welcome acidity. A nonstick skillet is easier to clean, but this recipe can be prepared in any 12-inch skillet with a lid.

1 Combine carrots, broth, 2 tablespoons sugar, and 1 teaspoon salt in 12-inch nonstick skillet; cover and bring to boil over medium-high heat. Reduce heat to medium and simmer, stirring occasionally, until carrots are almost tender when pierced with tip of paring knife, 5 to 8 minutes.

2 Uncover, increase heat to high, and simmer rapidly, stirring occasionally, until liquid is reduced to about 2 tablespoons, 3 to 6 minutes. Add butter and remaining ¼ cup sugar to skillet; toss carrots to coat and cook, stir-ring frequently, until carrots are completely tender and glaze is light gold, about 3 minutes. Off heat, add lemon juice and toss to coat. Transfer carrots to dish, scraping glaze from pan. Season with pepper to taste, and serve immediately.

Glazed Carrots with Ginger and Rosemary

Add 2-inch piece of ginger, cut crosswise into ¼-inch-thick coins, to skillet with carrots and 1½ teaspoons minced fresh rosemary with butter. Discard ginger before serving.

Glazed Curried Carrots with Currants and Almonds

Toast ½ cup sliced almonds in 12-inch nonstick skillet over medium heat until fragrant and lightly browned, about 5 minutes; transfer to small bowl and set aside. Off heat, sprinkle 1 tablespoon curry powder in skillet and stir until fragrant, about 2 seconds. Add curry powder to skillet with carrots, ½ cup dried currants with butter, and toasted almonds with lemon juice.

Honey-Glazed Carrots with Lemon and Thyme

Substitute honey for sugar and add 1 teaspoon minced fresh thyme and 1 teaspoon grated lemon zest with butter.

BRAISED CAULIFLOWER WITH GARLIC AND WHITE WINE

serves 4 to 6

1 teaspoon plus 3 tablespoons olive oil

3 garlic cloves, minced

⅛ teaspoon red pepper flakes

1 head cauliflower (2 pounds), cored and cut into 1½-inch florets

Salt and pepper

⅓ cup chicken or vegetable broth

⅓ cup dry white wine

2 tablespoons minced fresh parsley

Why This Recipe Works When properly cooked, braised cauliflower can be crisp-tender, nutty, and slightly sweet—a perfect backdrop for a variety of bold, imaginative flavors. However, too many recipes result in cauliflower that's waterlogged and bland or, worse, sulfurous and unappealing. Since these problems stem from long cooking times, we knew we'd need to quickly braise the florets. To this end, we cut the florets into small, 1½-inch pieces. Sautéing the cauliflower pieces in olive oil imparted nuttiness. Since the cauliflower would cook in our braising liquid for only a short amount of time, we maximized its impact by creating an ultraflavorful broth that the porous vegetable could absorb. White wine and broth made for a complexly flavored base, and a generous amount of garlic along with a pinch of red pepper flakes added punch and deeper flavor. Make sure to brown the cauliflower well in step 1.

1 Combine 1 teaspoon oil, garlic, and pepper flakes in small bowl. Heat remaining 3 tablespoons oil in 12-inch skillet over medium-high heat until shimmering. Add cauliflower and ¼ teaspoon salt and cook, stirring occasionally, until florets are golden brown, 7 to 9 minutes.

2 Push cauliflower to sides of skillet. Add garlic mixture to center and cook, mashing mixture into skillet, until fragrant, about 30 seconds. Stir garlic mixture into cauliflower.

3 Stir in broth and wine and bring to simmer. Reduce heat to medium-low, cover, and cook until cauliflower is crisp-tender, 4 to 6 minutes. Off heat, stir in parsley and season with salt and pepper to taste. Serve.

Braised Cauliflower with Capers and Anchovies

Add 2 anchovy fillets, rinsed and minced, and 1 tablespoon rinsed and minced capers to oil mixture in step 1. Stir 1 tablespoon lemon juice into cauliflower with parsley.

Braised Cauliflower with Sumac and Mint

Omit wine. Substitute 2 teaspoons ground sumac for pepper flakes and increase broth to ½ cup. In step 3, once cauliflower is crisp-tender, uncover and continue to cook until liquid is almost evaporated, about 1 minute. Substitute 2 tablespoons chopped fresh mint for parsley and stir ¼ cup plain yogurt into cauliflower with mint.

BRAISED BELGIAN ENDIVE

serves 4

3 tablespoons unsalted butter

½ teaspoon sugar

Salt and pepper

4 heads Belgian endive (4 ounces each), halved lengthwise

¼ cup dry white wine

¼ cup vegetable broth

½ teaspoon minced fresh thyme

1 tablespoon minced fresh parsley

1 teaspoon lemon juice

Why This Recipe Works You may find it in frilly salads or as a retro holder for a party appetizer, but Belgian endive takes well to cooking. And braising is your best bet: If done right, it transforms sharp, bitter endive into a side dish of uncommonly complex flavor—at once mellow, sweet, and rich, yet still faintly bitter. Plus, it really shows off the endive's intricate layered shape, looking great on the plate. We started the braise by browning halved endives in butter and sugar for maximum richness and sweetness and a beautiful caramelized look. Then we added the liquid and braised away—quickly—in white wine and vegetable broth, which added depth. Some lemon juice brightened the dish, and fresh parsley kept the vegetable fresh. To avoid discoloration, do not cut the endives far in advance of cooking. Delicate endive can fall apart easily if not handled gently. Move the halved endives in the pan by grasping the curved sides gingerly with tongs and supporting the cut sides with a spatula while lifting and turning.

1 Melt 2 tablespoons butter in 12-inch nonstick skillet over medium-high heat. Sprinkle sugar and ¼ teaspoon salt evenly over bottom of skillet, then lay endives cut sides down in single layer in skillet. Cook, shaking skillet occasionally, until first side is golden, about 5 minutes (reduce heat if endives brown too quickly). Turn endives over and cook until curved sides are golden, about 3 minutes.

2 Turn endives cut sides down; add wine, broth, and thyme. Reduce heat to low, cover, and simmer, checking occasionally, until leaves open up slightly and endives are tender throughout when poked with paring knife, 13 to 15 minutes. (If pan appears dry, add 2 tablespoons water.)

3 Gently transfer endives to platter, leaving liquid in skillet. Return liquid to simmer over medium-high heat and cook until syrupy, 1 to 2 minutes. Off heat, whisk in remaining 1 tablespoon butter, parsley, and lemon juice. Season with salt and pepper to taste. Spoon sauce over endives, and serve.

Braised Belgian Endive with Bacon and Cream

Cook 3 slices bacon, cut into ¼-inch pieces, in 12-inch skillet over medium heat until crisp, 5 to 7 minutes. Transfer bacon to paper towel–lined plate and set aside. Pour off all but 2 tablespoons fat from skillet. Substitute rendered fat for butter when browning endives in step 1, and substitute 2 tablespoons heavy cream for butter in step 3. Omit lemon juice. Sprinkle sauced endives with reserved bacon and serve.

Cider-Braised Belgian Endive with Apples

Omit lemon juice. Add 1 Granny Smith apple, peeled, cored, and cut into ¼-inch-thick wedges, to skillet with endives. Substitute ½ cup apple cider for vegetable broth and wine. Add 2 tablespoons cider to skillet before simmering to syrupy consistency in step 3.

BRAISED FENNEL

serves 4

3 tablespoons unsalted butter

½ teaspoon sugar

Salt and pepper

2 fennel bulbs, halved, each half cut into 4 wedges

¼ cup dry white wine

¼ cup chicken broth

½ teaspoon minced fresh thyme

1 tablespoon minced fresh parsley (optional)

1 teaspoon lemon juice

Why This Recipe Works Fennel has a beautiful flavor on its own—anise-y, floral, and slightly spicy—but it also tastes great cooked. During braising, it absorbs the flavors from the cooking liquid to great effect. We prepared the fennel by trimming the stalks, halving the fennel lengthwise, and then cutting each half into four wedges. As this was a simple side, we decided to brown the wedges on their cut sides only, thereby eliminating flipping. We sprinkled sugar into the skillet before adding the fennel—the caramelization of the sugar compensated for flavor lost by browning the fennel on only the cut sides. We liked a combination of chicken broth and white wine for our fennel—the broth gave the sauce savory backbone while the wine added acidity—and we threw in some thyme for pleasant herbal notes.

1 Melt 2 tablespoons butter in 12-inch nonstick skillet over medium-high heat. Sprinkle sugar and ¼ teaspoon salt evenly over bottom of skillet and add fennel, cut sides down, in single layer. Cook, shaking skillet occasionally, until golden brown, about 5 minutes, adjusting heat as needed if browning too quickly.

2 Add wine, broth, and thyme. Reduce heat to low, cover, and simmer until fennel loses its vibrant color and turns translucent and paring knife inserted into root end meets little resistance, 15 to 18 minutes.

3 Gently transfer fennel to platter, leaving liquid in skillet; cover fennel and set aside. Return liquid to simmer over medium-high heat and cook until syrupy, 1 to 2 minutes. Off heat, whisk in remaining 1 tablespoon butter; parsley, if using; and lemon juice and season with salt and pepper to taste. Spoon sauce over fennel, and serve.

BACON-BRAISED GREEN BEANS

serves 8

6 slices thick-cut bacon

1 onion, chopped fine

2 pounds green beans, trimmed and halved

1 cup chicken broth

2 tablespoons cider vinegar

1 tablespoon packed brown sugar

1 teaspoon minced fresh thyme

Salt and pepper

Why This Recipe Works In the South, green beans are often simmered for hours in a cast-iron pot with stock or water, a ham hock, sugar, and vinegar—in much the same way that fibrous collard greens are cooked. Although these beans are more soft than crisp and their color is muted, they offer something that quick-cooked beans never can: deep, sweet, smoky pork flavor. We wanted to develop the same rich flavor in minutes, not hours. First, we swapped out ham hock, which wouldn't give up its flavor in the shorter cooking time, for smoky, thick-cut bacon. After crisping the bacon, we sautéed onion in the drippings before adding the beans and chicken broth. Leaving a few slices of bacon in the skillet while the beans cooked infused them with meaty flavor. We crumbled the crisp bacon over the beans before serving for maximum impact. Adding cider vinegar twice—once to season the broth and again at the end of cooking for brightness—lent a nice tart element. A little brown sugar to complement the smoke and some herbal thyme rounded out the flavors. Large, thick green beans hold up best in this preparation.

1 Cook bacon in 12-inch skillet over medium heat until crispy, about 8 minutes. Transfer 4 slices bacon to paper towel–lined plate; when cool enough to handle, crumble bacon and reserve.

2 Add onion to skillet with remaining bacon and cook, stirring frequently, until onion is golden brown, about 8 minutes. Add green beans, broth, 1 tablespoon vinegar, sugar, thyme, ¼ teaspoon salt, and ¼ teaspoon pepper. Bring to boil, then reduce heat to medium-low and cook, covered, until beans are tender, about 12 minutes.

3 Uncover skillet and discard bacon slices. Increase heat to medium-high and cook until liquid evaporates, 3 to 5 minutes. Off heat, stir in remaining 1 tablespoon vinegar and crumbled bacon. Season with salt and pepper to taste, and serve.

MEDITERRANEAN BRAISED GREEN BEANS

serves 4 to 6

5 tablespoons extra-virgin olive oil

1 onion, chopped fine

4 garlic cloves, minced

Pinch cayenne pepper

1½ pounds green beans, trimmed and cut into 2- to 3-inch lengths

1½ cups water

½ teaspoon baking soda

1 (14.5-ounce) can diced tomatoes, drained with juice reserved, chopped coarse

1 tablespoon tomato paste

1 teaspoon salt

¼ teaspoon pepper

¼ cup chopped fresh parsley

Red wine vinegar

Why This Recipe Works While Southern-style green beans slowly braise until they pick up smoky flavor (see our Bacon-Braised Green Beans on page 362), Mediterranean cooks braise their green beans, too—but differently. They sauté garlic and onions in olive oil, add tomatoes and the green beans along with water, and then simmer until the sauce is thickened and the beans are infused with tomato and garlic flavor. The best part is the texture of the beans: The slow cooking renders them so tender that they're almost creamy. The problem: This traditionally takes about 2 hours. To get ultratender Mediterranean braised green beans in half the time, we first simmered them with a pinch of baking soda to weaken their cell walls. Once the beans were partially softened, we stirred in canned diced tomatoes to add sweet flavor; their acid also neutralized the baking soda and prevented the beans from over-softening. The beans turned meltingly tender after less than an hour of cooking in a low oven. Sautéed garlic and onion plus some red wine vinegar, parsley, and a drizzle of olive oil delivered bright flavor and richness. We like to serve the beans with a dollop of yogurt, which adds richness and tang.

1 Adjust oven rack to lower-middle position and heat oven to 275 degrees. Heat 3 tablespoons oil in Dutch oven over medium heat until shimmering. Add onion and cook, stirring occasionally, until softened, 3 to 5 minutes. Add garlic and cayenne and cook until fragrant, about 30 seconds. Add green beans, water, and baking soda and bring to simmer. Reduce heat to medium-low and cook, stirring occasionally, for 10 minutes. Stir in tomatoes and their juice, tomato paste, salt, and pepper.

2 Cover pot, transfer to oven, and cook until sauce is slightly thickened and green beans can be easily cut with side of fork, 40 to 50 minutes. Stir in parsley and season with vinegar to taste. Drizzle with remaining 2 tablespoons oil and serve warm or at room temperature.

Mediterranean Braised Green Beans with Mint and Feta
Add ¾ teaspoon ground allspice with garlic and cayenne. Substitute 2 tablespoons chopped fresh mint for parsley. Omit oil in step 2. Sprinkle green beans with ½ cup crumbled feta before serving.

Mediterranean Braised Green Beans with Potatoes and Basil
Substitute 2 teaspoons oregano for cayenne, 3 tablespoons chopped fresh basil for parsley, and 2 teaspoons lemon juice for red wine vinegar. In step 1, add 1 pound peeled Yukon Gold potatoes, cut into 2- to 3-inch lengths, to pot with green beans and increase salt to 2 teaspoons.

GREEN BEANS AND MUSHROOMS BRAISED IN CREAM

serves 4 to 6

2 tablespoons unsalted butter

1 tablespoon vegetable oil

4 shallots, sliced thin

1 pound green beans, trimmed

8 ounces white mushrooms, trimmed and quartered

⅔ cup heavy cream

2 teaspoons lemon juice

1½ teaspoons minced fresh thyme

Salt and pepper

Why This Recipe Works If the everlasting popularity of green bean casserole is any indication, earthy, hearty green beans are excellent napped with a mushroom cream sauce. We wanted to use these flavors and give them a lift, taking the green beans and mushrooms out of the casserole dish. Gently braising the green beans in the cream infused them with great richness; 15 to 20 minutes of braising was enough time for this transfer of flavors to take place—any longer and the color and texture of the beans suffered. Lemon juice perked up the braise, keeping it from being stodgy. Before cooking the beans and mushrooms, we even crisped up some shallots; a garnish of the crispy shallots gave a modern nod to this old-timey favorite and enhanced visual appeal.

1 Heat butter and oil in 12-inch skillet over medium-high heat. Add shallots and cook until golden brown and crisp, about 7 minutes. Transfer with slotted spoon to paper towel–lined plate; set aside.

2 Combine green beans, mushrooms, cream, lemon juice, and thyme in now-empty pan and bring to simmer. Reduce heat to low, cover, and simmer, stirring occasionally, until beans are crisp-tender, 15 to 20 minutes.

3 Uncover and, if sauce is too thin, simmer briskly to thicken cream. Season with salt and pepper to taste. Transfer to serving bowl, garnish with shallots, and serve immediately.

BRAISED HEARTY GREENS

serves 4 to 6

4 tablespoons unsalted butter

½ cup thinly sliced red onion

2½ pounds hearty greens
(kale, mustard, turnip, or collards),
stemmed and chopped coarse

1 cup chicken broth

1 tablespoon packed brown sugar

Salt and pepper

⅛ teaspoon cayenne pepper

2 tablespoons cider vinegar

Why This Recipe Works Hearty winter greens, braised Southern-style, long and slow until tender, silky, and deeply flavorful and pleasantly bitter, are a labor of love—sometimes even a 5-hour labor of love. We took a hard look at how long the greens really needed to cook, and we discovered that 40 minutes of simmering was perfect. We removed the lid during the last 10 minutes of cooking to help some of the liquid evaporate, leaving just a bit of the juice, which is affectionately known as "pot liquor" in the South. But we were having trouble fitting the volume of raw greens in the pot without it overflowing, so we quickly cooked down half the greens with a bit of liquid before stirring in the remaining greens. The result: a hearty recipe that highlighted the greens' cabbage-like flavor and firm texture. Don't be alarmed by the giant mound of greens—they wilt significantly when cooked. Collards may need a few extra minutes of covered cooking in step 1.

1 Melt 2 tablespoons butter in Dutch oven over medium heat. Add onion and cook until softened, about 5 minutes. Stir in half of greens, broth, sugar, ½ teaspoon salt, and cayenne. Cover and cook until greens begin to wilt, about 1 minute. Stir in remaining greens. Reduce heat to medium-low, cover, and cook, stirring occasionally, until greens are completely tender, about 30 minutes.

2 Uncover and increase heat to medium-high. Cook, stirring occasionally, until liquid is nearly evaporated, about 10 minutes. Stir in vinegar and remaining 2 tablespoons butter and cook until butter is melted, about 30 seconds. Transfer greens to serving dish and season with salt and pepper to taste. Serve.

Braised Hearty Greens with Chorizo and Pimentos

Omit 2 tablespoons butter and cayenne in step 1. Cook 8 ounces chorizo sausage, halved lengthwise and sliced ¼ inch thick, in Dutch oven over medium heat until browned, 6 to 8 minutes. Using slotted spoon, transfer chorizo to paper towel–lined plate. Cook onions as directed, substituting chorizo fat left in pot for butter. Substitute 2 tablespoons sherry vinegar for cider vinegar. Add chorizo and ½ cup chopped jarred pimento peppers with butter and vinegar in step 2.

Braised Hearty Greens with Pancetta and Pine Nuts

Omit butter. Before cooking onion, cook 6 ounces chopped pancetta in Dutch oven until crisp and browned, 6 to 8 minutes; transfer to paper towel–lined plate. Cook onions as directed, substituting pancetta fat left in pot for butter. Substitute 2 tablespoons red wine vinegar for cider vinegar. Sprinkle with ⅓ cup pine nuts, toasted, before serving.

Braised Hearty Greens with Raisins and Almonds

After removing lid in step 2, add ½ cup golden raisins. Substitute 2 tablespoons balsamic vinegar for cider vinegar. Sprinkle with ⅓ cup sliced almonds, toasted, before serving.

Braised Hearty Greens with White Beans

Add 1 (15-ounce) can rinsed small white beans to pot after uncovering in step 2. Substitute 2 tablespoons red wine vinegar for cider vinegar.

GARLICKY BRAISED KALE

serves 8

6 tablespoons extra-virgin olive oil

1 large onion, chopped fine

10 garlic cloves, minced

¼ teaspoon red pepper flakes

2 cups chicken or vegetable broth

1 cup water

Salt and pepper

4 pounds kale, stemmed and cut into 3-inch pieces

1 tablespoon lemon juice, plus extra for seasoning

Why This Recipe Works Kale is among the most nutrient-dense of all vegetables, but it can be difficult to turn the hearty green tender enough to enjoy. We wanted a simple approach to producing an abundance of tender kale without overcooking the greens or leaving them awash in liquid. We started with a generous 4 pounds of kale. To fit them in the pot, we sautéed one-third of the greens before adding the rest in two batches and covering the pot. In less than half an hour, the greens had almost the tender-firm texture we wanted. We removed the lid to allow the liquid to evaporate as the greens finished cooking. For flavorings, we added a substantial amount of garlic and chopped onion for aromatic character, and a pinch of red pepper flakes for heat. A squeeze of fresh lemon juice balanced the dish. For the best results, be sure the greens are fully cooked and tender in step 2 before moving on to step 3.

1 Heat 3 tablespoons oil in Dutch oven over medium heat until shimmering. Add onion and cook until softened and lightly browned, 5 to 7 minutes. Stir in garlic and pepper flakes and cook until fragrant, about 1 minute. Stir in broth, water, and ½ teaspoon salt and bring to simmer.

2 Add one-third of kale, cover, and cook, stirring occasionally, until wilted, 2 to 4 minutes. Repeat with remaining kale in 2 batches. Continue to cook, covered, until kale is tender, 13 to 15 minutes.

3 Remove lid and increase heat to medium-high. Cook, stirring occasionally, until most liquid has evaporated and greens begin to sizzle, 10 to 12 minutes. Off heat, stir in lemon juice and remaining 3 tablespoons oil. Season with salt, pepper, and extra lemon juice to taste. Serve.

Braised Kale with Coconut and Curry

Substitute 2 teaspoons grated fresh ginger and 1 teaspoon curry powder for red pepper flakes, and 1 (13.5-ounce) can coconut milk for water. Substitute lime juice for lemon juice, and sprinkle kale with ¼ cup toasted and chopped cashews before serving.

BRAISED RED POTATOES WITH LEMON AND CHIVES

serves 4 to 6

1½ pounds small red potatoes, unpeeled, halved

2 cups water

3 tablespoons unsalted butter

3 garlic cloves, peeled

3 sprigs fresh thyme

¾ teaspoon salt

1 teaspoon lemon juice

¼ teaspoon pepper

2 tablespoons minced fresh chives

Why This Recipe Works What if you could get red potatoes with the creamy interiors created by steaming and the crispy browned exteriors produced by roasting—without doing either? That's the result promised by recipes for braised red potatoes, but they rarely deliver. To make good on the promise, we combined halved small red potatoes, butter, and salted water (plus thyme for flavoring) in a 12-inch skillet and simmered the spuds until their interiors were perfectly creamy and the water was fully evaporated. Then we let the potatoes continue to cook in the now-dry skillet until their cut sides browned in the butter, developing the rich flavor and crisp edges of roasted potatoes. These crispy, creamy potatoes were so good they needed only a minimum of seasoning: We simply tossed them with some minced garlic (softened in the simmering water along with the potatoes), lemon juice, chives, and pepper. Use small red potatoes measuring about 1½ inches in diameter.

1 Arrange potatoes in single layer, cut sides down, in 12-inch nonstick skillet. Add water, butter, garlic, thyme sprigs, and salt and bring to simmer over medium-high heat. Reduce heat to medium, cover, and simmer until potatoes are just tender, about 15 minutes.

2 Remove lid and use slotted spoon to transfer garlic to cutting board; discard thyme sprigs. Increase heat to medium-high and vigorously simmer, swirling pan occasionally, until water evaporates and butter starts to sizzle, 15 to 20 minutes. When cool enough to handle, mince garlic to paste. Transfer paste to bowl and stir in lemon juice and pepper.

3 Continue to cook potatoes, swirling pan frequently, until butter browns and cut sides of potatoes turn spotty brown, 4 to 6 minutes longer. Off heat, add garlic mixture and chives and toss to thoroughly coat. Serve immediately.

Bacon-Braised Red Potatoes

Omit butter. Substitute 1 onion, halved and sliced ½ inch thick, for garlic and thyme sprigs. Add 2 slices thick-cut bacon, cut into 1 inch pieces, with water and onion. Reduce salt to ¼ teaspoon. Add pepper with salt in step 1. Cook as directed. In step 3, potatoes should be spotty brown and bacon should render completely. Off heat, stir in 2 teaspoons chopped fresh thyme and season with salt and pepper to taste.

Braised Red Potatoes with Dijon and Tarragon

Substitute 2 teaspoons Dijon mustard for lemon juice and 1 tablespoon minced fresh tarragon for chives.

Braised Red Potatoes with Miso and Scallions

Reduce salt to ½ teaspoon. Substitute 1 tablespoon red miso paste for lemon juice and 3 thinly sliced scallions for chives.

Nutritional Information for Our Recipes

To calculate the nutritional values of our recipes per serving, we used Edamam. When using this program, we entered all the ingredients, using weights for important ingredients such as most vegetables. We also used our preferred brands in these analyses. When the recipe called for seasoning with an unspecified amount of salt and pepper, we added ½ teaspoon of salt and ¼ teaspoon of pepper to the analysis. We did not include additional salt or pepper for food that's "seasoned to taste." If there is a range in the serving size, we used the highest number of servings to calculate the nutritional values.

	CALORIES	TOTAL FAT (G)	SAT FAT (G)	CHOL (MG)	SODIUM (MG)	TOTAL CARBS (G)	FIBER (G)	SUGAR (G)	PROTEIN (G)
Beef									
Simple Pot Roast	295	19 g	6 g	77 mg	701 mg	6 g	0 g	2 g	24 g
Simple Pot Roast with Root Vegetables	480	20 g	7g	78 mg	1408 mg	50 g	10 g	14 g	29 g
Italian Pot Roast	518	28 g	9 g	116 mg	378 mg	21 g	5 g	10 g	39 g
French-Style Pot Roast	379	16 g	7 g	63 mg	998 mg	16 g	2 g	6 g	19 g
Beef in Barolo	450	21 g	8 g	90 mg	951 mg	15 g	3 g	6 g	26 g
Brisket Carbonnade	862	63 g	24 g	248 mg	1029 mg	17 g	2 g	6 g	49 g
Atlanta Brisket	898	62 g	23 g	248 mg	1150 mg	35 g	2 g	25g	48 g
Braised Brisket with Pomegranate, Cumin, and Cilantro	795	55g	21 g	216 mg	927 mg	28 g	1 g	21 g	45 g
Beer-Braised Brisket with Prunes and Ginger	741	55 g	21 g	216 mg	881 mg	12 g	1 g	3 g	68 g
Red Wine–Braised Brisket and Thyme	739	55 g	21 g	217 mg	839 mg	1 g	1 g	3 g	45 g
Oaxacan-Style Beef Brisket	842	62 g	24 g	250 mg	1230 mg	18 g	3 g	9 g	51 g
Home-Corned Beef and Cabbage	918	60 g	24 g	253 mg	1253 mg	41 g	6 g	20 g	51 g
Braised Beef with Red Wine and Cherries	624	26 g	10 g	188 mg	885 mg	28 g	3 g	15 g	61 g
Beef en Cocotte with Caramelized Onions	686	47 g	17 g	211 mg	980 mg	7 g	1 g	2 g	55 g
Braised Boneless Beef Short Ribs	607	29 g	11 g	212 mg	1007 mg	12 g	2 g	5 g	56 g
Braised Boneless Beef Short Ribs with Guinness and Prunes	769	55 g	22 g	193 mg	956 mg	19 g	2 g	5 g	48 g
Red Wine–Braised Short Ribs with Bacon, Parsnips, and Pearl Onions	2126	176 g	76 g	368 mg	1023 mg	38 g	7 g	13 g	76 g
Porter-Braised Short Ribs with Prunes and Brandy	2124	167g	72 g	350 mg	804 mg	62 g	4 g	9 g	74 g
Pomegranate-Braised Short Ribs with Prunes and Sesame	1400	116 g	48 g	230 mg	480 mg	40 g	3 g	30 g	46 g
Ras el Hanout	53	2 g	0 g	0 mg	31 mg	11 g	5 g	0 g	2 g
Chinese-Style Braised Short Ribs	1830	169 g	72 g	345 mg	534 mg	11 g	2 g	0 g	67g
Shredded Beef Tacos (Carne Deshebrada)	895	51 g	22 g	179 mg	1451 mg	58 g	12 g	10 g	51 g
Cabbage-Carrot Slaw	37	0 g	0 g	0 mg	309 mg	8 g	2 g	5 g	1 g
Braised Oxtails with White Beans, Tomatoes, and Aleppo Pepper	698	47 g	18 g	153 mg	725 mg	13 g	3 g	4 g	49 g
Roman Braised Oxtails	659	46 g	17 g	153 mg	591 mg	11 g	2 g	5 g	46 g
Steak Tips with Mushroom-Onion Gravy	502	31 g	10 g	132 mg	1033 mg	13 g	2 g	5 g	40 g
Braised Steaks with Root Vegetables	498	20 g	7 g	87 mg	1267 mg	51 g	10 g	12 g	28 g
Braised Steaks with Mushrooms and Tomatoes	541	33 g	12 g	100 mg	417 mg	19 g	3 g	7 g	35 g
Braciole	453	20 g	5 g	39 mg	1269 mg	52 g	10 g	31 g	22 g

	CALORIES	TOTAL FAT (G)	SAT FAT (G)	CHOL (MG)	SODIUM (MG)	TOTAL CARBS (G)	FIBER (G)	SUGAR (G)	PROTEIN (G)
Beef (cont.)									
Cuban Braised Shredded Beef (Ropa Vieja)	629	49 g	14 g	145 mg	919 mg	13 g	3 g	5 g	30 g
Modern Beef Stew	593	35 g	12 g	96 mg	1097 mg	31 g	5 g	5 g	30 g
Beef Stew with Parsnips, Kale, and Mushrooms	517	14 g	4 g	99 mg	681 mg	49 g	10 g	13 g	42 g
Big Batch Beef Stew	499	17 g	7 g	156 mg	683 mg	35 g	5 g	8 g	54 g
Guinness Beef Stew	467	22 g	6 g	77 mg	1134 mg	40 g	6 g	8 g	29 g
Modern Beef Burgundy	1005	62 g	26 g	224 mg	1840 mg	27 g	3 g	7 g	63 g
Carne Guisada	885	36 g	10 g	114 mg	1342 mg	93 g	8 g	8 g	48 g
Daube Provençal	960	63 g	23 g	200 mg	1629 mg	27 g	6 g	8 g	57 g
Catalan-Style Beef Stew with Mushrooms	1401	121 g	47 g	215 mg	1460 mg	20 g	4 g	6 g	46 g
Chinese-Style Red-Cooked Beef	602	43 g	18 g	165 mg	1117 mg	10 g	0 g	6 g	42 g
Portuguese-Style Beef Stew (Alcatra)	542	23 g	8 g	121 mg	874 mg	10 g	1 g	2 g	59 g
Sichuan Braised Tofu with Beef (Mapo Tofu)	567	41 g	6 g	42 mg	584 mg	23 g	3 g	7 g	29 g
Flank Steak in Adobo	1308	54 g	16 g	232 mg	1825 mg	116 g	10 g	28 g	88 g
Ultimate Chili	843	42 g	12 g	164 mg	313 mg	50 g	12 g	7 g	60 g
Beef Short Rib Ragu	654	48 g	20 g	169 mg	1048 mg	13 g	4 g	6 g	44 g
Lamb and Veal									
Braised Lamb Shoulder Chops with Tomatoes and Red Wine	392	31 g	11 g	82 mg	498 mg	4 g	1 g	2 g	19 g
Braised Lamb Shoulder with Capers, Balsamic Vinegar, and Red Pepper	409	31 g	11 g	82 mg	596 mg	8 g	2 g	4 g	20 g
Braised Lamb Shoulder with Figs and North African Spices	426	31 g	11 g	82 mg	571 mg	16 g	2 g	12 g	20 g
Braised Lamb Shoulder with Tomatoes, Rosemary, and Olives	404	32 g	11 g	82 mg	522 mg	5 g	2 g	2 g	19 g
Braised Lamb Shanks with Lemon and Mint	840	51 g	20 g	245 mg	810 mg	12 g	2 g	5 g	66 g
Braised Lamb Shanks with North African Spices	850	51 g	20 g	245 mg	810 mg	19 g	5 g	4 g	89 g
Braised Lamb Shanks with Red Wine and Herbes de Provence	840	51 g	20 g	245 mg	810 mg	12 g	2 g	5 g	66 g
Leg of Lamb en Cocotte with Garlic and Rosemary	1157	80 g	33 g	359 mg	1256 mg	2 g	0 g	0 g	98 g
Moroccan Braised White Beans with Lamb	365	10 g	4 g	32 mg	466 mg	43 g	10 g	5 g	25 g
Irish Stew	1100	72 g	32 g	221 mg	268 mg	48 g	7 g	9 g	64 g
Irish Stew with Carrots and Turnips	1066	72 g	32 g	221 mg	310 mg	40 g	7 g	12 g	63 g
Italian-Style Lamb Stew with Green Beans, Tomatoes, and Basil	1141	72 g	32 g	221 mg	348 mg	55 g	10 g	13 g	65 g
Lamb Curry with Whole Spices	688	39 g	11 g	115 mg	409 mg	47 g	7 g	4 g	37 g
Lamb Curry with Figs and Fenugreek	526	39 g	11 g	115 mg	396 mg	10 g	2 g	4 g	33 g
Lamb Tagine with Apricots and Olives	357	18 g	3 g	13 mg	946 mg	43 g	7 g	24 g	10 g
Lamb Vindaloo	845	22 g	31 g	152 mg	181 mg	11 g	1 g	3 g	24 g
Osso Buco	591	27 g	4 g	225 mg	314 mg	12 g	3 g	5 g	60 g
Veal Stew with Fennel, Tarragon, and Cream (Blanquette de Veau)	445	21 g	11 g	139 mg	974 mg	23 g	5 g	9 g	37 g
Pork									
Pork with Red Cabbage, Apples, and Juniper	250	8 g	2 g	18 mg	817 mg	37 g	9 g	18 g	9 g
Milk-Braised Pork Loin	445	25 g	8 g	118 mg	719 mg	16 g	1 g	15 g	37 g
Cider-Braised Pork Roast	602	34 g	10 g	146 mg	1081 mg	28 g	2 g	21 g	42 g
Philadelphia Pork Sandwiches	712	39 g	15 g	138 mg	1051 mg	36 g	3 g	2 g	50 g
Braised Pork Loin with Black Mole Sauce	490	27 g	5 g	120 mg	791 mg	16 g	4 g	7 g	47 g
French-Style Pot-Roasted Pork Loin	493	25 g	8 g	162 mg	650 mg	10 g	2 g	5 g	52 g
French-Style Pot-Roasted Pork Loin with Port and Figs	500	33 g	11 g	130 mg	618 mg	10 g	2 g	5 g	39 g

	CALORIES	TOTAL FAT (G)	SAT FAT (G)	CHOL (MG)	SODIUM (MG)	TOTAL CARBS (G)	FIBER (G)	SUGAR (G)	PROTEIN (G)
Pork (cont.)									
Braised Country-Style Ribs with Black-Eyed Peas and Collard Greens	487	34 g	11 g	100 mg	800 mg	21 g	6 g	7 g	24 g
Spicy Pickled Onion	23	0 g	0 g	0 mg	96 mg	5 g	0 g	4 g	0 g
Sweet-and-Sour Pork Ribs	1172	31 g	27 g	335 mg	2160 mg	15 g	2 g	12 g	89 g
Pork Grillades	891	49 g	11 g	138 mg	1457 mg	57 g	3 g	5 g	50 g
Louisiana Seasoning	49	1 g	0 g	0 mg	949 mg	10 g	3 g	1 g	2 g
Red Wine–Braised Pork Chops	658	40 g	15 g	180 mg	1021 mg	11 g	2 g	3 g	53 g
Smothered Pork Chops	453	26 g	8 g	144 mg	755 mg	8 g	1 g	3 g	43 g
Smothered Pork Chops with Cider and Apples	584	32 g	9 g	151 mg	979 mg	25 g	2 g	16 g	45 g
Smothered Pork Chops with Spicy Collard Greens	539	32 g	9 g	151 mg	957 mg	11 g	2 g	1 g	48 g
Pork Chops with Vinegar Peppers	238	10 g	3 g	11 mg	652 mg	25 g	1 g	11 g	4 g
Pork Chops with Tomato Gravy	547	44 g	12 g	104 mg	729 mg	14 g	2 g	4 g	23 g
Mexican Pulled Pork (Carnitas)	668	35 g	12 g	164 mg	586 mg	36 g	5 g	3 g	51 g
French-Style Pork Stew	561	33 g	11 g	138 mg	626 mg	22 g	3 g	5 g	41 g
New Mexican Pork Stew (Posole)	849	55 g	17 g	137 mg	1730 mg	43 g	7 g	6 g	43 g
Colorado Green Chili	620	33 g	10 g	145 mg	1555 mg	31 g	4 g	14 g	48 g
Spicy Mexican Pork Tinga and Rice	560	25 g	8 g	96 mg	806 mg	49 g	2 g	5 g	33 g
Carne Adovado	555	35 g	11 g	142 mg	773 mg	18 g	5 g	6 g	43 g
Braised Greek Sausages with Peppers	479	38 g	12 g	67 mg	1182 mg	16 g	4 g	7 g	16 g
Stuffed Cabbage Rolls	732	43 g	14 g	123 mg	1850 mg	52 g	10 g	31 g	35 g
Pork Ragu	741	49 g	16 g	179mg	832 mg	18 g	5 g	6 g	53 g
Poultry									
Coq au Vin	1267	67 g	22 g	338 mg	1118 mg	20 g	1 g	6 g	107 g
Chicken Provençal	783	55 g	14 g	292 mg	1160 mg	11 g	2 g	3 g	52 g
Chicken Provençal with Saffron, Orange, and Basil	783	55 g	14 g	292 mg	1159 mg	11 g	2 g	3 g	52 g
Chicken with 40 Cloves of Garlic	950	52 g	15 g	337 mg	404 mg	20 g	2 g	3 g	97 g
Chicken Cacciatore	576	32 g	7 g	215 mg	311 mg	7 g	2 g	4 g	64 g
Chicken Paprikash	798	55 g	15 g	302 mg	379 mg	18 g	6 g	8 g	52 g
Filipino Chicken Adobo	884	70 g	31 g	292 mg	1425 mg	8 g	0 g	0 g	53 g
Quick Chicken Fricassee	448	17 g	6 g	219 mg	1170 mg	12 g	1 g	3 g	57 g
Chicken Florentine	727	42 g	19 g	294 mg	1427 mg	10 g	2 g	3 g	74 g
Chicken Scarpariello	923	60 g	16 g	273 mg	1391 mg	15 g	3 g	5 g	75 g
Chicken Vesuvio	615	20 g	6 g	213 mg	1400 mg	33 g	4 g	4 g	68 g
Mahogany Chicken Thighs	491	34 g	10 g	167 mg	1704 mg	15 g	0 g	10 g	33 g
Chicken with Pumpkin Seed Sauce	443	23 g	3 g	127 mg	792 mg	13 g	3 g	5 g	46 g
Chicken in a Pot with Red Potatoes, Carrots, and Shallots	1123	57 g	18 g	413 mg	953 mg	51 g	8 g	13 g	104 g
Chicken Bouillabaisse	1104	69 g	11 g	175 mg	1548 mg	54 g	6 g	10 g	58 g
Rouille	267	28 g	2 g	30 mg	93 mg	2 g	0 g	0 g	1 g
Spanish Braised Chicken with Sherry and Saffron (Pollo en Pepitoria)	863	63 g	15 g	372 mg	1330 mg	15 g	4 g	6 g	57 g
Lemon-Braised Chicken Thighs with Chickpeas and Fennel	834	48 g	11 g	210 mg	1239 mg	50 g	13 g	14 g	48 g
Chicken Curry	825	63 g	20 g	307 mg	578 mg	11 g	3 g	3 g	52 g
Chicken Curry with Sweet Potato and Cauliflower	807	59 g	19 g	237 mg	280 mg	10 g	3 g	3 g	59 g
Cilantro-Mint Chutney	37	0 g	0 g	2 mg	155 mg	6 g	1 g	3 g	1 g
Onion Relish	31	0 g	0 g	0 mg	79 mg	7 g	0 g	4 g	0 g
Chicken Tagine with Olives and Lemon	967	53 g	14 g	293 mg	1168 mg	20 g	4 g	9 g	99 g

	CALORIES	TOTAL FAT (G)	SAT FAT (G)	CHOL (MG)	SODIUM (MG)	TOTAL CARBS (G)	FIBER (G)	SUGAR (G)	PROTEIN (G)
Poultry (cont.)									
Southern-Style Smothered Chicken	992	66 g	16 g	258 mg	1353 mg	24 g	2 g	4 g	69 g
Braised Chicken Thighs with Chard and Mustard	890	62 g	16 g	337 mg	727 mg	17 g	3 g	4 g	62 g
Braised Chicken Thighs with Spinach and Garlic	884	61 g	16 g	337 mg	500 mg	15 g	3 g	3 g	62 g
Brunswick Stew	696	27 g	7 g	252 mg	1982 mg	52 g	5 g	16 g	59 g
Chicken Stew	644	30 g	11 g	257 mg	1468 mg	33 g	3 g	7 g	53 g
Cajun Chicken, Sausage, and Corn Stew	908	63 g	16 g	275 mg	1496 mg	30 g	4 g	10 g	56 g
Ethiopian-Style Spicy Chicken Stew (Doro Wat)	1073	60 g	17 g	593 mg	708 mg	16 g	2 g	3 g	92 g
Chicken and Dumplings	784	46 g	15 g	251 mg	1435 mg	41 g	2 g	4 g	49 g
White Chicken Chili	636	25 g	6 g	145 mg	195 mg	41 g	8 g	5 g	61 g
Indoor Pulled Chicken with Lexington Vinegar Barbecue Sauce	200	5 g	1 g	107 mg	498 mg	12 g	0 g	10 g	23 g
Indoor Pulled Chicken with South Carolina Mustard Barbecue Sauce	227	6 g	1 g	107 mg	676 mg	17 g	1 g	13 g	24 g
Indoor Pulled Chicken with Sweet and Tangy Barbecue Sauce	335	6 g	1 g	143 mg	871 mg	37 g	0 g	31 g	31 g
Turkey Breast en Cocotte with Pan Gravy	700	32 g	8 g	245 mg	1367 mg	11 g	1 g	1 g	87 g
Turkey Breast en Cocotte with Mole Sauce	889	46 g	10 g	287 mg	1423 mg	15 g	4 g	6 g	100 g
Turkey Breast en Cocotte with Orange-Chipotle Sauce	856	35 g	9 g	287 mg	1468 mg	29 g	1 g	24 g	98 g
Seafood									
Braised Cod with Leeks and Cherry Tomatoes	320	10 g	6 g	96 mg	557 mg	21 g	3 g	7 g	33 g
Braised Cod Provençal	262	8 g	1 g	73 mg	789 mg	11 g	4 g	6 g	32 g
Braised Cod with Peperonata	280	8 g	1 g	73 mg	840 mg	12 g	3 g	6 g	32 g
Braised Cod Veracruz	247	8 g	1 g	73 mg	705 mg	8 g	3 g	4 g	32 g
Braised Halibut with Leek and Mustard	316	15 g	2 g	56 mg	552 mg	17 g	2 g	5 g	23 g
Braised Halibut with Carrots and Coriander	335	15 g	12 g	56 mg	601 mg	22 g	5 g	10 g	24 g
Braised Halibut with Fennel and Tarragon	325	15 g	2 g	56 mg	583 mg	20 g	6 g	10 g	24 g
Hake in Saffron Broth with Chorizo and Potatoes	296	12 g	4 g	67 mg	775 mg	10 g	1 g	2 g	30 g
Catfish in Salty Caramel (Ca Kho To)	319	18 g	3 g	83 mg	1097 mg	14 g	1 g	12 g	24 g
Salmon en Cocotte with Leeks and White Wine	364	25 g	7 g	69 mg	416 mg	7 g	1 g	1 g	21 g
Salmon en Cocotte with Celery and Orange	383	26 g	7 g	69 mg	570 mg	15 g	2 g	7 g	21 g
Halibut en Cocotte with Roasted Garlic and Cherry Tomatoes	326	16 g	2 g	99 mg	720 mg	4 g	1 g	2 g	38 g
Halibut en Cocotte with Fennel and Saffron	352	16 g	2 g	99 mg	863 mg	9 g	3 g	4 g	39 g
Swordfish en Cocotte with Carrots and Chermoula	370	26 g	4 g	89 mg	460 mg	5 g	1 g	1 g	27 g
Swordfish en Cocotte with Shallots, Cucumbers, and Mint	406	26 g	4 g	89 mg	673 mg	13 g	3 g	4 g	29 g
Red Wine–Braised Octopus	452	8 g	2 g	218 mg	1053 mg	12 g	0 g	0 g	71 g
Cioppino	801	43 g	11 g	179 mg	1946 mg	26 g	6 g	8 g	68 g
Bouillabaisse	256	9 g	1 g	80 mg	939 mg	10 g	2 g	3 g	30 g
Spanish Shellfish Stew	863	20 g	3 g	85 mg	1194 mg	24 g	4 g	7 g	35 g
Spanish Shellfish Stew with Lobster	588	27 g	3 g	174 mg	1484 mg	29 g	7 g	9 g	43 g
Picada	92	7 g	0 g	0 mg	49 mg	5 g	0 g	0 g	1 g
Monkfish Tagine	174	7 g	1 g	28 mg	526 mg	8 g	2 g	3 g	20 g
Brazillian Shrimp and Fish Stew (Moqueca)	422	29 g	14 g	127 mg	1063 mg	15 g	4 g	6 g	27 g
Calamari Stew with Garlic and Tomatoes	499	19 g	3 g	528 mg	1013 mg	36 g	13 g	18 g	41 g
Vegetarian Mains									
Ratatouille	354	23 g	3 g	0 mg	1047 mg	36 g	12 g	19 g	7 g
Wild Mushroom Ragu	162	7 g	4 g	15 mg	430 mg	17 g	5 g	10 g	8 g
Hearty Ten-Vegetable Stew	209	5 g	0 g	0 mg	1379 mg	34 g	7 g	9 g	7 g

	CALORIES	TOTAL FAT (G)	SAT FAT (G)	CHOL (MG)	SODIUM (MG)	TOTAL CARBS (G)	FIBER (G)	SUGAR (G)	PROTEIN (G)
Vegetarian Mains (cont.)									
Ultimate Vegetarian Chili	396	10 g	1 g	0 mg	393 mg	64 g	16 g	10 g	19 g
Quinoa and Vegetable Stew	320	15 g	5 g	25 mg	328 mg	37 g	7 g	7 g	11 g
Quinoa and Vegetable Stew with Eggs	366	18 g	6 g	145 mg	374 mg	38 g	7 g	7 g	15 g
Artichoke, Pepper, and Chickpea Tagine	663	22 g	3 g	3 mg	1629 mg	100 g	25 g	34 g	23 g
Indian-Style Vegetable Curry with Potatoes and Cauliflower	256	13 g	4 g	0 mg	324 mg	31 g	8 g	7 g	8 g
Indian-Style Vegetable Curry with Sweet Potatoes and Eggplant	263	13 g	4 g	0 mg	300 mg	35 g	11 g	11 g	7 g
Potato Vindaloo	218	6 g	0 g	0 mg	798 mg	39 g	8 g	10 g	5 g
Braised Squash and Winter Greens with Coconut Curry	514	37 g	21 g	0 mg	369 mg	46 g	10 g	9 g	13 g
Caribbean-Style Swiss Chard and Butternut Squash Stew	366	24 g	14 g	18 mg	1474 mg	27 g	5 g	9 g	14 g
Chile-Braised Tofu	242	16 g	7 g	23 mg	645 mg	15 g	5 g	4 g	15 g
Asian Braised Tofu with Winter Squash and Coconut Milk	468	35 g	20 g	0 mg	40 mg	33 g	8 g	9 g	13 g
Braised Fennel with Radicchio and Parmesan	148	9 g	1 g	0 mg	73 mg	14 g	4 g	7 g	3 g
Beans									
Hearty Tuscan White Bean Stew	434	12 g	3 g	14 mg	1030 mg	59 g	13 g	6 g	23 g
Cranberry Beans with Warm Spices	329	9 g	1 g	4 mg	352 mg	44 g	10 g	5 g	16 g
Drunken Beans	470	11 g	4 g	21 mg	567 mg	58 g	13 g	5 g	22 g
Baked Navy Beans	344	4 g	0 g	0 mg	970 mg	62 g	12 g	17 g	18 g
Red Beans and Rice	308	12 g	4 g	23 mg	464 mg	33 g	12 g	3 g	17 g
Sicilian White Beans and Escarole	165	4 g	1 g	2 mg	386 mg	25 g	5 g	4 g	8 g
Stewed Chickpeas with Eggplant and Tomatoes	275	12 g	2 g	0 mg	583 mg	36 g	12 g	12 g	9 g
Chickpeas with Spinach, Chroizo, and Smoked Paprika	299	11 g	3 g	12 mg	772 mg	38 g	10 g	7 g	15 g
Black-Eyed Peas and Greens	291	13 g	4 g	18 mg	942 mg	31 g	9 g	4 g	14 g
Cuban-Style Black Beans and Rice	598	29 g	9 g	24 mg	894 mg	70 g	7 g	3 g	15 g
Black Bean Chili	437	10 g	1 g	0 mg	1303 mg	70 g	18 g	13 g	22 g
North African Vegetable and Bean Stew	136	3 g	0 g	0 mg	358 mg	23 g	5 g	3 g	6 g
Lentils with Spinach and Garlic Chips	174	5 g	1 g	0 mg	232 mg	25 g	5 g	2 g	9 g
French Lentils with Carrots and Parsley	173	5 g	1 g	0 mg	221 mg	25 g	5 g	3 g	8 g
Curried French Lentils with Golden Raisins	209	5 g	1 g	0mg	222 mg	35 g	5 g	10 g	9 g
French Lentils with Swiss Chard	173	5 g	1 g	0 mg	322 mg	25 g	5 g	2 g	9 g
Spiced Red Lentils (Masoor Dal)	169	5 g	2 g	7 mg	531 mg	23 g	4 g	2 g	8 g
Red Lentils with Coconut Milk	199	8 g	5 g	0 mg	519 mg	24 g	4 g	2 g	8 g
French Pork and White Bean Casserole	586	31 g	9 g	83 mg	705 mg	42 g	9 g	6 g	34 g
Brazilian Black Bean and Pork Stew	1236	69 g	23 g	263 mg	1259 mg	59 g	14 g	3 g	94 g
Brazilian Hot Sauce	50	4 g	1 g	0 mg	119 mg	3 g	1 g	2 g	0 g
Brazilian Toasted Manioc Flour (Farofa)	62	3 g	2 g	6 mg	1 mg	9 g	1 g	0g	1 g
Texas-Style Pinto Beans	197	1 g	0 g	0 mg	132 mg	35 g	9 g	1 g	12 g
Vegetable Sides									
Braised Spring Vegetables with Tarragon	140	9 g	1 g	0 mg	447 mg	11 g	4 g	4 g	4 g
Braised Artichokes with Tomatoes and Thyme	96	5 g	1 g	2 mg	323 mg	8 g	2 g	3 g	3 g
Beets with Lemon and Almonds	206	9 g	0 g	0 mg	683 mg	26 g	7 g	16 g	7 g
Beets with Ginger and Cashews	251	12 g	2 g	0 mg	705 mg	29 g	6 g	16 g	8 g
Beets with Lime and Pepitas	192	8 g	1 g	0 mg	680 mg	24 g	6 g	16 g	8 g
Beets with Orange and Walnuts	126	2 g	0 g	0 mg	652 mg	23 g	5 g	16 g	3 g

	CALORIES	TOTAL FAT (G)	SAT FAT (G)	CHOL (MG)	SODIUM (MG)	TOTAL CARBS (G)	FIBER (G)	SUGAR (G)	PROTEIN (G)
Vegetable Sides (cont.)									
Braised Bok Choy with Garlic	91	7 g	1 g	1 mg	263 mg	4 g	0 g	1 g	2 g
Braised Bok Choy with Shiitake Mushrooms	88	7 g	1 g	0 mg	256 mg	5 g	1 g	1 g	1 g
Braised Brussels Sprouts	110	6 g	3.5 g	0 mg	185 mg	13 g	5 g	4 g	4 g
Cream-Braised Brussels Sprouts	317	28 g	17 g	97 mg	200 mg	14 g	5 g	5 g	6 g
Curried Brussels Sprouts with Currants	133	6 g	4 g	15 mg	186 mg	18 g	6 g	8 g	5 g
Maple-Glazed Brussels Sprouts	156	8 g	5 g	20 mg	445 mg	18 g	5 g	7 g	5 g
Braised Red Cabbage	282	9 g	5 g	22 mg	866 mg	42 g	6 g	28 g	4 g
Beer-Braised Cabbage	126	6 g	3 g	15 mg	589 mg	15 g	5 g	7 g	3 g
Cream-Braised Cabbage with Lemon and Shallot	118	7 g	4 g	27 mg	434 mg	12 g	4 g	6 g	2 g
Braised Cabbage with Parsley and Thyme	57	3 g	2 g	8 mg	28 mg	7 g	3 g	4 g	2 g
Slow-Cooked Whole Carrots	59	2 g	0 g	0 mg	229 mg	9 g	3 g	5 g	1 g
Slow-Cooked Whole Carrots with Green Olive and Raisin Relish	127	6 g	1 g	0 mg	313 mg	18 g	4 g	10 g	2 g
Slow-Cooked Whole Carrots with Onion-Balsamic Relish	114	7 g	1 g	0 mg	166 mg	12 g	3 g	6 g	1 g
Slow-Cooked Whole Carrots with Pine Nut Relish	122	8 g	1 g	0 mg	280 mg	13 g	3 g	7 g	2 g
Glazed Carrots	115	3 g	1 g	7 mg	370 mg	21 g	3 g	14 g	1 g
Glazed Carrots with Ginger and Rosemary	119	3 g	1 g	7 mg	379 mg	21 g	3 g	14 g	1 g
Glazed Curried Carrots with Currants and Almonds	177	6 g	2 g	7 mg	379 mg	29 g	5 g	21 g	3 g
Honey-Glazed Carrots with Lemon and Thyme	127	3 g	1 g	7 mg	379 mg	24 g	3 g	18 g	1 g
Braised Cauliflower with Garlic and White Wine	118	8 g	1 g	0 mg	163 mg	9 g	3 g	3 g	3 g
Braised Cauliflower with Capers and Anchovies	122	8 g	1 g	2 mg	245 mg	9 g	3 g	3 g	4 g
Braised Cauliflower with Sumac and Mint	119	9 g	2 g	2 mg	176 mg	9 g	3 g	4 g	4 g
Braised Belgian Endive	99	8 g	5 g	22 mg	211 mg	3 g	1 g	0 g	0 g
Braised Belgian Endive with Bacon and Cream	136	11 g	4 g	24 mg	250 mg	3 g	1 g	1 g	3 g
Cider-Braised Belgian Endive with Apples	129	8 g	5 g	22 mg	326 mg	12 g	3 g	7 g	0 g
Braised Fennel	126	8 g	5 g	22 mg	357 mg	9 g	3 g	5 g	1 g
Bacon-Braised Green Beans	141	8 g	2 g	13 mg	431 mg	11 g	3 g	5 g	5 g
Mediterranean Braised Green Beans	241	17 g	2 g	0 mg	798 mg	20 g	7 g	10 g	4 g
Mediterranean Braised Green Beans with Mint and Feta	219	13 g	3 g	12 mg	926 mg	21 g	7 g	10 g	6 g
Mediterranean Braised Green Beans with Potatoes and Basil	269	10 g	1 g	0 mg	1230 mg	40 g	10 g	10 g	7 g
Green Beans and Mushrooms Braised in Cream	313	24 g	13 g	69 mg	660 mg	21 g	5 g	10 g	6 g
Braised Hearty Greens	191	12 g	7 g	30 mg	906 mg	17 g	5 g	7 g	6 g
Braised Hearty Greens with Chorizo and Pimentos	402	28 g	12 g	65 mg	1325 mg	19 g	5 g	7 g	20 g
Braised Hearty Greens with Pancetta and Pine Nuts	394	31 g	10 g	43 mg	1015 mg	19 g	5 g	8 g	13 g
Braised Hearty Greens with Raisins and Almonds	296	16 g	7 g	30 mg	968 mg	34 g	6 g	19 g	9 g
Braised Hearty Greens with White Beans	381	14 g	4 g	15 mg	1314 mg	53 g	12 g	13 g	16 g
Garlicky Braised Kale	180	12 g	2 g	2 mg	277 mg	15 g	5 g	4 g	7 g
Braised Kale with Coconut and Curry	354	25 g	11 g	2 mg	200 mg	28 g	9 g	7 g	13 g
Braised Red Potatoes with Lemon and Chives	202	8 g	5 g	22 mg	473 mg	28 g	3 g	2 g	3 g
Bacon-Braised Red Potatoes	193	5 g	1 g	9 mg	848 mg	30 g	3 g	3 g	5 g
Braised Red Potatoes with Dijon and Tarragon	205	9 g	5 g	22 mg	501 mg	28 g	3 g	2 g	3 g
Braised Red Potatoes with Miso and Scallions	214	9 g	5 g	22 mg	488 mg	30 g	3 g	2 g	4 g

Conversions and Equivalents

Some say cooking is a science and an art. We would say geography has a hand in it, too. Flours and sugars manufactured in the United Kingdom and elsewhere will feel and taste different from those manufactured in the United States. So we cannot promise that a loaf of bread you bake in Canada or England will taste the same as a loaf baked in the States, but we can offer guidelines for converting weights and measures. We also recommend that you rely on your instincts when making our recipes. Refer to the visual cues provided. If the dough hasn't come together as described, you may need to add more flour—even if the recipe doesn't tell you to. You be the judge.

The recipes in this book were developed using standard U.S. measures following U.S. government guidelines. The charts below offer equivalents for U.S. and metric measures. All conversions are approximate and have been rounded up or down to the nearest whole number.

EXAMPLE

| 1 teaspoon | = | 4.9292 milliliters, rounded up to 5 milliliters |
| 1 ounce | = | 28.3495 grams, rounded down to 28 grams |

VOLUME CONVERSIONS

U.S.	METRIC
1 teaspoon	5 milliliters
2 teaspoons	10 milliliters
1 tablespoon	15 milliliters
2 tablespoons	30 milliliters
¼ cup	59 milliliters
⅓ cup	79 milliliters
½ cup	118 milliliters
¾ cup	177 milliliters
1 cup	237 milliliters
1¼ cups	296 milliliters
1½ cups	355 milliliters
2 cups (1 pint)	473 milliliters
2½ cups	591 milliliters
3 cups	710 milliliters
4 cups (1 quart)	0.946 liter
1.06 quarts	1 liter
4 quarts (1 gallon)	3.8 liters

WEIGHT CONVERSIONS

OUNCES	GRAMS
½	14
¾	21
1	28
1½	43
2	57
2½	71
3	85
3½	99
4	113
4½	128
5	142
6	170
7	198
8	227
9	255
10	283
12	340
16 (1 pound)	454

CONVERSIONS FOR COMMON BAKING INGREDIENTS

Because measuring by weight is far more accurate than measuring by volume, and thus more likely to produce reliable results, in our recipes we provide ounce measures in addition to cup measures for many ingredients. Refer to the chart below to convert these measures into grams.

INGREDIENT	OUNCES	GRAMS
Flour		
1 cup all-purpose flour*	5	142
1 cup cake flour	4	113
1 cup whole-wheat flour	5½	156
Sugar		
1 cup granulated (white) sugar	7	198
1 cup packed brown sugar (light or dark)	7	198
1 cup confectioners' sugar	4	113
Cocoa Powder		
1 cup cocoa powder	3	85
Butter†		
4 tablespoons (½ stick or ¼ cup)	2	57
8 tablespoons (1 stick or ½ cup)	4	113
16 tablespoons (2 sticks or 1 cup)	8	227

* U.S. all-purpose flour, the most frequently used flour in this book, does not contain leaveners, as some European flours do. These leavened flours are called self-rising or self-raising. If you are using self-rising flour, take this into consideration before adding leaveners to a recipe.

† In the United States, butter is sold both salted and unsalted. We recommend unsalted butter. If you are using salted butter, take this into consideration before adding salt to a recipe.

OVEN TEMPERATURE

FAHRENHEIT	CELSIUS	GAS MARK
225	105	¼
250	120	½
275	135	1
300	150	2
325	165	3
350	180	4
375	190	5
400	200	6
425	220	7
450	230	8
475	245	9

CONVERTING TEMPERATURES FROM AN INSTANT-READ THERMOMETER

We include doneness temperatures in many of the recipes in this book. We recommend an instant-read thermometer for the job. Refer to the table above to convert Fahrenheit degrees to Celsius. Or, for temperatures not represented in the chart, use this simple formula:

Subtract 32 degrees from the Fahrenheit reading, then divide the result by 1.8 to find the Celsius reading.

example

"Flip chicken, brush with remaining glaze, and cook until breast registers 160 degrees, 1 to 3 minutes."

To convert
160°F − 32 = 128°
128° ÷ 1.8 = 71.11°C, rounded down to 71°C

Index

Note: Page references in *italics* indicate photographs.

A

Alcatra (Portuguese-Style Beef Stew), *96,* 97
Aleppo Pepper, White Beans, and Tomatoes, Braised
   Oxtails with, 68, *69*
Almonds
   and Currants, Curried Glazed Carrots with, 354
   and Lemon, Beets with, 338, *339*
   Picada, 92–93, 259
   and Raisins, Braised Hearty Greens with, 368
   Spanish Braised Chicken with Sherry and Saffron
     (Pollo en Pepitoria), *206,* 207
Anchovies and Capers, Braised Cauliflower with, 357
Apples
   Braised Red Cabbage, *346,* 347
     and Cider, Smothered Pork Chops with, 152
   Cider-Braised Belgian Endive with, 359
   Cider-Braised Pork Roast, *136,* 137
   French-Style Pot-Roasted Pork Loin, 142–43, *143*
   Red Cabbage, and Juniper, Pork with, 132, *133*
Apricots and Olives, Lamb Tagine with, *122,* 123
Artichoke(s)
   Braised, with Tomatoes and Thyme, *336,* 337
   Pepper, and Chickpea Tagine, *278,* 279
   preparing, 337
Asian Braised Tofu with Squash and Coconut Milk,
   290, *291*
Asparagus, in Braised Spring Vegetables with Tarragon,
   334, *335*
Atlanta Brisket, 46, *47*
Avocados
   Quinoa and Vegetable Stew, 276, *277*
   Quinoa and Vegetable Stew with Eggs, 276

B

Bacon
   Black-Eyed Peas and Greens, 312, *313*
   -Braised Green Beans, 362, *363*
   Braised Hearty Greens with Pancetta and Pine Nuts,
     368, *369*
   -Braised Red Potatoes, 373
   and Cream, Braised Belgian Endive with, 359
   Drunken Beans, *300,* 301
   Parsnips, and Pearl Onions, Red Wine–Braised Short
     Ribs with, 60–61, *61*
Baked Navy Beans, 302, *303*
Baking dish, 30
Balsamic Vinegar, Capers, and Red Pepper, Braised Lamb
   Shoulder Chops with, 108
Barbecue Sauce
   Lexington Vinegar, 230
   South Carolina Mustard, 231
   Sweet and Tangy, 231
Barolo, Beef in, 42, *43*
Basil
   Braciole, 74–75, *75*
   Green Beans, and Tomatoes, Italian-Style Lamb Stew
     with, 118, *119*
   and Potatoes, Mediterranean Braised Green Beans with,
     364, *365*
   Saffron, and Orange, Chicken Provençal with, 180
Basmati Rice Pilaf, 28
Bass, about, 21
Bean(s)
   adding baking soda to, 24
   Artichoke, Pepper, and Chickpea Tagine, *278,* 279
   Black, and Pork Stew, Brazilian, 328–29, *329*
   Black, and Rice, Cuban-Style, 314, *315*
   Black, Chili, *316,* 317
   Black-Eyed Peas and Greens, 312, *313*
   Braised Country-Style Ribs with Black-Eyed Peas and
     Collard Greens, *144,* 145
   braising with, 24

Bean(s) (*cont.*)

brining, 24

Brunswick Stew, *218,* 219

canned, cooking, 24

Chickpeas with Spinach, Chorizo, and Smoked Paprika, *310,* 311

Cranberry, with Warm Spices, 298, *299*

Drunken, *300,* 301

Indian-Style Vegetable Curry with Potatoes and Cauliflower, 280, *281*

Lemon-Braised Chicken Thighs with Chickpeas and Fennel, *208,* 209

Navy, Baked, 302, *303*

Pinto, Texas-Style, *330,* 331

Red, and Rice, 304, *305*

Stewed Chickpeas with Eggplant and Tomatoes, *308,* 309

Ultimate Chili, 102–3, *103*

Ultimate Vegetarian Chili, *274,* 275

and Vegetable Stew, North African, *318,* 319

White, and Escarole, Sicilian, 306, *307*

White, and Pork Casserole, French, 326–27, *327*

White, Braised Hearty Greens with, 368

White, Moroccan Braised, with Lamb, 114, *115*

White, Stew, Hearty Tuscan, *296,* 297

White, Tomatoes, and Aleppo Pepper, Braised Oxtails with, 68, *69*

White Chicken Chili, *228,* 229

see also Green Beans; Lentils

Beef

best cuts for braises, 11

Braised Oxtails with White Beans, Tomatoes, and Aleppo Pepper, 68, *69*

buying, 12

chuck/shoulder, about, 10

cutting up, for stew, 13

en Cocotte with Caramelized Onions, 56, *57*

grain-fed versus grass-fed, 12

organic, buying, 12

oxtails, about, 11

oxtails, storing and reheating, 9

prep tips, 13

primal cuts, 10

rib, about, 10

roasts, cutting a crosshatch into, 18

roasts, tying, 13

Roman Braised Oxtails, 69

round, about, 10

salting, 13

shank/brisket, plate, and flank, about, 10

shanks, about, 11

shanks, buying, 97

short loin, about, 10

Sichuan-Braised Tofu with (Mapo Tofu), 98, *99*

sirloin, about, 10

Stew, Portuguese-Style (Alcatra), *96,* 97

Stuffed Cabbage Rolls, 172–73, *173*

top sirloin roast, about, 11

trimming exterior fat from, 13

Beef (*cont.*)

USDA grades of, 12

Wagyu, about, 12

see also specific beef cuts below

Beef (Brisket)

about, 11

Atlanta, 46, *47*

Beer-Braised, with Prunes and Ginger, 49

Braised, with Pomegranate, Cumin, and Cilantro, 48–49, *49*

Carbonnade, *44,* 45

carving, 49

Home-Corned, and Cabbage, 52, *53*

Oaxacan-Style, *50,* 51

Red Wine–Braised, with Thyme, 49

Shredded, Cuban Braised (Ropa Vieja), *76,* 77

storing and reheating, 9

Beef (Chuck-Eye Roast)

about, 11

in Barolo, 42, *43*

Braised, with Red Wine and Cherries, *54,* 55

Burgundy, Modern, 86–87, *87*

Carne Guisada, *88,* 89

Daube Provençal, 90–91, *91*

French-Style Pot Roast, 40–41, *41*

Italian Pot Roast, *38,* 39

pot roasts, storing and reheating, 9

Simple Pot Roast, 36, *37*

Simple Pot Roast with Root Vegetables, 37

Stew, Big Batch, *82,* 83

stew, cutting up meat for, 13

Stew, Guinness, 84, *85*

Stew, Modern, 78–79, *79*

Stew with Parsnips, Kale, and Mushrooms, 80–81, *81*

Beef (Short Ribs)

about, 11

Braised Boneless, 58, *59*

Braised Boneless, with Guinness and Prunes, 58

Chinese-Style Braised, 64, *65*

Chinese-Style Red-Cooked, *94,* 95

Pomegranate-Braised, with Prunes and Sesame, 62–63, *63*

Porter-Braised, with Prunes and Brandy, 61

Ragu, *104,* 105

Red Wine–Braised, with Bacon, Parsnips, and Pearl Onions, 60–61, *61*

Shredded, Tacos (Carne Deshebrada), 66–67, *67*

Stew, Catalan-Style, with Mushrooms, 92–93, *93*

storing and reheating, 9

Beef (Steak)

blade or top blade, about, 11

Braciole, 74–75, *75*

Braised, with Mushrooms and Tomatoes, 72

Braised, with Root Vegetables, 72, *73*

buying, for steak tips, 71

flank, about, 11

Flank Steak in Adobo, 100–101, *101*

Steak Tips with Mushroom-Onion Gravy, *70,* 71

Ultimate Chili, 102–3, *103*

Beer
- Braised Boneless Beef Short Ribs with Guinness and Prunes, 58
- -Braised Brisket with Prunes and Ginger, 49
- -Braised Cabbage, 348, *349*
- Brisket Carbonnade, *44*, 45
- Drunken Beans, *300*, 301
- Guinness Beef Stew, 84, *85*
- Porter-Braised Short Ribs with Prunes and Brandy, 61
- Shredded Beef Tacos (Carne Deshebrada), 66–67, *67*
- Ultimate Chili, 102–3, *103*

Beets
- with Ginger and Cashews, 338
- with Lemon and Almonds, 338, *339*
- with Lime and Pepitas, 338
- with Orange and Walnuts, 338

Belgian Endive
- Braised, *358*, 359
- Braised, with Bacon and Cream, 359
- Cider-Braised, with Apples, 359

Big Batch Beef Stew, *82*, 83

Black Bean(s)
- Chili, *316*, 317
- and Pork Stew, Brazilian, 328–29, *329*
- and Rice, Cuban-Style, 314, *315*

Black-Eyed Peas
- and Collard Greens, Braised Country-Style Ribs with, *144*, 145
- and Greens, 312, *313*

Boiled Red Potatoes with Butter and Herbs, 27

Bok Choy
- Braised, with Garlic, 341
- Braised, with Shiitake Mushrooms, *340*, 341

Boning knife, 32

Bouillabaisse, 256, *257*

Bouillabaisse, Chicken, 204–5, *205*

Braciole, 74–75, *75*

Braised Artichokes with Tomatoes and Thyme, *336*, 337

Braised Beef with Red Wine and Cherries, *54*, 55

Braised Belgian Endive, *358*, 359

Braised Belgian Endive with Bacon and Cream, 359

Braised Bok Choy with Garlic, 341

Braised Bok Choy with Shiitake Mushrooms, *340*, 341

Braised Boneless Beef Short Ribs, 58, *59*

Braised Boneless Beef Short Ribs with Guinness and Prunes, 58

Braised Brisket with Pomegranate, Cumin, and Cilantro, 48–49, *49*

Braised Brussels Sprouts, 343

Braised Cabbage with Parsley and Thyme, 350

Braised Cauliflower
- with Capers and Anchovies, 357
- with Garlic and White Wine, *356*, 357
- with Sumac and Mint, 357

Braised Chicken Thighs with Chard and Mustard, 216, *217*

Braised Chicken Thighs with Spinach and Garlic, 216

Braised Cod
- with Leeks and Cherry Tomatoes, 236, *237*
- with Peperonata, 238
- Provençal, 238, *239*
- Veracruz, 238

Braised Country-Style Ribs with Black-Eyed Peas and Collard Greens, *144*, 145

Braised Fennel, 360, *361*

Braised Fennel with Radicchio and Parmesan, *292*, 293

Braised Greek Sausages with Peppers, *170*, 171

Braised Halibut
- with Carrots and Coriander, 241
- with Fennel and Tarragon, 241
- with Leek and Mustard, *240*, 241

Braised Hearty Greens, 368
- with Chorizo and Pimentos, 368
- with White Beans, 368

Braised Kale with Coconut and Curry, 370

Braised Lamb Shanks
- with Lemon and Mint, *110*, 111
- with North African Spices, 111
- with Red Wine and Herbes de Provence, 111

Braised Lamb Shoulder Chops
- with Capers, Balsamic Vinegar, and Red Pepper, 108
- with Figs and North African Spices, 108
- with Tomatoes, Rosemary, and Olives, 108
- with Tomatoes and Red Wine, 108, *109*

Braised Pork Loin with Black Mole Sauce, 140, *141*

Braised Red Cabbage, *346*, 347

Braised Red Potatoes
- with Dijon and Tarragon, 373
- with Lemon and Chives, *372*, 373
- with Miso and Scallions, 373

Braised Spring Vegetables with Tarragon, 334, *335*

Braised Squash and Winter Greens with Coconut Curry, *284*, 285

Braised Steaks with Mushrooms and Tomatoes, 72

Braised Steaks with Root Vegetables, 72, *73*

Braising
- benefits of, 3
- browning meat for, 6
- cooking *en cocotte*, about, 3
- defined, 3
- equipment for, 30–33
- internal cooking temperatures, 6
- making braises ahead, 9
- in oven, 6
- sequential steps for, 4
- starchy bases to pair with, 27–29
- on stovetop, 6
- techniques for, 6–7

Brandy and Prunes, Porter-Braised Short Ribs with, 61

Brazilian Hot Sauce (Molho Apimentado), 329

Brazilian Pork and Black Bean Stew, 328–29, *329*

Brazilian Shrimp and Fish Stew (Moqueca), 262–63, *263*

Brazilian Toasted Manioc Flour (Farofa), 329, *329*

Bread crumbs
Picada, 92–93, 259
Rouille, 205, *205*
Brisket Carbonnade, *44,* 45
Broccoli rabe, in Philadelphia Pork Sandwiches,
138–39, *139*
Brunswick Stew, *218,* 219
Brussels Sprouts
Braised, 343
Cream-Braised, *342,* 343
Curried, with Currants, 343
Maple-Glazed, 344, *345*
Bulgur, in Ultimate Vegetarian Chili, *274,* 275

C

Cabbage
Beer-Braised, 348, *349*
Braised, with Parsley and Thyme, 350
-Carrot Slaw, 67, *67*
Cream-Braised, with Lemon and Shallot, 350, *351*
French-Style Pork Stew, *160,* 161
and Home-Corned Beef, 52, *53*
Red, Apples, and Juniper, Pork with, 132, *133*
Red, Braised, *346,* 347
Rolls, Stuffed, 172–73, *173*
see also Bok Choy
Cajun Chicken, Sausage, and Corn Stew, *222,* 223
Ca Kho To (Catfish in Salty Caramel), *244,* 245
Calamari Stew with Garlic and Tomatoes, *264,* 265
Capers
and Anchovies, Braised Cauliflower with, 357
Balsamic Vinegar, and Red Pepper, Braised Lamb
Shoulder Chops with, 108
Caramel, Salty, Catfish in (Ca Kho To), *244,* 245
Caraway and Buttered Egg Noodles, 29
Carbonnade, Brisket, *44,* 45
Caribbean-Style Swiss Chard and Butternut Squash
Stew, *286,* 287
Carne Adovada, *168,* 169
Carne Deshebrada (Shredded Beef Tacos), 66–67, *67*
Carne Guisada, *88,* 89
Carnitas (Mexican Pulled Pork), *158,* 159
Carrot(s)
Beef Stew with Parsnips, Kale, and Mushrooms, 80–81, *81*
Big Batch Beef Stew, *82,* 83
Braised Boneless Beef Short Ribs, 58, *59*
Braised Boneless Beef Short Ribs with Guinness and
Prunes, 58
Braised Lamb Shanks with Lemon and Mint, *110,* 111
Braised Lamb Shanks with North African Spices, 111
Braised Lamb Shanks with Red Wine and Herbes
de Provence, 111
Braised Steaks with Root Vegetables, 72, *73*
-Cabbage Slaw, 67, *67*
and Chermoula, Swordfish en Cocotte with, *250,* 251
Chicken Stew, 220, *221*

Carrot(s) (*cont.*)
and Coriander, Braised Halibut with, 241
Curried French Lentils with Golden Raisins, 322
Daube Provençal, 90–91, *91*
French Lentils with Swiss Chard, 322
French-Style Pork Stew, *160,* 161
French-Style Pot Roast, 40–41, *41*
Glazed, 354, *355*
Glazed, with Ginger and Rosemary, 354
Glazed Curried, with Currants and Almonds, 354
Guinness Beef Stew, 84, *85*
Home-Corned Beef and Cabbage, 52, *53*
Honey-Glazed, with Lemon and Thyme, 354
Lamb Tagine with Apricots and Olives, *122,* 123
Mashed Potatoes and Root Vegetables, 28
Modern Beef Stew, 78–79, *79*
Monkfish Tagine, 260, *261*
and Parsley, French Lentils with, 322, *323*
Red Potatoes, and Shallots, Chicken in a Pot with,
202, *203*
Simple Pot Roast with Root Vegetables, 37
and Turnips, Irish Stew with, *116,* 117
Veal Stew with Fennel, Tarragon, and Cream
(Blanquette de Veau), 128, *129*
Whole, Slow-Cooked, 353
Whole, Slow-Cooked, with Green Olive and
Raisin Relish, 353
Whole, Slow-Cooked, with Onion-Balsamic Relish, 353
Whole, Slow-Cooked, with Pine Nut Relish, *352,* 353
Carving board, 32
Carving fork, 33
Carving knife, 33
Cashews
Braised Kale with Coconut and Curry, 370
and Ginger, Beets with, 338
Catalan-Style Beef Stew with Mushrooms, 92–93, *93*
Catfish in Salty Caramel (Ca Kho To), *244,* 245
Cauliflower
Braised, with Capers and Anchovies, 357
Braised, with Garlic and White Wine, *356,* 357
Braised, with Sumac and Mint, 357
and Potatoes, Indian-Style Vegetable Curry with, 280, *281*
and Sweet Potato, Indian-Style Chicken Curry with, 210
Celery and Orange, Salmon en Cocotte with, 246
Chard (Swiss)
and Butternut Squash Stew, Caribbean-Style, *286,* 287
French Lentils with, 322
Hearty Ten-Vegetable Stew, 272–73, *273*
and Mustard, Braised Chicken Thighs with, 216, *217*
North African Vegetable and Bean Stew, *318,* 319
Cheese
Braciole, 74–75, *75*
Braised Fennel with Radicchio and Parmesan, *292,* 293
Creamy Parmesan Polenta, 29
Drunken Beans, *300,* 301
Flank Steak in Adobo, 100–101, *101*
Mediterranean Braised Green Beans with Mint
and Feta, 364

Cheese (*cont.*)

Philadelphia Pork Sandwiches, 138–39, *139*

Shredded Beef Tacos (Carne Deshebrada), 66–67, *67*

Chef's knife, 32

Chermoula and Carrots, Swordfish en Cocotte with, *250*, 251

Cherries and Red Wine, Braised Beef with, *54*, 55

Chicken

browning, for braises, 6

in a Pot with Red Potatoes, Carrots, and Shallots, 202, *203*

see also specific chicken parts below

Chicken (Breasts)

Chili, White, *228*, 229

Florentine, 192, *193*

Fricassee, Quick, *190*, 191

with Pumpkin Seed Sauce, 200, *201*

Vesuvio, 196, *197*

Chicken (Pieces)

Bouillabaisse, 204–5, *205*

Cacciatore, *184*, 185

Coq au Vin, 178, *179*

Curry, 210, *211*

Curry, Indian-Style, with Sweet Potato and Cauliflower, 210

with 40 Cloves of Garlic, 182, *183*

Scarpariello, *194*, 195

Southern-Style Smothered, 214, *215*

Stew, Ethiopian-Style Spicy (Doro Wat), 224, *225*

Tagine with Olives and Lemon, 212, *213*

Chicken (Thighs)

Adobo, Filipino, *188*, 189

Braised, with Chard and Mustard, 216, *217*

Braised, with Spinach and Garlic, 216

Brunswick Stew, *218*, 219

and Dumplings, 226–27, *227*

Fricassee, Quick, *190*, 191

Lemon-Braised, with Chickpeas and Fennel, *208*, 209

Mahogany, 198, *199*

Paprikash, 186, *187*

Provençal, 180, *181*

Provençal with Saffron, Orange, and Basil, 180

Pulled, Indoor, 230, *231*

Sausage, and Corn Stew, Cajun, *222*, 223

Spanish Braised, with Sherry and Saffron (Pollo en Pepitoria), *206*, 207

Stew, 220, *221*

Chickpea(s)

Artichoke, and Pepper Tagine, *278*, 279

and Fennel, Lemon-Braised Chicken Thighs with, *208*, 209

Indian-Style Vegetable Curry with Potatoes and Cauliflower, 280, *281*

Indian-Style Vegetable Curry with Sweet Potato and Eggplant, 280

North African Vegetable and Bean Stew, *318*, 319

with Spinach, Chorizo, and Smoked Paprika, *310*, 311

Stewed, with Eggplant and Tomatoes, *308*, 309

Chile(s)

Braised Greek Sausages with Peppers, *170*, 171

Braised Lamb Shanks with North African Spices, 111

Braised Pork Loin with Black Mole Sauce, 140, *141*

-Braised Tofu, *288*, 289

Brazilian Hot Sauce (Molho Apimentado), 329

Caribbean-Style Swiss Chard and Butternut Squash Stew, *286*, 287

Carne Adovada, *168*, 169

Colorado Green Chili, 164, *165*

Drunken Beans, *300*, 301

Flank Steak in Adobo, 100–101, *101*

New Mexican Pork Stew (Posole), *162*, 163

Oaxacan-Style Beef Brisket, *50*, 51

Shredded Beef Tacos (Carne Deshebrada), 66–67, *67*

Turkey Breast en Cocotte with Orange-Chipotle Sauce, 233

Ultimate Chili, 102–3, *103*

Ultimate Vegetarian Chili, *274*, 275

White Chicken Chili, *228*, 229

Chili

Black Bean, *316*, 317

Colorado Green, 164, *165*

storing and reheating, 9

Ultimate, 102–3, *103*

Ultimate Vegetarian, *274*, 275

White Chicken, *228*, 229

Chinese-Style Braised Short Ribs, 64, *65*

Chinese-Style Red-Cooked Beef, *94*, 95

Chives and Lemon, Braised Red Potatoes with, *372*, 373

Chutney, Cilantro-Mint, 211

Cider

and Apples, Smothered Pork Chops with, 152

-Braised Belgian Endive with Apples, 359

-Braised Pork Roast, 136, 137

Cilantro

Brazilian Shrimp and Fish Stew (Moqueca), 262–63, *263*

Cabbage-Carrot Slaw, 67, *67*

Catfish in Salty Caramel (Ca Kho To), *244*, 245

Chicken with Pumpkin Seed Sauce, 200, *201*

Drunken Beans, *300*, 301

Flank Steak in Adobo, 100–101, *101*

-Mint Chutney, 211

Pomegranate, and Cumin, Braised Brisket with, 48–49, *49*

Spicy Mexican Pork Tinga and Rice, 166, *167*

Swordfish en Cocotte with Carrots and Chermoula, *250*, 251

Cioppino, 254, *255*

Clams

about, 21

Cioppino, 254, *255*

scrubbing, 22

Spanish Shellfish Stew, 258, *259*

Spanish Shellfish Stew with Lobster, 259

Classic Couscous, 29

Classic Mashed Potatoes, 27

Coconut and Curry, Braised Kale with, 370

Coconut Curry, Braised Squash and Winter Greens with, *284,* 285

Coconut Milk, Red Lentils with, 325

Cod
about, 21
Braised, Provençal, 238, *239*
Braised, Veracruz, 238
Braised, with Leeks and Cherry Tomatoes, 236, *237*
Braised, with Peperonata, 238
Brazilian Shrimp and Fish Stew (Moqueca), 262–63, *263*

Collard Greens
and Black-Eyed Peas, Braised Country-Style Ribs with, *144,* 145
Black-Eyed Peas and Greens, 312, *313*
Braised Hearty Greens, 368
Braised Hearty Greens with Chorizo and Pimentos, 368
Braised Hearty Greens with Pancetta and Pine Nuts, 368, *369*
Braised Hearty Greens with Raisins and Almonds, 368
Braised Hearty Greens with White Beans, 368
Hearty Tuscan White Bean Stew, *296,* 297
Spicy, Smothered Pork Chops with, 152

Colorado Green Chili, 164, *165*

Cooking *en cocotte,* about, 3

Coq au Vin, 178, *179*

Coriander and Carrots, Braised Halibut with, 241

Corn
Brunswick Stew, *218,* 219
Chicken, and Sausage Stew, Cajun, *222,* 223
Quinoa and Vegetable Stew, 276, *277*
Quinoa and Vegetable Stew with Eggs, 276

Cornmeal, in Creamy Parmesan Polenta, 29

Couscous
Classic, 29
with Garlic, Lemon, and Herbs, 29

Cranberry Beans with Warm Spices, 298, *299*

Cream
-Braised Brussels Sprouts, *342,* 343
-Braised Cabbage with Lemon and Shallot, 350, *351*
Green Beans and Mushrooms Braised in, *366,* 367

Creamy Parmesan Polenta, 29

Cuban Braised Shredded Beef (Ropa Vieja), *76,* 77

Cuban-Style Black Beans and Rice, 314, *315*

Cucumber, Shallots, and Mint, Swordfish en Cocotte with, 251

Cumin, Pomegranate, and Cilantro, Braised Brisket with, 48–49, *49*

Currants
and Almonds, Curried Glazed Carrots with, 354
Curried Brussels Sprouts with, 343

Curried Brussels Sprouts with Currants, 343

Curried French Lentils with Golden Raisins, 322

Curried Glazed Carrots with Currants and Almonds, 354

Curry
Chicken, 210, *211*
Chicken, Indian-Style, with Sweet Potato and Cauliflower, 210
and Coconut, Braised Kale with, 370

Curry (*cont.*)
Coconut, Braised Squash and Winter Greens with, *284,* 285
Lamb, with Figs and Fenugreek, 121
Lamb, with Whole Spices, *120,* 121
Vegetable, Indian-Style, with Potatoes and Cauliflower, 280, *281*
Vegetable, Indian-Style, with Sweet Potato and Eggplant, 280

Cutting board, 32

D

Daube Provençal, 90–91, *91*

Digital instant-read thermometer, 31

Doro Wat (Ethiopian-Style Spicy Chicken Stew), 224, *225*

Drunken Beans, *300,* 301

Dumplings, Chicken and, 226–27, *227*

Dutch oven, 30

E

Eggplant
Asian Braised Tofu with Squash and Coconut Milk, 290, *291*
Ratatouille, 268, *269*
and Sweet Potato, Indian-Style Vegetable Curry with, 280
and Tomatoes, Stewed Chickpeas with, *308,* 309

Eggs
Ethiopian-Style Spicy Chicken Stew (Doro Wat), 224, *225*
Quinoa and Vegetable Stew with, 276

Endive. *See* Belgian Endive

Equipment
baking dish, 30
boning knife, 32
carving board, 32
carving fork, 33
chef's knife, 32
cutting board, 32
digital instant-read thermometer, 31
Dutch oven, 30
fat separator, 32
fine-mesh strainer, 32
ladle, 33
Moroccan-style tagine, 31
nonstick skillet, 30
oven thermometer, 31
roasting pan, 30
slicing/carving knife, 33
tongs, 31
traditional skillet, 30
twine, 31

Escarole and White Beans, Sicilian, 306, *307*

Ethiopian-Style Spicy Chicken Stew (Doro Wat), 224, *225*

F

Farofa (Brazilian Toasted Manioc Flour), 329, *329*
Fat, skimming, 7
Fat separator, 32
Fennel
    Bouillabaisse, 256, *257*
    Braised, 360, *361*
    Braised, with Radicchio and Parmesan, *292,* 293
    Braised Cod Provençal, 238, *239*
    Chicken Bouillabaisse, 204–5, *205*
    and Chickpeas, Lemon-Braised Chicken Thighs with,
        208, 209
    and Saffron, Halibut en Cocotte with, 248
    Tarragon, and Cream, Veal Stew with
        (Blanquette de Veau), 128, *129*
    and Tarragon, Braised Halibut with, 241
Fenugreek and Figs, Lamb Curry with, 121
Figs
    and Fenugreek, Lamb Curry with, 121
    and North African Spices, Braised Lamb Shoulder
        Chops with, 108
    and Port, French-Style Pot-Roasted Pork Loin with, 143
Filipino Chicken Adobo, *188,* 189
Fine-mesh strainer, 32
Fish
    Bouillabaisse, 256, *257*
    Braised Cauliflower with Capers and Anchovies, 357
    Braised Cod Provençal, 238, *239*
    Braised Cod Veracruz, 238
    Braised Cod with Leeks and Cherry Tomatoes, 236, *237*
    Braised Cod with Peperonata, 238
    Braised Halibut with Carrots and Coriander, 241
    Braised Halibut with Fennel and Tarragon, 241
    Braised Halibut with Leek and Mustard, *240,* 241
    buying and storing, 20
    Catfish in Salty Caramel (Ca Kho To), *244,* 245
    Cioppino, 254, *255*
    cutting salmon into fillets, 22
    fillets, removing skin from, 22
    Hake in Saffron Broth with Chorizo and Potatoes,
        242, *243*
    Halibut en Cocotte with Fennel and Saffron, 248
    Halibut en Cocotte with Roasted Garlic and
        Cherry Tomatoes, 248, *249*
    halibut steaks, serving, 248
    monkfish, trimming, 260
    Monkfish Tagine, 260, *261*
    removing salmon pin bones, 22
    Salmon en Cocotte with Celery and Orange, 246
    Salmon en Cocotte with Leeks and White Wine, 246, *247*
    and Shrimp Stew, Brazilian (Moqueca), 262–63, *263*
    Swordfish en Cocotte with Carrots and Chermoula,
        250, 251
    Swordfish en Cocotte with Shallots, Cucumber,
        and Mint, 251
    types best suited for braises, 21

Flank Steak in Adobo, 100–101, *101*
Fork, carving, 33
French Lentils
    with Carrots and Parsley, 322, *323*
    Curried, with Golden Raisins, 322
    with Swiss Chard, 322
French Pork and White Bean Casserole, 326–27, *327*
French-Style Pork Stew, *160,* 161
French-Style Pot Roast, 40–41, *41*
French-Style Pot-Roasted Pork Loin, 142–43, *143*
French-Style Pot-Roasted Pork Loin with Port
    and Figs, 143
Fricassee, Quick Chicken, *190,* 191
Fruit. *See specific fruits*

G

Garlic
    Braised Bok Choy with, 341
    Chips and Spinach, Lentils with, *320,* 321
    40 Cloves of, Chicken with, 182, *183*
    Garlicky Braised Kale, 370, *371*
    Gremolata, *126,* 127
    Halibut en Cocotte with Fennel and Saffron, 248
    Lemon, and Herbs, Couscous with, 29
    Mashed Potatoes, 27
    Picada, 92–93
    Roasted, and Cherry Tomatoes, Halibut en Cocotte with,
        248, *249*
    and Rosemary, Leg of Lamb en Cocotte with, 112, *113*
    Rouille, 205, *205*
    and Spinach, Braised Chicken Thighs with, 216
    and Tomatoes, Calamari Stew with, *264,* 265
    and White Wine, Braised Cauliflower with, *356,* 357
Ginger
    and Cashews, Beets with, 338
    and Prunes, Beer-Braised Brisket with, 49
    and Rosemary, Glazed Carrots with, 354
Glazed Carrots, 354, *355*
    Curried, with Currants and Almonds, 354
    with Ginger and Rosemary, 354
    Honey-, with Lemon and Thyme, 354
Grains. *See* Polenta; Quinoa; Rice
Green Beans
    Bacon-Braised, 362, *363*
    Indian-Style Vegetable Curry with Sweet Potato
        and Eggplant, 280
    Mediterranean Braised, 364
    Mediterranean Braised, with Mint and Feta, 364
    Mediterranean Braised, with Potatoes and Basil, 364, *365*
    and Mushrooms Braised in Cream, *366,* 367
    Tomatoes, and Basil, Italian-Style Lamb Stew with,
        118, *119*
Greens
    Beef Stew with Parsnips, Kale, and Mushrooms, 80–81, *81*
    Braised Belgian Endive, *358,* 359

Greens (*cont.*)

Braised Belgian Endive with Bacon and Cream, 359
Braised Chicken Thighs with Chard and Mustard, 216, *217*
Braised Chicken Thighs with Spinach and Garlic, 216
Braised Fennel with Radicchio and Parmesan, *292*, 293
Braised Kale with Coconut and Curry, 370
Caribbean-Style Swiss Chard and Butternut Squash Stew, *286*, 287
Chicken Florentine, 192, *193*
Chickpeas with Spinach, Chorizo, and Smoked Paprika, *310*, 311
Cider-Braised Belgian Endive with Apples, 359
Collard, and Black-Eyed Peas, Braised Country-Style Ribs with, *144*, 145
Collard, Spicy, Smothered Pork Chops with, 152
French Lentils with Swiss Chard, 322
Garlicky Braised Kale, 370, *371*
Hearty, Braised, 368
Hearty, Braised, with Chorizo and Pimentos, 368
Hearty, Braised, with Pancetta and Pine Nuts, 368, *369*
Hearty, Braised, with Raisins and Almonds, 368
Hearty, Braised, with White Beans, 368
Hearty Ten-Vegetable Stew, 272–73, *273*
Hearty Tuscan White Bean Stew, *296*, 297
Lentils with Spinach and Garlic Chips, *320*, 321
North African Vegetable and Bean Stew, *318*, 319
preparing kale, 81
Sicilian White Beans and Escarole, 306, *307*
Gremolata, *126*, 127
Grillades, Pork, 148–49, *149*
Guinness Beef Stew, 84, *85*

H

Haddock, about, 21
Hake
about, 21
in Saffron Broth with Chorizo and Potatoes, 242, *243*
Halibut
about, 21
Bouillabaisse, 256, *257*
Braised, with Carrots and Coriander, 241
Braised, with Fennel and Tarragon, 241
Braised, with Leek and Mustard, *240*, 241
Cioppino, 254, *255*
en Cocotte with Fennel and Saffron, 248
en Cocotte with Roasted Garlic and Cherry Tomatoes, 248, *249*
steaks, serving, 248
Ham
French-Style Pork Stew, *160*, 161
hocks, about, 17
Texas-Style Pinto Beans, *330*, 331
Hearty Tuscan White Bean Stew, *296*, 297

Herbs
Braised Lamb Shanks with Red Wine and Herbes de Provence, 111
Garlic, and Lemon, Couscous with, 29
see also specific herbs
Home-Corned Beef and Cabbage, 52, *53*
Hominy, in New Mexican Pork Stew (Posole), *162*, 163
Honey-Glazed Carrots with Lemon and Thyme, 354
Horseradish and Scallions, Mashed Potatoes with, 27
Hot Sauce, Brazilian (Molho Apimentado), 329

I

Indian-Style Chicken Curry with Sweet Potato and Cauliflower, 210
Indian-Style Vegetable Curry with Potatoes and Cauliflower, 280, *281*
Indian-Style Vegetable Curry with Sweet Potato and Eggplant, 280
Indoor Pulled Chicken, 230, *231*
Instant-read thermometer, 31
Irish Stew, 117
Irish Stew with Carrots and Turnips, *116*, 117
Italian Pot Roast, *38*, 39
Italian-Style Lamb Stew with Green Beans, Tomatoes, and Basil, 118, *119*

J

Juniper, Red Cabbage, and Apples, Pork with, 132, *133*

K

Kale
Braised, with Coconut and Curry, 370
Braised Hearty Greens, 368
Braised Hearty Greens with Chorizo and Pimentos, 368
Braised Hearty Greens with Pancetta and Pine Nuts, 368, *369*
Braised Hearty Greens with Raisins and Almonds, 368
Braised Hearty Greens with White Beans, 368
Braised Squash and Winter Greens with Coconut Curry, *284*, 285
Garlicky Braised, 370, *371*
Hearty Tuscan White Bean Stew, *296*, 297
Parsnips, and Mushrooms, Beef Stew with, 80–81, *81*
preparing, 81
Knives
boning, 32
chef's, 32
slicing/carving, 33

L

Ladle, 33
Lamb
    buying, 15
    domestic versus imported, 15
    favorite cuts for braising, 15
    foreshank/breast, about, 14
    loin, about, 14
    prep tips, 15
    primal cuts, 14
    rib, about, 14
    shoulder, about, 14
    see also specific lamb cuts below
Lamb (Leg of)
    about, 14, 15
    boneless, trimming, 15
    Curry with Figs and Fenugreek, 121
    Curry with Whole Spices, *120,* 121
    en Cocotte with Garlic and Rosemary, 112, *113*
Lamb (Shanks)
    about, 15
    Braised, with Lemon and Mint, *110,* 111
    Braised, with North African Spices, 111
    Braised, with Red Wine and Herbes de Provence, 111
    Moroccan Braised White Beans with, 114, *115*
    storing and reheating, 9
    trimming, 15
Lamb (Shoulder Chops)
    blade chops, about, 15
    Braised, with Capers, Balsamic Vinegar, and
       Red Pepper, 108
    Braised, with Figs and North African Spices, 108
    Braised, with Tomatoes, Rosemary, and Olives, 108
    Braised, with Tomatoes and Red Wine, 108, *109*
    Irish Stew, 117
    Irish Stew with Carrots and Turnips, *116,* 117
    Italian-Style Lamb Stew with Green Beans, Tomatoes,
       and Basil, 118, *119*
    round chops, about, 15
Lamb (Shoulder Roast)
    Tagine with Apricots and Olives, *122,* 123
    Vindaloo, 124, *125*
Leek(s)
    and Cherry Tomatoes, Braised Cod with, 236, *237*
    and Mustard, Braised Halibut with, *240,* 241
    and White Wine, Salmon en Cocotte with, 246, *247*
Leg of Lamb en Cocotte with Garlic and Rosemary,
    112, *113*
Lemon
    and Almonds, Beets with, 338, *339*
    -Braised Chicken Thighs with Chickpeas and Fennel,
       208, 209
    and Chives, Braised Red Potatoes with, *372,* 373
    Gremolata, *126,* 127
    and Mint, Braised Lamb Shanks with, *110,* 111
    and Olives, Chicken Tagine with, 212, *213*
    Rouille, 205, *205*

Lemon (*cont.*)
    and Shallot, Cream-Braised Cabbage with, 350, *351*
    and Thyme, Honey-Glazed Carrots with, 354
Lentils
    French, Curried, with Golden Raisins, 322
    French, with Carrots and Parsley, 322, *323*
    French, with Swiss Chard, 322
    Red, Spiced (Masoor Dal), *324,* 325
    Red, with Coconut Milk, 325
    with Spinach and Garlic Chips, *320,* 321
Lexington Vinegar Barbecue Sauce, 230
Lime and Pepitas, Beets with, 338
Lobster, Spanish Shellfish Stew with, 259
Louisiana Seasoning, 149
Loukaniko sausage, about, 171

M

Mahogany Chicken Thighs, 198, *199*
Manioc Flour, Brazilian Toasted (Farofa), 329, *329*
Maple-Glazed Brussels Sprouts, 344, *345*
Mapo Tofu (Sichuan-Braised Tofu with Beef), 98, *99*
Mashed Potatoes
    Classic, 27
    Garlic, 27
    and Root Vegetables, 28
    with Scallions and Horseradish, 27
Masoor Dal (Spiced Red Lentils), *324,* 325
Meat
    bone-in cuts, for braising, 8
    browning, for braises, 7
    see also Beef; Lamb; Pork; Veal
Mediterranean Braised Green Beans, 364
    with Mint and Feta, 364
    with Potatoes and Basil, 364, *365*
Mexican Pork Tinga and Rice, Spicy, 166, *167*
Mexican Pulled Pork (Carnitas), *158,* 159
Milk-Braised Pork Loin, 134, *135*
Mint
    -Cilantro Chutney, 211
    Cucumber, and Shallots, Swordfish en Cocotte with, 251
    and Feta, Mediterranean Braised Green Beans with, 364
    and Lemon, Braised Lamb Shanks with, *110,* 111
    and Sumac, Braised Cauliflower with, 357
Miso and Scallions, Braised Red Potatoes with, 373
Modern Beef Burgundy, 86–87, *87*
Modern Beef Stew, 78–79, *79*
Mole Sauce, Black, Braised Pork Loin with, 140, *141*
Mole Sauce, Turkey Breast en Cocotte with, 232, *233*
Molho Apimentado (Brazilian Hot Sauce), 329
Monkfish
    about, 21
    Tagine, 260, *261*
    trimming, 260
Moqueca (Brazilian Shrimp and Fish Stew), 262–63, *263*
Moroccan Braised White Beans with Lamb, 114, *115*
Moroccan-style tagines, about, 31

Mushroom(s)
  Black Bean Chili, *316,* 317
  Catalan-Style Beef Stew with, 92–93, *93*
  Coq au Vin, 178, *179*
  French-Style Pot Roast, 40–41, *41*
  and Green Beans Braised in Cream, *366,* 367
  Hearty Ten-Vegetable Stew, 272–73, *273*
  Italian Pot Roast, *38,* 39
  Modern Beef Burgundy, 86–87, *87*
  -Onion Gravy, Steak Tips with, *70,* 71
  Parsnips, and Kale, Beef Stew with, 80–81, *81*
  Quick Chicken Fricassee, *190,* 191
  Shiitake, Braised Bok Choy with, *340,* 341
  and Tomatoes, Braised Steaks with, 72
  Wild, Ragu, *270,* 271
Mussels
  about, 21
  Bouillabaisse, 256, *257*
  buying, 20
  Cioppino, 254, *255*
  debearding, 22
  scrubbing, 22
  Spanish Shellfish Stew, 258, *259*
  Spanish Shellfish Stew with Lobster, 259
  storing, 20
Mustard
  Barbecue Sauce, South Carolina, 231
  Braised Red Potatoes with Dijon and Tarragon, 373
  and Chard, Braised Chicken Thighs with, 216, *217*
  and Leek, Braised Halibut with, *240,* 241
  Rouille, 205, *205*

N

New Mexican Pork Stew (Posole), *162,* 163
Nonstick skillet, 30
Noodles, Buttered Egg, and Caraway, 29
North African Spices, Braised Lamb Shanks with, 111
North African Spices and Figs, Braised Lamb Shoulder
    Chops with, 108
North African Vegetable and Bean Stew, *318,* 319
Nuts. *See* Almonds; Cashews; Pine Nut(s); Walnuts

O

Oaxacan-Style Beef Brisket, *50,* 51
Octopus
  about, 21
  preparing, 23, 253
  Red Wine–Braised, 252, *253*
Olive(s)
  and Apricots, Lamb Tagine with, *122,* 123
  Artichoke, Pepper, and Chickpea Tagine, *278,* 279
  Calamari Stew with Garlic and Tomatoes, *264,* 265
  Chicken Provençal, 180, *181*

Olive(s) (*cont.*)
  Chicken Provençal with Saffron, Orange, and Basil, 180
  Cuban Braised Shredded Beef (Ropa Vieja), *76,* 77
  Daube Provençal, 90–91, *91*
  Green, and Raisin Relish, Slow-Cooked Whole
      Carrots with, 353
  and Lemon, Chicken Tagine with, 212, *213*
  Lemon-Braised Chicken Thighs with Chickpeas and
      Fennel, *208,* 209
  Monkfish Tagine, 260, *261*
  Tomatoes, and Rosemary, Braised Lamb Shoulder
      Chops with, 108
Onion(s)
  Atlanta Brisket, 46, *47*
  -Balsamic Relish, Slow-Cooked Whole Carrots with, 353
  Braised Beef with Red Wine and Cherries, *54,* 55
  Brisket Carbonnade, *44,* 45
  Caramelized, Beef en Cocotte with, 56, *57*
  Coq au Vin, 178, *179*
  Cuban Braised Shredded Beef (Ropa Vieja), *76,* 77
  French-Style Pot Roast, 40–41, *41*
  Irish Stew, 117
  Irish Stew with Carrots and Turnips, *116,* 117
  Italian-Style Lamb Stew with Green Beans, Tomatoes,
      and Basil, 118, *119*
  Modern Beef Burgundy, 86–87, *87*
  Modern Beef Stew, 78–79, *79*
  -Mushroom Gravy, Steak Tips with, *70,* 71
  Pearl, Bacon, and Parsnips, Red Wine–Braised Short
      Ribs with, 60–61, *61*
  Portuguese-Style Beef Stew (Alcatra), *96,* 97
  Relish, 211
  Smothered Pork Chops, 152, *153*
  Spicy Pickled, *144,* 145
Orange
  and Celery, Salmon en Cocotte with, 246
  -Chipotle Sauce, Turkey Breast en Cocotte with, 233
  Saffron, and Basil, Chicken Provençal with, 180
  and Walnuts, Beets with, 338
Osso Buco, *126,* 127
Oven thermometer, 31
Oysters, buying and storing, 20

P

Pancetta and Pine Nuts, Braised Hearty Greens with,
    368, *369*
Paprika
  Chicken Paprikash, 186, *187*
  Louisiana Seasoning, 149
  Smoked, Spinach, and Chorizo, Chickpeas with, *310,* 311
Parsnips
  Bacon, and Pearl Onions, Red Wine–Braised Short
      Ribs with, 60–61, *61*
  Braised Steaks with Root Vegetables, 72, *73*
  Hearty Ten-Vegetable Stew, 272–73, *273*

Parsnips (*cont.*)

Kale, and Mushrooms, Beef Stew with, 80–81, *81*

Mashed Potatoes and Root Vegetables, 28

Simple Pot Roast with Root Vegetables, 37

Pasta and couscous

Classic Couscous, 29

Couscous with Garlic, Lemon, and Herbs, 29

North African Vegetable and Bean Stew, *318,* 319

Pork Ragu, *174,* 175

Peas

Beef Stew with Parsnips, Kale, and Mushrooms, 80–81, *81*

Big Batch Beef Stew, *82,* 83

Braised Spring Vegetables with Tarragon, *334, 335*

Chicken Curry, 210, *211*

Chicken Vesuvio, 196, *197*

Indian-Style Vegetable Curry with Potatoes and Cauliflower, 280, *281*

Modern Beef Stew, 78–79, *79*

Quinoa and Vegetable Stew, 276, *277*

Quinoa and Vegetable Stew with Eggs, 276

Veal Stew with Fennel, Tarragon, and Cream (Blanquette de Veau), 128, *129*

Peas, Black-Eyed

and Collard Greens, Braised Country-Style Ribs with, *144,* 145

and Greens, 312, *313*

Pepitas

Braised Squash and Winter Greens with Coconut Curry, *284,* 285

Chicken with Pumpkin Seed Sauce, 200, *201*

and Lime, Beets with, 338

toasting, 200

Pepper(s)

Artichoke, and Chickpea Tagine, *278, 279*

Black Bean Chili, *316,* 317

Braised Cod with Peperonata, 238

Braised Greek Sausages with, *170,* 171

Braised Hearty Greens with Chorizo and Pimentos, 368

Brazilian Hot Sauce (Molho Apimentado), 329

Brazilian Shrimp and Fish Stew (Moqueca), 262–63, *263*

Cajun Chicken, Sausage, and Corn Stew, *222,* 223

Carne Guisada, *88,* 89

Chicken Paprikash, 186, *187*

Chicken Scarpariello, *194,* 195

Cuban Braised Shredded Beef (Ropa Vieja), *76,* 77

Cuban-Style Black Beans and Rice, 314, *315*

Hearty Ten-Vegetable Stew, 272–73, *273*

Quinoa and Vegetable Stew, 276, *277*

Quinoa and Vegetable Stew with Eggs, 276

Ratatouille, 268, *269*

Red, Capers, and Balsamic Vinegar, Braised Lamb Shoulder Chops with, 108

Vinegar, Pork Chops with, *154,* 155

see also Chile(s)

Philadelphia Pork Sandwiches, 138–39, *139*

Picada, 92–93, 259

Pickled Onion, Spicy, *144,* 145

Pilaf

Basmati Rice, 28

Pine Nut(s)

and Pancetta, Braised Hearty Greens with, 368, *369*

Relish, Slow-Cooked Whole Carrots with, *352, 353*

Pinto Beans

Drunken Beans, *300,* 301

Texas-Style, *330,* 331

Ultimate Chili, 102–3, *103*

Polenta, Creamy Parmesan, 29

Pollo en Pepitoria (Spanish Braised Chicken with Sherry and Saffron), *206,* 207

Pomegranate

-Braised Short Ribs with Prunes and Sesame, 62–63, *63*

Cumin, and Cilantro, Braised Brisket with, 48–49, *49*

Pork

Berkshire, about, 18

buying, 18

Cuban-Style Black Beans and Rice, 314, *315*

favorite cuts for braises, 17

leg, about, 16

loin, about, 16

primal cuts, 16

shoulder, about, 16

side/belly, about, 16

unenhanced (or natural), about, 18

and White Bean Casserole, French, 326–27, *327*

see also Bacon; Ham; Sausage(s); *specific pork cuts below*

Pork (Butt Roast)

about, 17

Carne Adovada, *168,* 169

Cider-Braised, *136,* 137

Colorado Green Chili, 164, *165*

Pulled, Mexican (Carnitas), *158,* 159

Sandwiches, Philadelphia, 138–39, *139*

Stew, French-Style, *160,* 161

Tinga and Rice, Spicy Mexican, 166, *167*

Pork (Chops)

blade, about, 17

Grillades, 148–49, *149*

preventing curling of, 18

Red Wine–Braised, 150, *151*

rib, about, 17

Smothered, 152, *153*

Smothered, with Cider and Apples, 152

Smothered, with Spicy Collard Greens, 152

with Tomato Gravy, 156, *157*

with Vinegar Peppers, *154,* 155

Pork (Loin)

boneless blade-end roast, about, 17

boneless center-cut roast, about, 17

Braised, with Black Mole Sauce, 140, *141*

French-Style Pot-Roasted, 142–43, *143*

French-Style Pot-Roasted, with Port and Figs, 143

Milk-Braised, 134, *135*

with Red Cabbage, Apples, and Juniper, 132, *133*

roast, cutting a crosshatch into, 18

roast, double-butterflying, 143

Pork (Loin) (*cont.*)
    roast, tying up, 18
Pork (Ribs)
    and Black Bean Stew, Brazilian, 328–29, *329*
    Braised Country-Style, with Black-Eyed Peas and
        Collard Greens, *144,* 145
    country-style, about, 17
    Ragu, *174,* 175
    Stew, New Mexican (Posole), *162,* 163
    Sweet-and-Sour, *146,* 147
Port and Figs, French-Style Pot-Roasted Pork Loin
    with, 143
Porter-Braised Short Ribs with Prunes and Brandy, 61
Portuguese-Style Beef Stew (Alcatra), *96,* 97
Posole (New Mexican Pork Stew), *162,* 163
Potato(es)
    and Basil, Mediterranean Braised Green Beans with,
        364, *365*
    Beef Stew with Parsnips, Kale, and Mushrooms, 80–81, *81*
    Big Batch Beef Stew, *82,* 83
    Braised Steaks with Mushrooms and Tomatoes, 72
    Braised Steaks with Root Vegetables, 72, *73*
    Brunswick Stew, *218,* 219
    Carne Guisada, *88,* 89
    and Cauliflower, Indian-Style Vegetable Curry with,
        280, *281*
    Chicken Bouillabaisse, 204–5, *205*
    Chicken Stew, 220, *221*
    Chicken Vesuvio, 196, *197*
    and Chorizo, Hake in Saffron Broth with, 242, *243*
    French-Style Pork Stew, *160,* 161
    Guinness Beef Stew, 84, *85*
    Hearty Ten-Vegetable Stew, 272–73, *273*
    Home-Corned Beef and Cabbage, 52, *53*
    Irish Stew, 117
    Irish Stew with Carrots and Turnips, *116,* 117
    Italian-Style Lamb Stew with Green Beans, Tomatoes,
        and Basil, 118, *119*
    Lamb Curry with Whole Spices, *120,* 121
    Mashed, and Root Vegetables, 28
    Mashed, Classic, 27
    Mashed, Garlic, 27
    Mashed, with Scallions and Horseradish, 27
    Modern Beef Stew, 78–79, *79*
    Quinoa and Vegetable Stew, 276, *277*
    Quinoa and Vegetable Stew with Eggs, 276
    Red, Bacon-Braised, 373
    Red, Boiled, with Butter and Herbs, 27
    Red, Braised, with Dijon and Tarragon, 373
    Red, Braised, with Lemon and Chives, *372,* 373
    Red, Braised, with Miso and Scallions, 373
    Red, Carrots, and Shallots, Chicken in a Pot with,
        202, *203*
    red waxy, about, 25
    Simple Pot Roast with Root Vegetables, 37
    starchy, about, 25
    Sweet, and Cauliflower, Indian-Style Chicken
        Curry with, 210

Potato(es) (*cont.*)
    Sweet, and Eggplant, Indian-Style Vegetable
        Curry with, 280
    Vindaloo, 282, *283*
Pot Roast
    French-Style, 40–41, *41*
    Italian, *38,* 39
    Simple, 36, *37*
    Simple, with Root Vegetables, 37
    storing and reheating, 9
Prunes
    and Brandy, Porter-Braised Short Ribs with, 61
    and Ginger, Beer-Braised Brisket with, 49
    and Guinness, Braised Boneless Beef Short Ribs with, 58
    and Sesame, Pomegranate-Braised Short Ribs with,
        62–63, *63*
Pumpkin seeds. *See* Pepitas

Q

Quick Chicken Fricassee, *190,* 191
Quinoa
    and Vegetable Stew, 276, *277*
    and Vegetable Stew with Eggs, 276

R

Radicchio and Parmesan, Braised Fennel with, *292,* 293
Ragu
    Beef Short Rib, *104,* 105
    Pork, *174,* 175
    Wild Mushroom, *270,* 271
Raisin(s)
    and Almonds, Braised Hearty Greens with, 368
    Artichoke, Pepper, and Chickpea Tagine, *278,* 279
    Braciole, 74–75, *75*
    Golden, Curried French Lentils with, 322
    and Green Olive Relish, Slow-Cooked Whole
        Carrots with, 353
Ras el Hanout
    Braised Lamb Shanks with North African Spices, 111
    recipe for, 63
Ratatouille, 268, *269*
Red Beans and Rice, 304, *305*
Red-Cooked Beef, Chinese-Style, *94,* 95
Red Lentils
    with Coconut Milk, 325
    Spiced (Masoor Dal), *324,* 325
Red Wine
    Beef in Barolo, 42, *43*
    Braised Boneless Beef Short Ribs, 58, *59*
    –Braised Brisket with Thyme, 49
    –Braised Octopus, 252, *253*
    –Braised Pork Chops, 150, *151*
    Braised Red Cabbage, *346,* 347

Red Wine (*cont.*)

  –Braised Short Ribs with Bacon, Parsnips, and
    Pearl Onions, 60–61, *61*

  and Cherries, Braised Beef with, *54*, 55

  Coq au Vin, 178, *179*

  Daube Provençal, 90–91, *91*

  French-Style Pot Roast, 40–41, *41*

  and Herbes de Provence, Braised Lamb Shanks with, 111

  Modern Beef Burgundy, 86–87, *87*

  and Tomatoes, Braised Lamb Shoulder Chops with,
    108, *109*

Relish, Onion, 211

Rice

  Basmati, Pilaf, 28

  and Black Beans, Cuban-Style, 314, *315*

  Red Beans and, 304, *305*

  and Spicy Mexican Pork Tinga, 166, *167*

  White, Simple, 28

Roasting pan, 30

Roman Braised Oxtails, 69

Ropa Vieja (Cuban Braised Shredded Beef), 76, 77

Rosemary

  and Garlic, Leg of Lamb en Cocotte with, 112, *113*

  and Ginger, Glazed Carrots with, 354

  Tomatoes, and Olives, Braised Lamb Shoulder Chops
    with, 108

Rouille, 205, *205*

S

Saffron

  Bouillabaisse, 256, *257*

  Broth, Hake in, with Chorizo and Potatoes, 242, *243*

  Chicken Bouillabaisse, 204–5, *205*

  and Fennel, Halibut en Cocotte with, 248

  Monkfish Tagine, 260, *261*

  Orange, and Basil, Chicken Provençal with, 180

  Rouille, 205, *205*

  and Sherry, Spanish Braised Chicken with
    (Pollo en Pepitoria), *206*, 207

  Spanish Shellfish Stew, 258, *259*

  Spanish Shellfish Stew with Lobster, 259

Salmon

  about, 21

  cutting into fillets, 22

  en Cocotte with Celery and Orange, 246

  en Cocotte with Leeks and White Wine, 246, *247*

  pin bones, removing, 22

Sandwiches, Philadelphia Pork, 138–39, *139*

Sauces

  Beef Short Rib Ragu, *104*, 105

  Hot, Brazilian (Molho Apimentado), 329

  Lexington Vinegar Barbecue, 230

  Pork Ragu, *174*, 175

  Rouille, 205, *205*

  South Carolina Mustard Barbecue, 231

Sauces (*cont.*)

  Sweet and Tangy Barbecue, 231

  thickening, 7

Sausage(s)

  Braised Greek, with Peppers, *170*, 171

  Braised Hearty Greens with Chorizo and Pimentos, 368

  Brazilian Pork and Black Bean Stew, 328–29, *329*

  Brunswick Stew, *218*, 219

  Chicken, and Corn Stew, Cajun, *222*, 223

  Chicken Scarpariello, *194*, 195

  Chickpeas with Spinach, Chorizo, and Smoked Paprika,
    310, 311

  French Pork and White Bean Casserole, 326–27, *327*

  French-Style Pork Stew, *160*, 161

  Greek (loukaniko), about, 171

  Hake in Saffron Broth with Chorizo and Potatoes,
    242, *243*

  Portuguese-Style Beef Stew (Alcatra), *96*, 97

  Red Beans and Rice, 304, *305*

  Stuffed Cabbage Rolls, 172–73, *173*

Scallions

  and Horseradish, Mashed Potatoes with, 27

  and Miso, Braised Red Potatoes with, 373

Scallops

  about, 21

  Bouillabaisse, 256, *257*

  Spanish Shellfish Stew, 258, *259*

  Spanish Shellfish Stew with Lobster, 259

Seafood

  best suited for braises, 21

  Calamari Stew with Garlic and Tomatoes, *264*, 265

  octopus, preparing, 253

  preparing octopus, 23

  Red Wine–Braised Octopus, 252, *253*

  see also Fish; Shellfish

Seeds

  toasting, 200

  see also Pepitas; Sesame seeds

Sesame seeds

  Braised Pork Loin with Black Mole Sauce, 140, *141*

  Pomegranate-Braised Short Ribs with Prunes and
    Sesame, 62–63, *63*

  toasting, 200

Shallot(s)

  Cucumber, and Mint, Swordfish en Cocotte with, 251

  Green Beans and Mushrooms Braised in Cream, *366*, 367

  and Lemon, Cream-Braised Cabbage with, 350, *351*

  Red Potatoes, and Carrots, Chicken in a Pot with,
    202, *203*

Shellfish

  best suited for braises, 21

  Bouillabaisse, 256, *257*

  Brazilian Shrimp and Fish Stew (Moqueca), 262–63, *263*

  buying frozen shrimp, 20

  buying mussels and oysters, 20

  Cioppino, 254, *255*

  debearding mussels, 22

Shellfish (*cont.*)
    peeling and deveining shrimp, 23
    scrubbing mussels and clams, 22
    sorting out shrimp sizes, 20
    Stew, Spanish, 258, *259*
    Stew, Spanish, with Lobster, 259
    storing bivalves, 20

Sherry and Saffron, Spanish Braised Chicken with (Pollo en Pepitoria), *206*, 207

Shredded Beef Tacos (Carne Deshebrada), 66–67, *67*

Shrimp
    about, 21
    Bouillabaisse, 256, *257*
    and Fish Stew, Brazilian (Moqueca), 262–63, *263*
    frozen, buying, 20
    peeling and deveining, 23
    sizes and counts, 20
    Spanish Shellfish Stew, 258, *259*
    Spanish Shellfish Stew with Lobster, 259

Sichuan-Braised Tofu with Beef (Mapo Tofu), 98, *99*

Sicilian White Beans and Escarole, 306, *307*

Sides (starchy)
    Basmati Rice Pilaf, 28
    Boiled Red Potatoes with Butter and Herbs, 27
    Caraway and Buttered Egg Noodles, 29
    Classic Couscous, 29
    Classic Mashed Potatoes, 27
    Couscous with Garlic, Lemon, and Herbs, 29
    Creamy Parmesan Polenta, 29
    Garlic Mashed Potatoes, 27
    Mashed Potatoes and Root Vegetables, 28
    Mashed Potatoes with Scallions and Horseradish, 27
    Simple White Rice, 28

Sides (vegetable)
    Bacon-Braised Green Beans, 362, *363*
    Bacon-Braised Red Potatoes, 373
    Beer-Braised Cabbage, 348, *349*
    Beets with Ginger and Cashews, 338
    Beets with Lemon and Almonds, 338, *339*
    Beets with Lime and Pepitas, 338
    Beets with Orange and Walnuts, 338
    Braised Artichokes with Tomatoes and Thyme, *336*, 337
    Braised Belgian Endive, *358*, 359
    Braised Belgian Endive with Bacon and Cream, 359
    Braised Bok Choy with Garlic, 341
    Braised Bok Choy with Shiitake Mushrooms, *340*, 341
    Braised Brussels Sprouts, 343
    Braised Cabbage with Parsley and Thyme, 350
    Braised Cauliflower with Capers and Anchovies, 357
    Braised Cauliflower with Garlic and White Wine, *356*, 357
    Braised Cauliflower with Sumac and Mint, 357
    Braised Fennel, 360, *361*
    Braised Hearty Greens, 368
    Braised Hearty Greens with Chorizo and Pimentos, 368
    Braised Hearty Greens with Pancetta and Pine Nuts, 368, *369*

Sides (vegetable) (*cont.*)
    Braised Hearty Greens with Raisins and Almonds, 368
    Braised Hearty Greens with White Beans, 368
    Braised Kale with Coconut and Curry, 370
    Braised Red Cabbage, *346*, 347
    Braised Red Potatoes with Dijon and Tarragon, 373
    Braised Red Potatoes with Lemon and Chives, *372*, 373
    Braised Red Potatoes with Miso and Scallions, 373
    Braised Spring Vegetables with Tarragon, 334, *335*
    Cider-Braised Belgian Endive with Apples, 359
    Cream-Braised Brussels Sprouts, *342*, 343
    Cream-Braised Cabbage with Lemon and Shallot, 350, *351*
    Curried Brussels Sprouts with Currants, 343
    Curried Glazed Carrots with Currants and Almonds, 354
    Garlicky Braised Kale, 370, *371*
    Glazed Carrots, 354, *355*
    Glazed Carrots with Ginger and Rosemary, 354
    Green Beans and Mushrooms Braised in Cream, *366*, 367
    Honey-Glazed Carrots with Lemon and Thyme, 354
    Maple-Glazed Brussels Sprouts, 344, *345*
    Mediterranean Braised Green Beans, 364
    Mediterranean Braised Green Beans with Mint and Feta, 364
    Mediterranean Braised Green Beans with Potatoes and Basil, 364, *365*
    Slow-Cooked Whole Carrots, 353
    Slow-Cooked Whole Carrots with Green Olive and Raisin Relish, 353
    Slow-Cooked Whole Carrots with Onion-Balsamic Relish, 353
    Slow-Cooked Whole Carrots with Pine Nut Relish, *352*, 353

Simple Pot Roast, 36, *37*

Simple Pot Roast with Root Vegetables, 37

Simple White Rice, 28

Skillet, nonstick, 30

Skillet, traditional, 30

Slaw, Cabbage-Carrot, 67, *67*

Slicing/carving knife, 33

Slow-Cooked Whole Carrots, 353
    with Green Olive and Raisin Relish, 353
    with Onion-Balsamic Relish, 353
    with Pine Nut Relish, *352*, 353

Smothered Pork Chops, 152, *153*
    with Cider and Apples, 152
    with Spicy Collard Greens, 152

South Carolina Mustard Barbecue Sauce, 231

Southern-Style Smothered Chicken, 214, *215*

Spanish Braised Chicken with Sherry and Saffron (Pollo en Pepitoria), *206*, 207

Spanish Shellfish Stew, 258, *259*

Spanish Shellfish Stew with Lobster, 259

Spice Blends
    Louisiana Seasoning, 149
    Ras el Hanout, 63
    Whole Spice, 121

Spiced Red Lentils (Masoor Dal), *324*, 325

Spicy Mexican Pork Tinga and Rice, 166, *167*
Spicy Pickled Onion, *144,* 145
Spinach
    Chicken Florentine, 192, *193*
    Chorizo, and Smoked Paprika, Chickpeas with, *310,* 311
    and Garlic, Braised Chicken Thighs with, 216
    and Garlic Chips, Lentils with, *320,* 321
Squash
    Braised, and Winter Greens with Coconut Curry, *284,* 285
    Butternut, and Swiss Chard Stew, Caribbean-Style, *286,* 287
    and Coconut Milk, Asian Braised Tofu with, 290, *291*
    Hearty Ten-Vegetable Stew, 272–73, *273*
    Ratatouille, 268, *269*
Squid
    about, 21
    Calamari Stew with Garlic and Tomatoes, *264,* 265
Steak Tips with Mushroom-Onion Gravy, *70,* 71
Stewed Chickpeas with Eggplant and Tomatoes, *308,* 309
Stews
    Artichoke, Pepper, and Chickpea Tagine, *278,* 279
    Beef, Big Batch, *82,* 83
    Beef, Catalan-Style, with Mushrooms, 92–93, *93*
    beef, cutting up roasts for, 13
    Beef, Guinness, 84, *85*
    Beef, Modern, 78–79, *79*
    Beef, Portuguese-Style (Alcatra), *96,* 97
    Beef, with Parsnips, Kale, and Mushrooms, 80–81, *81*
    Bouillabaisse, 256, *257*
    Brunswick, *218,* 219
    Calamari, with Garlic and Tomatoes, *264,* 265
    Carne Adovada, *168,* 169
    Carne Guisada, *88,* 89
    Chicken, 220, *221*
    Chicken, Ethiopian-Style Spicy (Doro Wat), 224, *225*
    Chicken, Sausage, and Corn, Cajun, *222,* 223
    Chicken Bouillabaisse, 204–5, *205*
    Chicken Tagine with Olives and Lemon, 212, *213*
    Cioppino, 254, *255*
    Daube Provençal, 90–91, *91*
    Irish, 117
    Irish, with Carrots and Turnips, *116,* 117
    Lamb, Italian-Style, with Green Beans, Tomatoes, and Basil, 118, *119*
    Lamb Tagine with Apricots and Olives, *122,* 123
    Lamb Vindaloo, 124, *125*
    Modern Beef Burgundy, 86–87, *87*
    Monkfish Tagine, 260, *261*
    Pork, French-Style, *160,* 161
    Pork, New Mexican (Posole), *162,* 163
    Pork and Black Bean, Brazilian, 328–29, *329*
    Potato Vindaloo, 282, *283*
    Quinoa and Vegetable, 276, *277*
    Quinoa and Vegetable, with Eggs, 276
    Shellfish, Spanish, 258, *259*
    Shellfish, Spanish, with Lobster, 259

Stews (*cont.*)
    Shrimp and Fish, Brazilian (Moqueca), 262–63, *263*
    storing and reheating, 9
    Swiss Chard and Butternut Squash, Caribbean-Style, *286,* 287
    Ten-Vegetable, Hearty, 272–73, *273*
    thickening, 8
    Veal, with Fennel, Tarragon, and Cream (Blanquette de Veau), 128, *129*
    Vegetable and Bean, North African, *318,* 319
    White Bean, Hearty Tuscan, *296,* 297
    Wild Mushroom Ragu, *270,* 271
Strainer, fine-mesh, 32
Stuffed Cabbage Rolls, 172–73, *173*
Sumac and Mint, Braised Cauliflower with, 357
Sweet-and-Sour Pork Ribs, *146,* 147
Sweet and Tangy Barbecue Sauce, 231
Sweet Potato(es)
    and Cauliflower, Indian-Style Chicken Curry with, 210
    and Eggplant, Indian-Style Vegetable Curry with, 280
    Potato Vindaloo, 282, *283*
Swordfish
    about, 21
    en Cocotte with Carrots and Chermoula, *250,* 251
    en Cocotte with Shallots, Cucumber, and Mint, 251

T

Tacos, Shredded Beef (Carne Deshebrada), 66–67, *67*
Tagine
    Artichoke, Pepper, and Chickpea, *278,* 279
    Chicken, with Olives and Lemon, 212, *213*
    Lamb, with Apricots and Olives, *122,* 123
    Monkfish, 260, *261*
Tagines, Moroccan-style, about, 31
Tarragon
    Braised Spring Vegetables with, 334, *335*
    and Dijon, Braised Red Potatoes with, 373
    Fennel, and Cream, Veal Stew with (Blanquette de Veau), 128, *129*
    and Fennel, Braised Halibut with, 241
Texas-Style Pinto Beans, *330,* 331
Thermometer, digital instant-read, 31
Thermometer, oven, 31
Thyme
    and Lemon, Honey-Glazed Carrots with, 354
    and Parsley, Braised Cabbage with, 350
    Red Wine–Braised Brisket with, 49
    and Tomatoes, Braised Artichokes with, *336,* 337
Tofu
    Asian Braised, with Squash and Coconut Milk, 290, *291*
    Chile-Braised, *288,* 289
    Sichuan-Braised, with Beef (Mapo Tofu), 98, *99*

Tomatillos
Braised Pork Loin with Black Mole Sauce, 140, *141*
Chicken with Pumpkin Seed Sauce, 200, *201*
Tomato(es)
Beef Short Rib Ragu, *104,* 105
Black Bean Chili, *316,* 317
Black-Eyed Peas and Greens, 312, *313*
Braciole, 74–75, *75*
Braised Cod Provençal, 238, *239*
Braised Cod Veracruz, 238
Braised Cod with Peperonata, 238
Brazilian Hot Sauce (Molho Apimentado), 329
Brazilian Shrimp and Fish Stew (Moqueca), 262–63, *263*
Brunswick Stew, *218,* 219
Cherry, and Leeks, Braised Cod with, 236, *237*
Cherry, and Roasted Garlic, Halibut en Cocotte with, 248, *249*
Chicken Bouillabaisse, 204–5, *205*
Chicken Cacciatore, *184,* 185
Chicken Provençal, 180, *181*
Chicken Provençal with Saffron, Orange, and Basil, 180
Cioppino, 254, *255*
Colorado Green Chili, 164, *165*
and Eggplant, Stewed Chickpeas with, *308,* 309
and Garlic, Calamari Stew with, *264,* 265
Gravy, Pork Chops with, 156, *157*
Green Beans, and Basil, Italian-Style Lamb Stew with, 118, *119*
Halibut en Cocotte with Fennel and Saffron, 248
Italian Pot Roast, *38,* 39
Mediterranean Braised Green Beans, 364
Mediterranean Braised Green Beans with Mint and Feta, 364
Mediterranean Braised Green Beans with Potatoes and Basil, 364, *365*
and Mushrooms, Braised Steaks with, 72
Oaxacan-Style Beef Brisket, *50,* 51
Pork Grillades, 148–49, *149*
Pork Ragu, *174,* 175
Potato Vindaloo, 282, *283*
Ratatouille, 268, *269*
Red Lentils with Coconut Milk, 325
and Red Wine, Braised Lamb Shoulder Chops with, 108, *109*
Roman Braised Oxtails, 69
Rosemary, and Olives, Braised Lamb Shoulder Chops with, 108
Spanish Braised Chicken with Sherry and Saffron (Pollo en Pepitoria), *206,* 207
Spanish Shellfish Stew, 258, *259*
Spanish Shellfish Stew with Lobster, 259
Spiced Red Lentils (Masoor Dal), *324,* 325
Stuffed Cabbage Rolls, 172–73, *173*
and Thyme, Braised Artichokes with, *336,* 337

Tomato(es) (*cont.*)
Ultimate Vegetarian Chili, *274,* 275
White Beans, and Aleppo Pepper, Braised Oxtails with, 68, *69*
Tongs, 31
Tortillas
Carne Guisada, *88,* 89
Flank Steak in Adobo, 100–101, *101*
Mexican Pulled Pork (Carnitas), *158,* 159
Shredded Beef Tacos (Carne Deshebrada), 66–67, *67*
Traditional skillet, 30
Turkey Breast
en Cocotte with Mole Sauce, 232, *233*
en Cocotte with Orange-Chipotle Sauce, 233
en Cocotte with Pan Gravy, 232
Turnips
and Carrots, Irish Stew with, *116,* 117
Mashed Potatoes and Root Vegetables, 28
Tuscan White Bean Stew, Hearty, *296,* 297
Twine, 31

U

Ultimate Chili, 102–3, *103*
Ultimate Vegetarian Chili, *274,* 275

V

Veal
foreshank/breast, about, 19
leg, about, 19
loin, about, 19
Osso Buco, *126,* 127
primal cuts of, 19
rib, about, 19
shoulder, about, 19
Stew with Fennel, Tarragon, and Cream (Blanquette de Veau), 128, *129*
Vegetable(s)
and Bean Stew, North African, *318,* 319
braising with, 24
Curry, Indian-Style, with Potatoes and Cauliflower, 280, *281*
Curry, Indian-Style, with Sweet Potato and Eggplant, 280
and Quinoa Stew, 276, *277*
and Quinoa Stew with Eggs, 276
Root, and Potatoes, Mashed, 28
Root, Braised Steaks with, 72, *73*
Root, Simple Pot Roast with, 37
Spring, Braised, with Tarragon, 334, *335*
Ten- , Stew, Hearty, 272–73, *273*
see also specific vegetables

Vegetarian mains

    Artichoke, Pepper, and Chickpea Tagine, *278,* 279

    Asian Braised Tofu with Squash and Coconut Milk, 290, *291*

    Braised Fennel with Radicchio and Parmesan, *292,* 293

    Braised Squash and Winter Greens with Coconut Curry, *284,* 285

    Caribbean-Style Swiss Chard and Butternut Squash Stew, *286,* 287

    Chile-Braised Tofu, *288,* 289

    Hearty Ten-Vegetable Stew, 272–73, *273*

    Indian-Style Vegetable Curry with Potatoes and Cauliflower, 280, *281*

    Indian-Style Vegetable Curry with Sweet Potato and Eggplant, 280

    Potato Vindaloo, 282, *283*

    Quinoa and Vegetable Stew, *276,* 277

    Quinoa and Vegetable Stew with Eggs, 276

    Ratatouille, 268, *269*

    Ultimate Vegetarian Chili, *274,* 275

    Wild Mushroom Ragu, *270,* 271

Vindaloo

    Lamb, 124, *125*

    Potato, 282, *283*

Vinegar

    Balsamic, Capers, and Red Pepper, Braised Lamb Shoulder Chops with, 108

    Barbecue Sauce, Lexington, 230

Vinegar Peppers, Pork Chops with, *154,* **155**

W

Walnuts

    and Orange, Beets with, 338

    Ultimate Vegetarian Chili, *274,* 275

White Bean(s)

    Baked Navy Beans, 302, *303*

    Braised Hearty Greens with, 368

    and Escarole, Sicilian, 306, *307*

    Moroccan Braised, with Lamb, 114, *115*

    and Pork Casserole, French, 326–27, *327*

    Stew, Hearty Tuscan, *296,* 297

    Tomatoes, and Aleppo Pepper, Braised Oxtails with, 68, *69*

    White Chicken Chili, *228,* 229

White Chicken Chili, *228,* **229**

White Wine

    Braised Lamb Shanks with Lemon and Mint, *110,* 111

    Braised Lamb Shanks with North African Spices, 111

    and Garlic, Braised Cauliflower with, *356,* 357

    and Leeks, Salmon en Cocotte with, 246, *247*

    Osso Buco, *126,* 127

    Portuguese-Style Beef Stew (Alcatra), *96,* 97

Whole Spice Blend, 121

Wild Mushroom Ragu, *270,* **271**

Wine. *See* **Port; Red Wine; White Wine**

Z

Zucchini

    Hearty Ten-Vegetable Stew, 272–73, *273*

    Ratatouille, 268, *269*